ISBN 978-0-365-29763-5
PIBN 10148702

FB &c Ltd, Dalton House, 60 Windsor Avenue, London, SW19 2RR.
Company number 08720141. Registered in England and Wales.

For support please visit www.forgottenbooks.com

THE

HISTORY,

CIVIL AND COMMERCIAL,

OF THE

BRITISH COLONIES

IN THE

WEST INDIES.

By BRYAN EDWARDS, Esq. F. R. S. S. A.

FOURTH EDITION,

WITH CONSIDERABLE ADDITIONS.

ILLUSTRATED WITH PLATES.

IN THREE VOLUMES.

VOL. III.

LONDON:

PRINTED FOR JOHN STOCKDALE, PICCADILLY.

AN

HISTORICAL SURVEY

OF THE

FRENCH COLONY

IN THE

ISLAND OF ST. DOMINGO:

COMPREHENDING AN ACCOUNT OF

THE REVOLT OF THE NEGROES

IN THE YEAR 1791,

AND

A DETAIL OF THE MILITARY TRANSACTIONS OF THE BRITISH ARMY IN THAT ISLAND, IN THE YEARS 1793 & 1794.

PREFACE

TO THE

FIRST EDITION

OF THE

HISTORICAL SURVEY OF ST. DOMINGO,

1796.

SOON after I had published the History of the British Colonies in the West Indies, I conceived the design of compiling a general account of the settlements made by all the nations of Europe in that part of the New Hemisphere, but more particularly the French, whose possessions were undoubtedly the most valuable and productive of the whole Archipelago. This idea suggested itself to me on surveying the materials I had collected with regard to their principal colony in St. Domingo; not doubting, as the fortune of war had placed under the British dominion all or most of the other French islands, that I should easily procure such particulars of the condition, population, and culture of each, as would enable me to complete my design, with credit to myself, and satisfaction to the public. I am sorry to observe, that in this expectation I have hitherto found myself disappointed. The present publication

b 2 therefore,

therefore, is confined wholly to St. Domingo; concerning which, having personally visited that unhappy country soon after the revolt of the negroes in 1791, and formed connexions there, which have supplied me with regular communications ever since, I possess a mass of evidence, and important documents. My motives for going thither, are of little consequence to the public; but the circumstances which occasioned the voyage, the reception I met with, and the situation in which I found the wretched Inhabitants, cannot fail of being interesting to the reader; and I flatter myself that a short account of those particulars, while it confers some degree of authenticity on my labours, will not be thought an improper Introduction to my Book.

In the month of September 1791, when I was at Spanish Town in Jamaica, two French Gentlemen were introduced to me, who were just arrived from St. Domingo, with information that the negro slaves belonging to the French part of that island, to the number, as was believed, of 100,000 and upwards, had revolted, and were spreading death and desolation over the whole of the northern province They reported that the governor-general, considering the situation of the colony as a common cause among the white inhabitants of all nations in the West Indies, had dispatched commissioners to the neighbouring islands, as well as to the States of North America, to request immediate assistance of troops, arms, ammunition, and provisions; and that themselves were deputed

deputed on the same errand to the Government at Jamaica: I was accordingly desired to present them to the Earl of Effingham, the commander in chief. Although the dispatches with which these gentlemen were furnished, were certainly a very sufficient introduction to his lordship, I did not hesitate to comply with their request; and it is scarcely necessary to observe, that the liberal and enlarged mind which animated every part of Lord Effingham's conduct, needed no solicitation, in a case of beneficence and humanity. Superior to national prejudice, he felt, as a man and a christian ought to feel, for the calamities of *fellow men;* and he saw, in its full extent, the danger to which every island in the West Indies would be exposed from such an example, if the triumph of savage anarchy over all order and government should be complete. He therefore, without hesitation, assured the commissioners that they might depend on receiving from the government of Jamaica, every assistance and succour which it was in his power to give. Troops he could not offer, for he had them not; but he said he would furnish arms, ammunition, and provisions, and he promised to consult with the distinguished Officer commanding in the naval department, concerning the propriety of sending up one or more of his Majesty's ships; the commissioners having suggested that the appearance in their harbours of a few vessels of war might serve to intimidate the insurgents, and keep them at a distance, while the necessary defences and intrenchments were

were making to preserve the city of Cape François from an attack.

ADMIRAL AFFLECK (as from his known worth and general character might have been expected) very cheerfully co-operated on this occasion with Lord Effingham; and immediately issued orders to the captains of the Blonde and Daphne frigates to proceed, in company with a sloop of war, forthwith to Cape François. The Centurion was soon afterwards ordered to Port au Prince. The Blonde being commanded by my amiable and lamented friend, Captain William Affleck, who kindly undertook to convey the French commissioners back to St. Domingo, I was easily persuaded to accompany them thither; and some other gentlemen of Jamaica joined the party.

WE arrived in the harbour of Cape François in the evening of the 26th of September, and the first object which arrested our attention as we approached, was a dreadful scene of devastation by fire. The noble plain adjoining the Cape was covered with ashes, and the surrounding hills, as far as the eye could reach, every where presented to us ruins still smoking, and houses and plantations at that moment in flames. It was a sight more terrible than the mind of any man, unaccustomed to such a scene, can easily conceive.—The inhabitants of the town being assembled on the beach, directed all their attention towards us, and we landed amidst a crowd of spectators who, with uplifted hands and streaming eyes, gave welcome

to

to their deliverers (for such they considered us) and acclamations of *vivent les Anglois* resounded from every quarter.

THE governor of St. Domingo, at that time, was the unfortunate General Blanchelande; a *marechal de camp* in the French service, who has since perished on the scaffold. He did us the honour to receive us on the quay. A committee of the colonial assembly, accompanied by the governor's only son, an amiable and accomplished youth*, had before attended us on board the Blonde, and we were immediately conducted to the place of their meeting. The scene was striking and solemn. The hall was splendidly illuminated, and all the members appeared in mourning. Chairs were placed for us within the bar, and the Governor having taken his seat on the right hand of the President, the latter addressed us in an eloquent and affecting oration, of which the following is as literal a translation, as the idiom of the two languages will admit:

"We were not mistaken, Gentlemen, when we "placed our confidence in your generosity; but "we could hardly entertain the hope, that, besides "sending us succours, you would come in person "to give us consolation. You have quitted, with-"out reluctance, the peaceful enjoyment of hap-"piness at home, to come and participate in the "misfortunes of strangers, and blend your tears

* This young gentleman likewise perished by the guillotine under the tyranny of Robespierre. He was massacred at Paris, on the 20th July 1794, in the twentieth year of his age.

"with

" with ours. Scenes of misery (the contemplation " of which, to those who are unaccustomed to " misfortune, is commonly disgusting) have not " suppressed *your* feelings. You have been wil- " ling to ascertain the full extent of our distresses, " and to pour into our wounds the salutary balm " of your sensibility and compassion.

" The picture which has been drawn of our ca- " lamities, you will find has fallen short of the rea- " lity. That verdure with which our fields were " lately arrayed, is no longer visible; discoloured " by the flames, and laid waste by the devastations " of war, our coasts exhibit no prospect but that " of desolation. The emblems which we wear on " our persons, are the tokens of our grief for the " loss of our brethren, who were surprized, and " cruelly assassinated, by the revolters.

" It is by the glare of the conflagrations that " every way surround us, that we now deliberate: " we are compelled to sit armed and watchful " through the night, to keep the enemy from our " sanctuary. For a long time past our bosoms " have been depressed by sorrow; they experience " this day, for the first time, the sweet emotions of " pleasure, in beholding you amongst us.

" Generous islanders! humanity has operated " powerfully on your hearts;—you have yielded to " the first emotion of your generosity, in the hopes " of snatching us from death; for it is already too " late to save us from misery. What a contrast be- " tween your conduct, and that of other nations! " We will avail ourselves of your benevolence;

" but

" but the days you preserve to us, will not be suffi-
" cient to manifest our gratitude : our children
" shall keep it in remembrance.

" REGENERATED France, unapprized that such
" calamities might befal us, has taken no measures
" to protect us against their effects: with what
" admiration will she learn, that, without your
" assistance, we should no longer exist as a de-
" pendency to any nation.

" THE Commissioners deputed by us to the
" island of Jamaica, have informed us of your ex-
" ertions to serve us.—Receive the assurance of
" our attachment and sensibility.

" THE Governor-general of this island, whose
" sentiments perfectly accord with our own, par-
" ticipates equally in the joy we feel at your pre-
" sence, and in our gratitude for the assistance
" you have brought us."

AT this juncture, the French colonists in St. Domingo, however they might have been divided in political sentiments on former occasions, seemed to be softened, by the sense of common suffering, into perfect unanimity. All descriptions of persons joined in one general outcry against the National Assembly, to whose proceedings were imputed all their disasters. This opinion was indeed so widely disseminated, and so deeply rooted, as to create a very strong disposition in the white inhabitants of Cape François, to renounce their allegiance to the mother country. The black cockade was universally substituted in place of the

the tri-coloured one, and very earnest wishes were avowed in all companies, without scruple or restraint, that the British administration would send an armament to conquer the island, or rather to receive its voluntary surrender from the inhabitants. What they wished might happen, they persuaded themselves to believe was actually in contemplation; and this idea soon became so prevalent, as to place the author of this work in an awkward situation. The sanguine disposition observable in the French character, has been noticed by all who have visited them; but in this case their credulity grew to a height that was extravagant and even ridiculous. By the kindness of the Earl of Effingham, I was favoured with a letter of introduction to the Governor-general; and my reception, both by M. Blanchelande and the colonial assembly, was such as not only to excite the publick attention, but also to induce a very general belief that no common motive had brought me thither. The suggestions of individuals to this purpose, became perplexing and troublesome. Assurances on my part, that I had no views beyond the gratification of curiosity, had no other effect than to call forth commendations on my prudence. It was settled, that I was an agent of the English ministry, sent purposely to sound the inclinations of the Colonists towards the Government of Great Britain, preparatory to an invasion of the country by a British armament; and their wishes and inclinations co-operating with this idea, gave rise to many strange applications which were made to me;

some

some of them of so ludicrous a nature, as no powers of face could easily withstand.

This circumstance is not recorded from the vain ambition of shewing my own importance. The reader of the following pages will discover its application; and, perhaps, it may induce him to make some allowance for that confident expectation of sure and speedy success, which afterwards led to attempts, by the British arms, against this ill-fated country, with means that must otherwise have been thought at the time,—as in the sequel they have unhappily proved,—altogether inadequate to the object in view.

The ravages of the rebellion, during the time that I remained at Cape François, extended in all directions. The whole of the plain of the Cape, with the exception of one plantation which adjoined the town, was in ruins; as were likewise the Parish of Limonade, and most of the settlements in the mountains adjacent. The Parish of Limbé was every where on fire; and before my departure, the rebels had obtained possession of the bay and forts at l'Acul, as well as the districts of Fort Dauphin, Dondon, and La Grande Riviere.

Destruction every where marked their progress, and resistance seemed to be considered by the whites, not only as unavailing in the present conjuncture, but as hopeless in future. To fill up the measure of their calamities, their Spanish neighbours in the same island, with a spirit of bigotry and hatred which is, I believe, without an example in the world, refused to lend any assistance towards suppressing a revolt, in the issue of which common reason should have informed them, that their own preservation was implicated equally with that of the French. They were even accused not only of supplying the rebels with arms and provisions; but also of delivering up to them to be murdered, many unhappy French planters who had fled for refuge to the Spanish territories, and receiving money from the rebels as the price of their blood. Of these latter charges, however, no proof was, I believe, ever produced; and, for the honour of human nature, I am unwilling to believe that they are true.

To myself, the case appeared altogether desperate from the beginning; and many of the most respectable and best informed persons in Cape François (some of them in high stations) assured me, in confidence, that they concurred in this opinion. The merchants and importers of European manufactures, apprehending every hour the destruction of the town, as much from incendiaries within, as from the rebels without, offered their goods for ready money at half the usual prices; and applications were made to Captain Affleck, by persons of all descriptions, for permission to embark in the Blonde for Jamaica. The interposition of the colonial government obliged him to reject their solicitations; but means were contrived to send on board consignments of money to a great amount; and I know that other conveyances were found, by which effects to a considerable

derable value were exported both to Jamaica, and the states of North America.

UNDER these circumstances, it very naturally occurred to me to direct my enquiries towards the state of the colony previous to the revolt, and collect authentick information on the spot, concerning the primary cause, and subsequent progress, of the widely extended ruin before me. Strongly impressed with the gloomy idea, that the only memorial of this once flourishing colony would soon be found in the records of history, I was desirous that my own country and fellow-colonists, in lamenting its catastrophe, might at the same time profit by so terrible an example. My means of information were too valuable to be neglected, and I determined to avail myself of them. The Governor-general furnished me with copies of all the papers and details of office that I solicited, with a politeness that augmented the favour. The fate of this unhappy gentleman, two years afterwards, gave me infinite concern. Like his royal master, he was unfortunately called to a station to which his abilities were not competent; and in times when perhaps no abilities would have availed him.

THE President of the colonial assembly, at the time of my arrival, was M. de Caducsh, who some time afterwards took up his residence, and held an important office, in Jamaica. He was a man of very distinguished talents, and withal strongly and sincerely attached to the British government, of which, if it were proper, I could furnish unques-

tionable

tionable proof.* This gentlemen drew up, at my request, a short account of the origin and progress of the rebellion; and after my return to England, favoured me with his correspondence. Many important facts, which are given in this work, are given on his authority.

To M. Delaire, a very considerable and respectable merchant in the town of the Cape, who has since removed to the state of South Carolina, I was indebted for a similar narrative, drawn up by himself in the English language, of which he is a very competent master. It is brief, but much to the purpose; displays an intimate knowledge of the concerns of the colony, and traces, with great acuteness, its disasters to their source.

But the friend from whose superior knowledge I have derived my chief information in all respects, is the gentleman alluded to in the marginal note to p. 120 of the following sheets; and I sincerely regret, that ill fortune has so pursued him as to render it improper in this work to express to him, *by name*, the obligations I owe to his kindness. After a narrow escape from the vengeance of those merciless men, Santhonax and Polverel, he was induced to return to St. Domingo, to look after his property; and, I grieve to say, that he is again fallen into the hands of his enemies. He found

* He afterwards accompanied General Williamson back to St. Domingo, and was killed (or, as I have heard, basely murdered) in a duel at Port au Prince, by one of his countrymen.

means,

means, however, previous to his present confinement, to convey to me many valuable papers; and, among others, a copy of that most curious and important document, the dying deposition or testament of Ogè, mentioned in the fourth chapter, and printed at large among the additional notes and illustrations at the end of my work. Of this paper (the communication of which, in proper time, would have prevented the dreadful scenes that followed) although I had frequently heard, I had long doubted the existence. Its suppression by the persons to whom it was delivered by the wretched sufferer, appeared to be an act of such monstrous and unexampled wickedness, that, until I saw the paper itself, I could not credit the charge. Whether M. Blanchelande was a party concerned in this atrocious proceeding, as my friend asserts, I know not. If he was guilty, he has justly paid the forfeit of his crime; and although, believing him innocent, I mourned over his untimely fate, I scruple not to avow my opinion, that if he had possessed a thousand lives, the loss of them all had not been a sufficient atonement, in so enormous a case, to violated justice!

Such were the motives that induced me to undertake this Historical Survey of the French part of St. Domingo, and such are the authorities from whence I have derived my information concerning those calamitous events which have brought it to ruin. Yet I will frankly confess, that, if I have any credit with the publick as an author, I am not sure this work will add to my reputation. Every writer

writer must rise or sink, in some degree, with the nature of his subject; and on this occasion, the picture which I shall exhibit, has nothing in it to delight the fancy, or to gladden the heart. The prospects before us are all dark and dismal. Here is no room for tracing the beauties of unsullied nature. Those groves of perennial verdure; those magnificent and romantick landscapes, which, in tropical regions, every where invite the eye, and oftentimes detain it, until wonder is exalted to devotion, must now give place to the miseries of war, and the horrors of pestilence; to scenes of anarchy, desolation, and carnage. We have to contemplate the human mind in its utmost deformity: to behold savage man, let loose from restraint, exercising cruelties, of which the bare recital makes the heart recoil, and committing crimes which are hitherto unheard of in history; teeming

> ———— all monstrous, all prodigious things,
> Abominable, unutterable, and worse
> Than fables yet have feign'd, or fear conceiv'd!
>
> MILTON.

ALL therefore that I can hope and expect is, that my narrative, if it cannot delight, may at least *instruct*. On the sober and considerate, on those who are open to conviction, this assemblage of horrors will have its effect. It will expose the lamentable ignorance of some, and the monstrous wickedness of others, among the reformers of the present day, who, urging onwards schemes of perfection, and projects of amendment in the condition of

human

human life, faster than nature allows, are lighting up a consuming fire between the different classes of mankind, which nothing but human blood can extinguish. To tell such men that great and beneficial modifications in the established orders of society, can only be effected by a progressive improvement in the situation of the lower ranks of the people, is to preach to the winds. In their hands reformation, with a scythe more destructive than that of Time, mows down every thing, and plants nothing. Moderation and caution they consider as rank cowardice. Force and violence are the ready, and, in their opinion, the only proper application for the cure of early and habitual prejudice. Their practice, like that of other mountebanks, is bold and compendious; their motto is, *cure or kill.*

These reflections naturally arise from the circumstance which is incontrovertibly proved in the following pages, namely, that the rebellion of the negroes in St. Domingo, and the insurrection of the mulattoes, to whom Ogé was sent as ambassador, had one and the same origin. It was not the strong and irresistible impulse of human nature, groaning under oppression, that excited either of those classes to plunge their daggers into the bosoms of unoffending women and helpless infants. They were driven into those excesses—reluctantly driven—by the vile machinations of men calling themselves philosophers (the proselytes and imitators in France, of the Old Jewry associates in London) whose pretences to philanthropy were as gross a mockery of human reason, as their conduct was an outrage on all the feelings of our nature, and the ties which hold society together!

It is indeed true, that negro-rebellions have heretofore arisen in this and other islands of the West Indies, to which no such exciting causes contributed:—but it is equally certain, that those rebellions always originated among the newly-imported negroes only; many of whom had probably lived in a state of freedom in Africa, and had been fraudulently, or forcibly, sold into slavery by their chiefs. That cases of this kind do sometimes occur in the slave-trade, I dare not dispute, and I admit that revolt and insurrection are their natural consequences.

But, in St. Domingo, a very considerable part of the insurgents were—not Africans, but—Creoles, or natives. Some of the leaders were favoured domesticks among the white inhabitants, born and brought up in their families. A few of them had even received those advantages, the perversion of which, under their philosophical preceptors, served only to render them pre-eminent in mischief; for having been taught to read, they were led to imbibe, and enabled to promulgate, those principles and doctrines which led, and always will lead, to the subversion of all government and order.

Let me not be understood, however, as affirming that nothing is to be attributed on this occasion to the slave-trade. I scorn to have recourse to concealment or falshood. Unquestionably, the vast annual importations of enslaved Africans into St.

St. Domingo, for many years previous to 1791, had created a black population in the French part of that island, which was, beyond all measure, disproportionate to the white ;—the relative numbers of the two classes being as sixteen to one. Of this circumstance the leaders of the rebels could not be unobservant, and they doubtless derived encouragement and confidence from it. Here too, I admit, is a warning and an admonition to ourselves. The inference has not escaped me :—it constitutes my parting words with the reader, and I hope they are not urged in vain.

Having thus pointed out the motives which induced me to write the following narrative, the sources from whence my materials are derived, and the purposes which I hope will be answered by the publication; nothing farther remains but to submit the work itself to the judgment of my readers, which I do with a respectful solicitude.

ADVERTISEMENT.

(1800.)

IN presenting the present edition of the Historical Survey of St. Domingo *to the Publick, it is incumbent on me to acknowledge, that the many important corrections and improvements it has received in those chapters which relate to the constitution and political state of the French colony, under the ancient system, are chiefly derived from the very intelligent and interesting work of* M. LABORIE, *entitled,* The Coffee Planter of St. Domingo.

On this occasion also I hope I may be allowed, as well in justice to myself, as from a sense of gratitude and respect towards the memory of my lamented friend, SIR ADAM WILLIAMSON, *to boast that I had the honor and advantage of* his *assistance in that part of my work which details the proceedings and operations of the British army in this ill-fated country; most of the sheets having been revised by him, as they came from the press, and corrected by his own pen in many places. Motives of prudence and delicacy (which no longer exist) induced me to suppress this acknowledgement in the lifetime of my friend. Some errors and omissions which (perhaps unavoidably) escaped his notice, have since been corrected*

rected and supplied by a British officer of noble birth, and considerable rank in the army, who served on the spot; and whose name, if I were permitted to disclose it, would stamp indisputable authority on the communications he has kindly furnished. That many mistakes and oversights however still remain, I am too conscious of my own insufficiency to doubt; nor in truth could the greatest precaution on my part have enabled me, at all times, to guard against misrepresentation from some of the various persons whom the necessity of the case compelled me to consult. Thus, in giving an account of the French colonists;—their disposition towards the English, and their conduct towards each other;—to whom could I look for authentick information, but to some of themselves? Experience however has convinced me, that no great dependence can be placed on the charges and accusations which men raise against their fellow-citizens in times of civil commotion, and amidst the tumult of conflicting passions. A remarkable instance of the truth of this observation occurs in the case of a very respectable Gentleman, formerly an inhabitant of Cape Francois: I mean M. Augustus de Grasse, *(son of the late gallant Admiral* Count de Grasse*) to whom I now think myself bound in honour to make a publick reparation. In a paper formerly transmitted to me from St. Domingo, and annexed to the 8th chapter of my work, entitled,* Notes sur l'Evenement du Cap, *this gentleman was unjustly charged with having been present at the destruction of that town by the rebel negroes, aiding, abetting, and co-operating with their*

chiefs

Advertisement. (1800.)

chiefs. I am now convinced that this atrocious charge is altogether groundless, and I cannot sufficiently express the concern I feel on reflecting, that I was made the instrument of conveying it to the press.—I have therefore, in this edition, not only reprinted the sheet, and omitted the calumny, but I insert in this place, with great satisfaction, the following certificate, which M. DE GRASSE *has transmitted to me, in a very polite letter, from South Carolina, dated the* 22*d of October* 1799:

"NOUS soussignés, habitans de la ville du Cap et de ses dépendances, présent au pillage, au massacre et à l'incendié de cette ville, les 19, 20, 21 Juin 1793, et jours suivants, certifions, et attestons, sour la foy du serment, et pour rendre homage à la verité, Que M. Alexandre François Auguste De Grasse, habitant de la dépendance du Port de Paix, département du Cap, isle St. Domingue, fils du feu Comte de Grasse, &c. &c. etoit dans la ville du Cap avant et pendant le pillage, le massacre et l'incendiè de cette ville, en qualité d'adjutant général de l'armée des blancs en activité contre les noirs insurgés; qu'après ce funeste evénément il fut persécuté par les commissaires civiles, et mis par leurs ordres aux arrêts, au haut du Cap, sous la garde des negres armés, comme soupçonné d'avoir agi contre eux avec le Général Galbaud, mais, qu'après s'être justifie, il fut réintegré dans ses fonctions, et chargé immédiatement du commandement des casernes; où il a protége avec les troupes blanches, qui y étaient sous ses ordres, les hommes,

Advertisement. (1800.)

hommes, femmes et enfans, échappés au fer et aux flâmes, qui s'y étaient réfugiés. Et qu' enfin, forcé, comme une partie des soussignés, à fuir les dangers qui ménaçaient encore les tristes débris de la population blanche, il s'est embarqué avec sa femme, un enfant et quelques uns des soussignés, le 28 Juillet 1793, sur le brig le Thomas de Boston, destiné pour Charleston, Caroline du Sud, où il est arrivé et réside depuis le 14 Aout 1793, après avoir été, ainsi qu' environ 150 malheureux fugitifs, barbarement pillés par le corsaire Anglais La Susanna de Nassau, Cap. Tucker, (qui n'auroit pas dû les considerer ni les traiter comme des ennemis, étans d'ailleurs sur un batiment neutre qui ne contenoit uniquement que des passagers et leurs effets,) non seulement des negres domestiques qui les avaient volontairement suivis, mais encore du peu d'argent, de bijoux et de veselle d'argent qu'ils avaient sauvés du pillage par le secours de ces mêmes domestiques, (ce second pillage eut lieu à la Grande Inague des Isles Caiques, où le corsaire Anglais retint notre vaisseau deux jours, pour completter cet exploit.) Certifions et attestons pareillement, que M. de Grasse arrivé à St. Domingue avant la révolution, n'a jamais cessé, du moment que ses effets se sont manifestés dans cette infortuneé colonnie jusqu' à celui de son départ, d'étre uni authentiquement avec les habitans blancs, et en qualité de chef élû par eux-mêmes, soit au Port de Paix soit au Cap, pour repousser les dangers aux quels leurs vies et leurs propriétés étoient journellement exposés par les noirs insurgés,

Advertisement. (1800.)

surgés, et enfin, qu'aucunes circonstances, pendant le cours des funestes evénémens de St. Domingue, n'ont jamais donné lieu à former contre lui la moindre suspiçion contraire aux interets et à la sureté individuelle de la population blanche de St. Domingue.

En foy de quoi nous avons signés, a Charleston, Caroline du Sud, le 25 Octobre 1799.

(Signed by twenty respectable persons.)

Having thus made all the reparation in my power to this injured gentleman, I have farther to remark, in justice to myself, that my observations concerning the indisposition of the planters of St. Domingo towards the English, on the arrival of the first armament, appear, from a conversation I have had with some of them, to have been greatly misunderstood. Surely it reflects no dishonour on such of those gentlemen as had no concern in, or knowledge of, the invitation made to General Williamson, to say that they were not, in the first instance, very cordially disposed towards their invaders—especially too, as those invaders came with a force by no means sufficient to give them certain and permanent protection. Whatever might have been the sentiments of certain individuals among them on this occasion, and how strongly soever the inhabitants of Cape François *had, two years before, in a moment of irritation, expressed a wish for a British invasion, it seems to me that the chief planters throughout the colony were altogether unacquainted with the English,*

Advertisement. (1800.)

lish, and entertain no very favourable opinion of their laws, government, or manners. What then was their situation on the first arrival of the British troops? assailed, on the one hand, by a desperate and unprincipled faction of republicans and anarchists, whose principles they abhorred, and, on the other, called upon to co-operate with an insignificant foreign armament, which came, on the invitatian of a few obscure Frenchmen,—not to restore the country to the loyal inhabitants, but distinctly and avowedly to conquer and annex it to the British dominion! In this dilemma, the majority of the planters acted as conscientious men might be expected to act. A great many of them left the country, and went into honourable poverty and exile in a distant land. Others, who were unable to follow their example, remained in silent obscurity, in different parts of the Island, waiting patiently (and I grieve to say, without effect) for better times. If all this be duly considered, I trust I shall be no longer told, that I have calumniated the French planters, merely because, as an impartial historian, I have represented them to have acted as any other body of men, attached to their country, and faithful to their allegiance, would probably have acted, in similar circumstances.

London, 1800.

B. E.

CONTENTS

OF

VOLUME THE THIRD.

CHAP. VI.

CHAP. VII.

CHAP. VIII.

CHAP.

CHAP. IX.

CHAP. X.

CHAP. XI.

CHAP. XII.

CHAP. XIII.

CHAP. XIV.

APPENDIX.

HISTORY

HISTORY OF THE WAR IN THE WEST INDIES,

From its Commencement in February 1793.

POLYGYNIA.

Illicium	*floridanum*	Aniseed Tree	Florida	H. East, Esq. 1787
Liriodendron	*Tulipifera*	Tulip Tree	N. America	H. East, Esq. 1776
Magnolia	*grandiflora*	Laurel-leav'd Magnol	Carolina	Mr. Gale, 1772
	glauca	Swamp Magnolia	N. America	Mr. Gale, 1772
	acuminata	Blue Magnolia	N. America	H. East, Esq. 1788
Annona		Cherimoya	S. America	H. East, Esq. 1786
Anemone	*hortensis*	Garden Anemone	Italy	M. Wallen, Esq. 1773
Atragene	*indica*		S. America	H. East, Esq. 1788
Clematis	*Flammula*	Virgin's Bower	S. of France	
Adonis	*autumnalis*	Flos Adonis.	England	M. Wallen, Esq.
Ranunculus	*auricomus*	Wood Crowfoot	Britain	M. Wallen, Esq. 1773

Classis XIV.

DIDYNAMIA.

GYMNOSPERMIA.

Satureja	*hortensis*	Garden Savory	Italy	
Hyssopus	*officinalis*	Hyssop	S. of Europe	
Nepeta	*Cataria*	Catmint	Britain	H. East. Esq.
Lavandula	*Spica*	Common Lavender	S. of Europe	M. Wallen, Esq. 1774

* Two of these Plants were presented to Doctor Clarke by Monsieur Nectoux, from the King's Garden at Port au Prince; they appeared in a very luxuriant State of Growth on their Arrival, but have since died.

LAVANDULA	*Stœchas*	French Lavender	S. of Europe	H. East, Esq. 1787
	dentata	Tooth'd-leav'd Lav.	S. of Europe	H. East, Esq. 1787
	multifida	Canary Lavender	Canary Islands	Dr. Tho. Clarke, 1784
SIDERITIS	*candicans*	Iron-wort	Madeira	H. East, Esq.
MENTHA	*viridis*	it	England	
	piperita	it	England	
	Pulegium		Britain	
GLECOMA	*hederacea*		Britain	
BETONICA	*officinalis*		Britain	H. East, Esq.
MARRUBIUM	*vulgare*		Britain	M. Wallen, Esq.
ORIGANUM	*Onites*	Pot Ma ra	Sicily	
	Majorana	Sweet rjoram		
THYMUS	*vulgaris*	Garde hyme	Italy	
	mastichina	Mastic Thyme	Spain	H. East, Esq.
MELISSA	*officinalis*	Balm	Britain	
DRACOCEPHA-LUM	*Ruyschiana*		Sweden	H. East, Esq. 1788
	Moldavica	Moldavian Balm	Moldavia	M. Wallen, Esq. 1774
OCYMUM	*Basilicum*	Sweet Basil	Persia	M. Wallen, Esq.

ANGIOSPERMIA.

ANTIRRHINUM	*majus*	Snap-dragon	England	M. Wallen, Esq. 1773
	asarina	Toad-flax	Italy	H. East, Esq. 1773
DIGITALIS	*purpurea*	Purple Fox-glove	Britain	H. East, Esq. 1787
	ambigua	Yellow Fox-glove	Switzerland	H. East, Esq. 1784

AN

HISTORICAL SURVEY

OF

ST. DOMINGO,

&c. &c.

CHAPTER I.

Political State of St. Domingo previous to the Year 1789.

CHAP. I. Inhabitants.

THE inhabitants of the French part of St. Domingo, as of all the West Indian Islands, were composed of three great classes: 1st, Pure whites. 2d, People of colour, and blacks of free condition. 3d, Negroes in a state of slavery. The reader is apprised that the class which, by a strange abuse of language, is called *people of colour* originates from an intermixture of the whites and the blacks. The genuine offspring of a pure white with a negro is called a mulatto; but there are various casts, produced by subsequent connections, some of which draw near to the whites, until all visible distinction between them is lost; whilst others fall retrograde to the blacks. All these were known in St. Domingo by the term sang-melées, or *gens de couleur* (in familiar conversation they are collectively called *mulattoes)* and it must be attributed, I presume, to the greater discountenance which the married state reeeives from the national manners, that in all the French islands these people abound in far greater proportion to the

CHAP. I.

the whites than in those of Great Britain. In Jamaica, the whites out-number the people of colour as three to one. In St. Domingo, the whites were estimated at 30,000, the mulattoes at 24,000; of whom 4,700 were men capable of bearing arms, and accordingly, as a distinct people, actuated by an *esprit de corps,* they were very formidable. Of the policy which it was thought necessary in St. Domingo to maintain towards this unfortunate race, I shall presently treat; but it seems proper, in the first place, to give some account of the subordination in which, before the revolution of 1789, the parent state thought fit to hold the colony at large.

The laws of the mother country, as far as they were applicable, (as well the unwritten law, *or customs of Paris,* as the general laws of the king,), were laws of St. Domingo. These had been introduced without formal promulgation, being supposed to attach to all the subjects of France, whether abroad or at home; and the king issued, from time to time, colonial edicts, which were received with entire submission. Even mandatory letters written by the minister, in the king's name, were considered and obeyed as laws in the colony.

Government.

The government was exercised by a Governor General, and an officer called Intendant, both of whom were nominated by the crown, on the recommendation of the minister of the marine, and generally considered as established in their respective offices for three years. Their powers, in some cases, were administered jointly; in others, they possessed

possessed separate and distinct authority, which each of them exercised without the concurrence or participation of the other.

In their joint administration they were empowered to enact such regulations as the existing exigencies of the country required; and their provisional decrees had the force of laws, until revoked by the king. The grants of unclaimed lands and rivers; the erection of publick works and buildings; the opening publick roads and repairing bridges; the regulation and police of the several ports of shipping; the provisional appointment of the members of the superior councils or courts of justice in cases of vacancy, and the absolute nomination of the subordinate officers of those courts, were concerns of joint authority. With the consent of the king's attorney, the governor and intendant had power to stay execution in cases of capital conviction, until the king's pleasure should be known; and they were commissioned to try and condemn to capital punishment defrauders of the publick revenue, calling to their assistance five judges of the superior councils. The government of the clergy, the regulation of church establishments, and the erection of parishes, fell likewise under their joint cognizance; and they were empowered, in times of publick necessity (of which they were the judges) to suspend, in certain respects, the laws of navigation, by admitting importations of flour and bread, and allowing the exportation of colonial produce in foreign vessels. Against abuses in the exercise of these various

 powers

powers the people had no certain protection. Fortunately, it was rare that the governor and intendant agreed in opinion on the exercise of their joint authority, which therefore became necessarily relaxed; and the inhabitants derived some degree of security from the disputes and dissensions of the contending parties. In all such cases, however, the greatest weight of authority and right of deciding devolved on the governor. He was, in truth, an absolute prince, whose will, generally speaking, constituted law. He was authorized to imprison any person in the colony, for causes of which he alone was the judge; and having at the same time the supreme command of both the naval and military force, he had the means of exercising this power whenever he thought proper. On the other hand, no arrest, by any other authority, was valid without the governor's approbation. Thus he had power to stop the course of justice, and to hold the courts of civil and criminal jurisdiction in a slavish dependance on himself.

The peculiar province of the intendant, besides that of regulating the publick revenues or finances of the colony, was the administration of justice. His powers and functions were expressed in his title, *Intendant of justice, police, finance, war, and navy*. The collectors and receivers of all duties and taxes were subject to his inspection and controul. He passed or rejected their accounts, and made them such allowances as he alone thought proper. The application of all the publick monies in expenditures of all kinds for the army, the navy, fortifications,

fortifications, and publick hospitals, rested entirely with the intendant;—a province which created such temptation to himself as no virtue could resist, and furnished such means of corruption, as overcame all opposition from others.

The taxes and duties were laid and modified, as occasion required, by a court composed of the governor-general, the intendant, the presidents of the provincial councils, the attorney-general, the commissioner of the navy *(ordonnateur)* and the several commandants of the militia. This court was dignified by the title of the *Colonial Assembly,* although the colonists had not a single delegate in it. It ought not however to be suppressed that the taxes, were on the whole, very moderate. The total expenditure, comprehending all the contingencies of the colonial government, seldom exceeded 50,000*l.* sterling *per annum (a).*

For

(a) The colonial taxes were called *Octroi*, and consisted principally of duties on the exportation of the chief articles of produce. The latest assessment previous to the revolution was made in 1776. There was, besides those duties, a direct tax of $2\frac{1}{2}$ per cent. on the rents of houses in the towns, and a poll-tax of three dollars on slave servants or artificers belonging to estates or manufactures, the products of which were not exportable, as provision plantations, lime and brick kilns, &c. This system of taxing their exported produce is justified by Mons. Laborie on the following ground: "The difference of soil in St. Domingo" (he observes) "is such, that a plantation of double "the extent of land, and with twice the number of negroes "and cattle, and managed with equal skill, shall often yield "much less than another with half the same advantages: a "tax therefore on the produce, is more equal and proportionate than either a land-tax or a poll-tax upon the negroes."

Exterior

FOR the better administration of justice, and the easier collection of the revenues, the colony was divided into three provinces (which were distinguished, from their relative situation, by the names of the Northern, the Western, and Southern), and subdivided into ten districts. In each of those provinces resided a deputy governor, or commander *en second*, and in each district was established a subordinate court of justice, for the trial of causes both civil and criminal. Appeals however were allowed to the superior councils; of which there were two; one at *Cape Francois* for the Northern province, the other at *Port au Prince* for the Western and Southern. They were composed of the governor-general, the intendant, the deputy governors, the king's lieutenants (*b*), a president, and twelve counsellors, four *assesseurs*, or assistant judges, together with the attorney general and register. In these councils, or courts of supreme

Exterior expences, such as the navy, and extraordinaries of all kinds, were paid by the crown out of the duties which were levied on the produce of the colony imported into the mother country.

(*b*) These king's lieutenants were military officers residing in the several towns, commonly with the rank of colonel. There were also in each town *majors* and *aides-major*. All these officers were wholly independent of the civil power, and owned no superior but the governor-general, who could dismiss them at pleasure. It may be proper to observe too that the counsellors held their seats by a very uncertain tenure. One of the governors (the Prince de Rohan) sent the whole number state prisoners to France. They were seized on their seats of justice, and put on board a ship in irons, and in that condition conveyed to Paris, and shut up for a long time in the Bastille, without trial or hearing.

jurisdiction, as in the parliaments of France, the king's edicts, and those of the governor and intendant, were registered. Seven members constituted a quorum, but an appeal lay to the king in the last resort.

In most of the towns was a municipal establishment called *officers of the police;* consisting of inspectors, exempts, brigadiers, and serjeants. They were authorized to proceed summarily in quelling of riots; to arrest persons guilty of assault and battery, and thieves taken with *mainour*. They were appointed by the courts of justice, and were distinguished by a badge.

Another corps of nearly the same description, but of more extensive use, and of a more military character, was called the maréchaussée. It was partly composed of cavalry; and its functions were to watch over the general tranquillity; to protect travellers on the publick highways; to arrest negroes wandering without passports, and malefactors of all descriptions; to enforce the prompt execution of civil and criminal process, and lastly, to assist in the collection of the publick taxes.

The number of the king's troops on the colonial establishment was commonly from 2 to 3,000 men, composing two regiments of foot, and a brigade of artillery recruited from France; and each of the 51 parishes into which the colony was divided raised one or more companies of white militia, a company of mulattoes, and a company of free blacks. The whole number was reckoned between seven and eight thousand. The officers, both of the regular troops

troops and the militia, were commissioned provisionally by the governor-general, subject to the king's approbation; but the militia received no pay of any kind.

From this recapitulation, it is evident that the peace and happiness of the people of St. Domingo depended very much on the personal qualities and native disposition of the governor-general, who was commonly selected from the navy or army. At the same time it must be honestly admitted, that the liberality and mildness, which of late years have dignified and softened the military character among all the nations of Europe, had a powerful influence in the administration of the government in the French colonies. It must be allowed also, that the manifest importance to which, as mankind become divested of ancient prejudices, the commercial part of the community, even among the French, has imperceptibly risen, insured to the wealthy and opulent planters a degree of respect from persons in power, which, in former times, attached only to noble birth and powerful connections; while the lower orders among the whites derived the same advantage from that unconquerable distinction which nature herself has legibly drawn between the white and black inhabitants; and from their visible importance, in a country where, from the disproportion of the whites to the blacks, the common safety of the former class depends altogether on their united exertions.

To contend, as some philosophers have idly contended, that no natural superiority can justly belong

long to any one race of people over another, to Europeans over Africans, merely from a difference of colour, is to waste words to no purpose, and to combat with air. Among the inhabitants of every island in the West Indies, it is the colour, with some few exceptions, that distinguishes freedom from slavery: so long therefore as freedom shall be enjoyed exclusively by one race of people, and slavery be the condition of another, contempt and degradation will attach to the colour by which that condition is generally recognized, and follow it, in some degree, through its varieties and affinities. We may trace a similar prejudice among the most liberal and enlightened nations of Europe. Although nothing surely ought to reflect greater lustre on any man than the circumstance of his having risen by industry and virtue above the disadvantages of mean birth and indigent parentage, there are, nevertheless, but few persons in the world who delight to be reminded of this species of merit. There is a consciousness of something disgraceful in the recollection; and it seems therefore reasonable to conclude, that if nature had made the same distinction in this case as in the other, and stamped, by an indelible mark, the condition and parentage on the forehead, the same, or nearly the same, effect would have resulted from it, as results from the difference of colour in the West Indies. I mean however only to account for, in some degree, not to defend altogether, the conduct of the whites of St. Domingo towards the coloured people;

CHAP. I.

ple; whose condition was in truth much worse than that of the same class in the British colonies, and not to be justified on any principle of example or reason.

Free Mulattoes.

In many respects their situation was even more degrading and wretched than that of the enslaved negroes in any part of the West Indies; all of whom have masters that are interested in their preservation, and many of whom find in those masters powerful friends and vigilant protectors. Although released from the dominion of individuals, yet the free men of colour in all the French islands were still considered as the property of the publick, and as publick property they were obnoxious to the caprice and tyranny of all those whom the accident of birth had placed above them. By the colonial governments they were treated as slaves in the strictest sense; they are liable, on attaining the age of manhood, to serve three years in the military establishment called the maréchaussée, and on the expiration of that term they were compelled to serve in the militia of the parish or quarter to which they belonged, without pay or allowance of any kind, and in the horse or foot, at the pleasure of the commanding officer; and obliged also to supply themselves, at their own expence, with arms, ammunition, and accoutrements. The rigour with which the king's lieutenants, majors, and aides-major, enforced their authority over these people, had degenerated into the basest tyranny.

They were forbidden to hold any publick office,

fice, trust, or employment, however insignificant; they were not even allowed to exercise any of those professions, to which some sort of liberal education is supposed to be necessary. All the naval and military departments, all degrees in law, physick, and divinity, were appropriated exclusively by the whites. A mulatto could not be a priest, nor a lawyer, nor a physician, nor a surgeon, nor an apothecary, nor a schoolmaster. He could not even assume the sirname of the white man to whom he owed his being. Neither did the distinction of colour terminate, as in the British West Indies, with the third generation. The privileges of a white person were not allowed to any descendant from an African, however remote the origin. The taint in the blood was incurable, and spread to the latest posterity. Hence no white man, who had the smallest pretensions to character, would ever think of marriage with a negro or mulatto woman: such a step would immediately have terminated in his disgrace and ruin.

Under the pressure of these accumulated grievances, hope itself, too frequently the only solace of the wretched, was denied to these unfortunate people; for the courts of criminal jurisdiction, adopting the popular prejudices against them, gave effect and permanency to the system. A man of colour being prosecutor (a circumstance in truth which seldom occurred) must have made out a strong case indeed, if at any time he obtained the conviction of a white person. On the other hand, the whites never failed to procure

CHAP. I.

and speedy justice against the mulattoes. To mark more strongly the distinction between the two classes, the law declared, that if a free man of colour presumed to strike a white person of whatever condition, his right hand should be cut off; while a white man, for a similar assault on a free mulatto, was dismissed on the payment of an insignificant fine.

In extenuation of this horrible detail, it may be said with truth, that the manners of the white inhabitants softened, in some measure, the severity of their laws: thus, in the case last mentioned, the universal abhorrence which would have attended an enforcement of the penalty, made the law a dead letter. It was the same with the Roman law of the Twelve Tables, by which a father was allowed to inflict the punishment of death on his own child:—manners, not law, prevented the exertion of a power so unnatural and odious.

But the circumstance which contributed most to afford the coloured people of St. Domingo protection, was the privilege they possessed of acquiring and holding property to any amount. Several of them were the owners of considerable estates; and having happily the means of gratifying the venality of their superiors, these were secure enough in their persons; although the same circumstance made them more pointedly the objects of hatred and envy to the lower orders of the whites.

Enslaved negroes.

The next and lowest class of people in the French islands were the negroes in a state of slavery;

very; of whom, in the year 1789, St. Domingo contained no less than 480,000. It was in favour of this class that Louis XIV. in the year 1685, published the celebrated edict, or code of regulations, which is well known to the world under the title of the *Code Noir*; and it must be allowed, that many of its provisions breathe a spirit of tenderness and philanthropy which reflects honour on the memory of its author;—but there is this misfortune attending this, and must attend all other systems of the same nature, that most of its regulations are inapplicable to the condition and situation of the colonies in America. In countries where slavery is established, the leading principle on which government is supported, is *fear*; or a sense of that absolute coercive necessity, which, leaving no choice of action, supersedes all question of *right*. It is in vain to deny that such actually is, and necessarily must be, the case in all countries where slavery is allowed. Every endeavour, therefore, to extend positive rights to men in this state, as between one class of people and the other, is an attempt to reconcile inherent contradictions, and to blend principles together which admit not of combination. The great, and, I am afraid, the only certain and permanent security of the enslaved negroes, is the strong circumstance that the interest of the master is blended with, and, in truth, altogether depends on, the preservation, and even on the health, strength, and activity of the slave. This applies equally to all the European colonies in America; and accord-

ingly

CHAP. I.

ingly the actual condition of the negroes in all those colonies, to whatever nation they belong, is I believe nearly the same. Of that condition I have given an account in another place *(c)*: I have therefore only to observe in this, that in all the French islands the general treatment of the slaves is neither much better nor much worse, as far as I could observe, than in those of Great Britain. If any difference there is, I think that they are better clothed among the French, and allowed more animal food among the English. The prevalent notion that the French planters treat their negroes with greater humanity and tenderness than the British, I know to be groundless; yet no candid person, who has had an opportunity of seeing the negroes in the French islands, and of contrasting their condition with that of the peasantry in many parts of Europe, will think them, by any means, the most wretched of mankind.

On the whole, if human life, in its best state, is a combination of happiness and misery, and we are to consider that condition of political society as relatively good, in which, notwithstanding many disadvantages, the lower classes are easily supplied with the means of healthy subsistence; and a general air of cheerful contentedness, animates all ranks of people—where we behold opulent towns, plentiful markets, extensive commerce, and increasing cultivation—it must be pronounced that the government of the French part of St. Domingo (to whatever latent causes it might be owing) was

(c) Vol. II. Book 4. C. 2.

not

not altogether so practically bad, as some of the circumstances that have been stated might give room to imagine. With all the abuses arising from the licentiousness of power, the corruption of manners, and the system of slavery, the scale evidently preponderated on the favourable side; and, in spite of political evils and private grievances, the signs of publick prosperity were every where visible.

SUCH were the condition and situation of the French colony in St. Domingo in the year 1788— an eventful period; for the seeds of liberty which, ever since the war between Great Britain and her transatlantick possessions, had taken root in the kingdom of France, now began to spring up with a rank luxuriancy in all parts of her extensive dominions; and a thousand circumstances demonstrated that great and important changes and convulsions were impending. The necessity of a sober and well-digested arrangement for correcting inveterate abuses, both in the mother country and the colonies, was indeed apparent; but, unhappily, a spirit of subversion and innovation, founded on visionary systems inapplicable to real life, had taken possession of the publick mind. Its effects in St. Domingo are written in colours too lasting to be obliterated; for the pride of power, the rage of reformation, the contentions of party, and the conflict of opposing interests and passions, produced a tempest that swept every thing before it.

CHAP. II.

From the Revolution of 1789, *to the Meeting of the First General Colonial Assembly.*

CHAP. II.

ON the 27th of December 1788, the court of France came to the memorable determination to summon the States General of the kingdom; and resolved that the representation of the tiers état (or commons) should be equal to the sum of the representation of the other two orders.

THIS measure, as might have been foreseen, proved the basis of the great national revolution that followed; and it operated with immediate and decisive effect in all the French colonies. The governor of the French part of St. Domingo, at that period, was Mons Duchilleau, who was supposed secretly to favour the popular pretensions. He was allowed therefore to continue unmolested in the seat of government; but the king's sceptre dropped from his hand; for when he attempted to prevent the parochial and provincial meetings, which were every where summoned, from assembling, his proclamations were treated with indignity and contempt: the meetings were held in spite of the governor, and resolutions passed declaratory of the right of the colonists to send deputies to the States General. Deputies were accordingly elected for that purpose, to the number of eighteen (six for each province) who forthwith, without any authority either from the French ministry

ministry or the colonial government, embarked for France, as the legal representatives of a great and integral part of the French empire.

THEY arrived at Versailles the latter end of June, about a month after the States General had declared themselves the national assembly. But neither the minister nor the national assembly were disposed to admit the full extent of their claims. The number of eighteen deputies from one colony was thought excessive; and it was with some difficulty that six of them only were admitted to verify their powers, and seat themselves among the national representatives.

THERE prevailed at this time throughout the cities of France, a very strong and marked prejudice against the inhabitants of the Sugar Islands, on account of the slavery of their negroes. It was not indeed supposed, nor even pretended, that the condition of this people was worse at this juncture than in any former period: the contrary was known to be the truth. But declamations in support of personal freedom, and invectives against despotism of all kinds, had been the favourite topicks of many eminent French writers for a series of years: and the publick indignation was now artfully raised against the planters of the West Indies, as one of the means of exciting commotions and insurrections in different parts of the French dominions. This spirit of hostility against the inhabitants of the French colonies, was industriously fomented and aggravated by the measures of a society, who called themselves *Amis des*

 Noirs

CHAP. II. 1789. *Noirs* (Friends of the Blacks); and it must be acknowledged, that the splendid appearance, and thoughtless extravagance, of many of the French planters resident in the mother country, contributed by no means to divert the malice of their adversaries, or to soften the prejudices of the publick towards them.

The society in France called *Amis des Noirs,* was I believe originally formed on the model of a similar association in London, but the views and purposes of the two bodies had taken a different direction. The society in London *professed* to have nothing more in view than to obtain an act of the legislature for prohibiting the further introduction of African slaves into the British colonies. They disclaimed all intention of interfering with the government and condition of the negroes already in the plantations; publickly declaring their opinion to be, that a general emancipation of those people, in their present state of ignorance and barbarity, instead of a blessing, would prove to them a source of misfortune and misery. On the other hand, the society of *Amis des Noirs,* having secretly in view to subvert the ancient despotism of the French government, loudly clamoured for a general and immediate abolition, not only of the slave trade, but also of the slavery which it supported. Proceeding on abstract reasoning, rather than on the actual condition of human nature, they distinguished not between civilized and uncivilized life, and considered that it ill became them to claim freedom for themselves, and withhold it at the same time from the negroes: it is to be lamented that a principle so plausible in appearance, should, in its application to this case, be visionary and impracticable.

At this juncture, a considerable body of the mulattoes from St. Domingo and the other French islands, were resident in the French capital. Some of these were young people sent thither for education: others were men of considerable property, and many of them, without doubt, persons of intelligence and amiable manners. With these people the society of *Amis des Noirs* formed an intimate connection; pointed out to them the wretchedness of their condition; filled the nation with remonstrances and appeals on their behalf; and poured out such invectives against the white planters, as bore away reason and moderation in the torrent. Unhappily, there was too much to offer on the part of the mulattoes. Their personal appearance too, excited pity, and, co-operating with the temper of the times, and the credulity of the French nation, raised such an indignant spirit in all ranks of people against the white colonists, as threatened their total annihilation and ruin.

In this disposition of the people of France towards the inhabitants of their colonies in the West Indies, the national assembly, on the 20th day of August, voted the celebrated *declaration of rights;* and thus, by a revolution unparalleled in history, was a mighty fabrick (apparently established by every thing that was secure and unassailable) overturned in a moment. Happy had

 it

CHAP. II. 1789. it been for the general interests of the human race, if, when the French had gone thus far, they had proceeded no farther! Happy for themselves, if they had then known—what painful experience has since taught them—that the worst of all governments is preferable to the miseries of anarchy!

PERHAPS a diligent observer might have discovered, even in the first proceedings of this celebrated assembly, the latent seeds of that violence, injustice, and confusion which have since produced such a harvest of crimes and calamities. Many of the doctrines contained in the declaration of rights seem to have been introduced for no other purpose than to awaken a mischievous spirit of contention and cavil, and to destroy all subordination in the lower ranks of the people. Such, for instance, was the position, that "all men are "born, and continue, free and equal as to their "rights;" according to which, there ought to be no distinctions in society, nor (if the possession of property is *a right)* can any man have a right to possess or acquire any thing to the exclusion of others; a position not only false, but pernicious, and unfit for every condition of civilized life. To promulgate such lessons in the colonies, as the declared sense of the supreme government, was to subvert the whole system of their establishments. Accordingly, a general ferment prevailed among the French inhabitants of St. Domingo, from one end of the colony to the other. All that had passed in the mother country con-

cerning

cerning the colonists,—the prejudices of the metropolis towards them,—the efforts of the society of *Amis des Noirs* to emancipate the negroes,—and the conduct of the mulattoes,—had been represented to them through the medium of party, and perhaps with a thousand circumstances of exaggeration and insult, long before the declaration of rights was received in the colony; and this measure crowned the whole. They maintained that it was calculated to convert their peaceful and contented negroes into implacable enemies, and render the whole country a theatre of commotion and bloodshed.

In the meanwhile the French government, apprehensive that disorders of a very alarming nature might arise in the colonies from the proceedings in France, had issued orders to the governor general of St. Domingo, to convoke the inhabitants, for the purpose of forming a legislative assembly for interior regulation. These orders, however, being unaccountably delayed, the people had anticipated the measure. The inhabitants of the Northern district had already constituted a provincial assembly, which met at Cape François, and their example was followed in November in the Western and Southern provinces; the Western assembly met at Port au Prince, the Southern at *Les Cayes*. Parochial committees were, at the same time, every where established, for the sake of a more immediate communication between the people and their representatives.

A recital of the conduct and proceedings of these

CHAP. II. 1789.

these provincial assemblies, would lead me too much into detail. They differed greatly on many important questions; but all of them concurred in opinion concerning the necessity of a full and speedy colonial representation; and they unanimously voted, that if instructions from the king for calling such an assembly should not be received within three months thenceforward, the colony should take on itself to adopt and enforce the measure;—their immediate safety and preservation being, they said, an obligation paramount to all others.

DURING this period of anxiety and alarm, the mulattoes were not inactive. Instructed by their brethren in the metropolis in the nature and extent of their rights, and apprized of the favourable disposition of the French nation towards them, they became, throughout the colony, actuated by a spirit of turbulence and sedition; and disregarding all considerations of prudence, with regard to time and seasons, determined to claim, without delay, the full benefit of all the privileges enjoyed by the whites. Accordingly large bodies of them appeared in arms in different parts of the country; but acting without sufficient concert, or due preparation, they were easily overpowered. It is said, that the temper of the provincial assemblies at this juncture,—how much soever inflamed against the instigators and abettors of these people in the mother country,—was not averse to moderation and concession towards the mulattoes themselves. Thus, when the party which had taken arms at

Jacmel

Jacmel was defeated, and their chiefs imprisoned, the assembly of the West interposed with effect in favour of the whole number; and at Artibonite, where the revolt was much more extensive and alarming, a free and unconditional pardon was also chearfully granted on the submission of the insurgents.

Against such of the whites as had taken any part in these disturbances, in favour of the people of colour, the rage of the populace knew no limits. Mons. *Dubois*, deputy *procureur general*, had not only declared himself an advocate for the mulattoes, but, with a degree of imprudence which indicated insanity, sought occasions to declaim publickly against the slavery of the negroes. The Northern assembly arrested his person, and very probably intended to proceed to greater extremities; but the governor interposed in his behalf, obtained his release, and sent him from the country.

Mons. *Ferrand de Beaudierre*, who had formerly been a magistrate at Petit Goave, was not so fortunate. This gentleman was unhappily enamoured of a woman of colour, to whom, as she possessed a valuable plantation, he had offered marriage, and being a man of a warm imagination, with little judgment, he undertook to combat the prejudices of the whites against the whole class. He drew up, in the name and behalf of the mulatto people, a memorial to the parochial committee, wherein, among other things, they were made to claim, in express words, the full benefit of the national declaration of rights. Nothing could

CHAP. II. 1789. could be more ill-timed or injudicious than this proceeding: it was evident, that such a claim led to consequences of which the mulattoes themselves (who certainly at this juncture had no wish to enfranchise the slaves) were not apprized. This memorial therefore was considered as a summons to the negroes for a general revolt. The parochial committee seized the author, and committed him to prison; but the populace took him from thence by force, and in spite of the magistrates and municipality, who exerted themselves to stop their fury, put him to death.

January 1790. THE king's order for convoking a general colonial assembly was received in St. Domingo early in the month of January 1790. It appointed the town of Leogane, in the Western province, for the place of meeting; and instructions accompanied the order, concerning the mode of electing the members. These instructions, however, being considered by the provincial assemblies as inapplicable to the circumstances of the colony, were disapproved; and another plan, better suited, as they conceived, to the wealth, territory, and population of the inhabitants, was adopted. They resolved also to hold the assembly at the town of St. Marc instead of Leogane, and the 25th of March was fixed for the time of its meeting. It was afterwards prorogued to the 16th of April.

IN the meanwhile intelligence was received in France of the temper of St. Domingo towards the mother country. The inhabitants were very generally represented as manifesting a disposition either

to

CHAP. II. 1790.

to renounce their dependency, or to throw themselves under the protection of a foreign power; and the planters of Martinico were said to be equally discontented and disaffected. The trading and manufacturing towns took the alarm; and petitions and remonstrances were presented from various quarters, imploring the national assembly to adopt measures for composing the minds of the colonists, and preserving to the French empire its most valuable dependencies.

On the 8th of March 1790, the national assembly entered into the consideration of the subject, with a seriousness and solemnity suited to its importance; and, after full discussion, a very large majority voted, "That it never was the inten-"tion of the assembly to comprehend the inte-"rior government of the colonies in the consti-"tution which they had framed for the mother "country, or to subject them to laws which "were incompatible with their local establish-"ments; they therefore authorise the inhabi-"tants of each colony to signify to the national "assembly their sentiments and wishes concern-"ing that plan of interior legislation and com-"mercial arrangement, which would be most "conducive to their prosperity." It was required, however, that the plan to be offered should be conformable to the principles which had connected the colonies with the metropolis, and be calculated for the preservation of their reciprocal interests.—To this decree was annexed a declaration, "That the national assembly would "not

CHAP. II. 1790. "not cause any innovation to be made, directly or "indirectly, in any system of commerce in which "the colonies were already concerned."

NOTHING could equal the clamour which this decree occasioned among the people of colour resident in the mother country, and the philanthropick society of *Amis des Noirs*. The declaration concerning commerce was interpreted into a tacit sanction for the continuance of the slave trade; and it was even contended, that the national assembly, by leaving the adjustment of the colonial constitutions to the colonists themselves, had discharged them from their allegiance. It was said that they were no longer subject to the French empire, but members of an independent state.

NEVERTHELESS, if the circumstances of the times, and the disposition of the French colonists at this juncture, be taken into the account, candour must acknowledge that it was a decree not only justifiable on the motives of prudence and policy, but was founded also on the strong basis of moral necessity. The arguments that were urged against it seem to imply that the benefits of the French revolution were intended only for the people residing in the realm, in exclusion of their fellow subjects in the plantations. After that great event, to suppose that the inhabitants of those colonies (with the successful example too of the English Americans recent in their memories) would have submitted to be governed and directed in their local concerns by a legislature at the distance of 3,000 miles from them, is to manifest a very slender

CHAP. II. 1790.

slender acquaintance with human nature. How little inclined the colonial assembly was to such submission, their proceedings, from the first day of their meeting, to their final dissolution, will demonstrate.—Of those proceedings I shall endeavour to furnish a brief account in the next Chapter.

CHAP.

CHAP. III.

Proceedings of the General Colonial Assembly until its final Dissolution, and Embarkation of the Members for France, August 1790.

CHAP. II. 1790. THE General Assembly of St. Domingo met on the 16th of April, at the town of St. Marc. It was composed of 213 members, of whom the city of Cape François elected twenty-four, Port au Prince sixteen, and Les Cayes eight. Most of the other parishes returned two representatives each; and it is allowed that, on the whole, the colony was fairly, fully, and most respectably represented. The provincial assemblies, however, continued in the exercise of their functions as before, or appointed committees to act during their intermission.

THE session was opened by a discourse from the president, wherein, after recounting various abuses in the constitution and administration of the former colonial government, he pointed out some of the many great objects that seemed to require immediate attention: among others, he recommended the case of the mulattoes, and amelioration of the slave laws. The assembly concurred in sentiment with the orator; and one of their first measures was to relieve the people of colour from the hardships to which they were subject under the military jurisdiction. It was decreed, that in future no greater duty should be required of them in the militia than from the whites; and the harsh autho-

rity,

CHAP. III. 1790.

rity, in particular, which the king's lieutenants, majors, and aides-major, commanding in the towns, exercised over those people, was declared oppressive and illegal. These acts of indulgence were certainly meant as the earnest of greater favours, and an opening to conciliation and concession towards the whole class of the coloured people.

The general assembly proceeded, in the next place, to rectify some gross abuses which had long prevailed in the courts of judicature, confining themselves however to such only as called for immediate redress, their attention being chiefly directed to the great and interesting object of preparing the plan for a new constitution, or system of colonial government; a business which employed their deliberations until the 28th of May.

M. Peynier was now governor general, from whom the partizans and adherents of the ancient despotism secretly derived encouragement and support. The whole body of tax-gatherers, and officers under the fiscal administration, were of this number. These therefore began to recover from the panick into which so great and sudden a revolution had thrown them, and to rally their united strength. Nothing could be more opposite to their wishes, than the success of the general assembly in the establishment of order and good government throughout the colony. Nor were these the only men who beheld the proceedings of this body with an evil eye. All the persons belonging to the courts of civil and criminal jurisdiction (and their

CHAP. III. 1790.

numbers were considerable) who were interested in the maintenance of those abuses which the assembly had corrected, were filled with indignation and envy. To these were added most of the men who held military commissions under the king's authority. Habituated to the exercise of command, they indignantly beheld the subversion of all that accustomed obedience and subordination which they had been taught to consider as essential to the support of government, and offered themselves the willing instruments of the governor general in subverting the new system.

SUCH were the persons that opposed themselves to the new order of things in the colony, when the Chevalier Mauduit, colonel of the regiment of Port au Prince, arrived at St. Domingo. He had not come directly from France, but circuitously by way of Italy; and at Turin had taken leave of the Count d'Artois, to whose fortunes he was strongly attached. He was a man of talents; brave, active, and enterprizing; zealous for his party, and full of projects for a counter-revolution. By his dexterity and address, he soon acquired an ascendancy over the feeble and narrow genius of Peynier, and governed the colony in his name. His penetration easily made him discover that, in order effectually to disturb the new settlement, it was absolutely necessary to prevent a coalition of interests between the colonial assembly, and the free people of colour. He therefore proclaimed himself the patron and protector of the mulattoes, and courted them on all occasions, with

with such assiduity and success, as gained over the whole body.

It seems however extremely probable that the peace of the country would have been preserved, notwithstanding the machinations of Peynier, and Mauduit, if the planters, true to their own cause, had remained united among themselves. But, unfortunately, the provincial assembly of the North was induced, through misrepresentation or envy, to counteract, by all possible means, the proceedings of the general assembly at St. Marc. Thus, discord and dissention every where prevailed; and appearances seemed to indicate an approaching civil war, even before the plan for the new constitution was published. This was contained in the famous decree of the general colonial assembly of the 28th of May; a decree, which having been the subject of much animadversion, and made the ostensible motive, on the part of the executive power, for commencing hostilities, it is proper to state at large.

May.

It consisted of ten fundamental positions, which are preceded by an introductory discourse or preamble (as usual in the French decrees) wherein, among other considerations, it is stated, as an acknowledged principle in the French constitution, that the right in the crown to confirm the acts of the legislature, is a prerogative, inherent and *incommunicable*: of course that it cannot be delegated to a colonial governor, whose authority is precarious and subordinate. The articles are then subjoined, in the order and words following:

"1. The legislative authority, in every thing which relates to the internal concerns of the colony

CHAP. III. 1790.

lony (*regime interieur*), is vested in the assembly of its representatives, which shall be called *the General Assembly of the French Part of St. Domingo*.

2. No act of the legislative body, in what relates to the internal concerns of the colony, shall be considered *as a law definitive*, unless it be made by the representatives of the French part of St. Domingo, freely and legally chosen, and confirmed by the king.

3. In cases of urgent necessity, a legislative decree of the general assembly, in what relates to the internal concerns of the colony, shall be considered as a *law provisional*. In all such cases, the decree shall be notified forthwith to the governor general, who, within ten days after such notification, shall cause it to be published and enforced, or transmit to the general assembly his observations thereon.

4. The necessity of the case on which the execution of such provisional decree is to depend, shall be a separate question, and be carried in the affirmative by a majority of two-thirds of the general assembly; the names and numbers being taken down. (*Prises par l'appel nominel*).

5. If the governor general shall send down his observations on any such decree, the same shall be entered in the journals of the general assembly, who shall then proceed to revise the decree, and consider the observations thereon in three several sittings. The votes for confirming or annulling the decree shall be given in the words *Yes* or *No*, and a minute of the proceedings shall be signed by the members present, in which shall be enumerated the votes on each side of the question; and if there

there appears a majority of two-thirds for confirming the decree, it shall be immediately enforced by the governor-general.

6. As every law ought to be founded on the consent of those who are to be bound by it, the French part of St. Domingo shall be allowed to propose regulations concerning commercial arrangements, and the system of mutual connection (*rapports commerciaux, et autres rapports communs*), and the decrees which the national assembly shall make in all such cases *shall not be enforced in the colony, until the general assembly shall have consented thereto.*

7. In cases of pressing necessity, the importation of articles for the support of the inhabitants shall not be considered as any breach in the system of commercial regulations between St. Domingo and France; provided that the decrees to be made in such cases by the general assembly, shall be submitted to the revision of the governor-general, under the same conditions and modifications as are prescribed in articles 3 and 5.

8. Provided also, that every legislative act of the general assembly, executed provisionally, in cases of urgent necessity, shall be transmitted forthwith for the royal sanction. And if the king shall refuse his consent to any such act, its execution shall be suspended, as soon as the king's refusal shall be legally notified to the general assembly.

9. A new general assembly shall be chosen every two years, and none of the members who have

 served

CHAP. III. 1790.

served in the former assembly shall be eligible in the new one.

10. The general assembly decree that the preceding articles, as forming part of the constitution of the French colony in St. Domingo, shall be immediately transmitted to France for the acceptance of the national assembly, and the king. They shall likewise be transmitted to all the parishes and districts of the colony, and be notified to the governor-general."

THAT a decree of such comprehensiveness and magnitude should have excited very general disquisition in the colony, and have produced misrepresentation and clamour, even among men of very opposite sentiments and tempers, is no way surprising. It must be allowed, that some of the articles are irreconcileable to every just principle of colonial subordination. The refusing to allow a negative voice to the representative of the king, is repugnant to all the notions which an Englishman is taught to entertain of a monarchical government, however limited: and the declaration that no decree of the national assembly concerning the colony, in cases of exterior regulation, should be in force until confirmed by the colonial assembly, was such an extravagant assumption of imperial authority, in a subordinate part of the French empire, as I believe is without a precedent.

ALL that can be urged in extenuation seems to be, that the circumstances of the case were novel, and the members of the colonial assembly unexperienced in the business of legislation. That they

had

CHAP. III. 1790.

had any serious intention of declaring the colony an independent state, in imitation of the English American provinces, it is impossible to believe. Nevertheless, the decree was no sooner promulgated, than this notion was industriously propagated by their enemies from one end of the colony to the other; and when this report failed to gain belief, it was pretended that the colony was sold to the English, and that the members of the general assembly had received and divided among themselves 40 millions of livres as the purchase money.

If recent events had not demonstrated the extreme credulity and jealous temper of the French character, it would be difficult to believe that charges, thus wild and unsupported, could have made an impression on the minds of any considerable number of the people. So great however was the effect produced by them, as to occasion some of the Western parishes to recal their deputies; while the inhabitants of Cape François took measures still more decisive: they renounced obedience to the general assembly, and presented a memorial to the governor, requesting him to dissolve it forthwith; declaring that they considered the colony as lost, unless he proceeded with the utmost vigour and promptitude in depriving that body of all manner of authority.

M. Peynier received this address with secret satisfaction. It seemed indeed to be the policy of both parties to reject all thoughts of compromise by negociation; and there occurred at this junc-

CHAP. III. 1790. ture a circumstance which would probably have rendered all negociation abortive, had it been attempted. In the harbour of Port-au Prince lay a ship of the line, called the Leopard, commanded by M. Galisoniere. This officer, co-operating in the views of Peynier and Mauduit, made a sumptuous entertainment for the partizans of those gentlemen; and by this, or some other parts of his conduct, gave offence to his sailors. Whether these men had felt the influence of corruption (as asserted by one party) or were actuated solely by one of those unaccountable freaks to which seamen are particularly subject, the fact certainly is, that they withdrew their obedience from their proper officer, and declared themselves to be in the interests of the colonial assembly! Their conduct became at length so turbulent and seditious, as to induce M. Galisoniere to quit the ship; whereupon the crew gave the command to one of the lieutenants. The assembly, perceiving the advantages to be derived from this event, immediately transmitted a vote of thanks to the seamen (27th July.) for their patriotick conduct, and required them, in the name of the law and the king, to detain the ship in the road, and await their further orders. The sailors, gratified with this acknowledgment, promised obedience, and affixed the vote of thanks on the mainmast of the ship. Some partizans of the assembly, about the same time, took possession of a powder magazine at Leogane.

A CIVIL war seemed now to be inevitable. Two days after the vote of thanks had been transmitted from St. Marc's to the crew of the Leopard, M. Peynier

Peynier issued a proclamation to dissolve the general assembly. He charged the members with entertaining projects of independency, and asserted that they had treacherously possessed themselves of one of the king's ships by corrupting the crew. He pronounced the members, and all their adherents, traitors to their country, and enemies to the nation and the king: declaring that it was his intention to employ all the force he could collect to defeat their projects, and bring them to condign punishment; and he called on all officers, civil and military, for their co-operation and support.

His first proceedings were directed against the committee of the Western provincial assembly.—This body held its meetings at Port au Prince, and in the exercise of its subordinate functions, during the intermission of that assembly, had manifested such zealous attachment to the general assembly at St. Marc, as exposed its members to the resentment of the governor and his party. It was determined therefore, at a council held the same day, to arrest their persons the following night, and M. Mauduit undertook to conduct the enterprize. Having been informed that this committee held consultations at midnight, he selected about one hundred of his soldiers, and formed a scheme to seize the members at their place of meeting. On arriving however at the house, he found it protected by four hundred of the national guards *(g)*. A skirmish ensued; but the circumstances

(g) The troops in St. Domingo, called *the National Guards*, were

CHAP. III. 1790.

stances attending it are so variously related, that no precise account can be given of the particulars; nor is it ascertained which party gave the first fire. Nothing further is certainly known, than that two men were killed on the part of the assembly,—that several were wounded on both sides, and that M. Mauduit returned without effecting any purpose but that of seizing, and bearing away in triumph, the national colours;—a circumstance which afterwards (as will be seen in the sequel, cost him his life.

The general assembly, on receiving intelligence of this attack, and of the formidable preparations that were making for directing hostilities against themselves, summoned the people, from all parts of the colony, to hasten, properly armed, to protect their representatives; and most of the inhabitants of the neighbouring parishes obeyed the summons. The ship Leopard was brought from Port au Prince to St. Marc's for the same purpose. On the other hand, the Northern provincial assembly joined the party of the governor, and sent to his assistance a detachment from the regular troops in that quarter, which was joined by a body of two hundred people of colour. A much greater force was collected at the same time in the Western province by M. Mauduit, and the preparations on both sides threatened an obstinate and bloody conflict; when, by one of those won-

were originally nothing more than the colonial Militia. They were new organized in 1789, on the model of the national guards in the mother-country, and bore the same colours, and assumed the same name.

derful

derful eccentricities in the human mind which are seldom displayed except in times of publick commotion, a stop was put to the immediate shedding of blood, by the sudden and unexpected determination of the general assembly to undertake a voyage to France, and justify their conduct to the king and the national assembly in person. Their motives were thought the more laudable, as great part of the Western and Southern provinces gave a decided approbation of their conduct, and armed in a very short time two thousand men in their defence; which were in full march for Port au Prince. Their resolution however was fixed, and accordingly, of about one hundred members, to which the colonial assembly was reduced by sickness and desertion, no less than eighty-five (of whom sixty-four were fathers of families) actually embarked on board the Leopard, and on the 8th of August, took their departure for Europe: a proceeding which created as much surprize in the governor and his party, as admiration and applause among the people at large. Persons of all ranks accompanied the members to the place of embarkation, pouring forth prayers for their success, and shedding tears of sensibility and affection for a conduct which was very generally considered as noble a proof of self-denial, and as signal an instance of heroick virtue and christian forbearance as any age has exhibited. A momentary calm followed this event:—the parties in arms appeared mutually disposed to submit their differences to the wisdom and justice of the king and the national assembly, and M. Peynier resumed,

CHAP. III. 1790.

sumed, though with a trembling hand, the reins of government.

SUCH was the issue of the first attempt to establish a free constitution in the French part of St. Domingo, on the system of a limited monarchy; and it affords occasion for some important reflections. That the general colonial assembly, in their decree of the 28th of May, exceeded the proper boundary of their constitutional functions, has been frankly admitted. This irregularity, however, might have been corrected without bloodshed or violence; but there is this misfortune attending every deviation from the rule of right, that, in the conflict of contending factions, the excesses of one party are ever considered as the fullest justification for the outrages of the other. For some parts of their conduct an apology may be offered. The measure of securing to their interests the crew of the Leopard, and the seizure of the magazine at Leogane, may be vindicated on the plea of self-defence. It cannot be doubted that M. Peynier had long meditated how best to restore the ancient despotick system, and that, jointly with M. Mauduit and others, he had made preparations for that purpose. He had written to M. Luzerne, the minister in France, that he never intended the colonial assembly to meet; and let it be told in this place, in justice to the French ministry, that the answer which he received contained a tacit disapprobation of his measures; for M. Luzerne recommended moderate and conciliatory councils. The governor proceeded notwithstanding in the same career, and distrustful

trustful perhaps of the fidelity of the French soldiers, he made application (as appeared afterward) to the governor of the Havannah for a reinforcement of Spanish troops from Cuba. It is evident therefore that he concurred entirely in the plans of Mauduit for effectuating a counter-revolution; and hence it is reasonable to conclude, that the discord and distrust which prevailed among the inhabitants; and above all the fatal dissentions that alienated the provincial assembly of the North, from the general assembly at St. Marc's, were industriously fomented and encouraged by M. Peynier and his adherents. Concerning the members of the colonial assembly, their prompt and decisive determination to repair to France, and surrender their persons to the supreme government, obviates all impeachment of their loyalty. Their attachment to the mother-country was indeed secured by too many ties of interest and self-preservation to be doubted.

Of their reception by the national assembly, and the proceedings adopted in consequence of their arrival in Europe, I shall hereafter have occasion to speak. A pause in this place seems requisite;—for I have now to introduce to the reader the mournful history of an unfortunate individual, over whose sad fate (however we may condemn his rash and ill-concerted enterprize)

"One human tear may drop, and be forgiven!"

CHAP. IV.

Rebellion and Defeat of James Ogé, *a free Man of Colour.*

CHAP. IV.

1790.

FROM the first meeting of the general assembly of St. Domingo, to its dissolution and dispersion, as related in the preceding chapters, the coloured people resident within the colony remained on the whole more peaceable and orderly than might have been expected. The temperate and lenient disposition manifested by the assembly towards them, produced a beneficial and decisive effect in the Western and Southern provinces, and although 300 of them from these provinces, had been persuaded by M. Mauduit to join the force under his command, they very soon became sensible of their error, and, instead of marching towards St. Marc, as Mauduit proposed, they demanded and obtained their dismission, and returned quietly to their respective habitations. Such of the mulatto people however as resided at that juncture in the mother-country, continued in a far more hostile disposition; and they were encouraged in their animosity towards the white colonists by parties of very different descriptions. The colonial decree of the 28th of May, 1790, was no sooner made known in France, than it excited universal clamour. Many persons who concurred in nothing else, united their voices in reprobating the conduct of the inhabitants of St. Domingo. The

CHAP. IV. 1790.

The adherents of the ancient government were joined on this occasion by the partizans of democracy and republicanism. To the latter, the constitution of 1789 was even more odious than the old tyranny; and these men, with the deepest and darkest designs, possessed all that union, firmness, and perseverance which were necessary to their purposes; and which, as the world has beheld, have since rendered them irresistible. These two factions hoped to obtain very different ends, by the same means; and there was another party who exerted themselves with equal assiduity in promoting publick confusion: these were the discordant class of speculative reformers, whom it was impossible to reconcile to the new government, because every man among them had probably formed a favourite system in his own imagination which he was eager to recommend to others. I do not consider the philanthropick society, called *Amis des Noirs,* as another distinct body, because it appears to me that they were pretty equally divided between the democratick party, and the class last mentioned. Strengthened by such auxiliaries, it is not surprizing that the efforts of this society should have operated powerfully on the minds of those who were taught to consider their personal wrongs as the cause of the nation, and have driven some of them into the wildest excesses of fanaticism and fury.

Among such of these unfortunate people resident in France as were thus inflamed into madness, was a young man under thirty years of age, named James Ogé: he was born in St. Domingo,

CHAP. IV. 1790.

of a mulatto woman who still possessed a coffee plantation in the Northern province, about thirty miles from Cape François, whereon she lived very creditably, and found means out of its profits to educate her son at Paris, and even to support him there in some degree of affluence, after he had obtained the age of manhood. His reputed father, a white planter of some account, had been dead several years.

Ogé had been introduced to the meetings of the *Amis des Noirs*, under the patronage of Gregoire, Brissot *(h)*, La Fayette, and Robespierre *(i)*, the leading members of that society; and was by them initiated into the popular doctrine of *equality*, and *the rights of man*. Here it was that he first learnt the miseries of his condition; the cruel wrongs and contumelies to which he and all his mulatto brethren were exposed in the West Indies, and the monstrous injustice and absurdity of that prejudice, "which, (said Gregoire) estimating a "man's merit by the colour of his skin, has placed "at an immense distance from each other the "children of the same parent; a prejudice which "stifles the voice of nature, and breaks the bands "of fraternity asunder."

That these are great evils must be frankly admitted, and it would have been fortunate if such men as Brissot and Gregoire, instead of bewailing their existence and magnifying their extent, had applied their talents in considering of the best practicable means of redressing them.

(h) Guillotined 31 October, 1793.
(i) Guillotined 28 July, 1794.

But

But these persons had other objects in view:—their aim, as I have shewn, was not to reform, but to destroy; to excite convulsions in every part of the French empire; and the ill-fated Ogé became the tool, and was afterwards the victim, of their guilty ambition.

He had been led to believe, that the whole body of coloured people in the French islands were prepared to rise up as one man against their oppressors; that nothing but a discreet leader was wanting, to set them into action; and, fondly conceiving that he possessed in his own person all the qualities of an able general, he deternined to proceed to St. Domingo by the first opportunity. To cherish the conceit of his own importance, and animate his exertions, the society procured him the rank of lieutenant-colonel in the army of one of the German electors.

As it was found difficult to export a sufficient quantity of arms and ammunition from France, without attracting the notice of the government, and awakening suspicion among the planters resident in the mother-country, the society resolved to procure those articles in North America, and it was recommended to Ogé to make a circuitous voyage for that purpose. Accordingly, being furnished with money and letters of credit, he embarked for New England in the month of July 1790.

But, notwithstanding the caution that was observed in this instance, the whole project was publickly known at Paris previous to Ogé's embarkation;

CHAP. IV. 1790.

tion; and notice of the scheme, and even a portrait of Ogé himself, were transmitted to St. Domingo, long before his arrival in that island. He secretly landed there, from an American sloop, on the 12th of October 1790, and found means to convey undiscovered the arms and ammunition which he had purchased, to the place which his brother had prepared for their reception.

The first notice which the white inhabitants received of Ogé's arrival, was from himself. He dispatched a letter to the governor (Peynier) wherein, after reproaching the governor and his predecessors with the non-execution of the *Code Noir,* he demands, in very imperious terms, that the provisions of that celebrated statute should be enforced throughout the colony; he requires that the privileges enjoyed by one class of inhabitants (the whites) should be extended to all persons without distinction: declares himself the protector of the mulattoes, and announces his intention of taking up arms in their behalf, unless their wrongs should be redressed.

About six weeks had intervened between the landing of Ogé, and the publication of this mandate; in all which time he and his two brothers had exerted themselves to the utmost in spreading disaffection, and exciting revolt among the mulattoes. Assurances were held forth, that all the inhabitants of the mother-country were disposed to assist them in the recovery of their rights, and it was added, that the king himself was favourably inclined to their cause. Promises were distributed

tributed to some, and money to others. But, notwithstanding all these efforts, and that the temper of the times was favourable to his views, Ogé was not able to allure to his standard above 200 followers; and of these, the major part were raw and ignorant youths, unused to discipline, and averse to all manner of subordination and order.

He established his camp at a place called *Grande Riviere,* about fifteen miles from Cape François, and appointed his two brothers, together with one Mark Chavane, his lieutenants. Chavane was fierce, intrepid, active, and enterprizing; prone to mischief, and thirsty for vengeance. Ogé himself, with all his enthusiasm, was naturally mild and humane: he cautioned his followers against the shedding innocent blood; but little regard was paid to his wishes in this respect: the first white man that fell in their way they murdered on the spot: a second, of the name of Sicard, met the same fate; and it is related, that their cruelty towards such persons of their own complexion as refused to join in the revolt was extreme. A mulatto man of some property being urged to follow them, pointed to his wife and six children, assigning the largeness of his family as a motive for wishing to remain quiet. This conduct was considered as contumacious, and it is asserted, that not only the man himself, but the whole of his family, were massacred without mercy.

Intelligence was no sooner received at the town of Cape François of these enormities, than the

CHAP. IV. 1790. the inhabitants proceeded, with the utmost vigour and unanimity, to adopt measures for suppressing the revolt. A body of regular troops, and the Cape regiment of militia, were forthwith dispatched for that purpose. They soon invested the camp of the revolters, who made less resistance than might have been expected from men in their desperate circumstances. The rout became general; many of them were killed, and about sixty made prisoners: the rest dispersed themselves in the mountains. Ogé himself, one of his brothers, and Chavane his associate, took refuge in the Spanish territories. Of Ogé's other brother no intelligence was ever afterwards obtained.

After this unsuccessful attempt of Ogé, and his escape from justice, the disposition of the white inhabitants in general towards the mulattoes, was sharpened into great animosity. The lower classes in particular, (those whom the coloured people call *les petits blancs)* breathed nothing but vengeance against them; and very serious apprehensions were entertained, in all parts of the colony, of a proscription and massacre of the whole body.

Alarmed by reports of this kind, and the appearances which threatened them from all quarters, the mulattoes flew to arms in many places. They formed camps at Artibonite, Petit Goaves, Jeremie, and Les Cayes. But the largest and most formidable body assembled near the little town of *Verette*. The white inhabitants collected themselves in considerable force in the neighbourhood, and Colonel Mauduit, with a corps of two

two hundred men from the regiment of Port au Prince, hastened to their assistance; but neither party proceeded to actual hostility. M. Mauduit even left his detachment at the port of St. Marc, thirty-six miles from Verette, and proceeding singly and unattended to the camp of the mulattoes, had a conference with their leaders. What passed on that occasion was never publickly divulged. It is certain, that the mulattoes retired to their habitations in consequence of it; but the silence and secrecy of M. Mauduit, and his influence over them, gave occasion to very unfavourable suspicions, by no means tending to conciliate the different classes of the inhabitants to each other. He was charged with having traiterously persuaded them not to desist from their purpose, but only to postpone their vengeance to a more favourable opportunity; assuring them, with the utmost solemnity and apparent sincerity, that the king himself, and all the friends of the ancient government, were secretly attached to their cause, and would avow and support it whenever they could do it with advantage; and that the time was not far distant, &c. He is said to have pursued the same line of conduct at Jeremie, Les Cayes, and all the places which he visited. Every where he held secret consultations with the chiefs of the mulattoes, and those people every where immediately dispersed. At Les Cayes, a skirmish had happened before his arrival there, in which about fifty persons on both sides had lost their lives, and preparations were making to renew hostilities. The persuasions of M. Mauduit ef-

 fected

CHAP. IV. 1790. fected a truce; but Rigaud, the leader of the mulattoes in that quarter, openly declared that it was a transient and deceitful calm, and that no peace would be permanent, until one class of people had exterminated the other.

In November 1790, M. Peynier resigned the government to the lieutenant-general, and embarked for Europe;—a circumstance which proved highly pleasing to the major part of the planters:—and the first measure of M. Blanchelande (*k*), the new commander in chief, was considered as the earnest of a decisive and vigorous administration. He made a peremptory demand of Ogé and his associates from the Spaniards; and the manner in which it was enforced, induced an immediate compliance therewith. The wretched Ogé, and his companions in misery, were delivered over, the latter end of December, to a detachment of French troops, and safely lodged in the jail of Cape François, with the prisoners formerly taken; and a commission was soon afterwards issued to bring them to trial.

1791. Their examinations were long and frequent; and in the beginning of March 1791, sentence was pronounced. Twenty of Ogé's deluded followers, among them his own brother, were condemned to be hanged. To Ogé himself, and his lieutenant Chavane, a more terrible punishment was allotted:—they were adjudged to be broken

(*k*) Guillotined at Paris, 1793.

alive,

alive, and left to perish in that dreadful situation, on the wheel.

The bold and hardened Chavane met his fate with unusual firmness, and suffered not a groan to escape him during the extremity of his torture: but the fortitude of Ogé deserted him altogether. When sentence was pronounced, he implored mercy with many tears, and an abject spirit. He promised to make great discoveries if his life was spared, declaring that he had an important secret to communicate. A respite of twenty-four hours was accordingly granted; but it was not made known to the publick, at that time, that he divulged any thing of importance. His secret, if any he had, was believed to have died with him.

It was discovered, however, about nine months afterward, that this most unfortunate young man had not only made a full confession of the facts that I have related, but also disclosed the dreadful plot in agitation, and the miseries at that moment impending over the colony. His last solemn declarations and dying confession, sworn to and signed by himself the day before his execution, were actually produced; wherein he details at large the measures which the coloured people had fallen upon to excite the negro slaves to rise into rebellion. He points out the chiefs by name, and relates that, notwithstanding his own defeat, a general revolt would actually have taken place in the month of February preceding, if an extraordinary flood of rain, and consequent inundation from the rivers, had not prevented it. He declares

that

CHAP. IV. 1791.

that the ringleaders still maintained the same atrocious project, and held their meetings in certain subterranean passages, or caves, in the parish of La Grande Riviere, to which he offers, if his life might be spared, to conduct a body of troops, so that the conspirators might be secured.

The persons before whom this confession and narrative were made, were the commissioners appointed for the purpose of taking Ogé's examination, by the superior council of the Northern province, of which body they were also members (*l*). Whether this court (all the members of which were devotedly attached to the ancient system) determined of itself to suppress evidence of such great concern to the colony, or was directed on this occasion by the superior officers in the administration of the government, has never been clearly made known. Suppressed it certainly was, and the miserable Ogé hurried to immediate execution; seemingly to prevent the further communication, and full disclosure of so weighty a secret!

Christian charity might lead us to suppose that the commissioners by whom Ogé's examination was taken, disregarded and neglected (rather than suppressed) his information; considering it merely as the shallow artifice of a miserable man to obtain a mitigation of the dreadful punishment which awaited him, and utterly unworthy of credit. It does not appear, however, that the commissioners made this excuse for themselves; and the caution,

(*l*) Their names were Antoine Etienne Ruotte, and François Joseph de Vertierres.

circum-

circumspection, and secrecy which marked their conduct, leave no room for such a supposition. The planters at large scrupled not to declare, that the royalists in the colony, and the philanthropick and republican party in the mother-country, were equally criminal; and themselves made victims to the blind purposes, and unwarrantable passions, of two desperate and malignant factions.

Of men who openly and avowedly aimed at the subversion of all good order and subordination, we may easily credit the worst; but it will be difficult to point out any principle of rational policy by which the royalists could have been influenced to concur in the ruin of so noble and beautiful a part of the French empire. Their conduct therefore remains wholly inexplicable, or we must admit they were guided by a spirit of Machiavelian policy—a principle of refined cunning, which always defeats its own purpose. They must have encouraged the vain and fallacious idea that scenes of bloodshed, devastation, and ruin, in different parts of the French dominions, would induce the great body of the people to look back with regret to their former government, and lead them by degrees to co-operate in the scheme of effecting a counter-revolution; regarding the evils of anarchy as less tolerable than the dead repose of despotism. If such were their motives, we can only ascribe them to that infatuation with which Providence (as wise men have observed, and history evinces) *blinds a people devoted to destruction.*

CHAP.

CHAP. V.

Proceedings in France — Massacre of Colonel Mauduit in St. Domingo—and fatal Decree of the National Assembly of the 15th May 1791.

CHAP. V. 1791.

IN detailing the tragical story of the miserable Ogé, I have chosen to continue my narrative unbroken: but it is now time to call the reader homewards, and direct his attention to the measures adopted by the national assembly, in consequence of advices received from all parts of St. Domingo, concerning the proceedings of the colonial assembly which met at St. Marc's.

THE eighty-five members, whose embarkation for France has already been noticed, arrived at Brest on the 13th of September 1790. They were received on landing by all ranks of people, and even by men in authority, with congratulation and shouts of applause. The same honours were shewn to them as would have been paid to the national assembly. Their expences were defrayed, and sums of money raised for their future occasions by a voluntary and very general subscription; but these testimonies of respect and kindness served only to encrease the disappointment which they soon afterwards experienced in the capital; where a very different reception awaited them. They had the mortification to discover that their enemies had been beforehand with them. Depu-

ties

ties were already arrived from the provincial assembly of the North, who joining with the agents of Peynier and Mauduit, had so effectually prevailed with M. Barnave (a), the president of the committee for the colonies, that they found their cause prejudged, and their conduct condemned, without a hearing. The national assembly had issued a peremptory order, on the 21st of September, directing them to attend at Paris, and wait there for further directions. Their prompt obedience to this order procured them no favour. They were allowed a single audience only, and then indignantly dismissed from the bar. They solicited a second, and an opportunity of being confronted with their adversaries: the national assembly refused their request, and directed the colonial committee to hasten its report concerning their conduct. On the 11th of October, this report was presented by M. Barnave. It comprehended a detail of all the proceedings of the colonial assembly, from its first meeting at St. Marc's, and censured their general conduct in terms of great asperity; representing it as flowing from motives of disaffection towards the mother-country, and an impatience of subordination to constitutional authority and good government. The report concluded by recommending, "that "all the pretended decrees and acts of the said "colonial assembly, should be reversed, and pro-"nounced utterly null and of no effect; that the "said assembly should be declared dissolved, and

(a) Guillotined December 1, 1793.

CHAP. V. 1791. "its members rendered ineligible and incapable of "being delegated in future to the colonial assembly of St. Domingo; that testimonies of approbation should be transmitted to the Northern "provincial assembly, to Colonel Mauduit and "the regiment of Port au Prince, for resisting the "proceedings at St. Marc's; that the king should "be requested to give orders for the forming a "new colonial assembly on the principles of the "national decree of the 8th of March 1790, and "instructions of the 28th of the same month; "finally, that the *ci-devant* members, then in "France, should continue in a state of arrest, "until the national assembly might find time to "signify its further pleasure concerning them." A decree to this effect was accordingly voted on the 12th of October, by a very large majority; and the king was requested, at the same time, to send out an augmentation of force, both naval and military, for the better supporting the regal authority in St. Domingo.

It is not easy to describe the surprise and indignation which the news of this decree excited in St. Domingo, except among the partizans of the former government. By *them* it was regarded as the first step towards the revival of the ancient system; by most other persons it was considered as a dereliction by the national assembly of all principle; and the orders for electing a new colonial assembly were so little regarded, that many of the parishes positively refused to choose other deputies until the fate of their former members, at that time in France, should be decided; declaring,

ing, that they still considered those persons as the legal representatives of the colony. One immediate and apparent effect of this decree was, to heighten and inflame the popular resentment against Mauduit and his regiment. The reader has already been made acquainted with some particulars concerning this officer; and to what has been said of his general character, and his intemperate zeal for the re-establishment of the regal authority in its fullest extent, it may be added, that he was the more dangerous, because he was generous in his disposition, and even profuse in his bounty, towards his soldiers. In return, the attachment of his regiment towards his person appeared to exceed the usual limits of obedience and duty *(b)*.

THE massacre of this man by those very troops, a short time after the notification of the aforesaid decree, affords so striking an instance of that cruel and ungovernable disposition, equally impetuous and inconstant, which prevailed, and I am afraid still continues to prevail, amongst the lower classes of the people throughout all the French dominions, that I conceive a brief recital of the circumstances attending his murder will not be thought an unnecessary digression.

I HAVE, in a former place *(c)*, given some account of the proceedings of M. Peynier, the late governor, against certain persons who composed

(b) After his example they had rejected the national cockade, and wore a white feather in their hats, the symbol, or avowed signal, of the royal party.

(c) Chap. iii.

what

CHAP. V. 1791. what was called the committee of the Western provincial assembly, and of the attempt by M. Mauduit to seize by force the individuals who composed that committee. This happened on the 29th of July 1790; and I observed that the circumstance of M. Mauduit's carrying off the colours from a detachment of the national guards on that occasion, ultimately terminated in his destruction.

The case was, that not only the detachment from whom their ensign was taken, but the whole of the national guards throughout the colony, considered this act as the most outrageous and unpardonable insult that could possibly be offered to a body of men, who had sworn fidelity to the new constitution; and nothing but the dread of the superior discipline of the veterans composing the Port au Prince regiment (which Mauduit commanded) prevented them from exercising exemplary vengeance on the author of their disgrace. This regiment therefore, being implicated in the crime of their commanding officer, was regarded by the other troops with hatred and detestation.

On the 3d of March 1791, two ships of the line Le Fougueux and Le Borée, arrived from France, with two battalions of the regiments of Artois and Normandy; and when it is known that these troops had been visited by the crew of the Leopard, it will not appear surprising that, on their landing at Port au Prince, they should have manifested the same hostile disposition towards Mauduit's regiment, as was shewn by the national guards. They refused all manner of communication or intercourse with them, and even declined to enter into any of their places

of

CHAP. V 1791.

of resort. They considered, or affected to consider, them, as enemies to the colony, and traitors to their country. This conduct in the new-comers towards the ill-fated regiment, soon made a wonderful impression on the minds of both officers and privates of the regiment itself; and mutual reproach and accusation spread through the whole corps. The white feather was indignantly torn from their hats, and dark and sullen looks towards their once-loved commander, indicated not only that he had lost their confidence, but also that he was the object of meditated mischief. Mauduit soon perceived the full extent of his danger, and fearing to involve the governor (M. Blanchelande) and his family, in the ruin which awaited himself, he advised them to make the best of their way to Cape François, while they could do it with safety; and Blanchelande, for which he was afterwards much censured, followed this advice. Mauduit then harangued his grenadiers, to whom he had always shewn great kindness, and told them that he was willing, for the sake of peace, to restore to the national troops the colours which he had formerly taken from them; and even to carry them with his own hands, at the head of his regiment, and deposit them in the church in which they had been usually lodged: but he added, that he depended on their affection and duty to protect him from personal insult, while making this ample apology. The faithless grenadiers declared that they would protect him with their lives.

The next day the ceremony took place, and Mauduit

CHAP. V. 1791. Mauduit restored the colours, as he had promised, before a vast crowd of spectators. At that moment one of his own soldiers cried aloud, *that he must ask pardon of the national troops on his knees*; and the whole regiment applauded the proposal. Mauduit started back with indignation, and offered his bosom to their swords:—it was pierced with a hundred wounds, all of them inflicted by his own men, while not a single hand was lifted up in his defence. The spectators stood motionless, either through hatred to the man, or surprise at the treachery and cowardice of the soldiers. Such indeed was the baseness of these wretches, that no modern language can describe, but in terms which would not be endured, the horrible enormities that were practised on the dead body of their wretched commander. It was reserved for the present day to behold, for the first time, a civilized nation exceeding in feats of cruelty and revenge the savages of North America. I grieve to add, that many other dreadful instances might be recited in confirmation of this remark (*c*).

WHILE

(*c*) The following anecdote, though shocking to humanity, I have thought too extraordinary to omit. It was communicated to me by a French gentleman who was at St. Domingo at the time, and knew the fact; but decency has induced me to veil it in a learned language. MAUDUITO *vix mortuo, unus de militibus, dum cadaver calidum, et cruore adhuc fluente madidum, in pavimentum ecclesiæ episcopalis jacuit, sicam distringens, genitalia coram populo abscidit, et membra truncata in cistam componens ad feminam nobilem, quam amicam Mauduito statuit, ut legatum de mortuo attulit.*. It may afford the reader some consolation to find that the murder of their commanding officer, by his own regiment, excited in all the other troops no other sentiments than those

WHILE these shameful enormities were passing in St. Domingo, the society of *Amis des Noirs* in the mother-country were but too successfully employed in devising projects which gave birth to deeds of still greater horror, and produced scenes that transformed the most beautiful colony in the world into a field of desolation and carnage.

ALTHOUGH it must have occurred to every unprejudiced mind, from the circumstances that have been related concerning the behaviour of the mulattoes resident in the colony, that the general body of those people were by no means averse to conciliation with the whites, yet it was found impossible to persuade their pretended friends in Europe to leave the affairs of St. Domingo to their natural course. Barnave alone (hitherto the most formidable opponent of the prejudices and pretensions of the colonists) avowed his conviction that any further interference of the mother-country in the question between the whites and the coloured people, would be productive of fatal consequences. Such an opinion was entitled to greater respect, as coming from a man who, as president of the colonial committee, must be supposed to have acquired an intimate knowledge of the subject; but he was heard without conviction. There are enthusiasts in politicks as well as in religion, and it commonly happens with fanaticks in each, that the recantation of a few of their number serves only to strengthen the errors, and animate the pur-

those of indignation against his murderers. They were compelled to lay down their arms, and were sent prisoners to France; but I fear they escaped the punishment due to their crimes.

CHAP. V. 1791. poses of the rest. It was now resolved by Gregoire, La Fayette, Brissot, and some other pestilent reformers, to call in the supreme legislative authority of the French government to give effect to their projects; and that the reader may clearly understand the nature and complexion of the mischief that was meditated, and of those measures to which the ruin of the French part of St. Domingo is immediately to be attributed, it is necessary, in the first place, to recal his attention to the national decree of the 8th of March 1790, of which an account was given in the second chapter.

By that decree, as the reader must have remembered, the national assembly, among other things, disclaimed all right of interference in the local and interior concerns of the colonies; and it cannot be doubted, that if this declaration had been faithfully interpreted and acted upon, it would have contributed, in a very eminent degree, to the restoration of peace and tranquillity in St. Domingo. To render it therefore of as little effect as possible, and to add fuel to the fire which perhaps would otherwise have become extinguished, it had been insidiously proposed in the national assembly, within a few days after the decree of the 8th of March had passed, to transmit with it to the governor of St. Domingo, a code, or chapter, of instructions, for its due and punctual observance and execution. Accordingly, on the 28th of the same month, instructions which were said to be calculated for that purpose, were presented and decreed. They consisted of eighteen articles, and

and contained, among other things, a direction "that every person of the age of twenty-five and "upwards, possessing property, or having resided "two years in the colony, and paid taxes, should "be permitted to vote in the formation of the "colonial assembly."

THE friends of the colonists having at that time seats in the national assembly, opposed the measure chiefly on the ground of its repugnancy to the decree of the 8th; it being evidently, they urged, an interference in the local arrangements and interior regulations of the colonial government. It does not appear (notwithstanding what has since been asserted to the contrary) that they entertained an idea that the mulatto people were directly or indirectly concerned. The framers and supporters of the measure pretended that it went only to the modification of the privilege of voting in the parochial meetings, which it was well known, under the old government, had been constituted of white persons only. The coloured people had in no instance attended those meetings, nor set up a claim, or even expressed a desire, to take any part in the business transacted thereat. But these instructions were no sooner adopted by the national assembly, and converted into a decree, than its framers and supporters threw off the mask, and the mulattoes resident in the mother-country, as well as the society of *Amis des Noirs*, failed not to apprize their friends and agents in St. Domingo, that the people of colour, not being excepted, were virtually comprized in it. These, however, not thinking themselves sufficiently

CHAP. V. 1791. ficiently powerful to enforce the claim, or, perhaps, doubting the real meaning of the decree, sent deputies to France to demand an explanation of it from the national assembly.

In the beginning of May 1791, the consideration of this subject was brought forward by Abbé Gregoire, and the claim of the free mulattoes to the full benefit of the instructions of the 28th of March 1790, and to all the rights and privileges enjoyed by the white inhabitants, citizens of the French colonies, was supported with all that warmth and eloquence for which he was distinguished. Unfortunately, at this juncture, the news of the miserable death of Ogé arrived at Paris, and raised a storm of indignation in the minds of all ranks of people, which the planters resident in France were unable to resist. Nothing was heard in all companies but declamations against their oppression and cruelty. To support and animate the popular outcry against them, a tragedy or pantomime, formed on the story of Ogé, was represented on the publick theatres. By these, and other means, the planters were become so generally odious, that for a time they dared not to appear in the streets of Paris. These were the arts by which Gregoire, Condorcet, La Fayette, Brissot, and Robespierre disposed the publick mind to clamour for a new and explanatory decree, in which the rights of the coloured people should be placed beyond all future doubts and dispute. The friends and advocates of the planters were overpowered and confounded. In vain did they predict the utter destruction of the colonies

colonies if such a proposal should pass into a law. "Perish the colonies," said Robespierre, "rather "than sacrifice one iota of our principles." The majority reiterated the sentiment, and the famous decree of the 15th of May 1791 was pronounced amidst the acclamation and applause of the multitude.

CHAP. V. 1791.

By this decree it was declared and enacted, "that the people of colour resident in the French colonies, born of free parents, were entitled to, as of right, and should be allowed the enjoyment of, all the privileges of French citizens, and, among others, to those of having votes in the choice of representatives, and of *being eligible to seats both in the parochial and colonial assemblies.*" Thus did the national assembly sweep away in a moment all the laws, usages, prejudices, and opinions concerning these people, which had existed in the French colonies from their earliest settlement, and tear up by the roots the first principle of a free constitution:—a principle founded on the clearest dictates of reason and justice, and expressly confirmed to the inhabitants of the French West Indies by the national decree of the 8th of March 1790; I mean, *the sole and exclusive right of passing laws for their local and interior regulation and government.* The colonial committee, of which M. Barnave was president, failed not to apprize the national assembly of the fatal consequences of this measure, and immediately suspended the exercise of its functions. At the same time, the deputies from the colonies signified their purpose to decline any further attendance.

 The

CHAP. V. 1791.

The only effect produced by these measures however, on the national assembly, was an order that the three civil commissioners, who had been appointed in February preceding for regulating the affairs of the colonies on the spot, should immediately repair thither, and see the national decrees duly enforced. The consequences in St. Domingo will be related in the following chapter *(d)*.

(d) It has been confidently asserted, that *La Fayette*, in order to secure a majority on this question, introduced into the national assembly no less than eighty persons who were not members, but who sat and voted as such. This man had formerly been possessed of a plantation at Cayenne, with seventy negro slaves thereon, which he had sold, without any scruple or stipulation concerning the situation of the negroes, the latter end of 1789, and from that time enrolled himself among the friends of the blacks. The mere English reader, who may be personally unacquainted with the West Indies, will probably consider the clamour which was raised on this occasion by the French planters as equally illiberal and unjust. The planters in the British West Indies will perhaps bring the case home to themselves; and I have no hesitation in saying, that, supposing the English parliament should pass a law declaring, for instance, the free mulattoes of Jamaica to be eligible into the assembly of that island, such a measure would prove there, as it proved in St. Domingo, the declaration of civil war. On mere abstract reasoning this may appear strange and unjustifiable; but we must take mankind as we find them, and few instances occur in which the prejudices of habit, education, and opinion have been corrected *by force*.

CHAP.

CHAP. VI.

*Consequences in St. Domingo of the Decree of the 15th of May—Rebellion of the Negroes in the Northern Province, and Enormities committed by them—Revolt of the Mulattoes at Mirebalais —*Concordat *or Truce between the Inhabitants of Port au Prince and the Men of Colour, of the 11th of September—Proclamation by the National Assembly of the 20th of September.*

I AM now to enter on the retrospect of scenes, the horrors of which imagination cannot adequately conceive nor pen describe. The disputes and contests between different classes of French citizens, and the violences of malignant factions towards each other, no longer claim attention. Such a picture of human misery;—such a scene of woe presents itself, as no other country, no former age has exhibited. Upwards of one hundred thousand savage people, habituated to the barbarities of Africa, avail themselves of the silence and obscurity of the night, and fall on the peaceful and unsuspicious planters, like so many famished tygers thirsting for human blood. Revolt, conflagration, and massacre, every where mark their progress; and death, in all its horrors, or cruelties and outrages, compared to which immediate death is mercy, await alike the old and the young, the matron, the virgin, and the help-

CHAP. VI. 1791.

less

CHAP. VI. 1791.

less infant. No condition, age, or sex is spared. All the shocking and shameful enormities, with which the fierce and unbridled passions of savage man have ever conducted a war, prevail uncontrouled. The rage of fire consumes what the sword is unable to destroy, and, in a few dismal hours, the most fertile and beautiful plains in the world are converted into one vast field of carnage;—a wilderness of desolation!

There is indeed too much reason to believe, that these miseries would have occurred in St. Domingo, in a great degree, even if the proceedings of the National Assembly, as related in the latter part of the preceding chapter, had been more temperate, and if the decree of the 15th of May had never passed into a law. The declarations of the dying Ogé sufficiently point out the mischief that was meditated, long before that obnoxious decree was promulgated. But it may be affirmed, with truth and certainty, that this fatal measure gave life and activity to the poison. It was the brand by which the flames were lighted, and the combustibles that were prepared set into action. Intelligence having been received of it at Cape François on the 30th of June, no words can describe the rage and indignation which immediately spread throughout the colony; and in no place did the inhabitants breathe greater resentment than in the town of the Cape, which had hitherto been foremost in professions of attachment to the mother-country, and in promoting the spirit of disunion and opposition in the colonial assembly. They now unanimously determined

determined to reject the civick oath, although great preparations had been made for a general federation on the 14th of July. The news of this decree seemed to unite the most discordant interests. In the first transports of indignation it was proposed to seize all the ships, and confiscate the effects of the French merchants then in the harbour. An embargo was actually laid, and a motion was even made in the provincial assembly to pull down the national colours, and hoist the British standard in their room. The national cockade was every where trodden under foot, and the governor-general, who continued a sorrowful and silent spectator of these excesses, found his authority, as representative of the parent country, together with every idea of colonial subordination in the people, annihilated in a moment.

CHAP. VI. 1791.

The fears and apprehensions which the governor felt on this occasion have been well described by that officer himself, in a memorial which he afterwards published concerning his administration. "Acquainted (he observes) with the genius and temper of the white colonists, by a residence of seven years in the Windward Islands, and well informed of the grounds and motives of their prejudices and opinions concerning the people of colour, I immediately foresaw the disturbances and dangers which the news of this ill-advised measure would inevitably produce; and not having it in my power to suppress the communication of it, I lost no time in apprizing the king's ministers of the "general

CHAP. VI. 1791. "general discontent and violent fermentation "which it excited in the colony. To my own "observations, I added those of many respectable, "sober, and dispassionate men, whom I thought "it my duty to consult in so critical a conjunc-"ture; and I concluded my letter by expressing "my fears that this decree would prove the "death-warrant of many thousands of the inha-"bitants. The event has mournfully verified my "predictions!"

On the recommendation of the provincial assembly of the Northern department, the several parishes throughout the colony now proceeded, without further hesitation, to the election of deputies for a new general colonial assembly. These deputies, to the number of one hundred and seventy-six, met at Leogane, and on the 9th of August declared themselves *the general assembly of the French part of St. Domingo.* They transacted however but little business, but manifested great unanimity and temper in their proceedings, and resolved to hold their meetings at Cape François, whither they adjourned for that purpose, appointing the 25th of the same month for opening the session.

In the mean-while, so great was the agitation of the publick mind, M. Blanchelande found it necessary not only to transmit to the provincial assembly of the North, a copy of the letter which he mentions to have written to the king's ministers, but also to accompany it with a solemn assurance, pledging himself *to suspend the execution of the obnoxious decree, whenever it should come out to him properly*

properly authenticated; a measure which too plainly demonstrated that his authority in the colony was at an end.

JUSTLY alarmed at all these proceedings, so hostile towards them, and probably apprehensive of a general proscription, the mulattoes throughout the colony began to collect in different places in armed bodies; and the whites, by a mournful fatality, suffered them to assemble without molestation. In truth, every man's thoughts were directed towards the meeting of the new colonial assembly, from whose deliberations and proceedings the extinction of party, and the full and immediate redress of all existing grievances, were confidently expected. M. Blanchelande himself declares, that he cherished the same flattering and fallacious hopes. "After a long succession of "violent storms, I fondly expected (he writes) "the return of a calm and serene morning. The "temperate and conciliating conduct of the new "assembly, during their short sitting at Leogane, "the characters of most of the individual mem- "bers, and the necessity, so apparent to all, of "mutual concession and unanimity on this great "occasion, led me to think that the colony "would at length see the termination of its mise- "ries; when, alas, the storm was ready to burst, "which has since involved us in one common de- "struction!"

IT was on the morning of the 23d of August, just before day, that a general alarm and consternation spread throughout the town of the Cape. The inhabitants were called from their beds by

persons

CHAP. VI. 1791. persons who reported that all the negro slaves in the several neighbouring parishes had revolted, and were at that moment carrying death and desolation over the adjoining large and beautiful plain to the north-east. The governor, and most of the military officers on duty, assembled together; but the reports were so confused and contradictory, as to gain but little credit; when, as day-light began to break, the sudden and successive arrival, with ghastly countenances, of persons who had with difficulty escaped the massacre, and flown to the town for protection, brought a dreadful confirmation of the fatal tidings.

The rebellion first broke out on a plantation called Noé, in the parish of Acul, nine miles only from the city. Twelve or fourteen of the ringleaders, about the middle of the night, proceeded to the refinery, or sugar-house, and seized on a young man, the refiner's apprentice, dragged him to the front of the dwelling-house, and there hewed him into pieces with their cutlasses: his screams brought out the overseer, whom they instantly shot. The rebels now found their way to the apartment of the refiner, and massacred him in his bed. A young man lying sick in a neighbouring chamber, was left apparently dead of the wounds inflicted by their cutlasses: he had strength enough however to crawl to the next plantation, and relate the horrors he had witnessed. He reported, that all the whites of the estate which he had left were murdered, except only the surgeon, whom the rebels

rebels had compelled to accompany them, on the idea that they might stand in need of his professional assistance. Alarmed by this intelligence, the persons to whom it was communicated immediately sought their safety in flight. What became of the poor youth I have never been informed.

The revolters (consisting now of all the slaves belonging to that plantation) proceeded to the house of a Mr. Clement, by whose negroes also they were immediately joined, and both he and his refiner were massacred. The murderer of Mr. Clement was his own postilion, a man to whom he had always shewn great kindness. The other white people on this estate contrived to make their escape.

At this juncture, the negroes on the plantation of M. Flaville, a few miles distant, likewise rose and murdered five white persons, one of whom (the *procureur* or attorney for the estate) had a wife and three daughters. These unfortunate women, while imploring for mercy of the savages on their knees, beheld their husband and father murdered before their faces. For themselves, they were devoted to a more horrid fate, and were carried away captives by the assassins.

The approach of day-light served only to discover sights of horror. It was now apparent that the negroes on all the estates in the plain acted in concert, and a general massacre of the whites took place in every quarter. On some few estates indeed the lives of the women were spared, but they were

CHAP. VI. 1791.

were reserved only to gratify the brutal appetites of the ruffians; and it is shocking to relate, that many of them suffered violation on the dead bodies of their husbands and fathers!

In the town itself, the general belief for some time was, that the revolt was by no means an extensive, but a sudden and partial insurrection only. The largest sugar plantation on the plain was that of Mons. Gallifet, situated about eight miles from the town, the negroes belonging to which had always been treated with such kindness and liberality, and possessed so many advantages, that it became a proverbial expression among the lower white people, in speaking of any man's good fortune, to say *il est heureux comme un negre de Gallifet* (he is as happy as one of Gallifet's negroes). M. Odeluc, the attorney, or agent, for this plantation, was a member of the general assembly, and being fully persuaded that the negroes belonging to it would remain firm in their obedience, determined to repair thither to encourage them in opposing the insurgents; to which end, he desired the assistance of a few soldiers from the town-guard, which was granted him. He proceeded accordingly, but on approaching the estate, to his surprise and grief he found all the negroes in arms on the side of the rebels, and (horrid to tell!) *their standard was the body of a white infant, which they had recently impaled on a stake!* M. Odeluc had advanced too far to retreat undiscovered, and both he, and a friend that accompanied him, with most of the soldiers, were killed without

without mercy. Two or three only of the patrole escaped by flight; and conveyed the dreadful tidings to the inhabitants of the town.

By this time, all or most of the white persons that had been found on the several plantations, being massacred or forced to seek their safety in flight, the ruffians exchanged the sword for the torch. The buildings and cane-fields were every where set on fire; and the conflagrations, which were visible from the town, in a thousand different quarters, furnished a prospect more shocking, and reflections more dismal, than fancy can paint, or the powers of man describe.

Consternation and terror now took possession of every mind: and the screams of the women and children, running from door to door, heightened the horrors of the scene. All the citizens took up arms, and the general assembly vested the governor with the command of the national guards, requesting him to give such orders as the urgency of the case seemed to demand.

One of the first measures was to send the white women and children on board the ships in the harbour; and very serious apprehensions being entertained concerning the domestick negroes within the town, a great proportion of the ablest men among them were likewise sent on shipboard and closely guarded.

There still remained in the city a considerable body of free mulattoes, who had not taken, or affected not to take, any part in the disputes between their brethren of colour and the white inhabitants.

Their

CHAP. VI. 1791.

Their situation was extremely critical; for the lower class of whites, considering the mulattoes as the immediate authors of the rebellion, marked them for destruction; and the whole number in the town would undoubtedly have been murdered without scruple, if the governor and the colonial assembly had not vigorously interposed, and taken them under their immediate protection. Grateful for this interposition in their favour (perhaps not thinking their lives otherwise secure) all the able men among them offered to march immediately against the rebels, and to leave their wives and children as hostages for their fidelity. Their offer was accepted, and they were enrolled in different companies of the militia.

The assembly continued their deliberations throughout the night, amidst the glare of the surrounding conflagrations; and the inhabitants, being strengthened by a number of seamen from the ships, and brought into some degree of order and military subordination, were now desirous that a detachment should be sent to attack the strongest body of the revolters. Orders were given accordingly; and M. de Touzard, an officer who had distinguished himself in the service of the North Americans, took the command of a party of militia and troops of the line. With these he marched to the plantation of a M. Latour, and attacked a body of about four thousand of the rebel negroes. Many were destroyed, but to little purpose; for Touzard, finding the number of revolters to encrease in more than a centuple proportion to their losses, was at length obliged to

retreat;

retreat; and it cannot be doubted, that if the rebels had forthwith proceeded to the town, defenceless as it then was towards the plain, they might have fired it without difficulty, and destroyed all its inhabitants, or compelled them to fly to the shipping for refuge.

Sensible of this, the governor, by the advice of the assembly, determined to act for some time solely on the defensive; and as it was every moment to be apprehended that the revolters would pour down upon the town, the first measure resorted to was to fortify the roads and passes leading into it. At the eastern extremity, the main road from the plain is intersected by a river, which luckily had no bridge over it, and was crossed in ferry-boats. For the defence of this passage, a battery of cannon was raised on boats lashed together; while two small camps were formed at proper distances on the banks. The other principal entrance into the town, and contiguous to it towards the south, was through a mountainous district, called *le Haut du Cap*. Possession was immediately taken of these heights, and considerable bodies of troops, with such artillery as could be spared, were stationed thereon. But these precautions not being thought sufficient, it was also determined to surround the whole of the town, except the side next the sea, with a strong palisade and *chevaux de frize*; in the erecting and completing of which, all the inhabitants laboured without distinction or intermission. At the same time, an embargo was laid on all the shipping in the harbour; a measure of indispensable

CHAP. VI. 1791. indispensable necessity, calculated as well to obtain the assistance of the seamen, as to secure a retreat for the inhabitants in the last extremity.

To such of the distant parishes as were open to communication either by land or by sea, notice of the revolt had been transmitted within a few hours after advice of it was received at the Cape; and the white inhabitants of many of those parishes had therefore found time to establish camps, and form a chain of posts, which for a short time seemed to prevent the rebellion spreading beyond the Northern province *(a)*. Two of those camps however, one at *Grande Riviere*, the other at *Dondon*, were attacked by the negroes (who were here openly joined by the mulattoes) and forced with great slaughter. At Dondon, the whites maintained the contest for seven hours; but were overpowered by the infinite disparity of numbers, and compelled to give way, with the loss of upwards of one hundred of their body. The survivors took refuge in the Spanish territory.

These two districts therefore; the whole of the rich and extensive plain of the Cape, together with the contiguous mountains, were now wholly abandoned to the ravages of the enemy: and the cruelties which they exercised, uncontrouled, on such of the miserable whites as fell into their hands,

(a) It is believed that a general insurrection was to have taken place throughout the colony on the 25th of August (St. Louis's day); but that the impatience and impetuosity of some negroes on the plain, induced them to commence their operations two days before the time.

cannot

cannot be remembered without horror, nor reported in terms strong enough to convey a proper idea of their atrocity.

THEY seized Mr. Blen, an officer of the police, and having nailed him alive to one of the gates of his plantation, chopped off his limbs, one by one, with an axe.

A POOR man named *Robert*, a carpenter by trade, endeavouring to conceal himself from the notice of the rebels, was discovered in his hiding-place; and the savages declared *that he should die in the way of his occupatian:* accordingly they bound him between two boards, and deliberately sawed him asunder.

M. CARDINEAU, a planter of *Grande Riviere*, had two natural sons by a black woman. He had manumitted them in their infancy, and bred them up with great tenderness. They both joined in the revolt; and when their father endeavoured to divert them from their purpose, by soothing language and pecuniary offers, they took his money, and then stabbed him to the heart.

ALL the white, and even the mulatto children whose fathers had not joined in the revolt, were murdered without exception, frequently before the eyes, or clinging to the bosoms, of their mothers. Young women of all ranks were first violated by a whole troop of barbarians, and then generally put to death. Some of them were indeed reserved for the further gratification of the lust of the savages, and others had their eyes scooped out with a knife.

IN the parish of Limbè, at a place called the Great

CHAP. VI. 1791. Great Ravine, a venerable planter, the father of two beautiful young ladies, was tied down by a savage ringleader of a band, who ravished the eldest daughter in his presence, and delivered over the youngest to one of his followers: their passion being satisfied, they slaughtered both the father and the daughters.

Amidst these scenes of horror, one instance however occurs of such fidelity and attachment in a negro, as is equally unexpected and affecting. Mons. and Madame Baillon, their daughter and son-in-law, and two white servants, residing on a mountain plantation about thirty miles from Cape François, were apprized of the revolt by one of their own slaves, who was himself in the conspiracy, but promised, if possible, to save the lives of his master and his family. Having no immediate means of providing for their escape, he conducted them into an adjacent wood; after which he went and joined the revolters. The following night, he found an opportunity of bringing them provisions from the rebel camp. The second night he returned again, with a further supply of provisions; but declared that it would be out of his power to give them any further assistance. After this, they saw nothing of the negro for three days; but at the end of that time he came again; and directed the family how to make their way to a river which led to Port Margot, assuring them they would find a canoe on a part of the river which he described. They followed his directions, found the canoe, and got safely into it; but were overset by the rapidity of the current, and after a narrow escape, thought it best to return to their retreat in the mountains. The negro, anxious for their safety, again found them out, and directed them to a broader part of the river, where he assured them he had provided a boat; but said it was the last effort he could make to save them. They went accordingly, but not finding the boat, gave themselves up for lost, when the faithful negro again appeared like their guardian angel. He brought with him pigeons, poultry and bread; and conducted the family, by slow marches in the night, along the banks of the river, until they were within sight of the wharf at Port Margot; when telling them they were entirely out of danger, he took his leave for ever, and went to join the rebels. The family were in the woods nineteen nights*.

Let us now turn our attention back to the town of the Cape; where, the inhabitants being at length placed, or supposed to be placed, in some sort of security, it was thought necessary by the governor and assembly, that offensive operations against the rebels should be renewed, and a small army, under the command of M. Rouvray, marched to the eastern part of the plain, and encamped at a place called Roucrou. A very considerable body of the rebel negroes took possession, about the same time, of the large buildings

* This account was communicated by Madame Baillon herself to a friend of the author, who was with him at St. Domingo, and who spoke French like a native: from that friend I received it the same day, and immediately committed the particulars to writing.

 on

CHAP. VI. 1791.

on the plantation of M. Gallifet, and mounted some heavy pieces of artillery on the walls. They had procured the cannon at different shipping places and harbours along the coast, where it had been placed in time of war by the government, and imprudently left unprotected; but it was a matter of great surprize by what means they obtained ammunition (*b*). From this plantation they sent out foraging parties, with which the whites had frequent skirmishes. In these engagements, the negroes seldom stood their ground longer than to receive and return a single volley, but they appeared again the next day; and though they were at length driven out of their intrenchments with infinite slaughter, yet their numbers seemed not to diminish:—as soon as one body was cut off, another appeared, and thus they succeeded in the object of harassing and destroying the whites by perpetual fatigue, and reducing the country to a desert.

To detail the various conflicts, skirmishes, massacres, and scenes of slaughter, which this exterminating war produced, were to offer a disgusting and frightful picture; a combination of horrors;

(*b*) It was discovered afterwards, that great quantities of powder and ball were stolen by the negroes in the town of Cape François from the king's arsenal, and secretly conveyed to the rebels. Most of the fire-arms at first in their possession were supposed to have been part of *Ogé's* importation. But it grieves me to add, that the rebels were afterwards abundantly supplied, by small vessels from North America; the masters of which felt no scruple to receive in payment sugar and rum, from estates of which the owners had been murdered by the men with whom they trafficked.

CHAP. VI. 1791.

wherein we should behold cruelties unexampled in the annals of mankind; human blood poured forth in torrents; the earth blackened with ashes, and the air tainted with pestilence. It was computed that, within two months after the revolt first began, upwards of two thousand white persons, of all conditions and ages, had been massacred;—that one hundred and eighty sugar plantations, and about nine hundred coffee, cotton, and indigo settlements had been destroyed (the buildings thereon being consumed by fire), and one thousand two hundred christian families reduced from opulence to such a state of misery, as to depend altogether for their clothing and sustenance on publick and private charity. Of the insurgents, it was reckoned that upwards of ten thousand had perished by the sword or by famine; and some hundreds by the hands of the executioner;—many of them, I am sorry to say, under the torture of the wheel;—a system of revenge and retaliation, which no enormities of savage life could justify or excuse (c).

HITHERTO,

(c) Two of these unhappy men suffered in this manner under the window of the author's lodgings, and in his presence, at Cape François, on Thursday the 28th of September 1791. They were broken on two pieces of timber placed crosswise. One of them expired on receiving the third stroke on his stomach, each of his legs and arms having been first broken in two places; the first three blows he bore without a groan. The other had a harder fate. When the executioner, after breaking his legs and arms, lifted up the instrument to give the finishing stroke on the breast, and which (by putting the criminal out of his pain) is called *le coup de grace*, the mob, with the ferociousness of cannibals, called out *arretez!* (stop) and compelled him to

 leave

CHAP. VI. 1791.

HITHERTO, my narrative has applied chiefly to transactions in the Northern province; I grieve to relate, that the flames of rebellion soon began to break forth also in the Western division. Here, however, the insurgents were chiefly men of colour, of whom upwards of two thousand appeared in arms in the parish of Mirebalais. Being joined by about six hundred of the negro slaves, they began their operations by burning the coffee plantations in the mountains adjacent to the plain of Cul-de-Sac. Some detachments of the military which were sent against them from Port au Prince were repulsed; and the insurgents continued to ravage and burn the country through an extent of thirty miles, practising the same excesses and ferocious barbarities towards such of the whites as fell into their hands, as were displayed by the rebels in the North. They had the audacity at length to approach Port au Prince, with intention, as it was believed, to set it on fire; and so defenceless was the state of that devoted town, that its destruction seemed inevitable. Many of the mulatto chiefs, however, finding that their attempts to gain over the negro slaves on the sugar plantations in this part of the country, were not attended with that success which they expected, expressed an unwillingness

leave his work unfinished. In that condition, the miserable wretch, with his broken limbs doubled up, was put on a cart wheel, which was placed horizontally, one end of the axletree being driven into the earth. He seemed perfectly sensible, but uttered not a groan. At the end of forty minutes, some English seamen, who were spectators of the tragedy, strangled him in mercy.

2 to

to proceed to this extremity; declaring that they took up arms not to desolate the colony, but merely to support the national decree of the 15th of May, and that they were not averse to a reconciliation. These sentiments coming to the knowledge of M. de *Jumecourt*, a planter of eminence, he undertook the office of mediator, and through his well-timed and powerful interposition, a truce or convention, called the *concordat*, was agreed upon the 11th of September, between the free people of colour, and the white inhabitants of Port au Prince, of which the chief provisions were an oblivion of the past, and an engagement on the part of the whites, to admit in full force the national decree of the 15th of May, so often mentioned;—certainly the ostensible, though perhaps not the sole and original cause of the rebellion*.

INSTRUCTED by this example, and softened, it may be presumed, by the loyal and temperate conduct of the free mulattoes in the town of Cape François, as before related, the general assembly, by a proclamation of the 20th of September, declared that they would no longer oppose the operation of the same decree. They even went further, and announced an intention to grant considerable indulgences towards such free people of colour as were not comprehended in it, meaning those who

* It should also have been observed, that the condemnation and execution of Ogé is pronounced, in this *concordat*, "infa-"mous, and to be held in everlasting execration." These expressions were literally copied from a letter of Abbé Gregoire. I am obliged to the author of the history of Europe in the Annual Register for 1792 (Rivington's edit.) for reminding me of this circumstance.

were

CHAP. VI. 1791. were born of enslaved parents. They voted at the same time the formation of certain free companies of mulattoes, wherein the men of colour of all descriptions, possessed of certain qualifications, should be allowed to serve as commissioned officers.

These concessions, at an earlier period, would have operated with powerful effect in the salvation of the colony; but they now came too late, and produced only a partial truce, a temporary and fallacious cessation of miseries. The wounds that had been inflicted were yet green and bleeding; and the dark and sullen passions of disappointed pride, anger, malice, hatred and revenge, were secretly burning in the gloomy minds of all parties. The flames were smothered, not extinguished; soon to break out again, with aggravated violence and greater fury than ever.

CHAP.

CHAP. VII.

Of the Motives which induced the People of Colour to join the revolted Negroes.—Conduct of the British Association for the Abolition of the Slave Trade, and of the Society in Paris called Les Amis des Noirs—*Letter from* Abbé Gregoire *to the People of Colour—Repeal of the Decree of the* 15*th May* 1791—*Effects of that Measure—Civil War with the Mulattoes renewed—Port au Prince destroyed by Fire—Cruelties exercised by both Parties—Arrival at Cape François of the Civil Commissioners.*

CHAP. VII. 1791.

BEFORE I proceed to a renewal of those disgusting scenes of devastation, slaughter, and ruin, which my duty, as a faithful historian, calls upon me to describe (happy if they serve as an impressive lesson to other nations!) it seems necessary to remove some difficulties which may possibly have arisen in the mind of the reader, concerning the original and primary cause of the junction and co-operation of so large a number of the negro slaves, in this rebellion, with the men of colour. That the whole body of the latter in St. Domingo had solid ground of complaint and dissatisfaction, cannot be denied. There is a point at which oppression sometimes arrives, when forbearance under it ceases to be a virtue; and I should readily have admitted that the actual situation and condition of the mulattoes in the French islands

CHAP. VII. 1791.

islands would have made resistance a duty, if it did not appear, from what I have already related, that the redress of their grievances occupied the very first deliberations of the first general assembly of representatives that ever met in St. Domingo. Certainly, then, no justification can be offered for those pestilent reformers, who could persuade these unfortunate people to seek that relief by rebellion and massacre, which was offered to them by the supreme power of the country, as a spontaneous and voluntary concession;---the homage of enlightened reason on the altar of humanity. Concerning the enslaved negroes, however, it does not appear that the conduct of the whites towards them was in general reprehensible. I believe, on the whole, it was as lenient and indulgent as was consistent with their own safety. It was the mulatto people themselves who were the hard-hearted task-masters to the negroes. The same indignities which they received from the whites, they directed without scruple towards the blacks; exercising over the latter every species of that oppression which they loudly and justly complained of, when exercised on themselves; ---and this is a true picture of human nature. By what means, then, it will be asked, were the negroes induced to forget their resentments, and join with those who were the constant objects both of their envy and hatred?

In order to reply to this question with as much accuracy and precision as the subject will admit, it is necessary to recur to the proceedings of the two associations, of which mention was made in the

the Second Chapter of this History; namely, the British association for the abolition of the slave trade, which held its meetings in the Old Jewry in London; and the society called *Les Amis des Noirs* in Paris. A short review of the conduct of these societies will serve not only to lessen the surprize which may be felt at the revolt of the negroes of St. Domingo, but also raise a considerable degree of astonishment that the enslaved negroes in the British islands had not given them the example.

I HAVE observed, that the society in London *professed* to have nothing more in view than to obtain an act of the legislature for prohibiting the further introduction of African slaves into the British colonies. I have said, that "they disclaimed all intention of interfering with the government and condition of the negroes already in the plantations; publickly declaring their opinion to be, that a general emancipation of those people, in their present state of ignorance and barbarity, instead of a blessing, would prove to them the source of misfortune and misery." But although such were their ostensible declarations as a publick body, the leading members of the society, in the same moment, held a very different language; and even the society itself (acting as such) pursued a line of conduct directly and immediately repugnant to their own professions. Besides using every possible endeavour to inflame the publick of Great Britain against the planters, they distributed at a prodigious expence throughout the colonies, tracts and pamphlets

CHAP. VII. 1791.

pamphlets without number; the direct tendency of which was to render the white inhabitants odious and contemptible in the eyes of their own slaves, and excite in the latter such ideas of their natural rights and equality of condition, as should lead them to a general struggle for freedom through rebellion and bloodshed. In many of those writings, arguments are expressly adduced, in language which cannot be misunderstood, to urge the negroes to rise up and murder their masters without mercy.—"Resistance," say they, "is always justifiable where force is the substitute of right: *nor is the commission of a civil crime possible in a state of slavery.*" These sentiments are repeated in a thousand different forms; and in order that they might not lose their effect by abstract reasoning, a reverend divine of the church of England, in a pamphlet addressed to the chairman or president of the society, pours forth the most earnest prayers, in the most undisguised expressions, that the negroes would destroy all the white people, men, women, and children, in the West Indies: "Should we not (he exclaims), approve their conduct in their violence? Should we not crown it with eulogium, if they exterminate their tyrants with fire and sword! *Should they even deliberately inflict the most exquisite tortures on those tyrants, would they not be excusable* in the moral judgment of those who properly value those inestimable blessings, rational and religious liberty (a)?"

(a) This is a fair extract from a letter addressed to Granville Sharp, Esq; chairman of the society in the Old Jewry, by the Reverend

BESIDES distributing pamphlets of this complexion *gratis*, at the doors of all the churches and places of worship in the kingdom, and throughout the colonies, the society, or persons in their name, caused a medal to be struck, containing the figure of a naked negro, loaded with chains, and in the attitude of imploring mercy; thousands of which also were dispersed among the negroes in each of the sugar islands, for the instruction, I presume, of such of them as could not read; but, unhappily, this instance of provident caution was not requisite; for so many negro domesticks return annually from Europe to the West Indies, as constantly furnish a sufficient number of living instructors; and certain it is (I pronounce it from my own knowledge respecting Jamaica) that the labours of the society on their behalf, as well as many of the most violent speeches in the British parliament, wherein the whole body of planters were painted as a herd of blood-thirsty and remorseless tyrants, were explained to the negro slaves, in terms well adapted to their capacities, and suited, as might have been supposed, to their feelings. It will be difficult to say what other measures the Old Jewry associates could have taken to excite a rebellion, except that of furnishing the objects of their solicitude with fire arms and ammunition.

Reverend Percival Stockdale, A. M. Of such writers the planters may well exclaim, "*Forgive them, they know not what they* "*do!*" The same ejaculation I applied to the learned and pious Samuel Johnson, who possessed a negro servant, and before whom he frequently gave as a toast, "*A speedy rebellion of the* "*negroes in Jamaica, and success to them!*"

HITHERTO,

CHAP. VII. 1791.

HITHERTO, this society had served as a model and exemplar to that of Paris; but a disposition to stop at half measures constitutes no part of the French character; and the society of *Amis des Noirs* resorted, without scruple, to those measures which their fellow labourers in London still hesitated to adopt: beginning with the class of free mulattoes, because they found many of them in France, who became the willing instruments of their purposes; and who undertook to interpret to the negroes in the French colonies the wishes and good intentions towards them of their friends in the mother-country. Thus an opening was made towards conciliation and union between the two classes. The negroes, believing that it was only through the agency of the mulattoes, and the connections of those people in France, they could obtain a regular supply of arms and ammunition, forgot or suspended their ancient animosities; and the men of colour, sensible that nothing but the co-operation of the enslaved negroes (docile, as they supposed them to be, from their ignorance, and irresistible from their numbers) could give success to their cause, courted them with such assiduity as gained over at least nine-tenths of all the slaves in the Northern province of St. Domingo.

THERE seems however to have been some apprehensions entertained by the leading men among the *Amis des Noirs*, that the decree of the national assembly of the 15th of May, confined as the benefits of it were to the people of colour exclusively, (and of those, to such only as were born of free parents)

parents) might give rise to jealousies and suspicions, destructive of that unanimity between the different classes, the maintenance of which was an object of the last importance. To obviate any misapprehensions on this account, as well as to keep the mulattoes firm to their purpose, the Abbé Gregoire wrote and published his celebrated circular letter;—a performance which, if the intentions of the writer had been as pure as his expressions are eloquent, would have reflected lustre on his abilities *(b)*. What effect this distinguished piece of oratory may have had on the rugged and unenlightened minds of savage people, I pretend not to ascertain. It is certain that the Abbé Gregoire was considered by the negroes in St. Domingo as their great advocate and patron; a sort of guardian angel or tutelary deity; of the good effects of whose benevolent interposition and friendly offices their masters unjustly deprived them, and on whose support and assistance they might confidently rely, in the attempt, through rebellion and murder, to obtain justice for themselves.

Both classes of people being thus instructed and prepared, the decree of the 15th of May was the signal of revolt, the warhoop of massacre. From the clamour which it excited amongst all orders of the whites in St. Domingo (the lower classes especially) the people of colour, as I have shewn, had reason to apprehend that mischiefs of an extensive and alarming nature were meditated against them.

(b) The reader will find a translation of this letter at the end of the present Chapter.

They

CHAP. VII. 1791. They were thus furnished with a plausible, and, had they meant to have acted solely on the defensive, a justifiable cause for resorting to arms; but, unhappily, the strong tide of popular prejudice which prevailed in the mother country against the planters, and the great majority which voted for the fatal decree in the national assembly, were circumstances that inspired them with so dangerous a confidence in their own resources, as overpowered all considerations of prudence, policy, and humanity.

It must be considered, at the same time, that the enslaved negroes (ignorant and depressed as we suppose them to be) could not possibly be unobservant of these combined and concurring circumstances. They beheld the coloured people in open hostility against the whites. They were assured, that the former had the fullest support and encouragement from the supreme legislature of the mother country. They were taught to believe, that themselves also were become the objects of the paternal solicitude of the king and the national assembly, who wished to rescue them from the dominion of their masters, and invest them with their estates. It appeared from indisputable evidence, that assurances of this nature were held out to the enslaved negroes;—assurances which could not but excite their attention, awaken their faculties, and rouse them to action. Whoever shall calmly deliberate on these, and the other facts that have been stated, will find no difficulty in accounting for the dreadful extent of this insurrection; or in assigning it to its proper cause, and

and tracing to the fountain-head those rivers of blood which still continue to flow in this unfortunate and devoted colony *(c)*!

But it is now time to advert to the proceedings which occurred in France, where we left *Gregoire, La Fayette, Robespierre,* and the rest of the society of *Amis des Noirs,* exulting in the triumph they had obtained on the 15th of May; and perhaps waiting, in the ardent hope and expectation, that their obnoxious decree of that date, would produce those very evils which actually resulted from it. It was not until the beginning of September that information arrived at Paris concerning the reception which the account of this decree had met with in St. Domingo. The tumults, disorders, and confusions that it produced there, were now

(c) In September 1791, when the author was at Cape François, he dined with a large company on board the frigate *la Prudente*, commanded by Mons. *Joyeuse* (at present a distinguished admiral in the service of the new republick, by the name of *Villaret*) when, in the midst of the entertainment, a loud exclamation from the crew announced *that the gunner was returned.* This man, who had been missing some weeks, was immediately brought forward, and gave the following account of the cause of his absence. He said that, having gone on shore, to collect green meat for the pigs, he was surrounded by the rebel negroes, who were about putting him to death, when Jean François, the chief, finding that he was an officer in the king's service, ordered that his life should be spared, alledging *that the king was their friend.* They detained him however as a prisoner, and compelled him to load and point their artillery in the attack at M. Gallifet's plantation before-mentioned. On the defeat of the rebels in that engagement, he fortunately made his escape from them. Some of the shocking enormities and cruelties inflicted by the rebels on their white prisoners, as related in the preceding pages, were committed in this man's presence.

represented

CHAP. VII. 1791. represented in the strongest colouring, and the loss of the colony to France was universally apprehended. At this time, however, no suspicion was entertained concerning the enslaved negroes; but a civil war, between the whites and the mulattoes, was believed to be inevitable. The commercial and manufacturing towns, predicting the ruin of their trade and shipping, and the loss of their capitals from existing dangers, presented remonstrances and petitions to the national assembly, urging the necessity of an immediate repeal of all the decrees by which the rights of the planters were invaded; that of the 15th of May especially. The constituent national assembly was now on the point of dissolution, and perhaps wished to leave every thing in peace. At the same time the tide of popular prejudice, which had hitherto ran with such violence against the colonists, was beginning to turn. Most of those members whose opinions in colonial concerns, a few months before, had guided the deliberations of the national assembly, were now either silently disregarded, or treated with outrage;—a strong and striking proof of the lightness and versatility of the French character. At length a motion was made to annul the obnoxious decree, and (strange to tell!) on the 24th of September its repeal was actually voted by a large majority!—At this remarkable change of sentiment in the supreme legislature, it is necessary to pause, and remind the reader of what was doing at the same time in St. Domingo; where as we have seen, on the 11th of that very month, the *concordat*, or truce, took place between the people

people of colour and the white inhabitants of Port au Prince; and on the 20th, the colonial assembly at Cape François published the proclamation mentioned in the latter part of the preceding Chapter. Thus, almost in the very moment when the justice and necessity of the decree were acknowledged, and its faithful observance promised, by the colonial assembly, its repeal was pronounced by the national legislature in the mother country!

To such repugnancy and absurdity must every government be driven that attempts to regulate and direct the local concerns of a country three thousand miles distant. Of the two measures that have been mentioned, it is difficult to say which produced the greatest calamities; the decree of the 15th of May in the first instance; or its unexpected repeal, at the time and in the manner related! Doubts had already arisen in the minds of the mulattoes concerning the sincerity and good faith of the white people, with respect to the *concordat*. Their suspicions and apprehensions had indeed grown to such a height, as to induce them to insist on a renewal and confirmation of its provisions; which were accordingly granted them, by a new instrument, or treaty of the 11th of October, and a supplementary agreement of the 20th of the same month: but no sooner was authentick information received of the proceedings in France, in the repeal of the decree, than all trust and confidence, and every hope of reconciliation and amity between the two classes, vanished for ever. It was not possible to persuade the mulattoes that

CHAP. VII. the planters in the colony were innocent, and ignorant of the transaction. They accused the whites of the most horrid duplicity, faithlessness and treachery; and publickly declared that one party or the other, themselves or the whites, must be utterly destroyed and exterminated:—There was no longer, they said, an alternative.

In this disposition, exasperated to frenzy, the coloured people throughout the Western and Southern provinces flew to arms. In the Southern province, a body of them became masters of Port St. Louis; but the inhabitants of Port au Prince having been reinforced, a short time before, by the arrival of some troops from Europe, were better prepared, and drove the revolters from the city with great slaughter. They took post in the parish of *Croix des Bouquets*; but found means, however, before their retreat, to set fire to the city, and a dreadful conflagration ensued, in which more than one-third of the buildings were consumed.

Open war, and war in all its horrors, was now renewed. All the soft workings of humanity—what our great dramatick poet calls the *compunctious visitings of nature*—were now absorbed in the raging and insatiable thirst of revenge, which inflamed each class alike. It was no longer a contest for mere victory, but a diabolical emulation which party could inflict the most abominable cruelties on the other. The enslaved negroes in the district called *Cul-de-Sac* having joined the mulattoes, a bloody engagement took place, in which the negroes, being ranged in front, and acting

acting without any kind of discipline, left two thousand of their number dead on the field. Of the mulattoes about fifty were killed, and several taken prisoners. The whites claimed the victory; but for want of cavalry were unable to improve it by a pursuit, and contented themselves with satiating their revenge on their captives. Every refinement in cruelty that the most depraved imagination could suggest, was practised on the persons of those wretched men. One of the mulatto leaders was unhappily among the number: him the victors placed on an elevated seat in a cart, and secured him in it by driving large spiked nails through his feet into the boards. In this condition he was led a miserable spectacle through the city. His bones were afterwards broken, and he was then thrown alive into the flames!

The mulattoes scorned to be outdone in deeds of vengeance, and atrocities shameful to humanity. In the neighbourhood of *Jeremie* a body of them attacked the house of M. Sejourné, and secured the persons both of him and his wife. This unfortunate woman (my hand trembles while I write!) was far advanced in her pregnancy. The monsters, whose prisoner she was, having first murdered her husband in her presence, ripped her up alive, and threw the infant to the hogs. They then (how shall I relate it!) sewed up the head of the murdered husband in ——!!!—Such are thy triumphs, philanthropy!

With these enormities terminated the disastrous year 1791. Just before Christmas the three civil commissioners nominated by the national as-

CHAP. VII. sembly for St. Domingo, arrived at Cape François. Much was expected from their appointment by the friends of peace and good order; but the sequel will shew that they effected very little towards restoring the peace of the country.

Translation of the Letter of Abbé Gregoire, *Bishop of the Department of Loire and Cher, Deputy of the National Assembly, to the Citizens of Colour in the French West Indies, concerning the Decree of the* 15*th of May* 1791.

FRIENDS!

YOU *were* MEN;—your *are* now CITIZENS. Reinstated in the fulness of your rights, you will, in future, participate of the sovereignty of the people. The decree which the national assembly has just published respecting you, is not *a favour;* for a favour is *a privilege:* and a privilege to one class of people is an injury to all the rest.—They are words which will no longer disgrace the laws of the French.

IN securing to you the exercise of your political rights, we have acquitted ourselves of a *debt:*—not to have paid it, would have been a crime on our part, and a disgrace to the constitution. The legislators of a free nation certainly could not do less for you than our ancient despots have done.

IT is now above a century ago that Louis XIV. solemnly acknowledged and proclaimed your rights; but of this sacred inheritance you have been defrauded by pride and avarice, which have gradually increased your burthens, and embittered your existence.

THE regeneration of the French empire opened your hearts to hope, whose cheering influence has alleviated the weight of your

your miseries: miseries of which the people of Europe had no idea. While the white planters resident among us were loud in their complaints against *ministerial* tyranny, they took especial care to be silent *as to their own*. Not a hint was suggested concerning the complaints of the unhappy people of mixed blood; who, notwithstanding, are their own children. It is *we*, who, at the distance of two thousand leagues from you, have been constrained to protect those children against the neglect, the contempt, the unnatural cruelty of their fathers!

But it is in vain that they have endeavoured to suppress the justice of your claims. Your groans, notwithstanding the extent of the ocean which separates us, have reached the hearts of the European Frenchmen;—for *they* have *hearts*.

God Almighty comprehends all men in the circle of his mercy. His love makes no distinction between them, but what arises from the different degrees of their virtues. Can laws then, which ought to be an emanation of eternal justice, encourage so culpable a partiality? Can that government, whose duty it is to protect alike all the members of the same great family, be the mother of one branch, and the step-mother only of the others?

No, gentlemen:—you could not escape the solicitude of the national assembly. In unfolding to the eyes of the universe the great charter of nature, your titles were traced. An attempt had indeed been made to expunge them; but happily they are written in characters as indelible as the sacred image of the Deity, which is graven on your countenances.

Already had the national assembly, in the instructions which it prepared for the government of the colonies, on the 28th of March 1790, comprized both the whites and people of colour under one common denomination. Your enemies, in asserting the contrary, have published a falsehood. It is incontestably true, that when I demanded you should be expressly named, a great number of members, among whom were several planters, eagerly exclaimed, that you were already compre-

CHAP. VII.

hended under the general words contained in those instructions. M. Barnave himself, upon my repeated appeals to him on that head, has at length acknowledged, before the whole assembly, that this was the fact. It now appears how much reason I had to apprehend that a false construction would be put upon our decree!

New oppressions on the part of your masters, and new miseries on yours, until at length the cup of affliction is filled even to the brim, have but too well justified my apprehensions. The letters which I have received from you upon this head, have forced tears from my eyes. Posterity will learn with astonishment and indignation, that a cause like yours, the justice of which is so evident, was made the subject of debate for no less than five days successively. Alas! when humanity is obliged to struggle so long against vanity and prejudice, its triumph is dearly obtained!

It is a long time that the society of *Amis des Noirs* have employed themselves in finding out the means to soften your lot, as well as that of the slaves. It is difficult—perhaps impossible—to do good with entire impunity. The meritorious zeal of this society has drawn upon them much obloquy. Despicable writers have lanced their poisonous shafts at them, and impudent libels have never ceased to repeat objections and calumnies, which have been a hundred times answered and refuted. How often have we been accused of being sold to the English, and of being paid by them for sending you inflammatory writings and arms? You know, my friends, the weakness and wickedness of these charges. We have incessantly recommended to you attachment to your country, resignation and patience, while waiting the return of justice! Nothing has been able to cool our zeal, or that of your brethren of mixed blood who are at Paris. M. Raimond, in particular, has devoted himself most heroically to your defence. With what transport would you have seen this distinguished citizen, at the bar of the national assembly, of which he ought to be a member, laying before it the affecting picture of your miseries, and strenuously

strenuously claiming your rights! If that assembly had sacrificed them, it would have tarnished its glory. It was its duty to decree with justice, to explain itself clearly, and cause its laws to be executed with firmness: it has done so; and if (which God forbid!) some event, hidden in the womb of futurity, should tear our colonies from us, would it not be better to have a loss to deplore, than an injustice to reproach ourselves with?

CITIZENS! raise once more your humiliated countenances, and to the dignity of men, associate the courage and nobleness of a free people. The 15th of May, the day in which you recovered your rights, ought to be for ever memorable to you and to your children. This epoch will periodically awaken in you sentiments of gratitude towards the Supreme Being; and may your accents ascend to the vault of heaven, towards which your grateful hands will be extended! At length you have a country. Hereafter you will see nothing above you but the law; while the opportunity of concurring in the framing it, will assure to you that indefeasible right of all mankind, the right of obeying yourselves only.

You have a country: and it will no longer be a land of exile, where you meet none but tyrants on the one hand, and companions in misfortune on the other; the former distributing, and the latter receiving, contempt and outrage. The groans of your afflictions were punished as the clamours of rebellion; and situated between the uplifted poinard, and certain death, those unhappy countries were often moistened with your tears, and sometimes stained with your blood.

You have a country: and happiness will shine on the seat of your nativity. You will now enjoy in peace the fruits of the fields which you have cultivated without compulsion. Then will be filled up that interval, which, placing at an immense distance from each other, the children of the same father, has suppressed the voice of nature, and broke the bands of fraternity asunder. Then will the chaste enjoyments of conjugal union take place of those vile sallies of debauchery, by which the

CHAP. VII.

the majesty of moral sentiment has been insulted. By what strange perversion of reason can it be deemed disgraceful in a white man to marry a black or mulatto woman, when it is not thought dishonourable in him to be connected with her in the most licentious familiarity!

THE less real worth a man possesses, the more he seeks to avail himself of the appearances of virtue. What can be more absurd than to make the merit of a person to consist in different shades of the skin, or in a complexion more or less sallow? The man who thinks at all must sometimes blush at being a man, when he sees his fellow-creatures blinded by such ridiculous prejudices: but as unfortunately pride is one of those failings we most unwillingly part with, the empire of prejudice is the most difficult to subvert: man appears to be unable to arrive at truth, until he has exhausted his strength in travelling through the different paths of error.

THIS prejudice against the mulattoes and negroes has however no existence in our Eastern colonies. Nothing can be more affecting than the eulogium made on the people of colour by the inhabitants of that part of the world, in the instructions given by them, to those they have appointed their deputies to the national assembly. The members of the academy of sciences pride themselves in reckoning a mulatto of the Isle of France in the number of their correspondents. Among ourselves, a worthy negro is a superior officer of the district of St. Hypolite, in the department of Gard. We do not conceive that a difference of colour can be the foundation of different rights among members of the same political society. It is therefore we find no such despicable pride among our brave national guards, who offer themselves to embark for the West Indies to insure the execution of our decrees. Perfectly concurring in the laudable sentiments manifested by the inhabitants of Bourdeaux, they acknowledge with them, that the decree respecting the people of colour, framed under the auspices of prudence and wisdom, is an homage rendered to reason and justice. While the deputies from the colonies have endeavoured to calumniate

calumniate your intentions, and those of the mercantile part of the nation, the conduct of those deputies is perfectly contradictory. Ardently soliciting their own admission among us at Versailles; swearing with us in the Tennis Court not to separate from us, until the constitution should be established; and then declaring, when the decree of the 15th of May was passed, that they could no longer continue to sit with us! This desertion is a desertion of their principles, and a breach of their solemn oaths.

All those white inhabitants of the colonies who are worthy the name of Frenchmen, have hastened to abjure such ridiculous prejudices, and have promised to regard you in future as brothers and friends. With what delightful sensations do we cite the words of the citizens of Jacmel. "We "swear to obey, without reserve, the decrees of the national "assembly respecting our present and future constitution, "and even such of them as may substantially change it!" The citizens of Port au Prince tell the national assembly the same thing, in different words. "Condescend, gentlemen," say they, "to receive the oath which the municipality has "taken to you, in the name of the commons of Port au Prince, "punctually to obey and execute all your decrees, and never "to swerve from them in any respect whatsoever."

Thus has philosophy enlarged its horizon in the new world, and soon will absurd prejudices have no other supporters than a few inferior tyrants, who wish to perpetuate in America, the reign of that despotism which has been abolished in France.

What would these men have said, if the people of colour had endeavoured to deprive the whites of *their* political advantages? With what energy would they not have exclaimed at such an oppression! Inflamed into madness at finding that your rights have been pointed out to you, their irritated pride may perhaps lead them to make every effort to render our decrees ineffectual. They will probably endeavour to raise such disturbances, as, by wresting the colonies from the mother-

CHAP. VII.

mother-country, will enable them to defraud their creditors of their just debts. They have incessantly alarmed us with threats that St. Domingo will be lost, if justice be rendered to you. In this assertion we have found nothing but falsehood: we please ourselves in the belief, that our decree will draw the bands still closer which unite you to the mother country. Your patriotism, your interest, and your affections, will concur in inducing you to confine your commercial connections to France only; and the reciprocal tributes of industry will establish between her and her colonies a constant interchange of riches and good offices. If you act unfaithfully towards France, you will be the basest and most abandoned of the human race. But no! generous citizens, you will not become traitors to your country: you shudder at the idea. Rallied, with all other good Frenchmen, around the standard of liberty, you will defend our glorious constitution. The day shall arrive, when the representatives of the people of colour will cross the ocean to take their seats with us, and swear to live and die under our laws. The day shall arrive among you when the sun will shine on none but freemen; when the rays of light shall no longer fall on the fetters of slavery. It is true, the national assembly has not yet raised the condition of the enslaved negroes to a level with your situation; because suddenly granting the rights, to those who are ignorant of the duties of citizens, might perhaps have been a fatal present to them: but forget not, that they, like yourselves, are born to freedom and perfect equality. It is in the irresistible course of things that all nations, whose liberty has been invaded, shall recover that precious portion of their indefeasible inheritance!

You are accused of treating your slaves much worse than the whites: but, alas! so various have been the detractions with which you have been aspersed, that it would be weakness in us to credit the charge. If, however, there be any foundation for what has been advanced on this head, so conduct yourselves in future as to prove it will be a shameful calumny hereafter.

YOUR oppressors have heretofore endeavoured to hide from their slaves the light of christianity, because the religion of mildness, equality, and liberty, suits not with such blood-thirsty men. May *your* conduct be the reverse of *theirs*. Universal love is the language of the gospel; your pastors will make it heard among you. Open your hearts to receive this divine system of morality. We have mitigated *your* misfortunes: alleviate, on your part, those of the unhappy victims of avarice, who moisten your fields with their sweat, and often with their tears. Let the existence of your slaves be no longer their torment; but by your kind treatment of them, expiate the crimes of Europe!

BY leading them on progressively to liberty, you will fulfil a duty: you will prepare for yourselves the most comfortable reflections: you will do honour to humanity, and insure the prosperity of the colonies. Such will be your conduct towards your brethren, the negroes; but what ought it to be towards your fathers, the whites? Doubtless you will be permitted to shed tears over the ashes of *Ferrand de Baudiere*, and the unfortunate *Ogé*, assassinated under the forms of law, and dying on the wheel for having wished to be free! But may he among you perish, who shall dare to entertain an idea of revenge against your persecutors! They are already delivered over to the stings of their own consciences, and covered with eternal infamy. The abhorrence in which they are held by the present race of mankind, only precedes the execration of posterity. Bury then in eternal oblivion every sentiment of hatred, and taste the delicious pleasure of conferring benefits on your oppressors. Repress even too marked expressions of your joy, which, in causing them to reflect on their own injustice towards you, will make their remorse still more pungent.

STRICTLY obedient to the laws, teach your children to respect them. By a careful education, instruct them in all the duties of morality: so shall you prepare for the succeeding generation, virtuous citizens, honourable men, enlightened patriots, and defenders of their country!

CHAP. VII.

How will their hearts be affected when, conducting them to your shores, you direct their looks towards France, telling them, "beyond those seas is your parent country; it is from "thence we have received justice, protection, happiness, and "liberty. There dwell our fellow-citizens, our brethren, and "our friends: to them we have sworn an eternal friendship. "Heirs of our sentiments, and of our affections, may your "hearts and your lips repeat our oaths! Live to love them; "and, if necessary, die to defend them!"

Signed,

GREGOIRE.

Paris, 8th June, 1791.

CHAP.

CHAP. VIII.

Reception and Proceedings of the Civil Commissioners, and their Return to France—National Decree of the 4th of April 1792—Appointment of a new Governor (Mons. Desparbes) and three other Commissioners (Santhonax, Polverel, and Ailhaud)—Their Embarkation and Arrival, with a select Body of Troops—Their violent Proceedings — Appointment, by the Executive Council, of M. Galbaud as Chief Governor, in the Room of Desparbes—His Arrival, and Disputes with the Commissioners—Both Parties proceed to hostilities—The revolted Negroes called in to the Assistance of the Commissioners—A general Massacre of the White Inhabitants, and Conflagration of the Town of Cape Francois.

CHAP. VIII. January 1792.

THE civil commissioners who were to restore peace and subordination in St. Domingo, and whose arrival there was noticed in the last Chapter, were named Mirbeck, Roome, and St. Leger. Mirbeck and Roome had formerly been known as advocates in the parliaments of Paris; and St. Leger, who was a native of Ireland, had practised many years in France as a surgeon. Although the confusion of the times had elevated these men to power, not one of them was distinguished for extraordinary abilities, and their rank in life was not such as to command any great degree of consideration from the planters. They were received however,

CHAP. VIII. 1792. however, from respect to their appointment, with politeness and submission, both by the governor and the inhabitants. Military honours were shewn them, and they were led in publick procession to the cathedral, where the blessing of the Almighty was devoutly implored for success to their mission.

Their first proceeding, after announcing the new constitution and form of government for the mother-country, as confirmed by the king, was to publish the decree of the 24th of September 1791, by which the fatal decree of the 15th of May was annulled. So far all was well: but a few days afterwards they took upon them to proclaim a general amnesty and pardon to such people, of all descriptions, as should lay down their arms, and come in, within a certain prescribed time, and take the oaths required by the new constitution. This measure lost them the confidence of all the white inhabitants: a general amnesty to the men of colour and revolted slaves, was considered as a justification of the most horrible enormities, and as holding out a dangerous example to such of the negroes as preserved their fidelity; and it lost its effect on the mulattoes, by being accompanied with a repeal of their favourite decree. With what contempt and indignity it was received by the latter, the following circumstance will demonstrate. At *Petit Goave*, the mulattoes were masters, and held in close confinement thirty-four white persons whom they reserved for vengeance. On the publication of this amnesty, they led them to execution: but instead of putting them

to

to immediate death, they caused each of them to be broken alive; and in the midst of their tortures, read to them, in a strain of diabolical mockery, the proclamation aloud; affecting to consider it as a pardon for the cruelties they had just committed.

THE unlimited and indefinite authority which the commissioners seemed to claim, alarmed the colonial assembly, who desired to be informed of the nature and extent of their powers. To this request no satisfactory answer being given, the commissioners lost ground in the publick opinion daily; and their personal conduct, as individuals, contributed by no means to acquire them respect. Mirbeck spent the greatest part of his time in the practice of low debauchery, giving indulgence to his vicious propensities without restraint or decency. St. Leger considered his appointment as an authority to exact money, in which he was little scrupulous, and laid the few mulatto people who remained faithful, under a most unmerciful contribution. Roome alone conducted himself without reproach: he was a well-meaning inoffensive man, and attempted, though without effect, to act the part of a mediator between the different factions which desolated the country. This praise at least was given him—*that if he did no good, he did no harm.*

AFTER a short stay at Cape François, the commissioners visited other parts of the colony; but finding themselves every where very lightly regarded, and having no troops to support their authority, they returned separately to France in the months of March and April.

TROOPS

CHAP. VIII. 1792.

Troops however, as I have observed, had arrived from France to the number in the whole of about four thousand; but, in the spirit of the times, they manifested very little obedience either to the civil commissioners, or the governor of the colony; yet they served as a check to the revolters, who would otherwise, in all probability, before this time, have become masters both of Cape François and Port au Prince. In the Northern province, the rebel negroes indeed were supposed to be considerably reduced by disease and famine. Having destroyed all the provision grounds, and devoured the cattle of all kinds on the plain of the Cape, they had now taken possession of the surrounding mountainous districts, and were compelled by their chief leader, *Jean Francois*, a negro of great sagacity, to plant provisions for their future subsistence; a measure which has kept the flames of rebellion alive to the present hour.

In the meantime, the state of publick affairs in the mother-country was tending to a great and ominous change. Ever since the flight and seizure of their unhappy king, in the month of June 1791, the faction was hourly increasing in numbers which was soon to lay the kingdom in ruins, and bring the monarch himself to the scaffold. The Jacobin party, headed by a blood-thirsty triumvirate *(a)*, were becoming all-powerful; and the society of *Amis des Noirs* had once more acquired a fatal ascendancy in the legislative body. On the 29th of February, one of them, named *Garan de Coulon*, after a long and inflam-

(a) Danton, Robespierre, and Marat.

matory

matory harangue against the planters in general, proposed the form of a decree for abrogating that of the 24th of September; declaring a general amnesty throughout all the French colonies; and enacting, that new colonial assemblies should be formed, which should transmit their sentiments not only on the subject of the internal government of the colonies, *but also on the best method of effecting the abolition of negro slavery* IN TOTO.

CHAP. VIII. 1792.

FRANTICK as the new legislature *(b)* had shewn itself on many occasions since its first meeting, a majority could not at this time be found to vote for so senseless and extravagant a proposition: but in about two months afterwards, this assembly passed the famous decree of the 4th of April 1792, of which it is necessary the reader should be furnished with a copy at large; and it is conceived in the words following:

"THE national assembly acknowledges and declares, that the people of colour and free negroes in the colonies ought to enjoy an equality of political rights with the whites; in consequence of which it decrees as follows:

ARTICLE 1st. Immediately after the publication of the present decree, the inhabitants of each of the French colonies in the Windward and Leeward Islands, shall proceed to the re-election of colonial and parochial assemblies, after the mode prescribed by the decree of the 8th of March

(b) The former assembly is generally known by the name of the *Constituent* Assembly. The new one met the 1st of October 1791, and called itself the First *Legislative* Assembly.

CHAP. VIII. 1792. 1790, and the instructions of the national assembly of the 28th of the same month.

2d. The people of colour and free negroes shall be admitted to vote in all the primary and electoral assemblies, and shall be eligible to the legislature and all places of trust, provided they possess the qualifications prescribed by the 4th article of the aforesaid instructions.

3d. Three civil commissioners shall be named for the colony of St. Domingo, and four for the islands of Martinico, Guadaloupe, St. Lucia, and Tobago, to see this decree enforced.

4th. The said commissioners shall be authorized to dissolve the present colonial assemblies; to take every measure necessary for accelerating the convocation of the primary and electoral assemblies, and therein to establish union, order, and peace: as well as to determine provisionally (reserving the power of appeal to the national assembly) upon every question which may arise concerning the regularity of convocations, the holding of assemblies, the form of elections, and the eligibility of citizens.

5th. They are also authorized to procure every information possible, in order to discover the authors of the troubles in St. Domingo, and the continuance thereof, if they still continue; to secure the persons of the guilty, and to send them over to France, there to be put in a state of accusation, &c.

6th. The said civil commissioners shall be directed for this purpose to transmit to the national assembly minutes of their proceedings, and of the evidence

evidence they may have collected concerning the persons accused as aforesaid.

7th. THE national assembly authorizes the civil commissioners to call forth the publick force whenever they may think it necessary, either for their own protection, or for the execution of such orders as they may issue by virtue of the preceding articles.

8th. THE executive power is directed to send a sufficient force to the colonies, to be composed chiefly of national guards.

9th. THE colonial assemblies, immediately after their formation, shall signify, in the name of each colony respectively, their sentiments respecting that constitution, those laws, and the administration of them, which will best promote the prosperity and happiness of the people; conforming themselves nevertheless to those general principles by which the colonies and mother-country are connected together, and by which their respective interests are best secured, agreeably to the decree of the 8th of March 1790, and instructions of the 28th of the same month.

10th. THE colonial assemblies are authorized to send home delegates for the purposes mentioned in the preceding article, in numbers proportionate to the population of each colony; which proportion shall be forthwith determined by the national assembly, according to the report which its colonial committee is directed to make.

11th. FORMER decrees respecting the colonies shall be in force in every thing not contrary to the present decree.'

It may be supposed that the men who (rejecting all pretensions to consistency, and despising the lessons of experience) first proposed this decree, and finally prevailed in carrying it through the legislative assembly, had duly considered of the means for ensuring its execution in the colonies, and were provided with fit instruments for that purpose. The new commissioners nominated for St. Domingo were Messrs. Santhonax, Polverel, and Ailhaud, all of them among the most violent of the Jacobin faction; and it was resolved to furnish them with such a force as (if properly employed) would, it was alleged, not only establish their authority, but put a speedy end to all the disturbances which had so long afflicted and desolated the colony. Six thousand men, selected with great circumspection, from the national guards, with officers whose principles were well known to their employers, were accordingly ordered to embark forthwith for St. Domingo. M. Blanchelande, the governor-general, was recalled, and a new commission of commander in chief given to a Mons. Desparbes.

Thus appointed and provided, the civil commissioners and the new governor, accompanied by a fleet of thirty transports, took their departure from France in the month of July, probably in much the same disposition of mind towards the colonists, as was manifested by the Duke D'Alva and his Spanish and Italian troops in 1568, towards the inhabitants of the Low Countries. Inflamed like them with a spirit of avarice, fanaticism, and revenge, they meditated on nothing but

on

on the benefits to arise from seizure and confiscation; on schemes of mischief and projects of vengeance.

They landed at Cape François on the 13th of September, and finding M. Blanchelande at great variance with the colonial assembly, the commissioners took the shortest course possible to terminate the dispute, by forthwith dissolving the assembly and sending the unfortunate Blanchelande a state prisoner to France, where, as to be accused was to be condemned, he soon afterwards perished by the guillotine (c).

Dismay and terror now prevailed throughout the colony. Delegates were sent to the civil commissioners from all quarters, to demand an exposure and explanation of their views and intentions. Suspicions were already gone forth concerning the project, which the commissioners afterwards avowed, of declaring a general emancipation of the negro slaves; and all parties, as well among the republicans as the royalists, concurred on this occasion in reprobating the folly and iniquity of the measure. So general was the clamour on this account, that if a firm and extensive coalition of interests among the planters could at this time have been effected, it is probable the commissioners might have found that all the force they had brought with them would have proved insufficient for the purposes which they meditated. Dissimulation therefore was thought necessary for the present. They declared (and confirmed the de-

(c) 7th April 1793.

claration

CHAP. VIII. 1792. claration with the solemnity of an oath) that they had no wish nor intention to make any change in the system of colonial government concerning the slaves; avowing the fullest conviction that the emancipation of those people, under the then existing circumstances, was impracticable.—Their views, they said, extended no farther than to see the decree of the 4th of April, in favour of the free people of colour, properly enforced; to reduce the slaves in rebellion to obedience, and to settle the future government and tranquillity of the colony on a solid and permanent foundation.

These and similar declarations silenced, though they did not satisfy, the white inhabitants; who soon perceived, with unavailing indignation, that the commissioners held secret communications with the chiefs of the mulattoes in all parts of the colony. By the co-operation of those people, the commissioners soon found their strength sufficient to avow themselves openly the patrons and protectors of the whole body of the free negroes and mulattoes: and they now made no scruple of seizing the persons and effects of all such of the whites as opposed their projects; sending great numbers of them in a state of arrest to Europe, to answer before the national assembly to the accusations which they pretended to transmit against them. Among the persons thus imprisoned and transported to France, were comprehended the colonel, lieutenant-colonel, and many other officers of the Cape regiment.

The white inhabitants now called aloud for the election of a new colonial assembly, and hoped that

that the necessity of levying taxes would induce the commissioners to issue orders for that purpose; but instead of complying with the publick request, they substituted what was called *une commission intermediaire,* by nominating twelve persons, six of whom had been members of the last assembly, to act as a sort of legislative council: the other six were mulattoes. To this motley board, the commissioners delegated authority to raise money from the inhabitants; reserving to themselves, however, the right of appropriating and expending it, as they alone should think proper.

In the meanwhile, the new governor (Desparbes) began to manifest some signs of dissatisfaction and impatience. He complained that he was considered as a mere cypher in the government, or rather as an instrument in the commissioners' hands. His complaints were answered by a resolution to arrest his person; and he avoided the fate of his predecessor, Mons. Blanchelande, only by a speedy flight from the colony.

Two members out of the six whites that composed a moiety of the *commission intermediaire,* met with similar treatment. They ventured to offer their opinion on a measure of finance, in opposition to that of M. Santhonax. The commissioners commended their frankness, and M. Santhonax invited them to a supper. The invitation was accepted; but at the hour appointed, they found themselves surrounded by a detachment of the military, which conveyed them to very sorry entertainment

CHAP. VIII. 1793. entertainment in the hold of a ship, and there left them as state prisoners (*d*).

The commissioners, in the next place, fell out among themselves; and Santhonax and Polverel determined to get quit of their associate Ailhaud. Prudently judging, however, that the publick degradation of one of their own body would reflect some degree of ignominy on them all, they presuaded him to be content with a proportion of the common plunder, and silently quit the country. Ailhaud submitted with a good grace to what he could not avoid.

By these, and other means, above all by the practice of bestowing largesses on the troops, and the acquisition of a desperate band of auxiliaries, composed of some of the revolted slaves, and vagabonds of all colours and descriptions, mostly collected from the jails, Santhonax and Polverel, in the beginning of the year 1793, found themselves absolute masters of the colony. The lives and properties of all the white inhabitants lay at their mercy, and the dreadful scenes which were at that time passing in the mother-country, enabled these men to prosecute their purposes, and gratify their vindictive and avaricious passions, without notice or controul from any superior.

(*d*) To one of these gentlemen I am indebted for more valuable and extensive information than I have been able to collect through any other channel. In his voyage to Europe, the ship in which he was confined was (fortunately for him) captured by an English frigate, which brought him to England, where I had the happiness to render him some acceptable service.

But

CHAP. VIII. 1793.

But the tragedy which was acting in France, was no sooner brought to its catastrophe, by the foul murder of their amiable and unoffending sovereign, and war declared against Great Britain and Holland, than the persons who composed what was called the executive council, thought it necessary to pay some little attention to the safety of St. Domingo. Not having however leisure or inclination to enter into a full investigation of the complaints received from thence, they declined to revoke the powers exercised by the civil commissioners, and contented themselves with appointing a new governor, in the room of M. Desparbes. Their choice fell on Mons. Galbaud, an officer of artillery, and a man of fair character, whom they directed to embark for his new government without delay, in one of the national frigates, and put the colony into the best state of defence against a foreign enemy.

Galbaud, with his suite of attendants, landed at Cape François on the 7th of May 1793, to the great joy of the white inhabitants. At that period, the civil commissioners, with most of their troops, were employed in the Western province, endeavouring to quell an insurrection there which their tyranny had created; so that Galbaud was received with acclamations and submission by the municipality of the town of the Cape; to whose place of meeting he repaired with his attendants, took the necessary oaths, and entered on his government without opposition. He declared, at the same time, that he was not dependent on the civil commissioners, nor bound to execute, at all events, their proclamations.

CHAP. VIII. 1793.

A very quick interchange of letters took place between the new governor and the commissioners. He desired them to repair immediately to the Cape, that he might communicate the instructions he had received from the executive council. They answered that he was an entire stranger to them; that they had seen no decree of the national convention by which they themselves were superseded, and that being vested with authority to suspend or appoint a governor, as they alone might think proper, he could only be considered as an agent subordinate to themselves:—They added, that they were then assembling an army to suppress a rebellion in the town and neighbourhood of Port au Prince; but as soon as that business was at an end, they would repair to the Cape, and examine into the validity of his pretensions.

On the 10th of June the civil commissioners, having reduced Port au Prince and Jacmel, arrived at the Cape. The streets were lined with troops, and they were received by Galbaud with attention and respect. A very serious altercation however immediately took place between them, highly disadvantageous to the governor. There existed, it seems, a decree of the ancient government, unrepealed by the national assembly, enacting that no proprietor of an estate in the West Indies should hold the government of a colony wherein his estate was situated, and M. Galbaud was possessed of a coffee-plantation in St. Domingo. When therefore he was asked why he had not acquainted the executive council with this circumstance, he was utterly disconcerted and had no reply to make. CHAP. VIII. 1793.

On the 13th, the commissioners ordered M. Galbaud to embark forthwith on board the sloop of war La Normande, and return to France. At the same time they sent instructions to Mons. de la Salle, whom they had left commandant at Port au Prince, to repair to the Cape and receive from them, in the name of the French republick, the command of the colony.

The seven following days were spent on both sides in intrigues, and preparations for hostilities. Galbaud's brother, a man of spirit and enterprize, had collected from among the inhabitants, the Cape militia, and the seamen in the harbour, a strong party to support the governor's authority. On the 20th, the two brothers landed at the head of one thousand two hundred sailors, and being joined by a considerable body of volunteers, immediately marched in array towards the government house, in which the commissioners were stationed. The latter were defended by the people of colour, a body of regulars, and one piece of cannon. The conflict was fierce and bloody. The volunteers manifested great firmness, but the seamen getting possession of a wine cellar, soon became intoxicated and ungovernable; and the column was obliged to retire to the royal arsenal, where they remained the ensuing night unmolested.

The next morning many skirmishes took place in the streets, with various success, in one of which Galbaud's brother was taken prisoner by the commissioners'

CHAP. VIII. 1793. missioners' troops; and in another, the seamen that were fighting on the part of Galbaud made captive Polverel's son; and now an extraordinary circumstance occurred. The governor sent a flag proposing that his brother might be exchanged for the commissioner's son; but Polverel rejected the proposal with indignation; declaring in answer, that his son knew his duty, and was prepared to die in the service of the republick.

But a scene now opens, which, if it does not obliterate, exceeds at least, all that has hitherto been related of factious anarchy, and savage cruelty, in this unfortunate colony. On the first approach of Galbaud with so large a body of seamen, the commissioners dispatched agents to call in to their assistance the revolted negroes; offering them an unconditional pardon for past offences, perfect freedom in future, and the plunder of the city. The rebel generals Jean François and Biassou, rejected their offers; but on the 21st, about noon (just after that Galbaud and most of his adherents, finding their cause hopeless, had retired to the ships) a negro chief called *Macaya*, with upwards of three thousand of the revolted slaves, entered the town, and began an universal and indiscriminate slaughter of men, women, and children. The white inhabitants fled from all quarters to the sea-side, in hopes of finding shelter with the governor on board the ships in the harbour; but a body of the mulattoes cut off their retreat, and a horrid butchery ensued, which continued with unremitting fury from the 21st, to the evening of the 23d; when the savages,

having

having murdered all the white inhabitants that fell in their way, set fire to the buildings; and more than half the city was consumed by the flames. The commissioners themselves, either terrified at beholding the lamentable and extensive mischief which they had occasioned, or afraid to trust their persons with their rebel allies, sought protection under cover of a ship of the line. The proclamations which they published from time to time in palliation of their conduct, manifest a consciousness of guilt which could not be suppressed, and form a record of their villainies, for which the day of retribution awaits, but still lingers to overtake them *(f)* !

Such was the fate of the once flourishing and beautiful capital of St. Domingo !—a city which, for trade, opulence, and magnificence, was undoubtedly among the first in the West Indies,—perhaps in the new world : and here I shall close for the present, the disgusting detail of conspiracies, rebellions, crimes, cruelties, and conflagrations (a uniformity of horrors !) through which the nature of my work has compelled me to travel ;—rejoicing that I have at last

> Escap'd the Stygian pool, tho' long detain'd
> In that obscure sojourn ;——
>
> Milton.

(f) When this was written, the author did not know that Santhonax alone survives. Polverel died in 1794. Santhonax has lately appeared before the national assembly, and been pronounced *guiltless !*

CHAP. VIII. 1793.

and have the pleasing task to perform of rendering due homage to the gallant and enterprizing spirit of my countrymen in their noble—but alas! hitherto unavailing—endeavours to restore peace, subordination, and good government on this theatre of anarchy and bloodshed. Previous to which, however, it will be a relief and satisfaction to the reader to be presented with a picture or state of the colony, as it existed in the days of its prosperity;—its culture, population, and produce;—its growing importance and commercial value. Hitherto, we have contemplated nothing but scenes of desolation.—We shall now behold a pleasing contrast in the blessings of regular government: due subordination, social order, extensive commerce, peaceful industry, increasing cultivation, smiling plenty, and general happiness! The conclusions to be drawn from the contemplation of scenes so different in their nature, are of importance to all mankind.

The Account given above of the Destruction of the City of Cape François, *was drawn up with as much Caution as the Case seemed to require, from Information transmitted to the Author by Persons in Jamaica and St. Domingo, some of whom differed in many essential circumstances from others. He had afterwards an Opportunity of conversing personally on the Subject with a Gentleman of St. Domingo, on whose veracity and*

and Honour he could place the fullest Dependance, by whom he was favoured with the following Notes or Memoranda *in Writing, which he thinks best to lay before his Readers* verbatim.

CHAP. VIII.

NOTES SUR L'EVENEMENT DU CAP.

LE General Galbaud avoit mandé au Cap les commissaires Santhonax et Polverel, de la maniere la plus imperieuse; les commissaires se sont déterminés a s'y rendre par terre de S. Marc, d'où ils sont partis le 8 Juin, accompagnés de 400 mulâtres et 200 blancs, et compris leurs coupe tête les dragons d'Orleans. Ils ont fait leur entrée au Cap d'une maniere assez audacieuse pour en imposer.

GALBAUD avait deja indisposé les habitans du Cap par une addresse, ou proclamation, qui ordonnait une contribution de 450 mille livres, dont la perception a été faite de la façon la plus violente, et qui tenait plus du pillage que d'une contribution.

LE General Galbaud n'avait fait aucune dispositions pour se preserver des resolutions et des entreprises des commissaires, qui entrerent cependant d'une maniere menaçante.

A LA premiere entrevüe des General Galbaud et des commissaires, en la maison de la commission (le gouvernement) apres les premiers compliments, il y eut explication sur les pouvoirs du general; les commissaires lui oposerent un decret, qui deffendait qu'aucun proprietaire dans la colonie pût y commander ni y avoir d'autorité; et accuserent M. Galbaud d'avoir dissimulé au conseil executif qu'il avait des proprìetés.

PENDANT ce demêlé, qui dura près de deux jours, les agents des commissaires préparaient les esprits a les laisser faire, et a ne point se mêler de la discution, dans laquelle Santhonax prenait cependant une grande preponderance.

GALBAUD, voyant que personne ne s'empressait a le soutenir, et prevoyant sans doute une chute humiliante, demanda aux commissaires de s'en retourner en France, préférant la retraite, a des pouvoirs contestés; ce qui lui fut accordé sur le champ, et il s'embarqua le 14.

CHAP. VIII.

Le 17 Galbaud réünit tous les matelots de la rade et ceux des vaisseaux de guerre, et projette de descendre a la ville du Cap; il fait son débarquement le 18, et marche au gouvernement, où logeaient les commissaires, qui instruits des mouvemens de Galbaud, réünirent les troupes qui leurs etaient devouées, et particulierement les mulâtres, et les embusquerent derriere les murs du gouvernement, dans toutes les issües, sur les terrasses, &c. Aussitôt que les matelots furent a portée de pistolet, on fit des décharges, qui en tuerent et blesserent un grand nombre, néanmoins les mulâtres furent ebranlés deux fois; mais le désordre dans les matelots determina le General Galbaud a faire sa retraite a l'arsenal; là, il fit une proclamation pour inviter les bons citoyens a se réünir a lui, pour chasser les commissaires, qui voulaient usurper le gouvernement. Dès-lors les commissaires réünirent aux mulâtres tous les négres de la ville, qui avaient déja pris parti dans l'action en assassinant dans la ville toutes les troupes qui leurs avaient servis a leur expedition; et les placerent par pelotons a chaque coin des rües, et dès qu'un blanc voulait sortir de chéz lui, ou paraissait aux fenetres, il etait fusillé.

Pendant ce tems, et dès que les commissaires eurent appris les mouvemens de Galbaud, ils avaient depeché des exprès aux chefs des brigands, pour les engager a venir a leur secours, et leurs offraient le pillage de la ville.

Le 19 Galbaud capitule à l'arsenal, et se rend abord: il y en mis en état d'arrestation, ainsi que l'Amiral Cambis, et le Contre-Amiral Sercey, qui sont dépouillés de leur commandement.

Une proclamation des commissaires avait precedamment a cet évenement, mis a contribution 37 negociants, ou riches particuliers, pour une somme de 675 mille livres, qui parrait avoir été exigée et payée sur l'heure. Le 19, au soir, le 20, le 21, les brigands entrent de toutes parts dans la ville du Cap, ayant a leur tête leurs chefs, et on assure que M. de Grasse s'y est trouvé aussi. Le pillage, les massacrés, les flammes deviennent effroyables; les hommes, les femmes, les enfans, sont assassinés, massacrés, et éprouvent toutes les horreurs imaginables. Ils ont eu la barbarie de renfermer et de brûler dans une maison plus de 300 personnes toutes vives.

Les malheureux de tout sexe, de tout âge, qui cherchaient a se sauver en gagnant des embarcations, où a la nage, etaient fusillés même dans l'eau.

Il parrait que dans le massacre les négres ont frapés indistinctement tous les partis, blancs, mulâtres, et que les blancs se sont deffendus contre tous avec un grand acharnement; néanmoins il parrait certain, que la population blanche a été entierement détruite, et qu'il n'a pas resté un seul blanc au Cap; on estime, que, s'il s'est sauvé 12 a 1500 personnes abord, c'est plus qu'on n'ose l'esperer.

Le convoi est sortie du Cap le 23 pour l'Amerique, la majeure partie ayant très peu de vivres, très peu d'eau, et plusieurs sans être préparés a ce voyage, sans mats ni voilles, & ceux qui ont reçu les malheureux qui se sont sauvés abord, n'y auront trouvé aucune subsistance.

La ville incendiée, détruite, ses habitans massacrés, on assure qu'il ne reste que le gouvernement, une partie des casernes, l'arsenal, et les maisons du Petit Carenage;—l'église et les fontaines detruites.

Les commissaires ont resté spectateurs tranquilles pendant le carnage et le massacre; dans leur maison on a vu Santhonax serrer et presser dans ses bras les chefs des brigands, les appeller ses sauveurs, et leur témoigner leur reconnaissance.

Le 23 proclamation des commissaires, qui invite et appelle tous les bons citoyens à se réünir autour d'eux, et de laisser partir les scélerats, qui vont aller subir le juste chatiment de leurs crimes; le convoi en parti le jour même, & la ville fumait encore.

CHAP. IX.

Situation, Extent, and general Description of St. Domingo—Origin of the French Colony, and Topographical Description of the several Provinces into which the French Possessions were divided—Their Population, and Produce—Shipping and Exports—Compared with the Returns of Jamaica.

CHAP. IX.

THE island of St. Domingo is situated in the Atlantick Ocean, about three thousand five hundred miles from the land's end of England; the eastern point lying in north latitude 18° 20′, and in longitude 68° 40′ W. from Greenwich. The island extends about one hundred and forty miles in the broadest part, from north to south, and three hundred and ninety from east to west. In a country of such magnitude, diversified with plains of vast extent, and mountains of prodigious height, is probably to be found every species of soil which nature has assigned to all the tropical parts of the earth. In general, it is fertile in the highest degree; every where well watered, and producing almost every variety of vegetable nature, for use and beauty, for food and luxury, which the lavish hand of a bountiful Providence has bestowed on the richest portion of the globe; and the liberality of nature was laudably seconded by the industry of the inhabitants. Until those ravages and devastations which I have had the painful

painful task of recording, deformed and destroyed, with undistinguishing barbarity, both the bounties of nature, and the labours of art; the possessions of France in this noble island were considered as the garden of the West Indies; and for beautiful scenery, richness of soil, salubrity and variety of climate, might justly be deemed *the Paradise of the New World.*

Of the territories which remained exclusively in possession of the original conquerors, the Spaniards, my information is very imperfect. I shall hereafter give the best account I have been able to collect concerning them. On the southern coast, more especially in the neighbourhood of the ancient city from which the island derives its present name, the lands are said to be among the best, and without doubt a very large proportion of the remainder requires only the hand of the cultivator to become very productive. The interior country contains extensive savannahs, or plains, many of them occupied only by wild swine, horses, and horned cattle; for the Spaniards having exterminated the simple and unoffending natives, supplied their place with herds of domestick animals, which running wild, soon multiplied beyond computation. Thus does the tyranny of man convert the fruitful habitations of his fellow-creatures into a wilderness for beasts! In the present case, however, the crime brought down its own punishment;—a punishment which almost revenged the wrongs of the helpless Americans;—and who does not wish that avarice, ambition, and cruelty may be thus always entangled in their own projects?

CHAP. IX.

The reader is doubtless apprized that I here allude to the establishment in St. Domingo, of that daring and desperate band of adventurers, the *Bucaniers* ;—an association constituted of men of all countries and descriptions, but of whom it may truly be said, that if self-preservation be a law of nature, the hostilities which they maintained for upwards of fifty years against their oppressors, were more justifiable and legitimate in their origin, than all the wars which the pride and ambition of kings and nations have occasioned, from the beginning of the world to the present hour. As the cruelty of the Spaniards first compelled these men, from a sense of common danger, to unite their strength, so the blind policy of stocking with cattle a country of such extent, became their support; for the flesh of those animals supplied them with food, and they purchased arms, ammunition, and clothing with the skins.

Of the rise of these people, and the primary cause of their combining together to make reprisals on the Spanish settlements, a short account may be necessary: I have elsewhere treated the subject more at large (a).—They consisted originally of a body of French and English planters, whom, in the year 1629, a Spanish armament had expelled from the island of St. Christopher, with circumstances of outrageous barbarity. Driven from thence, by a force which they could not resist, as the only alternative of escaping from slaughter or slavery, they fled in open boats with their families, and possessed themselves of the

(a) Vol, I. Book ii. C. 2.

small

small unoccupied island of *Tortuga,* situated within a few miles of the northern coast of St. Domingo. Here they were joined by a considerable number of Dutch emigrants from *Santa Cruz,* whom the avarice and cruelty of the Spaniards had compelled, in like manner, to roam over the ocean for shelter, after having witnessed the massacre of many of their number, even to the women and children. Companions in adversity, these poor exiles learnt mutual forbearance from their common sufferings; for, although they were composed of three different nations, they appear to have lived for some years in perfect harmony with each other. Their mode of life contributed to produce the same beneficial effect: finding a country of immeasurable extent in their neighbourhood abounding in cattle, their time was chiefly occupied in hunting; an employment which left no leisure for dissension, and afforded them both exercise and food. The plains of St. Domingo were considered, however, merely as their hunting-grounds: Tortuga continued their home, and place of retreat. Here their women and young people cultivated small plantations of tobacco (an herb, of which, in hot and moist climates, the practice of inhaling the smoke, seems to be pointed out by nature); and as the coast was rugged, and of difficult approach, they fondly hoped that their obscurity would protect them from further persecution.

If the government of Spain had been actuated at this time by motives of wisdom, it would indeed have left these poor people to range over

the

CHAP. IX.

the wilderness unmolested. It ought to have known, that the occupation of hunting diverted them from projects of vengeance, and deeds of greater enterprize; but tyranny is without foresight, and the restless and remorseless bigotry of the Spanish nation allowed the fugitives no respite. An armament was collected, and preparations made to effect their utter extermination; the commanders of which, taking occasion when the ablest of the men had resorted to the larger island in their usual pursuit, landed a body of soldiers at Tortuga, and making captives of the women and children, the old and infirm, caused them all to be massacred without mercy.

It does not appear that the miserable people who were thus pursued to destruction, like beasts of prey, had been guilty of any outrages or depredations on the ships or subjects of Spain, which called for such exemplary vengeance. Neither was it imputed to them as a crime that they had possessed themselves of Tortuga, or that they roamed about the deserts of St. Domingo in pursuit of cattle which had no owners. Their guilt consisted in the circumstance of being born out of the Spanish territories, and presuming nevertheless to venture into any part of the New World; for the arrogant presumption and extravagant selfishness of this bigoted nation, led them to appropriate all the countries of America to themselves. They claimed even the sole and exclusive right of sailing on any such part of the main ocean as, in their judgment, constituted a portion of the newly-

newly-discovered hemisphere; and strict orders were issued to all their commanders, by sea and land, to seize the ships and subjects of oll other people that should be found within the boundaries which they had prescribed, and to punish the intruders with slavery or death. We have seen in what manner those orders were executed.

It is evident, therefore, that no alternative remained to the occupiers of Tortuga, but to turn on their pursuers, and wage offensive war on those who would allow of no peace with them. If the justice of their cause be still a question, let the records of time be consulted; let an appeal be made to that rule of conduct, which (to use an eloquent expression of Lord Coke) *is written by the finger of God on the heart of man;* and let history and reason determine, whether any instance of hostility, in the annals of mankind, can be defended on better grounds. To such men, in such a cause, no dangers were too formidable, no obstacles too great. Inured by their mode of life, to the vicissitudes of the climate, united among themselves, and animated by all the motives and passions which can inflame the human mind to great exertion, they became the most formidable antagonists which the Spaniards had ever encountered, and displayed such deeds of valour and successful enterprize, as (all circumstances considered) have never been equalled before or since.

From a party of these adventurers (chiefly natives of Normandy) the French colony in St. Domingo derived its origin. By what means they were induced to separate from their associates in danger,

CHAP. IX.

danger, to relinquish the gratification of revenge and avarice, and exchange the tumults of war for the temperate occupations of husbandry, it is neither within my province nor ability to explain. Many of them, without doubt, were men who had been driven from Europe by indigent circumstances and desperate fortunes; some, by the cruelty of creditors; and others, perhaps, by the consciousness of their crimes. Captivated by the renown, and allured by the wealth of the Bucaniers, they joined in their expeditions against the Spaniards from no better motives than those of plunder and rapine; and to such men must be imputed those outrages and excesses which have stamped the proceedings of the whole association with infamy (b). But there is a time for all

(b) I conceive, however, that these have been wonderfully magnified and exaggerated. The narrative called *The History of the Bucaniers*, published towards the latter end of the last century, which has been quoted by writers of all descriptions ever since as of unquestionable authority, was originally written in Dutch, by one John Esquemeling, who confesses that he had been one of the Bucaniers, and was expelled from their society. The reports of such a writer ought to have been received with great caution; but there is a still stronger circumstance to excite suspicion; and it is this: The English work is not taken from the Dutch original, but from *a Spanish translation*; and to suppose that a Spaniard would speak favourably of the Bucaniers, is the very excess of human credulity. Not having the original book to refer to, I cannot pronounce with certainty; but I am of opinion, that many of the tragical stories concerning the torture of the Spanish prisoners, and the violation of the women, are interpolations of the Spanish translator I form this conclusion from the malignity displayed towards the character of the famous Sir Henry Morgan. If we may believe the

CHAP. IX.

things; and the change of life in these men confirms the observation of an elegant writer, that "as there is no soil which will not shew itself "grateful to culture, so there is no disposition, "no character in mankind, which may not, by "dextrous management, be turned to the publick "advantage *(c)*." It was a happy circumstance in the infancy of their establishment, that while they were too obscure for the notice of the government, they had no check given to their industry by the chill influence of poverty. To a fortunate exemption from the hand of power, and the facility with which they were supplied with the common necessaries of life, they were indebted for their preservation and prosperity. A mediocrity of condition, and equal freedom, excited the spirit of emulation among them; but oppression would have produced discouragement; and

the account given of this gallant commander, he was the most inhuman monster that ever existed. Yet this very man (who by the way acted under a regular commission and letters of reprizal from government) after he had quitted the sea, was recommended by the earl of Carlisle to be his successor in the government of Jamaica, and was accordingly appointed lieutenant-governor in the earl's absence. He afterwards received the honour of knighthood from King Charles II. and passed the remainder of his life on his plantation in Jamaica. By the kindness of a friend in that island, I have had an opportunity of perusing some of Sir Henry Morgan's original private letters; and this I will say, that they manifest such a spirit of humanity, justice, liberality, and piety, as prove that he has either been grossly traduced, or that he was the greatest hypocrite living;—a character ill-suited to the frank and fearless temper of the man.

(c) European Settlements, Vol. II. p. 109.

sloth,

CHAP. IX. sloth, not industry, is the offspring of wretchedness.'

Of the progressive pursuits of those people in extending the footing which they had obtained, until the French government accepted their submission, acknowledged them as faithful subjects, and availed itself of their labours,—and the final cession to France of the western part of St. Domingo, by the peace of Ryswick, the reader will find an ample account in the history of this island by Pere Charlevoix. It is therefore unnecessary for me to detail what an author so well informed in the ancient transactions of the colony, has written. All that my English reader will expect, is an account of the political and topographical state of the colony; its population, produce, and exports at the time my History commences; and these particulars will be found in what remains of the present Chapter.

The possessions of the French in St. Domingo, as I have elsewhere observed, were divided into three great departments, called the Northern, the Western, and the Southern Provinces. The Northern Province comprehended a line of sea-coast extending about forty leagues, from the river Massacre to Cape St. Nicholas, and contained (including Tortuga) twenty-six parishes. Its population, in the beginning of 1790, consisted of 11,996 white inhabitants of all ages, and 164,656 negro slaves. The number of sugar plantations was 288, of which 258 made what is called *clayed*, or soft white sugar, and 30 *muscovado*, or raw sugar. It reckoned 2,009 plantations of coffee,

66 of cotton, 443 of indigo, and 215 smaller establishments, such as provision-grounds, cacao-groves, tan-pits, potteries, brick-kilns, &c. CHAP. IX.

Of the towns and harbours in the Northern Province, the chief were those of Cape François, Fort Dauphin, Port De Paix, and Cape St. Nicholas. I shall treat only of the first and the last.

The town of Cape François (which in time of war was the seat of the French government) would have ranked, for beauty and regularity, among the cities of the second class in any part of Europe. It consisted of between eight and nine hundred houses of stone and brick, many of them handsome and commodious, besides shops and warehouses; and it contained two magnificent squares, ornamented each with a publick fountain. The chief publick buildings were the church; the government-house (formerly a convent belonging to the Jesuits); a superb barrack for troops; a royal arsenal; a prison; a play-house; and two hospitals. The number of free inhabitants of all colours was estimated at eight thousand, exclusive of the king's troops and sea-faring people. The domestick slaves were said to be about twelve thousand. The situation of the town, however, was not to be commended. It was built at the foot of a very high mountain, called *Le Morne du Cap*, which abounds indeed with springs of excellent water, and furnished a great supply of garden vegetables, but it intercepted the land-wind, and reverberated the rays of the sun. The town arose to opulence chiefly from the commodiousness

CHAP. IX.

diousness of its harbour, and the extreme fertility of the plain adjoining it to the east, a district fifty miles in length, and twelve in breadth, appropriated solely to the cultivation of sugar (the plantations of which were divided from each other only by hedges of citrons and limes), and yielding greater returns than perhaps any other spot of the same extent in the habitable globe.

The town of Cape St. Nicholas consists of about 250 houses, which are chiefly built of American wood. It is sheltered by a hight bluff, called the *Mole;* and having been a free-port, was a place of considerable trade, and particularly resorted to by the ships of America. It is chiefly known, however, for the safety and extent of its harbour, which is justly called the key of the Windward passage; and the fortifications towards the sea are reckoned among the strongest in the West Indies. On the side of the land they are overlooked by the surrounding heights, and hence it is concluded, that although it might be difficult to take the place by an invading armament, it would be still more difficult to retain it afterwards, unless possession was obtained also of the interior country.

The Western Province began at Cape St. Nicholas, and extending along the line of coast which forms the bight of Leogane, for upwards of one hundred leagues, terminated at Cape Tiburon. It contained sixteen parishes, and four chief towns, namely, Port au Prince, St. Marc, Leogane, and Petit Goave; besides villages, of which those of Gonaives, Arcahaye, and Croix des Bouquets, are

not

not inconsiderable. The only good harbours in this great extent of coast are those of Port au Prince and Gonaives. All the other shipping-places are open roads, sometimes much exposed.

Port au Prince (except in time of war, when the Governor-General was directed to remove to Cape François) was considered as the metropolis of the colony. In 1790 it consisted of about 600 houses, and contained 2,754 white inhabitants *(d)*. The situation is low and marshy, and the climate, in consequence, very unhealthy. It is surrounded moreover by hills, which command both the town and the harbour; but both the hills and the valleys are abundantly fertile. To the east is situated the noble plain of Cul de Sac, extending from thirty to forty miles in length by nine in breadth, and it contained one hundred and fifty sugar-plantations, most of which were capable of being watered in times of drought, by canals admirably contrived and disposed for that purpose. The circumjacent mountains were at the same time clothed with plantations of coffee, which extended quite to the Spanish settlements.

The population and state of agriculture in the Western Province were as follow: white inhabitants of all ages 12,798; negroes in a state of slavery 192,961; plantations of clayed sugar 135, of muscovado 222. Plantations of coffee 894, of

(d) The free people of colour were estimated at 4,000, and the enslaved negroes at about 8,000: but being comprehended in the general return for the whole district, they are no where ascertained with precision.

cotton

CHAP. IX. cotton 489, of indigo 1,952, besides 343 smaller settlements.

THE Southern Province, extending upwards of sixty leagues from Cape Tiburon, along the southern coast of the island to L'Ance a Pitre, contained twelve parishes, and three chief towns, Les Cayes, Jeremie, and Jacmel; places of which I shall hereafter have occasion to speak. It possesses no safe harbours, and its roads are dangerous. The shipping that load at Les Coye take refuge, during the hurricane season, at La Baye des Flamands.

THE population in this department was composed of 6,037 whites, and 76,812 negro slaves. Its establishments consisted of 38 plantations of white sugar, and 110 of muscovado; 214 coffee-plantations, 234 of cotton, 765 of indigo, and 119 smaller settlements.

THE quantity of land in cultivation throughout all the parishes was 763,923 carreaux *(e)*, equal to 2,289,480 English acres, of which about two-thirds were situated in the mountains; and that the reader may have a state of the agriculture

(e) The carreau of land in St. Domingo is 100 paces square, of 3½ French feet each; the superficies 122,500 feet. The Paris foot is divided into twelve inches, and each into twelve lines; wherefore, if we suppose each line to be divided into 310 parts, the Paris foot will be 1440 parts, the London 1350. These proportions were settled by the Royal Academy of Sciences. The Jamaica acre contains 43,560 English feet superficial measure; which being multiplied by 1,350, and the total divided by 1,440, gives 40,837½, or about one-third part of the carreau of St. Domingo.

at

at one view, I shall subjoin a summary of the preceding accounts, from whence it will appear that the French colony contained, the beginning of 1790, CHAP. IX.

	431	plantations of clayed sugar,
	362	- of muscovado.
Total -	793	plantations of sugar,
	3,117	- of coffee,
	789	- of cotton,
	3,160	- of indigo,
	54	- of cacao, or chocolate,
	623	smaller settlements, chiefly for raising grain, yams, and other vegetable food.
Making	8,536	establishments of all kinds throughout the colony.

The population in 1790, on a like summary, appears to have been 30,831 whites of both sexes and all ages (exclusive of European troops and sea-faring people), and 434,429 negro slaves. In this account, however, the domestick slaves, and negro mechanicks employed in the several towns, are not comprehended. They amounted to about 46,000, which made the number of negro slaves throughout the colony 480,000.

Of the free people of colour, no very accurate account was obtained. Mons. Marbois, the intendant, reported them in 1787 at about 20,000. In 1790, the general opinion fixed them at 24,000.

The exterior appearance of the colony, as I have observed

CHAP. IX. observed in another place, every where demonstrated great and increasing prosperity. Cultivation was making rapid advances over the country. The towns abounded in warehouses, which were filled with the richest commodities and productions of Europe, and the harbours were crowded with shipping. There were freighted in 1787, for Europe alone, 470 ships, containing 112,253 tons, and navigated by 11,220 seamen. Many of them were vessels of very large burthen; and the following is an accurate account, from the intendant's return, of the general exports, on an average of the years 1787, 1788, and 1789; viz.

Average exports from the French part of St. Domingo, before the Revolution.

			Livres.
Clayed sugar - -	lbs.	58,642,214 -	41,049,549
Muscovado sugar	lbs.	86,549,829 -	34,619,931
Coffee - -	lbs.	71,663,187 -	71,663,187
Cotton - -	lbs.	6,698,858 -	12,397,716
Indigo - -	Hhds. -	951,607 -	8,564,463
Molasses - -	Hhds. -	23,061 -	2,767,320
An inferior sort of rum, called taffia	Hhds. -	2,600 -	312,000
Raw hides -		N° 6,500 -	52,000
Tan'd ditto		N° 7,900 -	118,500
The total value at the ports of shipping, in livres of St. Domingo, was			171,544,666

being equal to 4,956,780*l.* sterling money of Great Britain; and if all the smuggled articles

were

together with the value of mahogany and other woods, the whole amount would probably exceed five millions of pounds sterling *. CHAP. IX.

If this statement be compared by the rule of proportion with the exports from Jamaica, the result will be considerably in favour of St. Domingo, *i. e.* it will be found that the planters of Jamaica receive smaller returns from the labours of their negroes, in proportion to their numbers, than the planters of St. Domingo have received from theirs. For this difference various causes have been assigned, and advantages allowed, and qualities ascribed to the French planters, which I venture to pronounce, on full enquiry, had no existence. The true cause arose, undoubtedly, from the superior fertility of the soil, and the prodigious benefit which resulted to the French planters from the system of watering their sugar-lands in extreme dry weather. This is an advantage which nature has denied to the lands in Jamaica, except in a very few places; but has freely bestowed on many parts of St. Domingo; and the planters there availed themselves of it with the happiest success *(f)*.

And

* Vide Appendix, Table No. 2. from whence it will appear that the exports for 1791 greatly exceeded the average above given, both in quantities and value.

(f) Having made diligent enquiry into the average produce of the French sugar-lands in St. Domingo while on the spot, I venture to give the following estimate, as nearly founded in truth as the subject will admit.

In the North, the districts of Ouanaminthe, Maribaroux, and Quartier Dauphin, generally yielded from six to seven thousand

 pounds

CHAP. IX.

And such, in the days of its prosperity, was the French colony in the island of St. Domingo. I have now presented to my readers both sides of the medal. To Great Britain, above all other nations of the earth, the facts which I have related may furnish an important lesson; and it is such a one as requires no comment!

pounds weight of muscovado sugar for each carreau in canes; the average is - - 6,500
Jaquizi 7,000
Limonade 9,000
Quartier Morin - - 6,000
Plaine du Nord, Limbé, Petite Anse 5,000
——— 33,500

The average of the whole is 6,700 lbs. each carreau.—This part of St. Domingo was not watered.

In the West---St. Marc, L'Artibonite, and Gonaives, each carreau yielded - - 8,500
Vazes, Arcahaye, Boucassin 10,000
Cul de Sac - 9,000
Leogane 6,500
——— 34,000

The average is 8,500 lbs. the carreau.—All these districts were watered.

In the South---the districts of Grand Goave, Les-Cayes, Plaine du Fond, L'Islet, &c. which likewise were watered, yielded - - - 7,500

The general average, on the whole, is 7,500 lbs. from each carreau in canes; to which add 8½ per cent. for the difference between the English and French weights, the total is 8,137 lbs. for every three acres English, or 2,712 lbs. per acre; being nearly two-thirds more than the general yielding of all the land in canes throughout Jamaica.

CHAP. X.

Emigrations—Overtures to the British Government accepted—Situation and Strength of the Republican Party in St. Domingo, and Disposition of the Inhabitants—Negro Slavery abolished by the French Commissioners—Armament allotted for the Invasion of the Country—Surrender of Jeremie and the Mole at Cape St. Nicholas—Unsuccessful Attempt on Cape Tiburon—Further Proceedings of the British Army until the Arrival of General Whyte—Capture of Port au Prince.

CHAP. X.

THE destruction of the beautiful city of Cape François, and the massacre of most of the white inhabitants, were the sad events which terminated our historical detail at the close of the eighth Chapter. It was observed, however, that M. Galbaud and his partizans, among whom were comprehended many respectable families, had fortunately embarked on the ships in the harbour, just before the revolted negroes entered the town. Happy to fly from a country devoted to ruin, they directed their course to the United States of North America; and to the honour of the human character (debased as we have beheld it in other situations) they found there, what great numbers of their unhappy fellow-citizens had found before

them,

CHAP. X. them, a refuge from the reach of persecution, and an asylum from the pressure of poverty.

Emigrations from all parts of St. Domingo had indeed prevailed to a very great extent, ever since the revolt of the negroes in the Northern province. Many of the planters had removed with their families to the neighbouring islands: some of them had taken refuge in Jamaica; and it was supposed that not less than ten thousand had transported themselves, at various times, to different parts of the continent of America. Most of these were persons of peaceable tempers, who sought only to procure the mere necessaries of life in safety and quiet. The principal among the planters, having other objects in view, had repaired to Great Britain. It is a circumstance within my own knowledge, that so early as the latter end of 1791 (long before the commencement of hostilities between France and England) many of them had made application to the King's ministers, requesting that an armament might be sent to take possession of the country for the King of Great Britain, and receive the allegiance of the inhabitants. They asserted (—I am afraid with much greater confidence than truth—) that all classes of the whites wished to place themselves under the English dominion, and that, on the first appearance of a British squadron, the colony would surrender without a struggle. To these representations no attention was at that time given: but at length, after the national assembly had thought proper to declare war against Great Britain, the English ministry

ministry began to listen, with some degree of complacency, to the overtures which were again made to them, to the same effect, by the planters of St. Domingo. In the summer of 1793, a M. Charmilly (one of those planters) was furnished with dispatches from the secretary of state to General Williamson, the lieutenant-governor and commander in chief of Jamaica, signifying the king's pleasure (with allowance of great latitude however to the governor's discretion) that he should accept terms of capitulation from the inhabitants of such parts of St. Domingo as solicited the protection of the British government; and for that purpose the governor was authorized to detach, from the troops under his command in Jamaica, such a force as should be thought sufficient to take and retain possession of all the places that might be surrendered, until reinforcements should arrive from England. M. Charmilly, having thus delivered the orders and instructions with which he was entrusted, sent an agent without delay to *Jeremie (a)*, a small port and town in the district of *Grand Anse*, to which he belonged, to prepare the loyal inhabitants for a visit from their new allies and protectors the English.

But, before we proceed to detail the operations which followed this determination of the British cabinet, it seems necessary, as well for the satisfaction of the reader, as in justice to the gallantry and good conduct of the officers and men who were afterwards sent to St. Domingo, that

(a) It is situated just within the Bight of *Leogane*.

some

CHAP. X.

some account should be given of the difficulties which were to arise, and the force that was to be encountered in this attempt to annex so great and valuable a colony to the British dominion. I am well apprized that I am here treading on tender ground; but if it shall appear, as unhappily it will, that the persons at whose instance and entreaty the project was adopted, either meant to deceive, or were themselves grossly deceived, in the representations which they had made to the English government on this occasion, it is my province and my duty to place the failure which ensued to its proper account. The historian who, in such cases, from fear, favour, or affection, suppresses the communication of facts, is hardly less culpable than the factious or venal writer, who sacrifices the interests of truth and the dignity of history, to the prejudices of party.

THE republican commissioners, as the reader has been informed, had brought with them from France six thousand chosen troops; which, added to the national force already in the colony, and the militia of the country, constituted a body of fourteen or fifteen thousand effective men; to whom were joined a motley but desperate band of all complexions and descriptions, chiefly slaves which had deserted from their owners, and negroes collected from the jails. All these, amounting in the whole to about twenty-two thousand effectives, were brought into some degree of order and discipline; were well armed, and, what is of infinite

infinite importance, were, in a considerable degree, inured to the climate.* Being necessarily dispersed, however, in detachments throughout the different provinces, they were become on that account less formidable to an invading enemy. Aware of this circumstance, the commissioners, on the first intimation of an attack from the English, resorted to the most desperate expedient to strengthen their party, that imagination can conceive. They declared by proclamation all manner of slavery abolished, and pronounced the negro slaves to be from thenceforward a free people, on condition of resorting to their standard. From this moment it might have been foreseen that the colony was lost to Europe; for though but few of the negroes, in proportion to the whole, joined the commissioners, many thousands choosing to continue slaves as they were, and participate in the fortunes of their masters, yet vast numbers in

* The following detail was given me by a member of the colonial assembly.

Troops in St. Domingo on the arrival of Santhonax and Polverel, viz.

Troops of the line which arrived with the commissioners	6,000
The regiment of Cape François - - - -	700
The regiments of Artois and Normandy - - -	1,000
Stipendiary troops enlisted and paid for by the colony -	1,200
The colonial militia, including free people of colour	7,000
	15,900
Black companies raised by the authority of the commissioners - - - - -	6,000
Total - -	21,900

CHAP. X.

all parts of the colony (apprehensive probably that this offer of liberty was too great a favour to be permanent) availed themselves of it to secure a retreat to the mountains, and possess themselves of the natural fastnesses which the interior country affords. Successive bodies have since joined them, and have established themselves, in those recesses, into a sort of savage republick, like that of the black Charaibes of St. Vincent, where they subsist on the spontaneous fruits of the earth, and the wild cattle which they procure by hunting; prudently declining offensive war, and trusting their safety to the rocky fortresses which nature has raised around them, and from which, in my opinion, it will be no easy undertaking to dislodge them *(b)*.

(b) The proclamation alluded to was issued at Port au Prince the latter end of August, and was signed by Polverel alone, Santhonax being at that time in the Northern province. It begins by declaring, that neither himself nor Santhonax are recalled or disgraced. That, in order to encourage the negro slaves to assist in opposing the meditated invasion of the English, all manner of slavery is abolished; and the negroes are thenceforward to consider themselves as free citizens. It then expatiates upon the necessity of labour, and tells the negroes that they must engage to work as usual, from year to year; but that they are at liberty to make choice of their respective masters. That one-third of the crop shall be appropriated annually to the purchase of clothing and provisions for their maintenance; and that in the month of September in each year they are at liberty to make a new choice, or to confirm that of the preceding year. Such, to the best of my remembrance (for I speak from memory) are the chief provisions of this celebrated proclamation, which I think extended only to the Western and Southern provinces; Santhonax being empowered to make what other regulations he might think proper for the Northern province. The whole appears

CHAP. X.

Of the revolted negroes in the Northern province, many had perished of disease and famine; but a desperate band, amounting as it was supposed to upwards of 40,000, inured to war, and practised in devastation and murder, still continued in arms. These were ready to pour down, as occasion might offer, on all nations alike; and instead of joining the English on their landing, would rejoice to sacrifice both the victors and the vanquished, the invaders and the invaded, in one common destruction.

Concerning the white proprietors, on whom alone our dependance was placed, a large proportion, as we have seen, perhaps more than nine-tenths of the whole, had quitted the country. Of those that remained, *some* there were, undoubtedly, who sincerely wished for the restoration of order, and the blessings of regular government; but the greater part were persons of a different character: they were desperate adventurers who had nothing to lose, and every thing to gain, by confusion and anarchy: not a few of them had obtained possession of the effects and estates of absent proprietors. From people of this stamp, the most determined opposition was necessarily to be expected; and unfortunately, among those of better principle, I am afraid but a very small number were cordially attached to the English. The majority seem to have had nothing in view

pears to have been a matchless piece of absurdity; betraying a lamentable degree of ignorance concerning the manners and dispositions of the negroes, and totally impracticable in itself.

but

CHAP. X.

but to obtain by any means the restoration of their estates and possessions. Many of them, under their ancient government, had belonged to the lower order of *noblesse;* and being tenacious of titles and honours, in proportion as their pretensions to real distinction were disputable, they dreaded the introduction of a system of laws and government, which would reduce them to the general level of the community. Thus, as their motives were selfish, and their attachment feeble, their exertions in the common cause were not likely to be very strenuous or efficacious. I do not find that the number of French in arms, who joined us at any one period (I mean of white inhabitants) ever exceeded two thousand. It were unjust, however, not to observe, that among them were some distinguished individuals, whose fidelity was above suspicion, and whose services were highly important. (c).

From this recapitulation it is evident, that the

(c) A few men of colour also distinguished themselves in the common cause; *viz.* Monsieur *Le Point*, Lieutenant-colonel of the St Marc's legion, who, with about 300 Mulattoes under his command, kept the parish of L'Archaye in complete subjection for a considerable time. 2. *Boucquet*, Major of the *Milice Royale* of Verettes, a person much attached to the English. 3. *Charles Savory*, who commanded a very important post in the plain of Artibonite, upon the river D'Esterre. Great confidence was placed in this man by Colonel Brisbane, and it was never abused. All these men were well educated, and nourished deep resentment against the French planters, on account of the indignities which the class of coloured people had received from them. At Cape Tiburon, three or four hundred blacks were embodied very early, under a black general named Iean Kina, who served well and faithfully.

invasion

invasion of St. Domingo was an enterprize of greater magnitude and difficulty than the British government seem to have imagined. Considering the extent and natural strength of the country, it may well be doubted, whether all the force which Great Britain could have spared, would have been sufficient to reduce it to subjection, and restore it at the same time to such a degree of order and subordination, as to make it a colony worth holding. The truth seems to have been, that General Williamson, to whom, as hath been observed, the direction and distribution of the armament was entrusted, and whose active zeal in the service of his country was eminently conspicuous, was deceived, equally with the King's ministers, by the favourable accounts and exaggerated representations of sanguine and interested individuals, concerning the disposition of their countrymen, the white planters remaining in St. Domingo. Instead of the few hundreds of them which afterwards resorted to the British standard, the Governor had reason to expect the support and co-operation of at least as many thousands. In this fatal confidence, the armament allotted for this important expedition was composed of only the 13th regiment of foot, seven companies of the 49th, and a detachment of artillery, altogether amounting to about eight hundred and seventy, rank and file, fit for duty. Such was the force that was to annex to the crown of Great Britain, a country nearly equal in extent, and in natural strength infinitely superior, to Great Britain itself! Speedy and

CHAP. X. and effectual reinforcements from England were, however, promised, as well to replace the troops which were removed from Jamaica, as to aid the operations in St. Domingo.

In the meantime, the first division, consisting of six hundred and seventy-seven rank and file, under the command of Lieutenant-Colonel Whitelocke, sailed from Port-Royal the 9th of September, and arrived at Jeremie on the 19th of the same month. They were escorted by Commodore Ford, in the Europa, accompanied by four or five frigates.

As the propositions, or terms of capitulation, had been previously adjusted between the people of Jeremie, by their agent Mr. Charmilly, and General Williamson, it only remained for the British forces to take possession of the town and harbour. Accordingly, the troops disembarked early the next morning; the British colours were hoisted at both the forts, with royal salutes from each, which were answered by the Commodore and his squadron, and the oaths of fidelity and allegiance were taken by the resident inhabitants, with an appearance of great zeal and alacrity.

At the same time information was received, that the garrison at the Mole of Cape St. Nicholas were inclined to surrender that important fortress in like manner. As this was a circumstance not to be neglected, the Commodore immediately directed his course thither, and, on the 22d, took possession of the fortress and harbour, and received the allegiance of the officers and privates. The grenadier company of the 13th regiment, was forthwith

forthwith dispatched from Jeremie to take the command of the garrison; which was soon afterwards strengthened by the arrival of the second division of the armament ordered from Jamaica, consisting of five companies of forty men each.

THE voluntary surrender of these places raised expectations in the people of England, that the whole of the French colony in St. Domingo would submit without opposition; but the advantages hitherto obtained seem to have been greatly overvalued. The town of Jeremie is a place of no importance. It contains about one hundred very mean houses, and the country in the vicinage is not remarkably fertile; producing nothing of any account but coffee. At the Mole of Cape St. Nicholas, the country is even less productive than in the neighbourhood of Jeremie; but the harbour is one of the finest in the new world, and the fortifications vie with the strongest in the West Indies. Unfortunately, from the elevation of the surrounding heights, the place is not tenable against a powerful attack by land. The garrison consisted only of the regiment of Dillon, which was reduced by sickness or desertion to about one hundred and fifty men. The town itself was in the highest degree hostile: most of the inhabitants, capable of bearing arms, left the place on the arrival of the English, and joined the republican army.

ZEALOUS, however, to promote the glory of the British name, Colonel Whitelocke determined that his little army should not continue inactive at Jeremie. It was represented to him, that the acquisition of the neighbouring post of Tiburon would

CHAP. X.

prove of the utmost importance towards the security of Grand-Anse, and a M. Duval pledging himself to raise five hundred men to co-operate in its reduction, an expedition was undertaken for that purpose, and Colonel Whitelocke, with most of the British force from Jeremie, arrived in Tiburon Bay on the 4th of October.

But, on this occasion, as on almost every other, the English had a melancholy proof how little dependance can be placed on French declarations and assurances. Duval never made his appearance, for he was not able to collect more than fifty whites; the enemy's force was found to be far more formidable than had been represented, and the gallantry of our troops proved unavailing against superiority of numbers. They were compelled to retreat, with the loss of about twenty men killed and wounded.*

The defeat and discouragement sustained in this attack were the more grievously felt, as sickness soon afterwards began to prevail to a great extent in the army. The season of the year was unfavourable in the highest degree for military operations in a tropical climate. The rains were incessant; and the constant and unusual fatigue, and extraordinary duty to which the soldiers, from the smallness of their number, were necessarily subject, co-operating with the state of the weather, produced the most fatal consequences. That never-failing attendant on military expeditions in

* This Duval being afterwards suspected of corresponding with the enemy, was ordered to quit the island, and he went to America.

the

the West Indies, the yellow or pestilential fever, raged with dreadful virulence; and so many, both of the seamen and soldiers, perished daily, that the urvivors were stricken with astonishment and horror at beholding the havock made among their comrades!

General Williamson, with his usual humanity, exerted himself to give them all the relief in his power. Unhappily he had no alternative but either to withdraw the troops altogether from St. Domingo, leaving our allies and new subjects, the French planters who had sworn allegiance to our government, to the mercy of their enemies, or to send, from an already exhausted army, a small reinforcement of men, to perish probably in the same manner as those had done whose numbers they were scarcely sufficient to replace.

The latter measure was adopted: in truth, the circumstances of the case admitted of no other. The remainder of the 49th regiment, the 20th, and the royals, amounting all together to seven or eight hundred men, were therefore dispatched with all possible expedition; and the safety of Jamaica was at length entrusted to less than four hundred regular troops.

The sudden appearance in St. Domingo of a reinforcement, though small in itself, produced however a considerable effect among the French planters, by inducing a belief that the British government was now seriously resolved to follow up the blow. In the beginning of December, the parishes of Jean Rabel, St. Marc, Arcahaye, and Boucassin, surrendered on the same conditions as had

CHAP. X. had been granted to Jeremie; and their example was soon afterwards followed by the inhabitants of Leogane. All the former parishes are situated on the north side of the Bight: Leogane on the south.

The British commanders now directed their views once more towards the capture of Tiburon. The defeat which our troops had sustained in the late attack of that important post, served only to animate them to greater exertions; but a considerable time unavoidably elapsed before the expedition took place; the interval being employed in securing the places which had surrendered.
1794. On the 21st of January, however, the Commodore touched at Jeremie with the squadron, and received the troops on board; and the whole arrived off Cape Tiburon on the evening of the first of February.

The enemy appeared in considerable force, and seemed to wait the arrival of the British with great resolution; but a few broadsides from the ships soon cleared the beach. They came forward however again, as the flank companies approached the shore, and directed a general discharge of musquetry at the boats; but our troops landed and formed in an instant, routed their line with great slaughter, and immediately took possession of the post. The gallantry of Major Spencer who commanded, and of the officers and men who composed, the flank companies, was particularly conspicuous. It seems, indeed, to have been a spirited and well conducted enterprize throughout; and it was happily effected with the loss of only three of the English killed, and seven wounded. Of the enemy,

CHAP. X.

enemy, one hundred and fifty surrendered prisoners of war; and their magazines were found replete with ammunition*.

By the possession of this post on the south, and that of the Mole at Cape St. Nicholas on the north-western part of the island, the British squadron commanded the navigation of the windward passage, and the whole of that extensive bay which forms the Bight of Leogane, and the capture of the forts, shipping, and town of Port au Prince

* I have since been informed by an officer of rank, who took a distinguished part in this enterprize, that the real number of British killed and wounded was twenty-five. This gentleman was himself among the wounded. The generous gallantry of a common sailor named Allen, belonging to the Penelope, deserves to be recorded in this place. Instead of returning to his ship with the boats, according to orders, after the troops were landed, the sailor jumped on shore, swore *that he too would have a dash at the Brigands*. But it was necessary the troops should follow up their success, and it being found impossible to take all the wounded men along with them, many of those would have been left on the beach, in a dark night, liable to be massacred by a savage enemy; which honest Jack perceiving, he declared it was a more pleasing task to save the lives of these poor suffering men, than to kill half a score rebels. He therefore plunged into the water, the boats having pushed off, and by hard swimming, reached the Hound Sloop, lying near a mile from the shore, and from her was sent to his own ship. Captain Rowley being by this means informed of the situation of the wounded men, manned his barge, and brought them all off himself; and with a very commendable attention towards such of them as died in the removal, ordered the lieutenant to read the funeral service over them, by the light of a lanthorn, before their bodies were committed to the deep. Allen, the sailor, was reprimanded for his breach of discipline, but rewarded with five pounds for his humanity.

CHAP. X. 1794. Prince (the metropolis of the French colony) seemed more than probable, on the arrival of a large armament now daily expected, with much anxiety, from England.

In the meanwhile, it was determined (now that the season was favourable) in order that the troops might not continue inactive, as well as to facilitate the meditated reduction of Port au Prince, to attack *L'Acul*, an important fortress in the vicinity of Leogane. Accordingly, on the 19th of February, the flank companies, a detachment of the royal artillery, and of the 13th regiment, with some colonial troops, having two five-half-inch howitzers and two four-pounders, marched from thence under the command of Colonel Whitelocke, at four in the morning. Baron de Montalembert, with about two hundred colonial troops, and a few of the British artillery, were previously embarked in transports, and ordered to land and attack the fort at an hour appointed. Captain Vincent, with the light infantry of the 49th, and about eighty of the colonial troops, took a mountain road, while Colonel Whitelocke moved forward on the great road, and took post just out of cannon-shot, waiting the united attacks of the Baron and Captain Vincent's detachments. The enemy began to cannonade about seven o'clock, and continued it with intervals till eleven, when Colonel Whitelocke ordered Captain Smith, with the howitzers and cannon, to advance and fire upon the fort, supported by the light infantry of the royals and 13th regiments, under the command of Major Spencer, in order to give time for the

Baron's

Baron's people to land. Unfortunately, from the mismanagement of one of the transports, the troops under the orders of the Baron de Montalembert could not be landed. Colonel Whitelocke, therefore, finding he had nothing to expect from them, the day being considerably advanced, now came to the determination of attacking the fort by storm; and detached Major Spencer, with the grenadiers of the 49th regiment, and the light infantry of the 13th, to join Captain Vincent, and approach the fort by the mountain road, while he himself marched by the great road for the same purpose. At five o'clock, the two columns moved forward, and the moment the enemy discovered the march of Colonel Whitelocke's division, they commenced a very heavy fire of cannon and musquetry. Orders were immediately given for the column to advance and gain the fort, which orders were gallantly and rapidly executed. At this instant, Lieutenant M'Kerras of the engineers, and Captain Hutchinson of the royals, were both wounded; but they continued their exertions, notwithstanding, till the fort was in quiet possession of the victors. Our loss was not great; but Captain Morshead (who had before received a shot in the body, when gallantly mounting the hill) with Lieutenant Tinlin of the 20th grenadiers, Lieutenant Caulfield of the 62d regiment, and some privates, were unfortunately blown up by an explosion after the fort was taken; for the officer who commanded, finding he could no longer defend it, placed a quantity of powder and other combustibles in one of the buildings, which was

fired

CHAP. X.

fired by an unfortunate brigand, who perished in the explosion. Captain Morshead died the next day, and was interred with military honours, attended by the British garrison; Lieutenant Caulfield lingered some time longer, and then followed him to the grave; but Lieutenant Tinlin recovered*.

The next enterprize of our gallant little army had a less favourable termination. It was directed against a strong post and settlement at a place called *Bompard,* about eight miles from Cape St. Nicholas, where a hardy race of people, chiefly a colony of Germans, had established themselves, and lived in unambitious poverty. A detachment of two hundred men, from the different corps, were ordered on this service, in two divisions, one of which was commanded by Major Spencer, the brave and active officer already mentioned, the other by Lieutenant-Colonel Markham. Of their proceedings during the attack, and their retreat afterwards, I have not been furnished with the particulars. All that is known to the publick with certainty is, that our troops were repulsed by superior numbers, with the loss of forty men, but without any diminution of the national character. It

* I am indebted to the gentleman who favoured me with the information conveyed in the note to p. 161. for the following corrections and observations on the account, which I have given above, of the attack of *Acul.* "Our loss, that day (the 19th "February) was thirty-four killed and wounded, amongst "whom were six English officers and ten Frenchmen. Lieu- "tenant Lord Aylmer was wounded in the thigh, while ad- "vancing in Major Spencer's division to the attack."

It was allowed, even by the enemy, that they fought bravely. They were defeated, not dismayed, by circumstances which probably they did not foresee, and against which human prudence could not provide.

This afflicting loss was but ill compensated, by the very distinguished honour which was soon afterwards acquired by the few British troops that had been left in possession of Cape Tiburon, under the command of Captain Harlyman, of the 13th regiment, who were attacked on the 16th of April, by an army of brigands, amounting to upwards of two thousand. The enemy's force was led on by Andrew Rigaud, a man of colour, who commanded at Les Cayes, and was composed of revolted negroes, and desperadoes of all descriptions, rapacious after plunder, and thirsting for blood. This savage horde surrounded the fort about three o'clock in the morning. It was defended with much spirit until a quarter before nine, when the besieged, quitting the fort, assailed the assailants, and routed the besiegers with great slaughter, one hundred and seventy of their number being left dead on the field; but when it was discovered that no less than twenty-eight of our gallant soldiers had lost their lives, and that one hundred and nine others were severely wounded in the bloody contest, the shouts of triumph were suppressed by gloomy reflections on the forlorn condition of the army, it being mournfully evident that a few more such victories would annihilate the victors!

The defence of Fort L'Acul, early in the same month, is also deserving particular notice. Captain

CHAP. X. tain Napier had the command; and he was ably supported by Lieutenant Bambridge, of the artillery, and Lieutenant M'Kellan, of the royals. The latter was stationed in the adjoining block-house.

THE enemy, on this occasion, conducted their operations with such secrecy and concert, that it was supposed they must have lain concealed, a considerable part of the night, in the ditch; as the first notice the garrison had of their approach, was from a loud yell which they uttered in endeavouring to enter the embrasures.

THE firing of our morning gun was their signal of attack; but they seem not to have been apprized that previous thereto, by a full hour, it was the constant practice of the British officers to have their men at the out-posts under arms.

BEING twice repulsed from the fort and block-house, the enemy rallied, and made a third attempt; an instance of persevering bravery, unobserved until that time in their warfare. They were, however, finally driven off; and were afterwards pursued with great slaughter by a party of French royalists, under the command of the Baron de Montalembert, who had just arrived from Leogane.

THE whole of the British force at this time in all parts of St. Domingo did not, I believe, amount to nine hundred effective men, a number by no means sufficient to garrison the places in our possession; and the rapid diminution which prevailed among them, could not fail to attract observation among all classes of the French inhabitants; to dispirit our allies, and encourage our enemies. Such of the planters as had hitherto stood

stood aloof, now began to declare themselves hostile; and desertions were frequent from most of the parishes that had surrendered. At Jean Rabell, a place which, a few months before, had voluntarily declared for the British government, the garrison, consisting of two hundred and fifty of our supposed allies, rose on their officers, and compelled them to deliver up the post of Lavaux, the French general, and it was greatly apprehended that, unless a very powerful reinforcement should speedily arrive to strengthen the British army, many other places would follow their example.

Eight months had now elapsed since the surrender of Jeremie, and in all that interval, not a soldier had arrived from Great Britain; and the want of camp equipage, provisions, and necessaries, was grievously felt. The army seemed devoted to inevitable destruction, and disappointment and dismay were strongly marked in the countenance of every man. At length, however, on the 19th of May, when expectation was nearly lost May 1794. in despair, it was announced that his Majesty's ships the Belliqueux and the Irresistible, with the Fly sloop, had cast anchor in the harbour of Cape St. Nicholas, having a fleet of transports under their convoy, with the battalion companies on board of the 22d, 23d, and 41st regiments of infantry, under the command of Brigadier General Whyte. This event, as may well be imagined, afforded infinite relief and satisfaction to the harassed and worn-out troops on shore; and their animation on this occasion was heightened by the confident

CHAP. X.

confident hope and expectation that Port au Prince would be the object of an immediate attack. It was known that its harbour was crowded with ships, most of which were supposed to be laden with the richest productions of the colony; and although the regiments newly arrived did not exceed sixteen hundred men in the whole (of whom two hundred and fifty were sick and convalescent) the deficiency of numbers was no longer the subject of complaint. Every one anticipated to himself the possession of great wealth from the capture; and justly concluded that his share of the prize money would augment or diminish in an inverse proportion to the number of captors.

The belief that Port au Prince would be the first object of attack was well founded; and the road of Arcahaye was fixed on as a place of rendezvous for the men of war and transports. Accordingly, General Whyte, having landed his sick at Cape St. Nicholas, and taken one hundred and fifty of the garrison in their room, proceeded on the 23d to the place appointed, to concert measures with Commodore Ford, and receive on board such of the colonial troops as were to co-operate with the British in this enterprize. On the 30th the squadron sailed from Arcahaye, and cast anchor off Port au Prince on the evening of the same day. It was composed of four ships of the line, the Europa, the Belliqueux, the Irresistible, and the Sceptre, three frigates, and four or five smaller vessels; the whole under the immediate command of Commodore Ford; and the land forces, under the orders of General Whyte, consisted

sisted of one thousand four hundred and sixty-five rank and file fit for duty.

The whole force being thus collected, and the necessary preparations made, a flag was sent, early the next morning, to demand the surrender of the place; but the officer charged with the dispatch was informed that no flag would be admitted, and the letter was returned unopened. It was now determined to commence operations by the cannonade of Fort Bizotton, a fortress situated on a commanding eminence, well adapted to guard the approach to the harbour, and defended by five hundred men, eight pieces of heavy cannon, and two mortars. Two line of battle ships were ordered to attack the sea-front, and a frigate was stationed close to the shore, to flank a ravine to the eastward. From these vessels a brisk and well-directed fire was maintained for several hours; but as no great impression appeared to be made, Major Spencer, with three hundred British, and about five hundred of the colonial troops, was put on shore in the evening, within a mile of the fort, with orders to commence an attack on the side towards the land. On their arrival at a small distance from the scene of action, about eight o'clock at night, a most tremendous thunder-storm arose, accompanied with a deluge of rain, of which, as it overpowered the sound of their approach, the advanced guard, commanded by Captain Daniel, of the 41st, determined to take advantage. These brave men, sixty only in number, accordingly rushed forward, and finding a breach in the walls, entered with fixed bayonets, and

CHAP. X.

and became instantly masters of the fortress; the besieged every where throwing down their arms, and calling for mercy. So rapid were the movements of this gallant band, and so unexpected was their success, that Major Spencer, the commander, had his fears for the safety of the whole party, of whose situation he was unapprized for some hours. I grieve to add, that Captain Daniel, who so gallantly led the advanced guard on this occasion, received a severe wound in the attack, while his brave associate, Captain Wallace, the second in command, was most unfortunately killed on the glacis.

The possession of Fort Bizotton determined the fate of the capital, which was evacuated by the enemy on the 4th of June; and the British commanders were so fortunate as to preserve, not only the town itself, but also the shipping in the harbour, from conflagration, although the republican commissioners had given orders and made preparations for setting fire to both. The commissioners themselves, with many of their adherents, among whom was the Mulatto Montbrun, commandant of their troops, made their escape over the mountains to Jacmel, carrying with them, it is said, money and effects to a great amount.

Thus was achieved the conquest of Port au Prince; an event which has proved not less profitable than honourable to such of the officers and soldiers by whom it was effected, as have lived to enjoy the fruits of their victory; for there were captured in the harbour, two-and-twenty top-sail vessels, fully laden with sugar, indigo, and coffee, of which thirteen were from three to five hundred

tons

tons burthen, and the remaining nine, from one hundred and fifty to three hundred tons; besides seven thousand tons of shipping in ballast; the value of all which, at a moderate computation, could not be far short of 400,000*l*. sterling*.

CHAP. X.

* Three days after the surrender of Port au Prince, the enemy made a second attempt on the British post at Tiburon; at that time under the command of Captain (now Lieutenant Colonel) Bradshaw. This attack took place on the 7th of June; but the assailants were prevented bringing their artillery to bear on the fort, by a heavy and well-directed fire from the Success Frigate (Captain Roberts), stationed off the point, close to which the cannon must have been conveyed; about midnight, therefore, the enemy, from the covert of an adjoining wood, began a general discharge of small arms, and continued to fire very vigorously for several hours, but with little execution; the fort having been made proof against musquetry. During this attack, as the great guns of the fort could not be pointed towards the enemy with any certainty of effect, Captain Bradshaw directed his men to remain quiet. By this judicious conduct the enemy were completely deceived; for interpreting the silence and inactivity of the garrison to proceed from the effects of terror and the loss of men, they were encouraged, about six in the morning, to attempt, in full force, to storm. The consequences were fatal to them: Captain Bradshaw allowed them to approach within a small distance of the walls, when he opened so tremendous a fire, both from artillery and small arms, as instantly laid nearly one half of their number breathless, and compelled the remainder to retreat in the utmost confusion. A sortie being, at the same time, made from the garrison, a great many were killed in the pursuit, and their discomfiture was decisive.

☞ The circumstances here related were unfortunately omitted in the first edition of the Historical Survey of St. Domingo.

CHAP.

CHAP. XI.

Sickness among the Troops, and the causes thereof.—Reinforcement.—Dreadful Mortality.—General Whyte is succeeded by Brigadier General Horneck.—Leogane taken by the Rebels.—Temporary Successes of Lieutenant-Colonel Brishane at Artibonite.—Revolt of the Mulattoes at St. Marc.—Attack of Fort Bizotton.—Preparations by Rigaud for another Attempt on Tiburon.—The Post attacked on Christmas Day, and carried.—Gallant Defence and Escape of the Garrison, and melancholy Fate of Lieutenant Baskerville.—Lieutenant-Colonels Brisbane and Markham killed.—Observations and Strictures on the Conduct of the War.

CHAP. XI.

From the success which attended the British arms in the conquest of Port au Prince, it might have been hoped that we were now to enter on the survey of brighter prospects than those which have hitherto presented themselves to our contemplation; but a melancholy reverse of fortune was soon to await the conquerors; for, immediately after possession was taken of the town, the same dreadful scourge—disease, exasperated to contagion, which had been so fatally prevalent among our troops in the preceding autumn, renewed its destructive progress; and, on this occasion, it is not difficult to trace the proximate causes of so terrible a calamity. The situation of the town of Port au Prince has already been noticed. Unhealthy

healthy in itself, it is surrounded by fortified heights, which command both the lines and the harbour; and these heights are again commanded by others. Here the enemy on their retreat from town, made their stand, in the well-founded confidence of receiving regular supplies of men, ammunition, and necessaries, from Les Cayes, a seaport on the southern coast, distant only from Port au Prince, by a very easy road, about forty miles *(a)*. No part of St. Domingo possesses a more ready communication with the French Islands to windward or with the states of America, than the port last mentioned; and from both these sources, reinforcements were actually received, and constantly poured into the enemy's camp. On this account the British commanders found it indispensably necessary to strengthen the lines, and raise additional intrenchments and works on that side of the town which fronts the mountains. Thus a most severe and unusual burthen was imposed on the soldiers. They were compelled with but little intermission, to dig the ground in the day, and to perform military duty in the night; exposed, in the one case, to the burning

(a) The harbour of Les Cayes was guarded by two small forts, each of which was furnished with only six pieces of cannon, and a smaller battery, which mounted only five pieces. The number of white inhabitants belonging to the town were computed at eight hundred; but the people of colour had taken possession of it in the latter end of 1792, and Andrew Rigaud, a Mulatto, was made commander in chief and governor-general of the south side of the French part of St. Domingo. His power was absolute, and his brother, of the same cast, was appointed next in command. These men were invested with this authority by the two commissioners, Polverel and Santhonax.

CHAP. XI. burning rays of the sun; in the other, to the noxious dews and heavy rains of the climate. Such extraordinary and excessive labour imposed on men, most of whom had been actually confined six months on ship-board without fresh provisions or exercise, co-operating with the malignancy of the air, produced its natural consequences. They dropt like the leaves in autumn, until at length the garrison became so diminished and enfeebled, that deficiencies of the guards were oftentimes made up from convalescents, who were scarcely able to stand under their arms *(b)*.

It is true, that a reinforcement came from the Windward Islands, soon after the surrender of the town;—but, by a mournful fatality, this apparent augmentation of the strength of the garrison, contributed in an eminent degree to the rapid encrease and aggravation of its miseries. On the 8th of June, eight flank companies belonging to the 22d, 23d, 35th, and 41st regiments, arrived at Port au Prince, under the command of Lieutenant-Colonel Lenox. They consisted, on their embarkation, of about seventy men each, but the aggregate number, when landed, was not quite three hundred. The four grenadier companies, in particular, were nearly annihilated. The frigate in which they were conveyed, became *a house of pestilence*. Upwards of one hundred of their number were buried in the deep, in the short passage between

(b) It was fortunate for the British army, that the French troops suffered by sickness almost as much as our own: Port au Prince would otherwise have been but a short time in our possession.

between Guadaloupe and Jamaica, and one hundred and fifty more were left in a dying state at Port Royal. The wretched remains of the whole detachment discovered, on their landing at Port au Prince, that they came—not to participate in the glories of conquest, but—to perish themselves within the walls of a hospital! So rapid was the mortality in the British army, after their arrival, that no less than forty officers and upwards of six hundred rank and file met an untimely death, without a contest with any other enemy than sickness, in the short space of two months after the surrender of the town!

General Whyte, his health much impaired, and hopeless, it may be presumed, of further triumphs with an army thus reduced and debilitated, now solicited and obtained permission to return to Europe. He was succeeded in the chief command by Brigadier-General Horneck, who arrived from Jamaica about the middle of September; 1794.
and if the requisite qualifications for such a station—firmness without arrogance, and conciliating manners without weakness, could always ensure success to the possessor, General Horneck would have brought good fortune with him. But the difficulties which the former commander would have had to encounter, had he remained in his station, devolved with aggravated weight on his successor. The only reinforcement which followed General Horneck, consisted of fifty men from Jamaica. Whatever troops were promised or expected from Great Britain, none arrived, until the expiration of seven months after General

CHAP. XI. Oct. 1794. Horneck had taken the command. Instead therefore of attempting new achievements, he was compelled, by irresistible necessity, to act chiefly on the defensive. The rebel Mulattoes, under Rigaud, even became masters of Leogane, and satiated their vengeance by putting to death all such of the French planters, our allies, as unfortunately fell into their power.

On the other hand, the judicious exertions and rapid successes of Lieutenant-Colonel Brisbane on the plain of Artibonite, had been for some time the subject of much applause, and had given birth to great expectation. The French inhabitants of the town and neighbourhood of St. Marc, had been all along more heartily disposed to co-operate with the English, than any of their countrymen. Colonel Brisbane had not above fourscore British under his command. The rest of his little army was composed of the remains of Dillon's regiment, the St. Marc's legion, the militia of the neighbouring parishes, and a body of about three hundred reluctant Spaniards from Verette; the whole not exceeding twelve hundred men in arms. With this force, properly distributed, he had routed the republican troops and rebel negroes in every quarter; and even brought the negro chiefs to solicit permission to capitulate. Eight or ten thousand of these deluded wretches had actually submitted unconditionally, and many returned, of their own accord, to the plantations of their masters. But these promising appearances were of short continuance. While Colonel Brisbane was following up his successes in a distant part of

Artibonite,

Artibonite, the men of colour in the town of St. Marc, finding the town itself without troops, had violated their promises of neutrality, and on the 6th of September, taken up arms on the part of the republick; putting to death every man that fell in their way, whom they considered as an enemy to the French commissioners.—The garrison, consisting of about forty British convalescents, threw themselves into a small fort on the seashore, which they gallantly defended for two days, when a frigate came to their relief from the Mole of Cape St. Nicholas, and took them off.—The triumph of the Mulattoes, however, was transient. Colonel Brisbane returning in force, attacked them on the side of the land, and recovered the town; making upwards of three hundred of the insurgents prisoners, and driving the rest over the Artibonite river; but the advantages which he had obtained on the plain were lost in the interim. The negro chiefs no longer offered to capitulate, but appeared in greater force than ever. Being joined by the fugitive Mulattoes, they soon repassed the river; and having procured in the mean time, plenty of arms and ammunition, they threatened so formidable an attack on the town of St. Marc, early in October, as to excite the most serious apprehensions for its safety.

Such was the situation of affairs, in the western parts of St. Domingo, about the period of General Horneck's arrival. The northern province (the Mole St. Nicholas and the town of Fort Dauphin excepted) was entirely in possession of the rebel negroes; and unhappily, in all other

CHAP. XI. 1794.

parts of the colony, the weakness of the British was so apparent, as not only to invite attacks from the enemy, but also to encourage revolt and conspiracy in the posts in our possession (c). Rigaud, who commanded in the south, now determined to make a bold effort for the recovery of Fort Bizotton. The fort was attacked early in the morning of the 5th of December by three columns of the enemy, amounting in the whole to about two thousand men; but they were defeated with great slaughter on their part, and with little loss on ours. Captain Grant, however, and both his lieutenants, Clunes and Hamilton, were severely wounded early in the attack; yet they continued their efforts, and nobly succeeded; and General Williamson bore testimony to their good conduct and valour.

Baffled in this attack, Rigaud resolved to make another, and a more formidable attempt, for the recovery of Tiburon. His intentions were known, and his project might have been defeated, if

(c) Colonel Brisbane had scarcely driven the Mulattoes from St. Marc, and restored order and tranquillity in the town, before a dark conspiracy was agitated among some of the French inhabitants, under the British protection, to cut him off; but it was happily discovered and defeated before it broke out into action. This happened the beginning of January 1795; and a still more daring and dangerous plot was carried on, a month afterwards, in Port au Prince, to seize on the garrison, and put all the English to death. This conspiracy also was fortunately discovered, and twenty of the conspirators being brought to trial before a council of war, composed of the principal commanders by sea and land (among whom were five French field officers) they were all adjudged to suffer death, and fifteen of them were accordingly shot on the 18th of February.

CHAP. XI. 1794.

if any one English ship of war could have been spared to watch his motions off the harbour of Les Cayes, where Rigaud commanded, and from whence he conveyed his artillery, ammunition, and provisions. He proceeded, however, without interruption, in his preparations for the attack; and his armament sailed from Les Cayes on the 23d of December. His naval force consisted of one brig of sixteen guns, and three schooners of fourteen guns each; and he had collected a body of three thousand men, of all colours and descriptions, eight hundred of which were troops of the line. The attack commenced on Christmas-day. The harbour was defended with infinite spirit, by the sloop King Gray, until a red-hot shot from the enemy took her magazine, and caused her to blow up. The garrison, consisting of only four hundred and fifty men, made a vigorous defence for four days, when, having lost upwards of three hundred of their number, and finding the post no longer tenable, the survivors, with unexampled bravery, fought their way for five miles through the enemy, and got safe to Irois. On this occasion, the British acknowledged themselves much indebted to the gallantry and good conduct of Monsieur de Sevré, commandant of the French troops. M. du Plessis, the Lieutenant Colonel, and two other officers of the south legion were killed in the fort. The loss of du Plessis was greatly felt and lamented. Lieutenant Baskerville was the only British officer who, by some unfortunate circumstance, was unable to join his companions in their retreat; and this high-spirited young man, with a resolution which, though a Christian

CHAP. XI.

must condemn it, a Roman would have approved, to defeat the triumph of his savage enemy, who would probably have made him suffer a shameful death, put a period to his own existence as Rigaud entered the fort.

WITH this disastrous occurrence terminated the year 1794, *(d)* and here I shall close my account of the military transactions of the British army in St. Domingo; for, although hostilities are still continued in this ill-fated country, it is, I think, sufficiently apparent, that all hopes and expectations of ultimate success are vanished for ever! The historian who shall recount the events of 1795, will have to lament the mournful and untimely deaths of many brave and excellent young men who perished in this fruitless contest. Among the foremost of these was Lieutenant Colonel Thomas Brisbane, of whom honourable notice is taken in the foregoing pages, and whose gallantry and good conduct were not more the subject of universal admiration, than his untimely fate of universal regret. He was killed on a reconnoitring party in February. By his death, his country was deprived, at a most critical juncture, of an able, indefatigable, and intelligent officer, who had gained the affections of most of the various descriptions of people under his command by his kindness, and the confidence of all by his courage *(e)*. The

(d) Major General Williamson, the latter end of the year, was appointed Governor General of St. Domingo. He arrived at Port au Prince in May 1795.

(e) He was a captain in the 49th regiment, and lieutenant colonel of the colonial corps called the St. Marc's Legion.

CHAP. XI.

26th March 1795.

The same fate, a month afterwards, awaited Lieutenant-Colonel Markham, who perished in attacking an out-post of the enemy's forces which were, at that time, laying siege to Fort Bizotton. He fell as the detachment was rapidly advancing to the charge. His survivor in command (the hon. Captain Colville) proceeded however with equal animation: the out-post was carried; the colours of the enemy, and five pieces of their cannon, were taken, and some hundreds of their number slain on the spot; but the victory was dearly obtained by the loss of so enterprizing and accomplished a leader. Yet it affords some consolation to reflect, that these brave young men, though cut off in the bloom of life, fell in the field of glory, nobly exerting themselves in the cause of their country, and dying amidst the blessings and applauses of their compatriots. Alas, how many of their youthful associates, in this unhappy war, might have envied them so glorious an exit! What numbers have perished—not in the field of honour—but on the bed of sickness!—not amidst the shouts of victory—but the groans of despair!—condemned to linger in the horrors of pestilence; to fall without a conflict, and to die without renown! *(f)*.

THESE

(f) The disease of which so many gallant men have perished is commonly known by the name of the *yellow fever*. Two writers of great ability (Dr. Rush of Philadelphia, and Dr. Benjamin Moseley of Pall Mall, London) have treated fully of this dreadful calamity. The picture which the latter has given of an unhappy patient of his in the West Indies, a young officer of great merit, in the last stage of this disease, after four days illness, is drawn by the hand of a master. "I arrived at the

lodgings

CHAP. XI.

These reflections, and the observations which I have made in the preceding pages, on the insufficiency of the means to the objects in view, are not written in the spirit of accusation against men in authority; nor (if I know myself) is there any bias of party zeal on my judgment. I am far from asserting, that the situation and resources of Great Britain were such as to afford a greater body of troops for service in St. Domingo, at the proper moment, than the number that was actually sent thither. I presume not to intrude into the national councils, and am well-apprized that existing alliances and pre-engagements of the state, were objects of important consideration to his Majesty's ministers. Neither can I affirm, that the

lodgings of this much esteemed young man (says the doctor) about four hours before his death. When I entered the room, he was vomiting a black muddy cruor, and was bleeding at the nose. A bloody ichor was oozing from the corners of his eyes, and from his mouth and gums. His face was besmeared with blood, and, with the dulness of his eyes, it presented a most distressing contrast to his natural visage. His abdomen was swelled, and inflated prodigiously. His body was all over of a deep yellow, interspersed with livid spots. His hands and feet were of a livid hue. Every part of him was cold excepting about his heart. He had a deep strong hiccup, but neither delirium nor coma; and was, at my first seeing him, as I thought, in his perfect senses. He looked at the changed appearance of his skin, and expressed, though he could not speak, by his sad countenance, that he knew life was soon to yield up her citadel, now abandoning the rest of his body. Exhausted with vomiting, he at last was suffocated with the blood he was endeavouring to bring up, and expired."

Moseley on Tropical Diseases, 3d edit. p. 449.

the delays and obstructions, which prevented the arrival at the scene of action of some of the detachments, until the return of the sickly season, were avoidable. A thousand accidents and casualties continually subvert and overthrow the best-laid schemes of human contrivance. We have seen considerable fleets detained by adverse winds, in the ports of Great Britain, for many successive months, and powerful armaments have been driven back by storms and tempests, after many unavailing attempts to rech the place of their destination. Thus much I owe to candour ; but, at the same time, I owe it also to truth, to avow my opinion, that in case no greater force could have been spared for the enterprize against St. Domingo, the enterprize itself ought not to have been undertaken. The object of the British ministers was avowedly to obtain possession of the whole of the French part of the country. That they placed great dependance on the co-operation of the French inhabitants, and were grossly deceived in this expectation, I believe and admit ; but they ought surely to have foreseen, that a very formidable opposition was to be expected from the partizans and troops of the republican government ; and they ought also to have known, that no considerable body of the French planters could be expected to risk their lives and fortunes in the common cause, but in full confidence of protection and support. In my own judgment, all the force which Great Britain could have sent thither, would not have been sufficient for the complete subjugation of the colony. It is asserted by competent judges, that no less than six thousand

men

CHAP. XI.

men were necessary for the secure maintenance of Port au Prince alone; yet I do not believe that the number of British, in all parts of St. Domingo, at any one period previous to the month of April 1795, exceeded two thousand two hundred, of whom, except at the capture of Port au Prince, not one half were fit for active service; and during the hot and sickly months of August, September, and October, not one third *(g)*.

Perhaps the most fatal oversight in the conduct of the whole expedition, was the strange and unaccountable neglect of not securing the little port of Jacmel on the south side of the Island, previous to the attack of Port au Prince. With that post on the one side of the peninsula, and the post of Acul in our possession on the other, all communication between the southern and the two other provinces

(g) The following returns are authentick;

Return of the provincial troops in the service of the British government at St. Domingo, 31st December, 1794.

	Rank and file fit for duty.	Sick.	Total.
At Port au Prince	496	48	544
Mole St. Nicholas	209	38	247
St. Marc	813	321	1134
	1518	407	1925

Return of the British forces in the island of St. Domingo, 31st December 1794.

	Rank and file effective.	Sick.	Total.
Port au Prince	366	462	828
Mole St. Nicholas	209	166	375
Jeremie	95	59	154
Tiburon	34	18	52
St. Marc	48	33	81
	752	738	1490

CHAP. XI.

provinces would have been cut off; the navigation from the Windward Islands to Jamaica would have been made secure, while the posession of the two Capes which form the entrance into the Bight of Leogane (St. Nicholas and Tiburon) would have protected the homeward trade in its course through the Windward Passage. All this might have been accomplished; and I think it is all that, in sound policy, ought to have been attempted. As to Port au Prince, it would have been fortunate if the works had been destroyed, and the town evacuated immediately after its surrender.

THE retention by the enemy of Jacmel and Les Cayes, not only enabled them to procure reinforcements and supplies, but also most amply to revenge our attempts on their coasts, by reprisals on our trade. It is known, that upwards of thirty privateers, some of them of considerable force, have been fitted out from those ports, whose rapacity and vigilance scarce a vessel bound from the Windward Islands to Jamaica could escape. The prizes which they made, in a few short months, abundantly compensated for the loss of their ships at Port au Prince *(h)*.

AFTER

(h) The following is a list of vessels bound to Jamaica, which were taken and carried into Les Cayes, between June 1794 and June 1795, most of them laden with dry goods, provisions, and plantation stores, and many of them of great value.

	From
The Edward, Wm. Marshall, 13th June 1794,	Bristol.
Fame, Robt. Hall, July - -	L. and Cork.
Bellona, Thos. White, - -	Liverpool.
Hope, Wm. Swan.	

The

CHAP. XI.

After all, though I have asserted nothing which I do not believe to be true, I will honestly admit, that many important facts and circumstances, unknown to me, very probably existed, an acquaintance with which is indispensably necessary to enable any man to form a correct judgment of the measures which were pursued on this occasion. To a writer, sitting with composure in his closet, with a partial display of facts before him, it is no difficult task to point out faults and mistakes in the conduct of publick affairs; and even where mistakes are discovered, the wisdom of after-knowledge is very cheaply acquired. It is the lot of our nature, that the best-concerted plans

From

The Molly, Peter Mawdsley, 5th Mar. 1795, Africa, 300 negroes.
Hodge, Geo. Brown, 19th Ditto, - Liverpool.
William, Thos. Calloine, 20th Ditto.
Bell, Archd. Weir, Ditto, - - Greenock.
Bustler, —— Sewell, - a transport.
Druid, ——Wilson, 14th March, Leith.
Martha, Wm. Reid, 31st March, London.
Alexander, Benjn. Moor, 17th April, - Glasgow.
Lovely Peggy, Peter Murphy.
Swallow, Lachlan Vass, 10th May.
Dunmore, Stephen Conmick, 26th May, London.
Maria, ——— Wilkinson, - - Ditto.
Minerva, ——— Robertson, 4th June, Africa, 450 negroes.
General Mathew, Thos. Douglas, 8th Ditto, - London.
A schooner, name forgot, Adam Walker, 22d Do. Glasgow.
Hope, —— Hambleton, 22d Ditto, - Ditto.
Caledonia, —— Hunter, 25th Ditto, Leith, last from London.
Molly, —— Simpson, 27th Ditto, - - Glasgow.
Resolution, —— Taunton, 29th Ditto, - - Hull.

And several vessels belonging to Kingston, names frgot.

plans of human policy are subject to errors which the meanest observer will sometimes detect. "The hand (says an eminent writer) that "cannot build a hovel, may demolish a pa-"lace."

CHAP. XI.

But a new scene new opens for contemplation and reflection, arising from intelligence received since I began my work, that the Spanish government has formally ceded to the Republick of France the whole of this great and noble island in perpetual sovereignty! So extraordinary a circumstance will doubtless give birth to much speculation and enquiry, as well concerning the value and extent of the territory ceded, as the present disposition and general character of the Spanish inhabitants. Will they relish this transfer of their allegiance from a monarchical to a republican government, made, as it confessedly is, without their previous consent or knowledge: or may reasonable expectations be encouraged, that they will now cordially co-operate with the English, in reducing the country to the British dominion? Will such assistance effect the re-establishment of subordination and good government among the vast body of revolted negroes? These are deep questions, the investigation of which will lead to enquiries of still greater magnitude; for, whether we consider the possession, by an active and industrious people, of so vast a field for enterprize and improvement on the one hand, or the triumph of successful revolt and savage anarchy on the other, it appears to me that the future fate and profitable existence of the British territories in this

CHAP. XI. this part of the world, are involved in the issue. On all these, and various collateral subjects, I regret that I do not possess the means of giving much satisfaction to the reader. Such information, however, as I have collected on some of the preceding enquiries, and such reflections as occur to me on others, will be found in the ensuing chapter, which concludes my work.

CHAP.

CHAP. XII.

Ancient State of the Spanish Colony.—The Town of St. Domingo established by Bartholomew Columbus in 1498.—Pillaged by Drake in 1586.—Conjectures and Reflections concerning its present Condition, and the State of Agriculture in the interior Country.—Numbers and Character of the present Inhabitants.—Their Animosity towards the French Planters, and Jealousy of the English.—Conjectures concerning the future Situation of the whole Island; and some concluding Reflections.

THE Spanish colony in Hispaniola (the name St. Domingo being properly applicable to the chief city only) was the earliest establishment made by the nations of Europe in the New World; and unhappily, it is too notorious to be denied, that it was an establishment founded in rapacity and cemented with human blood! The sole object of the first Spanish adventurers was to ransack the bowels of the earth for silver and gold; in which frantick pursuit, they murdered at least a million of the peaceful and inoffensive natives! As the mines became exhausted, a few of the more industrious of the Spaniards entered on the cultivation of cacao, ginger, and sugar; but the poverty of the greater part of the inhabitants, and the discovery of new mines in Mexico, occasioned a prodigious emigration;—the experience of past disappointments not proving sufficiently powerful to

CHAP. XII. to cure the rage for acquiring wealth by a shorter course than that of patient industry. In less than a century, therefore, Hispaniola was nearly deserted, and nothing preserved it as a colony, but the establishment of archiepiscopal government in its chief city, St. Domingo; and its being for many years the seat of civil and criminal jurisdiction, in cases of appeal, from all the territories of Spain in this part of the world *(a)*.

The settlement of the French in the western part of the island, of the origin of which I have already given an account, though the primary cause of hereditary and irreconcilable enmity between the two colonies was however productive of good even to the Spaniards themselves. As the French settlers increased in number, and their plantations became enlarged, they wanted oxen for their markets, and horses for their mills. These, their neighbours were able to supply without much exertion of labour; and thus an intercourse was created, which has continued to the present day; the Spaniards receiving, through the French, the manufactures of Europe, in exchange for cattle. The example too, before their eyes, of successful industry and growing prosperity, was not wholly without its effect. The cultivation of sugar, which had diminished nearly to nothing, was revived in different parts of the Spanish territory, and plantations were established of cacao, indigo, ginger, and tobacco. The quantity

(a) The administration of justice throughout Spanish America is at present divided into twelve courts of *audience*, one only of which is at St. Domingo.

tity of sugar exported in the beginning of the present century, is said to have amounted yearly to 15,000 chests, each of 7 cwt.

The country itself being evidently more mountainous in the central and eastern than in the western parts, it is probable, that the Spanish territory is, on the whole, naturally less fertile than that of the French; but much the greater portion of the island remained, until the late treaty, under the Spanish dominion; and of that, by far the major part continues at this hour an unproductive wilderness. On the northern coast, the line of division began at the river Massacre, and, crossing the country somewhat irregularly, terminated on the southern side, at a small bay called Les Ances à Pitre; leaving nearly two-thirds of the whole island in the possession of Spain. Proceeding eastward along the shore from the boundary on the north, the first place of note is Monte Christi, a town which formerly grew to importance by contraband traffick with North America, but is now reduced to a miserable village, the abode of a few fishermen; and the surrounding country exhibits a melancholy prospect of neglect and sterility. The river St. Jago runs into the sea at this place; on the banks of which, at some distance inland, are grazing farms of considerable extent. From the mouth of this river, for the space of fifteen leagues, to Punta Isabella (the site of the first settlement established by Christopher Columbus) the soil, though capable of improvement, exhibits no sign of cultivation. From Isabella to old Cape François (with the exception of

CHAP. XII. of Puerto de Plata) the coast seems entirely deserted; nor, after passing the bay of Samana, does a much better prospect offer, until coasting round the eastern extremity, we reach a vast extent of level country called Llos Llanos, or the Plains; at the west end of which, on the banks of the river Ozama, stands the metropolis.

THIS city, which was long the most considerable in the new world, was founded by Bartholomew Columbus, in the year 1498, and named, after a saint of great renown in those days, St. Dominick. There is preserved in Oviedo, a Spanish historian, who resided here about thirty years after its first establishment, an account of its state and population at that period, which being equally authentick and curious, I shall present to the reader at length.

" BUT nowe (says the historian) to speake sum-" what of the principall and chiefe place of the " islande, whiche is the citie of *San Domenico:* I " saye, that as touchynge the buildynges, there is " no citie in Spaine, so much for so-muche (no " not *Barsalona,* whiche I have oftentymes seene) " that is to bee preferred before this generallye. " For the houses of San Domenico are for the " moste parte of stone, as are they of Barsalona. " The situation is muche better thā that of *Bar-" salona,* by reason that the streates are much " larger and playner, and without comparyson " more directe and strayght furth. For beinge " buylded nowe in our tyme, besyde the commoditie " of the place of the foundation, the streates were " also directed with corde, compase and measure; " werein it excelleth al the cities that I have sene.

" It

"It hath the sea so nere, that of one syde there is "no more space betwen the sea and the citie, "then the waules. On the other parte, hard by "the syde and at the foote of the houses, passeth "the ryver *Ozama*, whiche is a marveylous porte; "wherein laden shyppes ryse very nere to the "lande, and in manner under the house wyn-"dowes. In the myddest of the citie is the for-"tresse and castle; the port or haven also, is so "fayre and commodious to defraight or unlade "shyppes, as the lyke is founde but in fewe places "of the worlde. The chymineis that are in this "citie are about syxe hundreth in number, and "such houses as I have spoken of before; of the "which sum are so fayre and large that they "maye well receave and lodge any lorde or noble "manne of Spayne, with his trayne and familie; "and especially that which Don *Diego Colon*, "viceroy under your majestie, hath in this citie, "is suche that I knowe no man in Spayne that "hath the lyke, by a quarter, in goodnesse, con-"syderynge all the commodities of the same. "Lykewyse the situation thereof as beinge above "the sayde porte, and altogyther of stone, and "havynge many faire and large roomes, with as "goodly a prospect of the lande and sea as may "be devysed, seemeth unto me so magnifical and "princelyke, that your majestie may bee as well "lodged therein as in any of the moste exquisite "builded houses of Spayne. There is also a ca-"thedrall churche buylded of late, where, as well "the byshop accordyng to his dygnitie, as also "the canones, are wel indued. This church is

CHAP. XII.

"well buylded of stone and lyme, and of good "workemanshyppe.* There are further-more "three monasteries bearyng the names of Saynt "Dominike, Saynt Frances, and Saynt Mary of "Mercedes; the whiche are well buylded, al-"though not so curiouslye as they of Spayne. "There is also a very good hospitall for the ayde "and succour of pore people, whiche was found-"ed by Michaell Passamont, threasurer to your "majestie. To conclude, this citie frō day to day "increaseth in welth and good order, as wel for "that the sayde admyrall and viceroy, with the "lorde chaunceloure and counsayle appoynted "there by your majestie, have theyr continuall "abydynage here, as also that the rychest men of "the ilande resort hyther, for thyre moste com-"modious habitation and trade of such merchaun-"dies as are eyther brought owt of Spayne, or "sent thyther from this iland, which nowe so "abundeth in many thynges, that it serveth "Spayne with many commodities, as it were with "usury requityng such benefites as it fyrst re-"ceaved from thense *(b)*."

It is probable that St. Domingo had now attained the summit of its prosperity. About sixty years afterwards (1st January 1586) it was attacked by Sir Francis Drake; a narrative of whose

* To this cathedral were conveyed, from the Carthusian Monastery in Seville, the remains of Christopher Columbus, who expired at Valladolid on the 20th of May 1506. It was his dying request that his body should be interred in St. Domingo.

(b) From a translation by Richard Eden, printed, London 1555, in black letter.

expedition,

expedition, by an eye-witness, is preserved in Hakluyt's Collection; from which it appears, that it was, even then, a city of great extent and magnificence; and it is shocking to relate, that, after a month's possession, Drake thought himself authorized, by the laws of war, to destroy it by fire. "We spent the early part of the mornings (says the historian of the voyage) in fireing the outmost houses; but they being built very magnificently of stone, with high loftes, gave us no small travell to ruin them. And albeit, for divers dayes together, we ordeined ech morning by day-break, until the heat began at nine of the clocke, that two hundred mariners did nought els but labour to fire and burn the said houses, whilst the souldiers in a like proportion, stood forth for their guard; yet did we not, or could not, in this time, consume so much as one third part of the towne; and so in the end, wearied with firing, we were contented to accept of five and twenty thousand ducats, of five shillings and sixpence the peece, for the ransome of the rest of the towne *(c)*."

(c) The following anecdote, related by the same author, is too striking to be overlooked. I shall quote his own words: During the stay of the English army in the city, "it chanced that the general sent on a message to the Spanish governor, a negro boy with a flag of white, signifying truce, as is the Spanyards ordinarie manner to do there, when they approach to speak to us; which boy unhappily was first met withall by some of those who had been belonging as officers for the king in the Spanish galley, which, with the towne, was lately fallen into our hands, who, without all order or reason, and contrary to that good usage wherewith wee had intertained their messengers, furiously strooke the poor boy thorow the body, with which wound the boy returned to the general, and, after he had de-

 clared

CHAP. XII.

Of the present condition of this ancient city, the number of its inhabitants, and the commerce which they support, I can obtain no account on which I can depend. That it hath been long in its decline, I have no doubt; but that it is wholly depopulated and in ruins, as Raynal asserts, I do not believe. The cathedral and other publick buildings are still in being, and were lately the residence of a considerable body of clergy and lawyers. The city continued also, while under the Spanish government, the diocese of an archbishop, to whom, it is said, the bishops of St. Jago in Cuba, Venezuela in New Spain, and St. John's in Porto Rico, were suffragans. These circumstances have hitherto saved St. Domingo from entire decay, and may possibly continue to save it. With this very defective information the reader must be content. As little seems to be known concerning the state of agriculture in the Spanish

clared the manner of this wrongfull crueltie, died forthwith in his presence; wherewith the generall being greatly passion'd, commanded—the provost martiall to cause a couple of friers, then prisoners, to be carried to the same place where the boy was stroken, and there presently to be hanged; dispatching, at the same instant, another poor prisoner, with the reason wherefore this execution was done, and with this further message, that untill the party who had thus murdered the general's messenger, were delivered into our hands to receive condigne punishment, there should no day passe wherein there should not two prisoners be hanged, until they were all consumed which were in our hands. Whereupon the day following, hee that had been captaine of the king's galley, brought the offender to the towne's end, offering to deliver him into our hands; but it was thought to be a more honourable revenge to make them there, in our sight, to performe the execution themselves, which was done accordingly."

possessions

possessions in this island, as of their capital and commerce. A few planters are said to cultivate cacao, tobacco, and sugar, for their own expenditure; and perhaps some small quantities of each are still exported for consumption in Spain. The chief article of exportation, however, continues to be, what it always has been since the mines were abandoned, *the hides of horned cattle*: which have multiplied to such a degree, that the proprietors are said to reckon them by thousands; and vast numbers (as I believe I have elsewhere observed) are annually slaughtered solely for the skins.*

It seems therefore extremely probable, that the cultivation of the earth is almost entirely neglected throughout the whole of the Spanish dominion in this island; and that some of the finest tracts of land in the world, once the paradise of a simple and innocent people, are now abandoned to the beasts of the field, and the vultures which hover round them *(d)*.

Of this description, probably, is the country already mentioned, called Los Llanos, which stretches eastward from the capital upwards of fourscore British miles in length, by twenty or twenty-five in width; and which, abounding in rivers throughout, may be supposed adapted for

* It is said that a Company was formed at Barcelona in 1757, with exclusive privileges, for the re-establishment of agriculture and commerce in the Spanish part of St. Domingo: I know not with what success.

(d) The *Gallinazo*, or American vulture, a very ravenous and filthy bird that feeds on carrion. These birds abound in St. Domingo, and devour the carcases of the cattle as soon as the skins are stripped off by the hunters.

the

CHAP. XII.

the growth of every tropical production: it seems capable also of being artificially flooded in dry weather.

NEXT to Los Llanos in magnitude, but superior, it is believed, in native fertility, is the noble valley to the north, called Vega Real; through the middle of which flows the river Yuna, for the space of fifty miles, and disembogues in Samana bay to the east. Perhaps it were no exaggeration to say, that this and the former districts are alone capable of producing more sugar, and other valuable commodities, than all the British West Indies put together.

THESE plains, however, though in contiguity the largest, are not the only parts of the country on which nature has bestowed extraordinary fertility. Glades abundantly rich, easy of access, and obvious to cultivation, are every where found even in the bosom of the mountains; while the mountains themselves contribute to fertilize the valleys which they encircle.

PROCEEDING westward along the southern coast, from the capital to the river Nieva, the country is said to be subject to excessive droughts; but here too, the beneficence of nature has provided a remedy for this inconvenience, in a thousand beautiful rivulets, which, descending from the distant mountains, intersect the low lands in various directions. Of this never-failing resource, even the aboriginal natives, ignorant as we suppose them to have been, knew how to avail themselves by flooding their lands therefrom in the dry season;*

* Vide vol. i. p. 102.

—and

—and it is probable that some of the earliest of the Spanish settlers followed their example; for it is evident that many spots in this great tract were formerly covered with plantations both of sugar and indigo; their sites being marked out by the ruins of ancient buildings, which could have been erected only for the manufacture of those articles. Amidst the wilderness of thickets and weeds, which now deform and encumber the ground, are discovered many valuable growths in a state of wild luxuriance, such as the *cactus* of several varieties, the indigo plant,—a species of cotton of which the wool is reddish, and some others; pointing out to the present slothful possessors, that line of cultivation which would turn to profitable account, even in spots to which water could not easily be conducted. With this auxiliary there is no reason to doubt that every production of the tropicks might be raised throughout this district, in the utmost plenty and perfection.

By much the greater part of this extensive range, however, remains as Nature originally created it; covered with woods of immense growth and luxuriant foliage, with very little underwood. The mahogany, the cedar, the guaiacum, the bitter-ash, the fustick, and a thousand others, here flourish, and die unmolested. In some places are vast groves of the latanier or thatch-palm, the sight of which always gives pleasure to the beholder, not more from the singular conformation and beauty of the tree itself, than from the circumstance that it indicates, with unerring certainty, a rich and deep soil underneath.

THE

CHAP. XII.

The great obstacle to the re-establishment of towns and settlements on the southern coast, arises from the insufficiency of its ports and harbours;—many of the shipping places being nothing more than open bays, which, in the autumnal months, lie exposed to the fury of storms and hurricanes. The harbour of St. Domingo, which was formerly supposed to be commodious and secure, has become, in the course of years, too shallow to admit ships of large burthen;—but its loss might be happily supplied, at the distance of fourteen leagues to the westward, in the bay of Ocoa; a capacious inlet, comprehending two most safe and commodious ports, named *Caldera* and *Puerto Riejo*. The very advantageous position of this great bay, in the centre of the southern part of the island:—in the track, and almost in sight, of ships bound to Jamaica, and the Mexican Gulph;—the safety and security which it offers at all seasons of the year, in the two subordinate ports before mentioned;—all these are circumstances of importance; and they will, without doubt, attract the notice of the French Government, whenever it shall hereafter attempt to form any considerable establishment in the late Spanish part of this great country.*

* Most of what is given in the above and the preceding page, is added since the former edition. The author derived his information from a letter to the French Directory, written in 1798, by certain commissioners employed to examine the eastern part of St. Domingo, and report to the Directory concerning its agriculture and production. This letter, which is one only of a large series, having been sent by a vessel that was captured by a British cruiser, was put into the hands of the author, and, as far as it goes, is very intelligent and satisfactory. It is to be hoped the

remainder

CHAP. XII.

THUS scanty and uninteresting is the best account I have to give of the territory itself; nor is my information much more perfect concerning the number and condition of the people by whom it is at present inhabited. The earliest detachments from Old Spain were undoubtedly numerous. Herrera, an accurate and well-informed historian, reckons that there were, at one period, no less than 14,000 Castillians in Hispaniola. Such was the renown of its riches, that men of all ranks and conditions resorted thither, in the fond expectation of sharing in the golden harvest. Its mines, indeed, were very productive. Robertson relates, that they continued for many years to yield a revenue of 460,000 pesos *(e)*. In contrasting this fact with an anecdote which I have elsewhere * recorded, that the inhabitants, at the time of Drake's invasion, were so wretchedly poor, as to be compelled to use, in barter among themselves, *pieces of leather* as a substitute for money, we are furnished with a striking proof, that the true way to acquire riches, is not by digging into the bowels, but by improving the surface of the earth. Not having any manufactures, nor the productions of agriculture, to offer in exchange for the necessaries and conveniences of life, all their gold had soon found its way to Europe; and when the mines became exhausted, their penury

remainder of the correspondence will some time or other be made publick, as the writers appear to be men of science and observation.

(e) Upwards of 100,000*l.* sterling.

* Vol. i. Book 2d.

CHAP. XII. penury was extreme; and sloth, depopulation, and degeneracy, were its necessary consequences (*f*).

The introduction into this island of negroes from Africa, of which I have elsewhere traced the origin and cause (*g*), took place at an early period. This resource did not, however, greatly contribute to augment the population of the colony; for such of the whites as removed to the continent, in search of richer mines and better fortune, commonly took their negroes with them; and the small-pox, a few years afterwards, destroyed prodigious numbers of others. In 1717, the whole number of inhabitants under the Spanish dominion, of all ages and conditions, enslaved and free, were no more than 18,410, and since that time, I conceive, they have rather diminished than increased. Of pure whites (in contradistinction to the people of mixed blood) the number is undoubtedly very inconsiderable; perhaps not 3,000 in the whole.

The

(*f*) The gross ignorance of considering gold and silver as *real* instead of *artificial* wealth, and the folly of neglecting agriculture for the sake of exploring mines, have been well exposed by Abbé Raynal; who compares the conduct of the Spaniards in this respect, to that of the dog in the fable, dropping the piece of meat which he had in his mouth, to catch at the shadow of it in the water.

(*g*) Book iv. c. 2. A curious circumstance was, however, omitted. When the Portuguese first began the traffick in negroes, application was made to the Pope to sanctify the trade by a bull, which his Holiness issued accordingly. In consequence of this permission and authority, a very considerable slave-market was established at Lisbon, insomuch, that about the year 1539, from 10 to 12,000 negroes were sold there annually.

The hereditary and unextinguishable animosity between the Spanish and French planters on this island has already been noticed. It is probable, however, that the knowledge of this circumstance created greater reliance on the co-operation of the Spaniards with the British army, than was justified by subsequent events. At the earnest and repeated solicitations of Lieutenant Colonel Brisbane, in 1794, orders were indeed transmitted from the city of St. Domingo to the Commandant at Verettes, Don Francisco de Villa Nevva, to join the English with the militia of that part of the country; the British garrison at St. Marc undertaking to supply them with provisions and ammunition: but these orders were ill obeyed. Not more than three hundred men were brought into the field, and even those were far from being hearty in the common cause. The French loyalists appeared in greater numbers in the neighbourhood of St. Marc than in any other district; and the Spaniards detested the French colonists of all descriptions. It was evident, at the same time, that they were almost equally jealous of the English; betraying manifest symptoms of discontent and envy, at beholding them in possession of St. Marc, and the fertile plains in its vicinage. They proceeded, however, and took the town and harbour of Gonaive; but their subsequent conduct manifested the basest treachery, or the rankest cowardice. The town was no sooner attacked by a small detachment from the revolted negroes, than the Spaniards suffered themselves to be driven out of it, in the most unaccountable manner; leaving the

the French inhabitants to the fury of the savages, who massacred the whole number (as their comrades had done at Fort Dauphin) and then reduced the town itself to ashes *(h)*.

On the whole, there is reason to suppose that a great proportion of the present Spanish proprietors in St. Domingo are a debased and degenerate race; a motley

(h) In the northern province of the French colony, the inhabitants of Fort Dauphin, a town situated on the Spanish borders, having no assistance from the English, and being apprehensive of an attack from the rebel negroes, applied for protection, and delivered up the town, to the Spanish government. The Spanish commandant, on accepting the conditions required, which were chiefly for personal safety, issued a proclamation, importing, that such of the French planters as would seek refuge there should find security. Seduced by this proclamation, a considerable number repaired thither; when, on Monday the 7th of July 1794, *Jean Francois*, the negro general, and leader of the revolt in 1791, entered the town with some thousands of armed negroes. He met not the smallest resistance, either at the advanced posts, or at the barriers occupied by the Spanish troops; the inhabitants keeping their houses, in the hope of being protected by the commandant. In an instant, every part of the city resounded with the cry of "Long live the King of Spain! Kill all the French; but offer no violence to the Spaniards;" and a general massacre of the French commenced, in which no less than 771 of them, without distinction of sex or age, were murdered on the spot: the Spanish soldiers standing by, spectators of the tragedy. It is thought, however, that if the Spaniards had openly interposed, they would have shared the fate of the French. It is said that Mont-Calvos, commander of the Spanish troops, moved by compassion towards some French gentlemen of his acquaintance, admitted them into the ranks, dressing them in the Spanish uniform for their security; others were secretly conveyed to the fort, and sent off in the night to Monte Christi, where they got on board an American vessel belonging to Salem.

a motley mixture from European, Indian, and African ancestry; and the observation which has been made in another place (*i*), concerning the Spanish inhabitants of Jamaica, at the conquest of that island in 1655, will equally apply to these. They are neither polished by social intercourse, nor improved by education; but pass their days in gloomy languor, enfeebled by sloth, and depressed by poverty. From such men, therefore, great as their antipathy is to the French nation, and however averse they may be to a change of laws and government, I am afraid that no cordial co-operation with the British can ever be expected. The best families among them, rather than submit to the French dominion, will probably remove to Cuba, or seek out new habitations among their countrymen on the neighbouring continent; while those which remain will necessarily sink into the general mass of coloured people, French and Spanish; a class that, I think, in process of time, will become masters of the towns and cultivated parts of the island on the sea-coast; leaving the interior country to the revolted negroes. Such, probably, will be the fate of this once beautiful and princely colony; and it grieves me to say, that the present exertions of Great Britain on this blood-stained theatre, can answer no other end than to hasten the catastrophe!

I MIGHT here expatiate on the wonderful dispensations of Divine Providence, in raising up the enslaved Africans to avenge the wrongs of the injured aborigines; I might also indulge the fond but fallacious

(*i*) Vol. i. Book 2d.

CHAP. XII.

cious idea, that as the negroes of St. Domingo have been eye-witnesses to the benefits of civilized life among the whites;—have seen in what manner, and to what extent, social order, peaceful industry, and submission to laws, contribute to individual and general prosperity (advantages which were denied to them in their native country;) some superior spirits may hereafter rise up among them, by whose encouragement and example they may be taught, in due time, to discard the ferocious and sordid manners and pursuits of savage life; to correct their vices, and be led progressively on to civilization and gentleness, to the knowledge of truth, and the practice of virtue. This picture is so pleasing to the imagination, that every humane and reflecting mind must wish it may be realized; but I am afraid it is the mere creation of the fancy—"the fabrick of a vision!" Experience has demonstrated, that a wild and lawless freedom affords no means of improvement, either mental or moral. The Charaibes of St. Vincent, and the Maroon negroes of Jamaica, were originally enslaved Africans; and *what they now are*, the freed negroes of St. Domingo *will hereafter be*—savages in the midst of society; without peace, security, agriculture, or property; ignorant of the duties of life, and unacquainted with all the soft and endearing relations which render it desirable; averse to labour, though frequently perishing of want; suspicious of each other, and towards the rest of mankind revengeful and faithless, remorseless and bloody-minded; pretending to be free, while groaning beneath the capricious despotism of their chiefs, and feeling all the miseries of servitude, without the benefits of subordination!

If what I have thus—not hastily, but—deliberately predicted, concerning the fate of this unfortunate country, shall be verified by the event, all other reflections must yield to the pressing consideration how best to obviate and defeat the influence which so dreadful an example of successful revolt and triumphant anarchy may have in our own islands. This is a subject which will soon force itself on the most serious attention of Government; and I am of opinion, that nothing less than the co-operation of the British parliament with the colonial legislatures can meet its emergency. On the other hand, if it be admitted that the object is infinitely too important, and the means and resources of France much too powerful and abundant, to suffer a doubt to remain concerning the ultimate accomplishment of her views, in seizing on the whole of this extensive country: if we can suppose that (convinced at length, by painful experience, of the monstrous folly of suddenly emancipating barbarous men, and placing them at once in all the complicated relations of civil society) she will finally succeed in reducing the vast body of fugitive negroes to obedience; and in establishing security, subordination, and order, under a constitution of government suited to the actual condition of the various classes of the inhabitants:—if such shall be her good fortune, it will not require the endowment of prophecy to foretel the result. The middling, and who are commonly the most industrious, class of

Planters,

CHAP. XII. Planters, throughout every island in the West Indies, allured by the cheapness of the land and the superior fertility of the soil, will assuredly seek our settlements in St. Domingo; and a West Indian empire will fix itself in this noble island, to which, in a few short years, all the tropical possessions of Europe will be found subordinate and tributary. Placed in the centre of British and Spanish America, and situated to windward of those territories of either nation which are most valuable, while the commerce of both must exist only by its good pleasure, all the riches of Mexico will be wholly at its disposal. Then will the vassal Spaniard lament, when it is too late, the thoughtless and improvident surrender he has made, and Great Britain find leisure to reflect how deeply she is herself concerned in the consequences of it. The dilemma is awful, and the final issue known only to that omniscient Power, in whose hand is the fate of empires! But whatever the issue may be,—in all the varieties of fortune,—in all events and circumstances, whether prosperous or adverse,—it infinitely concerns both the people of Great Britain, and the inhabitants of the British colonies,—I cannot repeat it too often,—to derive admonition from the story before us. To Great Britain I would intimate, that if, disregarding the present example, encouragement shall continue to be given to the pestilent doctrines of those hot-brained fanaticks, and detestable incendiaries, who, under the vile pretence of philanthropy and zeal for the interests of suffering humanity, preach up rebellion and murder

murder to the contented and orderly negroes in our own territories, what else can be expected, but that the same dreadful scenes of carnage and desolation, which we have contemplated in St. Domingo, will be renewed among our countrymen and relations in the British West Indies? May God Almighty, of his infinite mercy, avert the evil! To the resident Planters I address myself with still greater solicitude; and, if it were in my power, would exhort them, "with more than mortal voice," to rise above the foggy atmosphere of local prejudices, and, by a generous surrender of temporary advantages, do that, which the Parliament of Great Britain, in the pride and plenitude of imperial dominion, cannot effect, and ought not to attempt. I call on them, with the sincerity and the affection of a brother, of themselves to restrain, limit, and finally abolish the further introduction of enslaved men from Africa; ---not indeed by measures of sudden violence and injustice, disregarding the many weighty and complicated interests which are involved in the issue; but by means which, though slow and gradual in their operation, will be sure and certain in their effect. The Colonial Legislatures, by their situation and local knowledge, are alone competent to this great and glorious task: and this example of St. Domingo, and the dictates of self-preservation, like the hand-writing against the wall, warn them no longer to delay it! Towards the poor negroes over whom the statutes of Great Britain, the accidents of fortune, and the laws of inheritance, have invested them with

 power,

CHAP. XII.

power, their general conduct for the last twenty years (notwithstanding the foul calumnies with which they have been loaded) may court enquiry, and bid defiance to censure. A perseverance in the same benevolent system, progressively leading the objects of it to civilization and mental improvement, preparatory to greater indulgence, is all that humanity can require; for it is all that prudence can dictate. Thus will the Planters prepare a shield of defence against their enemies, and secure to themselves that serenity and elevation of mind, which arise from an approving conscience; producing assurance in hope, and consolation in adversity. Their persecutors and slanderers in the mean time will be disregarded or forgotten; for calumny, though a great, is a temporary evil, but truth and justice will prove triumphant and eternal!

ILLUSTRATIONS,

ILLUSTRATIONS, AND ADDITIONAL NOTES, TO THE HISTORICAL SURVEY OF ST. DOMINGO.

The following TABLES were drawn up by order of the Legislative Assembly of France, which met the 21st of October 1791, and seem to have been framed in the view of ascertaining the actual state of the Colony, and its Commerce, immediately before the breaking out of the rebellion of the Negroes in the month of August of that year. The totals will be found to differ, in some of the particulars, from the statement which has been given in the preceding pages. The difference arises partly from the actual change of circumstances, in the course of two years which intervened between the periods when each statement was made up, and partly, I am afraid, from errors and omissions of my own.

No. I.

Etat Général des Cultures et des Manufactures de la Partie Françoise de St. Domingue.

1791.

	Chefs lieux ou jurisdictions.	Quartiers ou paroisses.	Sucreries. En Blanc.	Sucreries. En brut.	Cafeteries.	Cotonneries.	Indigoteries.	Tanneries.	Guildiveries.	Cacaoteries.	Fours à Chaux	Briqueries et Poteries.	Nombre de Négres.
Partie du Nord.	Le Cap	Le Cap et dépendances	1	—	2	—	—	1	3	—	2	1	21,613
		La petite Ance et la plaine du Nord	43	7	37	1	5	2	3	—	4	2	11,122
		L'acul, Limonade et Ste. Suzanne	52	4	157	3	6	—	9	—	1	1	19,876
		Morien et la Grande Rivière	35	1	255	2	1	—	5	5	7	—	18,554
		Le Dondon et Marmelade	—	—	216	1	—	—	1	1	32	2	17,376
		A Limbé et Port Magot	22	3	272	5	11	—	7	1	2	2	15,978
		Plaisance et le Borgne	—	—	324	2	4	—	—	—	3	5	15,018
	Le Fort Dauphin	Le Fort Dauphin	29	7	71	2	10	—	4	—	3	8	10,004
		Ouanaminthe et Valliere	25	2	151	—	2	—	4	—	—	3	9,987
		Le Terrier rouge et le trou	56	1	123	1	37	—	5	—	4	1	15,476
	Le Port de Paix	Le Port de Paix le petit St. Louis Jean Rabel et le gros Morne	6	2	218	9	369	—	4	18	26	4	29,540
	Le Mole	Le Mole et Bombarde	—	—	31	14	15	—	—	—	—	—	3,183

Partie de l' Ouest.	Port au Prince	Port au Prince et la Croix des Bouquets	65	75	151	22	15	—	29	1	20	1	48,843
		L'Arcahaye - - -	11	36	62	24	48	—	14	—	23	5	15,553
		Mirebalais - - -	3	—	27	19	322	—	—	2	5	—	10,902
	Léogane -	Léogane - - - -	27	39	58	18	78	—	25	1	14	1	14,896
	St. Marc -	St. Marc, la petite Rivière - - Les Verettes et les Gonaives - -	22	21	298	815	1,184	—	10	1	71	12	67,216
	Le petit Goave	Le petit Goave, le grand Goave, et le fonds des Négres - - -	11	16	52	25	31	—	11	2	9	—	18,829
		L'Anse à Veau et le petit trou -	6	11	11	7	185	—	7	1	9	2	13,229
	Jérémie -	Jérémie et le Cap Dame Marie - -	3	5	105	30	44	—	6	25	14	—	20,774
Partie du Sud.	Les Cayes	Les Cayes et Torbeck - - -	24	86	69	76	175	—	18	2	32	8	30,937
	Le Cap Tiburon	Le Cap Tiburon et les Côteaux - -	1	1	24	12	169	—	—	4	7	1	8,153
	St. Louis -	St. Louis, Cavaillon et Aquin	9	23	39	28	157	—	8	2	18	1	18,785
	Jacmel -	Jacmel, les Cayes, et Baynel - -	—	1	57	89	129	—	—	3	7	1	21,151
	Total -	51 Paroisses - -	451	341	2,810	705	3,097	3	173	69	313	61	455,000

No. II.

Etat des Denrées de St. Domingue exportées en France depuis le 1er Janvier 1791 au 31 Décembre inclusivement.

Départemens.	Sucre.		Café.	Coton.	Indigo.	Cuirs.		Sirop.	Tafia.
	Blanc.	Brut.				en Poil.	Tannés.		
	Livres.	Livres.	Livres.	Livres.	Livres.	Banettes.	Côtes.	Boucauts.	Barique.
Partie du Nord.									
Le Cap	43,864,552	1,517,489	29,367,382	—	195,099	2,006	6,975	10,654	
Le Fort Dauphin	8,609,258	1,639,900	2,321,610	1,200	2,005	1,134	160	2,731	
Le Port de Paix	473,800	824,500	1,829,754	38,752	61,472	120	—	272	25
Le Mole	22,500	105,680	294,550	29,236	6,294	31	—	84	6
Partie de l'Ouest.									
Le Port au Prince	7,792,219	53,648,923	14,584,023	1,370,021	176,918	1,601	752	8,350	36
Léogane	1,492,983	7,688,537	1,786,484	154,084	12,520	112	—	95	45
Saint Marc	3,244,673	6,993,966	5,521,237	3,008,163	357,530	—	—	73	49
Le Petit Goave	218,866	855,237	1,395,690	84,865	320	—	—	206	6
Jérémie	19,804	476,445	4,453,331	189,194	1,075	100			
Partie du Sud.									
Les Cayes	4,375,627	18,984,425	1,843,403	720,770	105,456	67	—	6,938	136
Le Cap Tiburon	63,150	278,500	305,740	34,325	1,954	—	—	99	
St. Louis	2,000	9,600	90,706	42,497	2,064				
Jacmel	48,266	67,910	4,357,270	613,019	7,309	15			
Total	70,227,708	93,177,512	68,151,180	6,286,126	930,016	5,186	7,887	29,502	303

No. II.—*continued.*

Valeur commune des Exportations et des Droits perçus dans la Colonie sur toutes les Denrées.

Indication de la Nature des Denrées.	Quotité en nature.	Estimation en raison du prix Commun.			Du 1er Janvier 1791 au 31 Xbre de la même année.		Vendus en France.
					Valeur Commune	Droits perçus.	
Sucre { Blanc ou terré - -	70,227,708	Livres - à	—	12	67,670,781	2,528,197	65,142,584
Sucre { Brut - - - -	93,177,512	Livres - à	—	6	49,041,567	1,677,195	48,264,372
Café - - - -	68,151,180	Livres - à	—	16	51,890,748	1,226,720	50,664,028
Coton - - - -	6,286,126	Livres - à	2	—	17,572,252	785,766	16,786,486
Indigo - - - -	930,016	Livres - à	7	10	10,875,120	465,008	10,410,112
Cacao - - - - -	150,000	Livres - à	—	16	120,000	—	120,000
Sirop - - - - -	29,502	Boucauts à	66	—	1,947,132	221,275	1,725,857
Tafia - - - - -	303	Bariques - à	72	—	21,816	1,821	19,995
Cuirs Tannés - - -	7,887	Côtes - à	10	—	78,870	10,377	68,493
Cuirs en poil - - -	5,186	Banettes - à	18	—	93,348	7,807	85,541
Caret (tortoise shell) - -	5,000	Livres - à	10	—	50,000	—	50,000
Gayac Acajou, et Campêche -	1,500,000	Livres - à	Estimés.		40,000	—	40,000
Total de la Valeur commune de toutes les Denrées - - -					200,301,634	6,924,166	193,377,468

OBSERVATION ESSENTIELLE.

Toutes les sommes dont il est question dans ce tableau sont Argent des Colonies. Le change y est à 33$\frac{1}{3}$, et la Livre Tournois comptée pour une livre dix sous.

1er Exemple.

Le montant des Exportations s'éleve Argent des Colonies à la somme de - - - - - - 200,301,634
Réduite Argent de France à - - - 133,534,423

Différence sur cet Article de - - - 66,767,211

2me Exemple.

La totalité des denrées exportées, et vendues en France montant ensemble à la somme de - - - 193,377,468
Réduite en Livres Tournois à - - - - 128,918,312

Différence sur cet Article de - - - 64,459,156

On obtiendra le même résultat article par article, ayant l'attention de réduire le tiers sur chaque somme.

No. III.

Apperçu des Richesses territoriales des habitations en grande Culture de la Partie Françoise de St. Domingue.

Indication de la Nature des Capitaux.	Nombre.	Estimation particulière de chaque Objet en raison du prix moyen.	Evaluation des Capitaux.		Totalité de la Valeur Générale.
			En Terres, Batimens, et Plantations.	En Négres et animaux employés à l'exploitation.	
Sucreries { en Blanc - - -	451	à - 230,000	103,730,000	—	103,730,000
Sucreries { en Brut - - -	341	à - 180,000	61,380,000	—	61,380,000
Cafeteries - - - - - -	2,810	à - 20,000	56,200,000	—	56,200,000
Cotonneries - - - -	705	à - 30,000	21,150,000	—	21,150,000
Indigoteries - - - - -	3,097	à - 30,000	92,910,000	—	92,910,000
Guildiveries - - -	173	à - 5,000	865,000	—	865,000
Cacaotéries - - -	69	à - 4,000	275,000	—	275,000
Tanneries - - - -	3	à - 160,000	480,000	—	480,000
Fours à Chaux, Briqueries et Poteries	374	à - 15,000	5,510,000	—	5,510,000
Négres anciens et nouveaux, grands et petits - - -	455,000	à - 2,500	—	1,137,500,000	1,137,500,000
Chevaux et Mulets - - -	16,000	à - 400	—	6,400,000	6,400,000
Bêtes à cornes - - - -	12,000	à - 120	—	1,440,000	1,440,000
Total des Richesses employées à la Culture - - -			342,500,000	1,145,340,000	1,487,840,000

ADDITIONAL TABLES,

Containing Information not comprehended in the preceding;

Collected by the Author when at Cape François.

No. IV.

TRADE of the French Part of St. Domingo with old France.
Imports for the Year 1788.

Quantity.	Nature of Goods.	Amount in Hispaniola Currency.
		Liv.
186,759	Barrels of Flour	12,271,247
1,366	Quintals of Biscuit	38,684
3,309	Ditto - Cheese	217,450
2,044	Ditto - Wax Candles	602,010
27,154	Ditto - Soap	1,589,985
16,896	Ditto - Tallow Candles	1,479,510
20,762	Ditto - Oil	1,973,750
1,359	Ditto - Tallow	55,770
121,587	Casks of Wine	13,610,960
7,020	Cases of Do	584,770
5,732	Casks of Beer	328,175
6,174	Hampers of Beer	157,380
10,375	Cases of Cordials	340,070
6,937	Ankers of Brandy	140,238
2,284	Ditto of Vinegar	23,784
19,457	Baskets of Aniseed Liquor	254,398
5,999	Quintals of Vegetables	322,130
14,613	Cases of preserved Fruit	320,477
2,486	Quintals of Cod Fish	85,607
1,308	Ditto - Salt Fish	26,700
17,219	Ditto - Butter	1,650,150
24,261	Ditto - Salt Beef	998,300
14,732	Ditto - Salt Pork	1,101,395
4,351	Ditto - Ditto	376,560
1,627	Ditto - Hams	177,340
	Dry Goods, viz. Linens, Woollens, Silks, Cottons, and Manufactures of all kinds	39,008,600
	Sundry other Articles, valued at	8,685,600
	Amount of all the Goods imported	86,414,040

These Importations were made in 580 Vessels, measuring together 189,679 Tons, or by Average 325½ Tons each Vessel; viz.

224 from Bourdeaux.
129 from Nantes.
90 from Marseilles.
80 from Havre de Grace.
19 from Dunkirk.
11 from St. Malo.
10 from Bayonne.
5 from La Rochelle.
3 from Harfleur.
2 from Cherbourg.
2 from Croisic.
1 from Dieppe.
1 from Rouen.
1 from Granville.
1 from Cette.
1 from Rhedon.

Add to the 580 Vessels from France, 98 from the Coast of Africa, and the French Part of Hispaniola will be found to have employed 678 Vessels belonging to France in the year 1788.

No. V.

Foreign TRADE in 1788 (exclusive of the Spanish.)

Imported by Foreigners (Spaniards excepted) to the Amount of - - - - - -	6,821,707 Livres.
Exported by the same - - - - -	4,409,922
Difference - - - -	2,411,785

N. B. This Trade employed 763 small Vessels, measuring 55,745 Tons. The Average is 73 Tons each. Vessels from North America (American built) are comprehended in it: but there were also employed in the North American Trade 45 French Vessels, measuring 3,475 Tons (the Average 77 Tons each), which exported to North America Colonial Products, Value - - 525,571 Livres.

And imported in return Goods to the Amount of -	465,081
Difference - - -	60,490

Spanish TRADE in 1788.

259 Spanish Vessels, measuring 15,417 Tons, or 59 Tons each, imported to the Amount of (chiefly Bullion) - -	9,717,113
And exported Negro Slaves, and Goods, chiefly European Manufactures, to the Amount of - -	5,587,515
Difference - - - - -	4,129,598

N. B. This is exclusive of the Inland Trade with the Spaniards, of which there is no Account.

No. VI.

AFRICAN TRADE.

Negroes imported into the French Part of Hispaniola, in 1788.

Ports of Importation.	Men.	Women.	Boys.	Girls.	Amount.	Number of Vessels.
Port au Prince -	4,732	2,256	764	541	8,293	24
St. Marc - -	1,665	645	230	60	2,600	8
Léogane - -	1,652	798	469	327	3,246	9
Jérémie - -	88	75	23	18	204	1
Cayes - -	1,624	872	1,245	849	4,590	19
Cape François -	5,913	2,394	1,514	752	10,573	37
	15,674	7,040	4,245	2,547	29,506	98

In 1787, 30,839 Negroes were imported into the French Part of St. Domingo.

The 29,506 Negroes imported in 1788, were sold for 61,936,190 Livres (Hispaniola Currency) which on an average is 2,099 liv. 2s. each, being about 60*l*. sterling.

ILLUSTRATIONS, &c.

CHAP. IV: p. 51.

It was discovered, however, about nine months afterwards, that this most unfortunate young man (Ogé) *had made a full confession. His last solemn declaration, sworn to and signed by himself the day before his execution, was actually produced,* &c.

The following is a copy of this important document.

TESTAMENT DE MORT D'OGÉ.

Extrait des minutes du Conseil Supérieur du Cap, l'an mil sept cent quatre-vingt-onze et le neuf mars, nous Antoine-Etienne Ruotte, conseiller du roi, doyen au Conseil Supérieur du Cap, et Marie-François Pourcheresse de Vertieres, aussi conseiller du roi au Conseil Supérieur du Cap, commissaires nommés par la cour, à l'effet de faire exécuter l'arrêt de la dite cour, du 5 du présent mois, portant condamnation de mort contre le nommé Jacques Ogé, dit Jacquot, quarteron libre; lequel, étant en la chambre criminelle, et après lecture faite du dit arrêt, en ce qui le concerne, a dit et déclaré, pour la décharge de sa conscience, serment préalablement par lui prêté, la main levée devant nous, de dire vérité.

QUE dans le commencement du mois du février dernier, si les rivières n'avoient pas été débordées, il devoit se faire un attroupement de gens de couleur, qui devoient entraîner avec eux les ateliers, et devoient venir fondre sur la ville du Cap en

CHAP. IV. p. 51.

en nombre très considérable ; qu'ils étoient même déjà réunis au nombre de onze mille hommes ; que le débordement des rivières est le seul obstacle qui les a empêchés de se réunir ; cette quantité d'hommes de couleur étant composée de ceux du Mirebalais, de l'Artibonite, du Limbe, d'Ouanaminthe, de la Grande Rivière, et généralement de toute la Colonie. Qu'à cette époque, il étoit sorti du Cap cent hommes de couleur pour se joindre à cette troupe. Que l'accusé est assuré que les auteurs de cette révolte sont les Declains, négres libres de la Grande-Rivière, accusés au procès : Dumas, n. l. ; Yvon, n. l. ; Bitozin, m. l. espagnol ; Pierre Godard et Jean-Baptiste, son frère, n. l. de la Grande-Rivière ; Legrand Mazeau et Toussaint Mazeau, n. l. ; Pierre Mauzi, m. l. ; Ginga Lapaire, Charles Lamadieu, les Sabourins, Jean Pierre Goudy, Joseph Lucas, mulâtres libres ; Maurice, n. l. ; tous accusés au procès,

Que les grands moteurs, au bas de la côte ; sont les nommés Daguin, accusé au procès ; Rebel, demeurant au Mirebalais ; Pinchinat, accusé au procès ; Labastille, également accusé au procès ; et que l'accusé, ici présent, croit devoir nous déclarer être un des plus ardens partisans de la révolte, qui a mu en grande partie celle qui a éclaté dans les environs de Saint-Marc, et qui cherche à en éxciter une nouvelle ; qu'il y a dans ce moment plusieurs gens de couleur, dans différens quartiers, bien résolus à tenir à leurs projets, malgré que ceux qui trempéroient dans la révolte perdroient la vie ; que l'accusé, ici présent, ne peut pas se ressouvenir du nom de tous ; mais qu'il se rappelle que le fils de Laplace, q. l. ; dont lui accusé a vu la sœur dans les prisons, a quitté le Limbé pour aller faire des récrues dans le quartier d'Ouanaminthe ; et que ces récrues et ces soulévemens de gens de couleur sont soutenus ici par la présence des nommés Fleury et l'Hirondelle Viard, députés des gens de couleur auprès de l'assemblée nationale ; que lui accûsé, ici présent, ignore si les députés se tiennent chez eux ; qu'il croit que le nommé Fleury se tient au Mirebalais, et le nommé l'Hirondelle Viard dans le quartier de la Grande-Rivière.

Que

Que lui accusé, ici présent, déclare que l'insurrection des revoltés existe dans les souterrains qui se trouvent entre la Crête à Marcan et le Canton du Giromon, paroisse de la Grande-Rivière ; qu'en conséquence, si lui accusé pouvoit être conduit sur les lieux, il se feroit fort de prendre les chefs des révoltés ; que l'agitation dans laquelle il se trouve, rélativement à sa position actuelle, ne lui permet pas de nous donner des détails plus circonstanciés : qu'il nous les donnera par la suite, lorsqu'il sera un peu plus tranquil ; qu'il lui vient en ce moment à l'esprit que le nommé Castaing, mulâtre libre de cette dépendance, ne se trouve compris en aucune manière dans l'affaire actuelle ; mais que lui accusé, nous assure que si son frère Ogé eût suivi l'impulsion du dit Castaing, il se seroit porté à de bien plus grandes extrémités ; qui est tout ce qu'il nous a dit pouvoir nous déclarer dans ce moment, dont lui avons donné acte, qu'il a signé avec nous et le gréffier.

CHAP. IV. p. 51.

Signé à la minute J. OGE', RUOTTE, POURCHERESSE DE VERTIERES, et LANDAIS, gréffier.

EXTRAIT des minutes du grêffe du Conseil Supérieur du Cap, l'an mil sept cent quatre-vingt-onze, le dix mars, trois heures de rélévé, en la chambre criminelle, nous Antoine-Etienne Ruotte, conseiller du roi, doyen du Conseil Supérieur du Cap, et Marie-François-Joseph de Vertieres, aussi conseiller du roi au dit Conseil Supérieur du Cap, commissaires nommés par la cour, suivant l'arrêt de ce jour, rendu sur les conclusions du procureur général du roi de la dite cour, à l'éffet de procéder au recolement de la déclaration faite par le nommé Jacques Ogé, q. l. ; lequel, après serment par lui fait, la main levée devant nous de dire la vérité, et après lui avoir fait lecture, par le gréffier, de la déclaration du jour d'hier, l'avons interpellé de nous déclarer si la dite déclaration contient vérité, s'il veut n'y rien ajouter, n'y diminuer, et s'il y persiste.

A répondu que la dite déclaration du jour d'hier contient vérité, qu'il y persiste, et qu'il y ajoute que les deux Didiers frères,

CHAP. IV. p. 51. frères, dont l'un plus grand que l'autre, mulâtres ou quarterons libres, ne les ayant vu que cette fois; Jean-Pierre Gerard, m. l. du Cap, et Caton, m. l aussi du Cap, sont employés à gagner les ateliers de la Grand-Rivière, qu'ils sont ensemble de jour, et que de nuit ils sont dispersés.

Ajoute encore que lors de sa confrontation avec Jacques Lucas, il a été dit par ce dernier, que lui accusé, ici présent, l'avoit menacé de le faire pendre; à quoi, lui accusé, a répondu au dit Jacques Lucas, qu'il devoit savoir pourquoi que le dit Jacques Lucas, n'ayant pas insisté, lui accusé n'a pas déclaré le motif de cette menace, pour ne pas perdre le dit Jacques Lucas; qu'il nous déclare les choses comme elles se sont passées; que le dit Lucas lui ayant dit qu'il avoit soulevé les ateliers de M. Bonamy et de divers autres habitans de la Grande-Rivière, pour aller égorger l'armée chez M. Cardineau; qu'au premier coup de corne, il étoit sûr que ces ateliers s'attrouperoient et se joindroient à la troupe des gens de couleur; alors lui accusé, tenant aux blancs, fut révolté de cette barbarie, et dit au nommé Jacques Lucas, que l'auteur d'un pareil projet méritoit d'être pendu; qu'il eût à l'instant à faire rentrer les négres qu'il avoit apposté dans différens coins avec des cornes; que lui accusé, ici présent, nous déclare qu'il a donné au dit Lucas trois pomponelles de tafia, trois bouteilles de vin et du pain; qu'il ignoroit l'usage que le dit Lucas en faisoit; que la troisième fois que le dit Lucas en vint chercher; lui accusé, ici présent, lui ayant demandé ce qu'il faisoit de ces boissons et vivres; le dit Lucas répondit que c'étoit pour les négres qu'il avoit dispersé de côté et d'autre; que ce qui prouve que le dit Lucas avoit le projet de souléver les nègres esclaves contre les blancs, et de faire égorger ces derniers par les premiers; c'est la proposition qu'il fit à Vincent Ogé, frère de lui accusé, de venir sur l'habitation de lui Jacques Lucas, pour être plus a portée de se joindre aux nègres qu'il avoit débauché; que si lui accusé n'a pas révélé ces faits à sa confrontation avec le dit Jacques Lucas, c'est qu'il s'est apperçu qu'ils n'étoient pas connus, et qu'il n'a pas voulu le perdre; qu'il a dû moins la satisfaction d'avoir détourné ce crime horrible et cannibale; qu'il s'étoit réservé de révéler en justice, lors de son élargissement; que ce même Lucas est celui qui a voulu couper la tête a deux blancs prisonniers, et notamment au sieur Belisle, pour lui avoir enlevé une femme; que Pierre Roubert ôta le sabre des mains de Jacques Lucas, et appella Vincent Ogé, frère de lui accusé, ici présent, qui fit des rémontrances au dit Lucas; que cependant ces prisonniers ont déclarés en justice que c'étoit lui accusé qui avoit eu ce dessein; que même à la confrontation ils le lui ont soutenu: mais que le fait s'étant passé de nuit, les dits prisonniers ont pris, lui accusé, pour le dit Lucas, tandis que lui accusé n'a cessé de les combler d'honnêtetés; qu'à la confrontation, lui accusé a cru qu'il étoit suffisant de dire que ce n'étoit pas lui, et d'affirmer qu'il n'avoit jamais connu cette femme; mais qu'aujourd'hui il se croyoit obligé, pour la décharge de sa conscience, de nous rendre les faits tels qu'ils sont, et d'insister à jurer qu'il ne l'a jamais connue.

CHAP. IV. p. 51.

Ajoute l'accusé que le nommé Fleury et Perisse, le premier, l'un des députés des gens de couleur près de l'assemblée nationale, sont arrivés en cette Colonie par un bâtiment Bordelais avec le nommé l'Hirondelle Viard; que le capitaine a mis les deux premiers à Acquin, chez un nommé Dupont, homme de couleur; et le nommé l'Hirondelle Viard, également député des gens de couleur, au Cap. Ajoute encore l'accusé, qu'il nous avoit déclaré, le jour d'hier, que le nommé Laplace, dont le père est ici dans les prisons, faisant des récrues à Ouanaminthe, est du nombre de ceux qui ont marché du Limbé contre le Cap; que pour éloigner les soupçons, il est allé au Port-Margot, où il s'est tenu caché plusieurs jours, feignant d'avoir une fluxion; que le dit Laplace père a dit, à lui accusé, qu'il étoit sûr que son voisin, qui est un blanc, ne déposera pas contre lui, malgré qu'il sache toutes ses démarches; qu'il étoit assuré, que le nommé Girardeau, détenu en prison, ne déclareroit rien, parce qu'il étoit trop son ami pour le découvrir; qu'ensuite,

CHAP. IV. p. 51. s'il le dénonçoit, il seroit forcé d'en dénoncer beaucoup d'autres, tant du Limbé que des autres quartiers.

Observe l'accusé que lorsqu'il nous a parlé des moyens employés par Jacques Lucas pour soulever les nègres esclaves, il a omis de nous dire que Pierre Maury avoit envoyé une trentaine d'esclaves chez Lucas; que lui accusé, avec l'agrément d'Ogé le jeune, son frère, les renvoya, ce qui occasionna une plainte générale, les gens de couleur disant que c'étoit du renfort; que lui accusé eut même à cette occasion une rixe avec le plus grand des Didiers, avec lequel il manqua de se battre au pistolet, pour vouloir lui soutenir qu'étant libre et cherchant à être assimilé aux blancs, il n'étoit pas fait pour être assimilé aux nègres esclaves; que d'ailleurs soulevant les esclaves, c'étoit détruire les propriétés des blancs, et qu'en les détruisant, ils détruisoient les leurs propres; que dépuis que lui accusé étoit dans les prisons, il a vu un petit billet écrit par ledit Pierre Maury à Jean-François Tessier, par lequel il lui marque qu'il continue à ramasser, et que le nègre nommé Coquin, alla à la dame veuve Castaing aînée, armé d'une paire de pistolets garnis en argent et d'une manchette que le dit Maury lui a donnée, veille à tout ce qui se passe, et rend compte tous les soirs audit Maury; qui est tout ce que l'accusé, ici present, nous déclare, en nous conjurant d'être persuadés que, s'il lui étoit possible d'obtenir miséricorde, il s'exposeroit volontiers à tout les dangers pour faire arrêter les chefs de ces révoltés; et que dans toutes les circonstances, il prouvera son zèle et son respect pour les blancs.

Lecture à lui faite de sa déclaration, dans laquelle il persiste pour contenir vérité, lui en donnons acte, qu'il a signé avec nous et le gréffier.

Signé à la minute J. OGE', RUOTTE, POUCHERESSES DE VERTIERES, et LANDAIS, gréffier.

Pour expédition collationée, signé, LANDAIS, gréffier.

A Copy of the preceding document, the existence of which I had often heard of, but very much doubted, was trans-

transmitted to me from St. Domingo in the month of July 1795, inclosed in a letter from a gentleman of that island, whose attachment to the British cannot be suspected, and whose means for information were equal to any: This Letter is too remarkable to be omitted, and I hope, as I conceal his name, that the writer will pardon its publication: It here follows: CHAP. IV. p. 51.

Je vous envoye ci-joint, le testament de Jaques Ogé, executé au Cap le 9 Mars 1791. Voici mes réflexions sur les dates et les faits:

1. Jaques Ogé depose le projet connu dépuis long tems par les Brissotins dont il étoit un des Agents. Il nomme les chefs des Mulâtres, qui dans toutes les parties de la Colonie devoient exécuter un plan digne des Suppôts de l'enfer.

2. Il depose que l'abondance des pluies et les crues des rivières avoient empêché l'exécution du projet au mois de Février.

3. Il déclare que si on veut lui accorder miséricorde, il s'exposera aux dangers de faire arrêter les chefs.

Ogé est exécuté, avec vingt de ses complices, le 9 Mars 1791. Son testament est gardé secret jusqu'à la fin de 1791 (après l'incendie générale de la partie du Nord) qu'un arrêté de l'Assemblée Coloniale oblige impérieusement le Gréffier du Conseil du Cap à en délivrer des copies. Que conclure? Hélas, que les coupables sont aussi nombreux qu'atroces et cruels!

1ers. Coupables: Les hommes de couleur nommés par la déposition d'Ogé.

2. (et au moins autant s'ils ne sont plus.) Le Conseil du Cap, qui a osé faire exécuter Ogé, et qui a gardé le secret sur ses dépositions si interessantes.

CHAP. IV. p. 51. 3. Le Général Blanchelande et tous les chefs militaires qui n'ont pas fait arrêter sur le champ toutes les personnes de Couleur nommées par Ogé et ne les ont pas confrontées avec leur accusateur. Mais non: on a précipité l'exécution du malheureux Ogé; on a gardé un secret dont la publicité sauveroit la Colonie. On a laissé libres tous les chefs des révoltés; on les a laissé pour suivre leurs projets destructifs.

Si les Chefs militaires, le conseil, les magistrats civils, avoient fait arrêter au mois de Mars 1791, les mulâtres Pinchinat, Castaing, Viard, et tous les autres, ils n'auroient pas pu consommer leur crime le 25 Août suivant. Les Régimens de Normandie et d'Artois qui venoient d'arriver de France, étoient assez forts pour arrêter tous les gens de couleur coupables, et s'ils ne l'avoient pas été, et que ce fut le motif, qui eut empêché Blanchelande d'agir, pourquoi Blanchelande envoyat-il, au mois de Mai 1791, des troupes de ligne que lui envoyoit de la Martinique, M. de Behague?

La série de tous ces faits prouve évidemment la coalition des contre-révolutionnaires avec les Mulâtres, dont ils ont été la dupe, et la victime après l'arrivée des Commissaires Polverel et Santhonax.

CHAP. VI. p. 85.

A truce or convention called the CONCORDAT *was agreed upon the* 11*th of September between the free people of colour and the white inhabitants of Port-au-Prince, &c.* The following is a true copy of this curious and important document:

CONCORDAT de MM. les citoyens blancs du Port-au-Prince avec MM. les citoyens du couleur.

L'AN mil sept cent quatre-vingt-onze, & le onze du mois de Septembre.

Les commissaires de la garde nationale des citoyens blancs du Port-au-Prince, d'une part;

Et

CHAP. VI. p. 85.

Et les commissaires de la garde nationale des citoyens de couleur, d'autre part: et ceux fondés de pouvoir par arrêté de ce jour, & du neuf Septembre présent mois.

Assemblés sur la place d'armes du bourg de la Croix-des-Bouquets, à l'effet de délibérer sur les moyens les plus capable d'opérer la réunion des citoyens de toutes les classes, & d'arrêter les progrès & les suites d'une insurrection qui menace également toutes les parties de la colonie.

L'assemblée ainsi composée s'étant transportée dans l'église paroissale du dit bourg de la Croix-des-Bouquets, pour éviter l'ardeur du soleil, il a été procédé de suite, des deux côtés, à la nomination d'un président & d'un secrétaire.

Les commissaires de la garde nationale du Port-au-Prince ont nommé pour leur président M. Gamot, & pour leur secrétaire M. Hacquet; & les commissaires de la garde nationale des citoyens de couleur ont nommé pour leur président M. Pinchinat, & secrétaire M. Daguin fils.

Lesquels présidens & secrétaires ont respectivement accepté les dites charges, & ont promis de bien & fidellement s'en acquitter.

Après quoi il a été dit de la part des citoyens de couleur, que la loi faite en leur faveur en 1685, avoit été méprisée & violée par les progrès d'un préjugé ridicule, & par l'usage abusif et le despotisme ministériel de l'ancien régime, ils n'ont jamais joui que très-imparfaitement du bénéfice de cette loi.

Qu'au moment où ils ont vu l'assemblée des représentans de la nation se former, ils ont pressenti que les principes qui ont dicté la loi constitutionnelle de l'état, entraîneroit nécessairement la réconnoissance de leurs droits qui, pour avoir été long-temps méconnus, n'en étoient pas moins sacrés.

Que cette réconnoissance a été consacrée par les décrets & instructions des 8 & 28 Mars 1790, & par plusieurs autres rendus depuis; mais qu'ils ont vu avec la plus vive douleur que les citoyens blancs des colonies leur refusoient avec obstination l'exécution de ces décrets, pour ce qui

CHAP. VI. p. 85. qui les y concerne, par l'interprétation injuste qu'ils en ont faite.

Qu'outre la privation du bénéfice des dits décrets, lorsqu'ils ont voulu les réclamer, on les a sacrifiés à l'idole du préjugé, en exerçant contre eux un abus incroyable des lois & de l'autorité du gouvernement, au point de les forcer d'abandonner leurs foyers.

Qu'enfin, ne pouvant plus supporter leur existence malheureuse, & étant résolus de l'exposer à tous les évènemens, pour se procurer l'exercice des droits qu'ils tiennent de la nature & qui sont consacrés par les lois civiles & politiques, ils se sont réunis sur la montagne de la Charbonnière, où ils ont pris les armes, le 31 Août dernier, pour se mettre dans le cas d'une juste défense.

Que l'envie d'opérer la réunion des tous les citoyens indistinctement leur fait accueillir favorablement la députation de MM. les commissaires blancs de la garde nationale du Port-au-Prince; qu'ils voyent avec une satisfaction difficile à exprimer le retour des citoyens blancs aux vrais principes de la raison, de la justice, de l'humanité & de la saine politique, qu'ayant tout lieu de croire à la sincérité de ce retour ils se réuniront de cœur, d'esprit & d'intention aux citoyens blancs, pourvu que la précieuse & sainte égalité soit la base & le résultat de toutes opérations, qu'il n'y ait entre-eux & les citoyens blancs, d'autre différence que celle qu'entraînent nécessairement le mérite & la vertu, & que la fraternité, la sincérité, l'harmonie & la concorde, cimentent à jamais les liens qui doivent les attacher réciproquement : en conséquence, ils ont demandé l'exécution des articles suivans, auxquels les sus dits commissaires blancs ont répondu, ainsi qu'il est mentionné en la colonne parallele à celle des demandes.

Demandes des commissaires de la garde nationale des citoyens de couleur.

Article premier. Les citoyens blancs feront cause commune avec les citoyens de couleur, & contribueront de toutes leurs forces & de tous leurs moyens à l'exécution littérale de tous les points & articles des décrets & instructions de l'assemblée nationale, sanctionnés par le roi, & ce, sans restriction & sans se permettre aucune interprétation, conformément à ce qui est prescrit par l'assemblée nationale qui defend d'interprêter ses décrets ——Accepté. CHAP. VI. p. 85.

II. Les citoyens blancs promettent & s'obligent de ne jamais s'opposer directement ni indirectement à l'exécution du décret du 15 Mai dernier, qui dit-on n'est pas encore parvenu officiellement dans cette colonie ; de protester même contre toutes protestations & réclamations contraires aux dispositions du sus dit décret, ainsi que contre toutes adresses à l'assemblée nationale, au roi, aux quatre-vingt-trois départemens & aux différentes chambres de commerce de France, pour obtenir la révocation de ce décret bienfaisant.——Accepté.

III. Ont demandé les sus dits citoyens de couleur, la convocation prochaine & l'ouverture des assemblées primaires & coloniales, par tous les citoyens actifs, aux termes de l'article IV des instructions de l'assemblée nationale, du 28 Mars 1790.——Accepté.

IV. De députer directement à l'assemblée coloniale, & de nommer des députés choisis parmi les citoyens de couleur, qui auront, comme ceux des citoyens blancs, voix consultative & délibérative.——Accepté.

V. Déclarent les sus dits citoyens blancs & de couleur protester contre toute municipalité provisoire ou non, de même contre toutes assemblées provinciales & coloniales ; les dites municipalités assemblées provinciales & coloniales n'étant point formées sur le mode prescrit par les décrets & instructions des 8 & 28 Mars 1790.——Accepté.

VI. Demandent les citoyens de couleur qu'il soit reconnu par les citoyens blancs, que leur organisation présente, leurs opérations récentes & leur prise d'armes, n'ont eu pour but & pour motif, que leur sûreté individuelle, l'exécution des décrets de l'assemblée nationale, la réclamation de leurs droits méconnus & violés & le desir de parvenir par ce moyen

CHAP. VI. p. 85.

à la tranquillité publique, qu'en conséquence ils soient déclarés inculpables pour les événemens qui ont résulté de cette prise d'armes, & qu'on ne puisse dans aucun cas exercer contre-eux collectivement ou individuellement, aucune action directe ou indirecte pour raison de ces mêmes événemens, qu'il soit en-outre reconnu que leur prise d'armes tiendra jusqu'au moment ou les décrets de l'assemblée nationale seront ponctuellement & formellement exécutés; qu'en conséquence, les armes, canons & munitions de guerre enlevés pendant les combats qui ont eu lieu, resteront en la possession de ceux qui ont eu le bonheur d'être vainqueurs; que cependant les prisonniers [si toute-fois il en est] soient remis en liberté de part & d'autre.——Accepté.

VII. Demandent les dits citoyens de couleur que, conformément à la loi du 11 Février dernier & pour ne laisser aucun doute sur la sincérité de la réunion prête à s'opérer, toutes proscriptions cessent & soient révoquées dès ce moment, que toutes les personnes proscrites, décrétées, & contre lesquelles il seroit intervenu des jugemens ou condamnations quelconques pour raison des troubles survenus dans la colonie depuis le commencement de la révolution, soient de suite rapelés & mis sous la protection sacrée & immédiate de tous les citoyens, que réparation solemnelle & authentique soit faite à leur honneur, qu'il soit pourvu par des moyens convenables, aux indemnités que nécessitent leur exil, leurs proscriptions & les décrets décernés contre-eux; que toutes confiscations de leurs biens soient levées & que restitution leur soit faite de tous les objets qui leur ont été enlevés, soit en exécution des jugemens prononcés contre-eux, soit à main armée. Demandant que le présent article soit strictement & religieusement observé par tous les citoyens du ressort du conseil supérieur de Saint-Domingue, & sur-tout à l'égard des sieurs Poisson, Desmares, les frères Regnauld & autres compris au même jugement que ceux-ci, tous les habitans de la paroisse de la Croix-des-Bouquets, de même qu'à l'égard du sieur Jean-Baptiste la Pointe habitant de l'Arcahaye, contre lequel il n'est intervenu un jugement sévère

que

CHAP. VI. p. 85.

que par une suite de persécutions exercées contre les citoyens de couleur, & qui proscrit par les citoyens de Saint-Marc & de l'Arcahaye, n'a pu se dispenser d'employer une juste défense contre quelqu'un qui vouloit l'assassiner & qui l'assassinoit en effet; se réservant les citoyens de couleur de faire dans un autre moment & envers qui il appartiendra, toutes protestations & réclamations relatives aux jugemens prononcés contre les sieurs Oger, Chavannes & autres compris dans les dits jugemens, regardant dès à présent les arrêts prononcés contre les sus dits sieurs, par le conseil supérieur du Cap, comme infâmes, dignes d'être voués à l'exécration contemporaine & future, & comme la cause fatale de tous les malheurs qui affligent la province du nord.——Accepté, en ce qui nous concerne.

VIII. Que le secret des lettres & correspondance soit sacré & inviolable, conformément aux décrets nationaux.——Accepté.

IX. Liberté de la presse, sauf la responsabilité dans les cas déterminés par la loi.——Accepté.

X. Demandent en-outre les citoyens de couleur, qu'en attendant l'exécution ponctuelle & littérale des décrets de l'assemblée nationale, & jusqu'au moment où ils pourront se retirer dans leurs foyers, Messieurs les citoyens blancs de la garde nationale du Port-au-Prince s'obligent de contribuer à l'approvisionnement de l'armée des citoyens de couleur pendant tout le tems que durera son activité contre les ennemis communs & du bien public, & de faciliter la libre circulation des vivres dans les différens quartiers de la partie de l'ouest. ——Accepté.

XI. Observent en-outre les sus dits citoyens de couleur, que la sincérité dont les citoyens blancs viennent de leur donner une preuve authentique, ne leur permet pas de garder le silence sur les craintes dont ils sont agités; en conséquence ils déclarent qu'ils ne perdront jamais de vue la reconnoissance de tous droits & de ceux de leurs frères des autres quartiers; qu'ils verroient avec beaucoup de peine & de douleur la réunion prête à s'opérer au Port-au-Prince & autres

CHAP. VI. p. 85. tres lieux de la dépendance souffrir des difficultés dans les autres endroits de la colonie, auquel cas ils déclarent que rien au monde ne sauroit les empêcher de se réunir à ceux des leurs qui par une suite des anciens abus du régime colonial, éprouveroient des obstacles à la reconnoissance de leurs droits & par conséquent à leur félicité.——Accepté.

Après quoi l'assemblée revenue à la place d'armes, la matière mise en délibération, mûrement examinée & discutée, l'assemblée considérant qu'il est d'une nécessité indispensable de mettre en usage tous les moyens qui peuvent contribuer au bonheur de tous les citoyens qui sont égaux en droits.

Que la réunion des citoyens de toutes les classes peut seule ramener le calme & la tranquillité si nécessaires à la prospérité de cette colonie qui se trouve aujourd'hui menacée des plus grands malheurs.

Que l'exécution ponctuelle & littérale de tous les articles des décrets & instructions de l'assemblée nationale sanctionnés par le roi, peut seule opérer cette réunion désirable sous quelque point de vue qu'on l'envisage.

Il a été arrêté, savoir : de la part des citoyens blancs, qu'ils acceptent tous les articles insérés au présent concordat.

Et de la part des citoyens de couleur, que, vu l'acceptation de tous les articles sans restriction insérés au présent concordat, ils se réuniront & se réunissent en effet de cœur, d'esprit & d'intention aux citoyens blancs, pour ramener le calme & la tranquillité, pour travailler de concert à l'exécution ponctuelle des décrets de l'assemblée nationale sanctionnés par le roi, & pour employer toutes leurs forces & tous leurs moyens contre l'ennemi commun.

A été arrêté par Messieurs les citoyens blancs & Messieurs les citoyens de couleur, que ce jour devoit éteindre toute espèce de haine & de division entre les citoyens de la colonie en général, les citoyens de couleur du Port-au-Prince qui, par une fausse pusillanimité, ne se sont pas réunis à leurs frères d'armes, seront compris dans l'amnistie générale ; que jamais aucun reproche ne leur sera fait de leur conduite ;

CHAP. VI. p. 85.

duite; entendant qu'ils participent également aux avantages que promet notre heureuse réunion entre toutes les personnes & tous les citoyens indistinctement.

De plus, que protection égale devoit être accordée au sexe en général, les femmes & filles de couleur en jouiront de même que les femmes & filles blanches, & que mêmes précautions & soins seront pris pour leur sûreté respective.

Arrêté que le présent concordat sera signé par l'état major de la garde nationale du Port-au-Prince.

Il a été arrêté que le présent concordat sera rendu public par la voie de l'impression, que copies collationées d'y celui seront envoyées à l'assemblée nationale, au roi, aux quatre-vingt-trois départemens, à toutes les chambres de commerce de France, & à tous autres qu'il appartiendra.

Arrêté que mercredi prochain quatorze du présent mois MM. les citoyens blancs du Port-au-Prince se réuniront à l'armée de MM. les citoyens de couleur en la paroisse de la Croix-des-Bouquets, qu'il sera chanté dans l'église de cette paroisse à dix heures du matin un *Te Deum* en action de grâce de notre heureuse réunion; que MM. des bataillons de Normandie & d'Artois, et des corps d'Artillerie, de la marine royale & marchande, seront invités à s'y faire représenter par des députations particulières, que de même les citoyens en général de la Croix-des-Bouquets, du Mirebalais & autres endroits circonvoisins seront invités à s'y rendre, afin d'unir leurs vœux aux nôtres pour le bonheur commun.

Arrêté en-outre que le présent concordat sera passé en triple minute dont la première sera déposée aux archives de la municipalité future, la seconde entre les mains des chefs de l'armée des citoyens de couleur, & la troisième dans les archives de la garde nationale du Port-au-Prince.

Faite triple entre nous et de bonne foi, le jour, mois & an que dessus. *Signé, &c.*

Discours

CHAP. VI. p. 85. *Discours de M. Gamot, président des commissaires représentans les citoyens blancs du Port-au-Prince, à MM. les commissaires représentans l'armée des citoyens de couleur.*

MESSIEURS,

Nous vous apportons enfin des paroles de paix. Nous ne venons plus *traiter avec vous;* nous ne venons plus vous *accorder des demandes,* nous venons, animés de l'esprit de justice, reconnoître authentiquement vos droits, vous engager à ne plus voir dans les citoyens blancs que des amis, des frères, auxquels la patrie en danger vous invite, vous sollicite de vous réunir pour lui porter un prompt secours.

Nous acceptons entièrement & sans aucune réserve, le concordat que vous nous proposez. Des circonstances malheureuses que vous connoissez sans doute, nous ont fait hésiter un instant; mais notre courage a franchi tous les obstacles; nous avons imposé silence aux petits préjugés, au petit esprit de domination.

Que le jour où le flambeau de la raison nous éclaire tous, soit à jamais mémorable! qu'il soit un jour d'oubli pour toutes les erreurs, de pardon pour toutes les injures, & ne disputons désormais que d'amour & de zèle pour le bien de la chose publique.

CHAP. V. p. 60.

CHAP. V. p. 60. *Mauduit started back, &c.—while not a single hand was lifted up in his defence.*

IN this last particular I was misinformed, and rejoice that I have an opportunity of correcting my mistake. The following detail of that bloody transaction has been transmitted to me from St. Domingo since the first sheets were printed; "Les grenadiers du regiment de Mauduit, & d'autres voix parties de la foule, demandent que le Colonel fasse réparation à la garde nationale. On exige qu'il fasse des excuses

pour

pour l'insulte qu'il lui a faite. Il prononce les excuses qu'on lui demande; ses grenadiers ne sont points satisfaits, ils veulent qu'il les fasse à genoux. Une rumeur terrible se fait entendre: ce fut alors que plusieurs citoyens, *meme de ceux que Mauduit avoit le plus vexé,* fendent la foule, et cherchent à le soustraire au mouvement qui se préparoit. On a vu dans ce moment le brave *Beausoleil,* après avoir été atteint d'un coup de feu à l'affaire du 29 au 30 Juillet, et défendant le comité (*see Page* 34.) recevoir un coup de sabre en protégeant les jours de Mauduit. On peut rendre justice aussi à deux officiers de Mauduit: *Galeseau* et *Germain* n'ayant pas abandonné leur Colonel jusqu'au dernier moment; mais l'indignation des soldats étoit à son comble, et il n'étoit plus temps. CHAP. V. p. 60.

Mauduit pressé par ses grenadiers de s'agénouiller pour demander pardon à la garde nationale, et refusant constamment de s'y soumettre, reçut un coup de sabre à la figure, qui le terrassa; un autre grenadier lui coupa à l'instant la tête, *qui fut portée au bout d'une bayonette.* Alors le ressentiment des soldats et des matelots livrés à eux mêmes, n'eut plus de bornes: ils se transporterent chez Mauduit, où ils trainairent son corps, tout y fut brisé, rompu, meubles &c. on décarela même la maison, &c. &c.

CHAP. X. p. 151.

CHAP. X. p. 151.

They declared by proclamation all manner of slavery abolished, &c.—This proceeding was ratified in February, followed by the National Convention in a Decree, of which follows a Copy.

Decret de la Convention Nationale, du 16 Jour de Pluviôse; an second de la Republique Françoise, une et indivisible. 5 Feb. 1794.

La Convention Nationale déclare que l'esclavage des Nègres dans toutes les Colonies est aboli; en conséquence elle

CHAP. X. p. 151. 

elle decrète que tous les hommes, sans distinction de couleur, domiciliés dans les Colonies, sont citoyens François, et jouiront de tous les droits assurés par la constitution.

Elle renvoie au comité de salut public, pour lui faire incessament un rapport sur les mesures à prendre pour assurer l'éxécution du présent décret.

Visé par les inspecteurs. *Signé*

Auger,
Cordier,
S. E. Monnel.

Collationné à l'original, par nous président et sécrétaires de la Convention Nationale, à Paris le 22 Germinal, an second de la République Françoise une et indivisible. *Signé*, Amar, *Président*. A. M. Baudot. Monnot. Ch. Pottier, et Peyssard, *Secrétaires*.

As most of the French islands fell into possession of the English soon after this extraordinary decree was promulgated, the only place where it was attempted to be enforced was in the southern province of St. Domingo, and the mode of enforcing it, as I have heard, was as singular as the decree itself. The negroes of the several plantations were called together, and informed *that they were all a free people*, and at liberty to quit the service of their masters whenever they thought proper. They were told however, at the same time, that as the Republic wanted soldiers, and the state allowed no man to be idle, such of them as left their masters would be compelled to enlist in one or other of the black regiments then forming. At first many of the negroes accepted the alternative, and enlisted accordingly; but the reports they soon gave of the rigid discipline and hard fare to which they were subject, operated in a surprising manner on the rest, in keeping them more than usually quiet and industrious, and they requested that no change might be made in their condition.

CHAP. X. p. 153.

CHAP. X. p. 153.

Of the revolted Negroes in the northern province, many had perished of disease and famine, &c.

FROM the vast number of negroes that had fallen in battle, and the still greater number that perished from the causes above mentioned, it was computed in the year 1793 that this class of people at that period had sustained a diminution of more than one hundred thousand. *(Reflexions sur la Colonie, &c.* tom. 2. p. 217.) Since that time the mortality has been still more rapid, and, including the loss of whites, by sickness and emigration, I do not believe that St. Domingo at this juncture (June 1796) contains more than two-fifths of the whole number of inhabitants (white and black) which it possessed in the beginning of 1791.—According to this calculation, upwards of 300,000 human beings have miserably perished in this devoted country within the last six years!

CHAP. XI. p. 180.

CHAP. XI. p. 180.

The same fate awaited Lieutenant Colonel Markham, &c.

I CANNOT deny myself the melancholy satisfaction of preserving in this work the following honourable tribute to the memory of this amiable officer, which was given out in general orders after his death by the Commander in Chief.

Head Quarters, 28 *March* 1795.

Brigadier General Horneck begs the officers, non-commissioned officers, and privates of the detachment, which on the 26th inst, proceeded under the command of Lieutenant Colonel Markham on a party of observation, to receive his very sincere thanks for their gallant behaviour at the attack of the enemy's advanced post, taking their colours and cannon, and destroying their stores.

At

CHAP. XI. p. 180.

At the same time he cannot sufficiently express his feelings on the late afflicting loss that has been sustained in Lieutenant Colonel Markham, who, equally excellent and meritorious as an officer and a man, lived universally respected and beloved, and died leaving a bright example of military, social, and private virtue.

The Brigadier General likewise requests Captains Martin and Wilkinson, of the Royal Navy, to receive his acknowledgments and thanks for the important assistance they have afforded; not only on this occasion alone, but on every other, wherein his Majesty's service has required their co-operation. He also begs Captain Martin to do him the favour to impart the like acknowledgments to the officers of the Royal Navy, and to the respective ships' companies under his command, for the zeal and good conduct they have shewn whenever employed.

HISTORY OF THE WEST INDIES,

&c. &c.

A

T O U R

THROUGH THE SEVERAL ISLANDS

OF

BARBADOES, St. VINCENT, ANTIGUA, TOBAGO,

AND GRENADA,

IN THE YEARS 1791 AND 1792:

BY SIR WILLIAM YOUNG, BART.

M.P. F.R.S. &c. &c.

A TOUR,

&c. &c.

CHAP. XIII.

ON Sunday October 30, 1791, Sir William Young embarked in the ship Delaford at Spithead, which sailed the same evening, and after a pleasant voyage of thirty-eight days, came in sight of the island of Barbadoes. Here then the Tour may be said to commence; and the following extracts are, by favour of Sir William Young, transcribed literally from a rough journal, in which he entered such observations as occurred to him from the impressions of the moment. They may be considered therefore as a picture drawn from the life; and the reader must be a bad judge of human nature, and have a very indifferent taste, who does not perceive that it is faithfully drawn, and by the hand of a master.—For the few notes at foot I am accountable. CHAP. XIII.

B. E.

TUESDAY, December 6.—Early in the morning Barbadoes appeared in sight, bearing on the starboard bow W. N. W. At two o'clock P. M. the passengers landed in the six-oared pinnace. We went to a noted tavern, formerly Rachel's, now kept by Nancy Clark, a mulatto woman, where I Barbadoes, 1791.

first

CHAP. XIII. Barbadoes.

first tasted avocado-pear, a mawkish fruit*. Walking about the streets of Bridge-Town, my impressions gave me far from a disagreeable sensation as to the negroes. The town is extensive, and seems crowded with people, mostly negroes; but the negroes, with few exceptions, seemed dressed in a style much above even our common artizans, the women especially, and there was such a swagger of importance in the gait of those (and many there were) who had gold ear-rings and necklaces, that I told my friend Mr. O., on his pressing me for my opinion of what struck me on first landing in the West Indies, *That the negro women seemed to me the proudest mortals I had ever seen.* A Guinea ship was then in the harbour, and had lain there for some time; but none of the disgusting sights of ulcerated and deserted seamen appeared in the streets. Nor did I see any thing relative to the conduct of the slaves that implied the situation of abject acquiescence, and dread of cruel superiority, attributed to them in Great Britain. Many pressed their services on our first landing; and some first begged, and then joked with us, in the style of a *Davus* of Terence, with great freedom of speech. and some humour. I had a higher opinion of their minds, and a better opinion of their masters and government, than before

* There is no disputing about tastes. In Jamaica this fruit is very highly esteemed by all classes of people. It is usually eaten with pepper and salt, and has something of the flavour of the Jerusalem artichoke, but is richer and more delicate. It is sometimes called *vegetable marrow*, and it is remarkable that animals, both granivorous and carnivorous, eat it with relish.

before I set my foot on shore.—Such are my first impressions, written this evening on returning aboard: further-more, the squares or broader streets are crowded with negroes; their wrangles and conversation forcibly struck me, as analogous to what might have been looked for from the slaves in the Forum of Rome. Said a negro boy about twelve years of age to a young mulatto: *You damn my soul? I wish you were older and bigger, I would make you change some blows with me.—Upon my honour!* said an old negro.—*I'll bet you a joe,* (johannes) answered another, who had nothing but canvas trowsers on. I gave him no credit for possessing a six-and-thirty shilling piece, but I gave him full credit for a language which characterizes a presumption of self-importance. Perhaps, however, liberty of speech is more freely allowed, where licence can most promptly be suppressed. The *liberti* of the Roman Emperors, as we find in Tacitus, and the domestick slaves of the Roman people, as we deduce from scenes of Plautus and Terence, sometimes talked a language, and took liberties, with their lords and masters, which in free servants and citizens would not have been allowed. Liberty of the press is a proof of political freedom, but liberty of tongue is rather a proof of individual slavery. The feast of the *Saturnalia* allowed to slaves freedom of speech for the day, without controul. In my estimate of human nature, I should say that such freedom could not be used but moderately indeed; for the slave knew, that if he abused *his* power on the Thursday, the master might abuse *his* power

CHAP. XIII. Barbadoes. power on the Friday. His best security was on those days, when every word might be forbidden, and therefore every word might be forgotten, or forgiven. In qualification of all inference from my first view of negroes I should observe, that they were *town* negroes, many of them probably *free* negroes, and many, or most of them, if not all, *domestick* or *house* negroes. One small country cart, drawn by twelve oxen, and with three carters, gave me no favourable idea of the owner's feeding of either beasts or men. But accounts of distress, and objects of distress in the streets, are exaggerations. I saw as little of either as in any market town in England.

At six in the evening we returned on board; Captain and Mrs. W. of the 60th regiment, and their little girl, joining us on the passage to St. Vincent's, for which island we immediately bore away.

Barbadoes is an island rising with gentle ascent to the interior parts, called the Highlands of Scotland. As we sailed along the coast from East to West, it appeared wonderfully inhabited; dotted with houses as thick as on the declivities in the neighbourhood of London or Bristol, but with no woods, and with very few trees, even on the summits of the hills;—two or three straggling cocoas near each dwelling-house were all the trees to be seen.

St. Vincent. 1791. Wednesday, December 7, at day-break, St. Vincent's in sight. At 3 P. M. the ship came to an anchor in Nanton's Harbour, off Calliaqua. Mr. H. came immediately on board, and in half an hour we went on shore in the pinnace; horses were

were ready to carry us up to the villa, or mansion-house of my estate, distant about half a mile. A number of my negroes met us on the road, and stopped my horse, and I had to shake hands with every individual of them. Their joy was expressed in the most lively manner, and there was an ease and familiarity in their address, which implied no habits of apprehension or restraint: the circumstance does the highest honour to my brother-in-law, Mr. H. who has the management of them. On my arriving at my house, I had a succession of visitors. The old negro nurse brought the grass gang, of twenty or thirty children, from five to ten years old, looking as well and lively as possible. The old people came one by one to have some chat with *Massa* (Master), and among the rest "*Granny** Sarah," who is a curiosity. She was born in Africa, and had a child before she was carried from thence to Antigua. Whilst in Antigua she remembers perfectly well the rejoicing on the *Bacra's* (white men's) being let out of gaol, who had killed Governor Park. Now this happened on the death of Queen Anne, in 1713-4! which gives, to Christmas 1791-2,

	Years 78
Add two years in Antigua, for passage, &c. - - -	- - - 2
Suppose her to have had a child at fourteen, and to have been sold the year after	- - - 15
The least probable age of Granny Sarah is - -	- - - 95

and she is the heartiest old woman I ever saw. She

* Grandmother.

CHAP. XIII. St. Vincent.

She danced at a Negro-ball last Christmas; and I am to be her partner, and dance with her next Christmas. She has a garden, or provision-ground, to herself, in which, with a great-grand-child, about six years old, she works some hours every day, and is thereby rich. She hath been exempted from all labour, except on her own account, for many years.

The villa at Calliaqua is an excellent house for the climate: it hath ten large bed-chambers, and it accommodated all our party from the ship with great ease.

Thursday, December 8. This morning I rode over the estate, which seems in the most flourishing condition: the negroes seem under a most mild discipline, and are a very cheerful people. This day again I had repeated visits from my black friends: Granny Sarah was with me at least half a dozen times, telling me, "*Me see you, Massa; now me go die*!*" (I behold you, my Master; now let me die!)

"Friday, December 9. We mounted our horses at one o'clock to ride to Kingston, where a negro boy had carried our clothes to dress: the distance

* This is a stroke of nature. The sight of her master was a blessing to old Sarah beyond all expectation; and not having any thing further to hope for in life, she desires to be released from the burthen of existence. A similar circumstance occurred to myself in Jamaica; but human nature is the same in all countries and ages.—"And Joseph made ready his chariot, "and went up to meet Israel his father, to Goshen; and presented himself unto him: and he fell on his neck, and wept "on his neck a good while.—And Israel said unto Joseph, *Now* "*let me die, since I have seen thy face,*" &c. Genesis, chap. 46. v. 29, 30.

distance is about three miles of very hilly road. I particularly noticed every negro whom I met or overtook on the road: of these I counted eleven, who were dressed as field negroes, with only trowsers on; and adverting to the evidence on the Slave Trade, I particularly remarked that not one of the eleven had a single mark or scar of the whip. We met or overtook a great many other negroes, but they were dressed. Passing through Mr. Greatheed's large estate, I observed in the gang one well-looking negro woman, who had two or three wheals on her shoulders, which seemed the effect of an old punishment.*

A FREE mulatto woman, named Burton, came this day to complain before Mr. H. of her negro slave, a lad of about seventeen. The boy was confronted, and seemed in truth a bad subject, having absented himself the three last days. The only threat the woman used to her slave, was that she would sell him. Mr. H. advised her to do it; and it ended in ordering the boy *to look out himself for a master, who would purchase him.*

KINGSTON is a small and scattered, but very neat and well-built town. We dressed ourselves there, and proceeded at three to the government house, about a mile up the country. It is a good

* In the West Indies the punishment of whipping is commonly inflicted, not on the *backs* of the negroes, (as practised in the discipline of the British soldiers) but more humanely, and with much less danger, on *partes posteriores*. It is therefore no proof that the negroes whom Sir William Young inspected had escaped flagellation, because their shoulders bore no impression of the whip. This acknowledgment I owe to truth and candour.

house,

CHAP. XIII. St. Vincent.

house, hired from the Alexander estate. The governor gave me a most polite reception. Riding home, I had the company and conversation of Mr. L. speaker of the assembly, who told me that a new slave act was prepared, and under consideration of the legislature, which he himself had drawn up; and, above all, had studied to frame such clauses and provisions as might ensure the execution and full effect of the law in favour of the negroes.—*Nous verrons.*—We had likewise some talk on the subject of building a church at Kingston: he said, if moved in the assembly, he had not a doubt of unanimity. I promised, in addition to my quota of tax for such purpose, to subscribe £.200 towards ornamental architecture or additional expence, which the conservators of the public purse might not think themselves warranted to admit in their plan and estimate; he promised to set the business on foot.

Saturday, December 10.—This day (as usual) a half-holiday from twelve o'clock for the negroes.

Friday, December 16.—Three Guinea ships being in the harbour, full of slaves from Africa, I testified a wish to visit the ships previous to the sale. I would have visited them privately and unexpectedly, but it was not practicable. Every thing was prepared for our visit, as the least observing eye might have discovered: in particular I was disgusted with a general jumping or dancing of the negroes on the deck, which some, and perhaps many of them, did voluntarily, but some under force or controul; for I saw a sailor, more than once, catch those rudely by the arm who had ceased

ceased dancing, and by gesture menace them to repeat their motion, to clap their hands, and shout their song of *Yah! Yah!* which I understood to mean "Friends."—Independent of this, and when I insisted on the dance being stopped, I must say that the people, with exception to one single woman (perhaps ill) seemed under no apprehensions, and were cheerful for the most part, and all anxious to go ashore, being fully apprised of what would be their situation and employment, when landed, by some of their countrymen, who were permitted to visit them from the plantations for that purpose.

Never were there ships or cargoes better suited for the ground of general observation; for the ships came from distant districts, and with people of different nations on board: the Pilgrim of Bristol, with 370 Eboes from Bonny. The Eolus of Liverpool, with 300 Windward negroes from Bassa. The Anne of Liverpool, with 210 Gold Coast negroes from Whydah.

The Pilgrim (Taylor, commander) was in the best possible order; she was six feet in height between decks, without shelves or double tier in the men's apartments, and as clean as a Dutch cabinet. We visited every part of the ship; in the hospital there was not one sick, and the slaves mustered on the deck, were to all appearance, and uniformly, not only with clean skins, but with their eyes bright, and every mark of health. This Captain Taylor must be among the best sort of men in such an employment; having in three voyages, and with full cargoes, lost on the whole but eight

slaves,

CHAP. XIII.

St. Vincent.

slaves, and not one seaman. In general, I should give a favourable account too of the Eolus, but the Pilgrim had not a scent that would offend, and was indeed sweeter than I should have supposed possible, in a crowd of any people of the same number, in any climate. One circumstance in all the three was particularly striking, in relation to the evidence on the Slave Trade: A full half of either cargo consisted of children (and generally as fine children as I ever saw) from six to fourteen years of age; and, on enquiry, I found but very few indeed of these were connected with the grown people on board. I could not but suppose, then, that these little folks were stolen from their parents, and perhaps (in some instances) sold by their parents.* I again remark, that these slaves were from Bonny and from Bassa.

The Anne was from the Gold Coast, a small vessel, scarcely clean, disagreeably offensive in smell, with only three feet six inches between the main decks, yet apparently with no sick on board. These Gold Coast negroes were in themselves a

* Nothing is more common in all parts of Africa, than the circumstance of parents of free condition selling their children in times of scarcity, which frequently happen, for a supply of food. Mr. Park has recorded many instances of it among the Mandingoes, (vide his Travels, p. 248, and again, p. 295.) "Perhaps by a philosophick and reflecting mind (observes Mr. Park) death itself would scarcely be considered as a greater calamity than slavery: but the poor negro, when fainting with hunger, exclaims, like Esau of old, *Behold I am at the point to die, and what profit shall this birthright do to me?* These are dreadful evils; ordained, without doubt, for wise and good purposes, but, concerning the causes of them, human wisdom is doomed to silence."

worse

worse looking people, but they bore too a sickly complexion and heaviness of mien and mind which the others did not; and it was remarkable in the contrast of the cargoes, that among the last there was not even a common proportion of children or young people: I should suppose not above 20 in the 210.

Mr. B. of the Custom House, told me that at St. Vincent's more certificates for bounties were given than at all the other islands, and that the reason was, because it was situated next to Barbadoes, the most windward of the islands, and the Guinea Ships arriving thus far in health, the masters, to avail themselves of the parliamentary bounty, took up their certificates before proceeding on to Jamaica or elsewhere, inasmuch as every day, at the close of a long voyage, might be marked by disease or death, and thus eventually preclude them from the benefit of the law. This should be rectified.

Mr. B. allowed, in conversation with me, that the regulations of tonnage proportioned to numbers, on which such outcry had been raised, had ultimately proved advantageous to the trader, as well as to the poor slave. The preservation of the slaves had well and fully repaid for the diminution in freight.

Saturday, December 17. At ten this morning all my negroes were mustered at the works, and had ten barrels of herrings distributed among them: afterwards, such of the women as had reared children, came to the villa, and each received, as a present, five yards of fine cotton, at 2*s*. 6*d*. *per* yard, of the gayest pattern, to make a petticoat,

CHAP. XIII.

St. Vincent.

Sunday, 18. Mr. H. read prayers to a congregation of my negroes.

Tuesday, 20. Went to Kingston to attend the sale of the Eboe, Windward, and Gold Coast slaves, in all 880. The slaves were seated on the floor in two large galleries, divided into lots of ten each. Those purchasers who, by previous application, had gained a title of pre-emption, (for there was a demand for three times the number imported) drew for the lots in succession, until each had his number agreed for. In lotting the slaves, some broken numbers occurred, and a little lot of four (two girls and two boys) of about twelve years old, were purchased for me. The slaves did not seem under any apprehension, nor did they express any uneasiness, with exception to the Gold Coast negroes, who gave many a look of sullen displeasure. Returning home in the evening, I found my four little folks in old Mrs. H——'s room, where they eat a hearty supper, had some of their country folks got round them, and went to sleep as much at their ease as if born in the country. These children were unconnected with any on board the ship. The girls were remarkably straight, and with finer features than negroes ordinarily have. They had each a bead necklace, and small cotton petticoat of their country make, and must I think have been kidnapped or stolen from their parents. I cannot think that any parents would have sold such children.

Friday, 23. This morning I passed an hour or more, observing the process of sugar-making in the boiling house. Of the best cane-juice, a gallon of liquor gives one lb. of sugar; of the middling-rich, 20 gallons give 16 lbs.; of the watery canes, 24 gallons give 16 lbs.

THIS afternoon ANSELM, chief of the Charaibes in the quarter of Morne-Young, and BRUNAU, chief of Grand Sable, at the head of about twenty, came into the parlour after dinner, and laid a *don d'amitié* at my feet of Charaibe baskets, and of fowls and pine apples. We treated them with *wine*, and afterwards about a dozen of their ladies were introduced, who preferred *rum*. I had much courteous conversation with Anselm, accepted a basket, and a couple of pines, and bought some baskets of the other Charaibes. They were all invited to sleep on the estate, and a keg of rum was ordered in return for Anselm's present, and for Brunau's, &c.

LA LIME, one of the chiefs who had signed the treaty in 1773, and a dozen others, had before visited me at different times, but this was a formal address of ceremony, and all in their best attire, that is, the men, and perhaps the women too, for though they had no clothes, saving a petticoat resembling two children's pocket handkerchiefs sewed at the corners, and hanging one before and one behind, yet they had their faces painted red, pins through their under lips, and bracelets; and about their ancles strings of leather and beads.

DECEMBER 25. About ten in the forenoon the negroes of my estate, both men and women, exceedingly well dressed, came to wish us a merry Christmas: soon after came two negro fidlers and a tamborine, when we had an hour's dancing, and

carpenter

CHAP. XIII. St. Vincent.

carpenter Jack, with Phillis, danced an excellent minuet, and then four of them began a dance not unlike a Scotch reel. After distributing among them different Christmas boxes, to the number of about fifty, we attended prayers in a large room; myself read select parts of the service, and Mr. H—— closed our church attendance with a chapter from our Saviour's sermon on the mount, and a dialogue of practical christianity on the heads of resignation towards God, and peace towards men. This day, and almost every day, I had many Charaibe visitors tendering presents. I laid down a rule to receive no presents but from the chiefs, for the person presenting expects double the value in return, and the Charaibes are too numerous for a general dealing on such terms, either with views to privacy or economy. I should not omit that yesterday morning the chiefs, Anselm and Brunau, who had visited me the evening before, came to see me, and politely having observed that they would not intermingle, in their first visit of congratulation, on my coming to St. Vincent's, any matter of another nature, proceeded to demand *quelles nouvelles de la France,* and then *quelles nouvelles de l'Angleterre;* and thus proceeded gradually to open the tendency of the question, as relating to the designs of government touching themselves. It seems that some persons of this colony, travelling into their country, and looking over the delightful plains of Grand Sable from Morne Young, had exclaimed, "*what a pity this country yet belongs to the savage Charaibes!*" and this kind of language repeated among them, had

awakened

awakened jealousies and apprehensions, and some French discontented fugitives from Martinico and elsewhere had (as had been heard from the Charaibes at Kingston) given a rumour that I was come out with some project for dispossessing them by the English government. To remove these jealousies, I told them, 'That private a man as I was, and come merely to look at my estate, and settle my private affairs, I would venture, on personal knowledge of the minister, and character of our common king, and unalterable principles of our government, to assure them, that whilst they continued their allegiance, and adhered to the terms of the treaty of 1773, no one dare touch their lands, and that Grand Sable was as safe to them as was Calliaqua to me: it was treason to suppose that the king would not keep his word, according to the conditions of that treaty; and if any subjects ventured to trespass on them, they would, on proper representations, be punished. For myself, I assumed a mien of anger, that they should forget their national principle in exception of me. If friendships and enmities descended from father to son, they must know me for their steadiest friend, and incapable of any injustice towards them.' They seemed very much pleased with this sort of language, and assured me of their strongest regard and confidence, and would hear no more lies or tales to the prejudice of myself, or of the designs of government. They invited me to come and taste their hospitality, and I promised to do so, and we parted as I could wish—the best friends in the world.

DECEMBER

CHAP. XIII. St. Vincent.

December 26. This was a day of Christmas gambols. In the morning we rode out, and in the town of Calliaqua saw many negroes attending high mass at the popish chapel. The town was like a very gay fair, with booths, furnished with every thing good to eat and fine to wear. The negroes (with a very few exceptions) were all dressed in pattern cottons and muslins, and the young girls with petticoat on petticoat; and all had handkerchiefs, put on with fancy and taste, about their heads. Returning to the villa, we were greeted by a party which frightened the boys. It was the *Moco Jumbo* and his suite.* The *Jumbo* was on stilts, with a head, mounted on the actor's head, which was concealed: the music was from two baskets, like strawberry baskets, with little bells within, shook in time. The swordsman danced with an air of menace, the musician was comical, and Jumbo assumed the "antic terrible," and was very active on his stilts. We had a large company to dinner; and in the evening I opened the ball in the great court, with a minuet, with black Phillis, Granny Sarah being indisposed: our music consisted of two excellent fiddles, *Johnny* and *Fisher*, from my Pembroke estate, and *Grandison*, tamborin of the villa: there stood up about eighteen couple; the men negroes were dressed in the highest beauism, with muslin frills, high capes, and white hats; and one beau had a large fan. The negro girls were all dressed gay and fine, with handkerchiefs folded

* Without doubt the *Mumbo Jumbo* of the Mandengoes.—Vide Park's Travels, c. 3, p. 39.

tastefully

tastefully about their heads, and gold ear-rings and necklaces: the girls were nearly all field negroes; there are but four female slaves as domesticks in the villa. In England, no idea of "jolly Christmas" can be imagined, in comparison with the three days of Christmas in St. Vincent's. In every place is seen a gaiety of colours and dress, and a corresponding gaiety of mind and spirits; fun and finery are general. This moment a new party of musicians are arrived with an African *Balafo*, an instrument composed of pieces of hard wood of different diameters, laid on a row over a sort of box: they beat on one or the other so as to strike out a good musical tune. They played two or three African tunes; and about a dozen girls, hearing the sound, came from the huts to the great court, and began a curious and most lascivious dance, with much grace as well as action; of the last plenty in truth.

1792. Sunday, January 1, 1792. Rode over to my Pembroke estate in the valley of Buccament, about six miles distant, to the leeward of Kingston. The road is over the most rugged and towering hills, with occasional precipices of rock of a reddish dark hue, and for the rest covered with bushes and some fine tress. In the vales, between the ridges, and on every practicable ascent, are cultivated grounds, and the whole is a mixture of the rich and the romantick. The road winds much, to avoid the deep ravines and gullies. The flight of a bird cannot be more than three miles from Kingston to Buccament. We entered

CHAP. XIII. St. Vincent. the valley of Buccament by a ravine, called Keillan's land, belonging to me.

The vale of Buccament brings to mind the happy and secluded valley of Rasselas, prince of Abyssinia. The valley, containing about 3,000 acres, is hemmed on each side by towering hills, whose steep ascents have in parts peeled off or split in the storm, and now are left precipices of bare rock, appearing between streaks of the highest verdure, from which occasionally shoots the *mountain cabbage-tree.** In the centre of the valley stands an insulated mountain, whose height, through an interstice in the rugged boundary of the vale, looks down on the garrison of Berkshire-hill, and Berkshire-hill is 627 feet above the sea. The hills or rocks that shut in the valley, again command the hill in the centre. Down the vale runs a fine and rapid river, abounding with the finest mullet and other fish; its bed is obstructed with fragments of rocks from the skirting mountains. Its murmurs fill the vale. It winds round the centre hill, and then pours straight into the sea. The valley, as it coasts the sea, is about one mile over. It stretches inland about five miles; its greatest breadth, half-way from the sea, is two miles. From the mount, in the centre, it forms a most luxuriant picture of cultivation, contrasted with romantic views, and seems wholly secluded from all the world. My Pembroke estate takes in the hill in the centre, and thence runs along the

* Called also the *Palmeto-Royal.* See it described at large, vol. i. p. 20.

river-

4

river-side, comprehending all the valley on one side, to within a quarter of a mile of the sea. CHAP. XIII. St. Vincent.

A NEGRO gave signal of my approach to the house, and all the negroes came forth to greet me, and with a welcome as warm as that at Calliaqua. They caught hold of my bridle, my feet, and my coat; every one anxious for a share in leading me up to the house; and indeed they attempted to take me off my horse and carry me, but I begged them to desist.

FRIDAY, January 6. I visited Berkshire-hill, and went over the fortifications. The hill itself is a rock, and, from its precipices, is scarcely assailable; where it is so, parts have been cut away, and, take art and nature together, the place may be deemed impregnable. The point above hath been flatted off, so as to admit room on its surface for most commodious barracks for a complete regiment, stores, reservoirs, &c. all bomb-proof. In my different excursions, I continued to inspect the persons of the negroes, and I can assert, that not one in fifty of those I have seen has been marked with the whip, with exception to the gang employed at the public works on Berkshire-hill. This gang may be supposed to consist for the most part of reprobate and bad negroes, who have been sold from estates for riddance of their practices and examples. They chiefly belong, as an entire gang, to the overseer of the works, who may be supposed to pick them up cheap, being bad characters, though competent to their business, under the controul of the military. The inhabitants, not willing to send their able men to the publick

CHAP. XIII. St. Vincent.

lick works, for fear of evil communication, commute their quota of labourers, by paying the overseer a certain sum to find others in their room.

FRIDAY, January 13, 1792. The Charaibe chief of all, *Chatoyer*, with his brother *du Vallee*, and six of their sons, came to pay me a visit, and brought their presents; a stool of Charaibe workmanship, and a very large cock turkey of the wild breed, which with a hen I mean for England. Chatoyer and du Vallèe were well dressed; as a mark of respect, they came without arms. We had much conversation with them, and I gave in return a silver-mounted hanger to Chatoyer, and a powder-horn to du Vallee. The latter is possessed of nine negro slaves, and has a cotton plantation. He is the most enlightened of the Charaibes, and may be termed the founder of civilization among them. Chatoyer and his sons dined at the villa, and drank each a bottle of claret. In the evening they departed in high glee, with many expressions of friendship.

JANUARY 17. I visited the king's botanic garden; Dr. Anderson went round the garden with me. It consists of about thirty acres, of which sixteen are in high garden cultivation. The variety, beauty, growth, and health of the plants, from all quarters of the globe, is most striking. It is a scene for a painter as well as a botanist. The quickness of vegetation is astonishing: some English oak of three years growth are above seven feet high. The Indian teak wood, full eighteen feet high, and six inches diameter, of only four years growth. This being a remarkable hard and durable

Grignion sculp.

CHATOYER the CHIEF of the BLACK CHARAIBES in S.

Drawn from the life by Agostino Brunyas — 1773. From an original painting in the possession of Sir W.m Young Bar.t F.R.S

Publish'd March 12. 1796. by I. Stockdale, Piccadilly.

durable wood, leads me to note the general remark of Dr. *Anderson*, "that in this country, "where vegetation never stops or is checked, "the hardest woods are of growth as quick as "the most pulpous or soft texture." Dr. *Anderson* is multiplying to a great extent all the useful trees; the Chinese tallow tree, the gum arabic, the Peruvian bark, the balsam of Capivi, the cinnamon, &c. &c. *N. B.* I name them from their produce.

January 23. Never passing a slave without observing his back, either in the field or in the road, or wenches washing in the rivers, I have seen not one back marked, besides that of the woman observed before on Mr. Greathead's estate (in whom I may be mistaken as to the cause) and one new negro unsold at Kingston, who found means to explain to me that he was fumfumm'd (flogged) by the surgeon of the ship; and he seemed to have had two or three strokes with a cat. I note it in the language of one accustomed to attend military punishments.—At my estate, and I believe on most others, confinement is the usual punishment. Three have been punished at Calliaqua since my arrival; Sampson has received ten lashes, and two men were put into the stocks, of whom Indian Will was one, for getting drunk and cutting a negro lad's head open in his passion; he was released the next morning. The other was a watchman at the mill, from which the sails had been stolen; he was confined for two nights in terrorem, and then, no discovery being made of the theft, he was released.

January

CHAP. XIII. St. Vincent. JANUARY 26. Sailed from Nanton's harbour in the Maria schooner of 28 tons, took our departure at ten in the forenoon, coasted to leeward, and came off St. Lucia in the evening.

FRIDAY, 27. Off Dominica in the morning, becalmed. In the evening a breeze sprung up; and,

SATURDAY, 28, Came at day-break off Basseterre, in Guadaloupe; hailed a fishing boat, and bought some fish; the people said all was quiet; *tout va bien a la Guadaloupe*.

SAW a very large spermaceti whale spouting and playing close a-head in the channel between Guadaloupe and Antigua. Came to an anchor at

Antigua, 1792. 5 P. M. in *Old Road bay*, Antigua. Walking up an excellent level coach road half a mile, to the old-road plantation house. A mulatto boy getting before, gave notice of *Massa* being on the way. Every hoe was now thrown down, and a general huzza followed; and my good creoles, man, woman, and child, ran to meet me with such ecstacy of welcome, embracing my knees, catching my hands, clothes, &c. &c. that I thought I should never have reached the house. At length, in joyous procession, with handkerchiefs for flags, I was conveyed to the old mansion of my ancestors, and gave my good people a treat of rum, and all was dance and song.

SUNDAY, 29. Enquiring into the condition of the estate and situation of the negroes, I found the latter generally dissatisfied with their manager, Mr. R——. Their complaints were directed chiefly to his curtailing the allowance of the old people,

people, and such others as were incapable of labour; and his frequency and severity of punishments. The first complaint I removed instantly, by ordering the full allowance of industrious youth to meritorious age. For the second, (on examining into the grounds of allegation, and finding them just) I immediately discharged Mr. R. and appointed Mr. H——, who had been ten years on the estate, and much liked by the negroes, to be their manager. Their satisfaction on both accounts seemed complete and general.

Monday, 30. Went to St. John's, a large, and in many parts a well-built town, and the church an excellent building, as is likewise the town or court house; but the town itself has the appearance of ruined trade and deserted habitancy. The country for twelve miles, from the old road plantation to St. John's, is open, with very few trees or even shrubs, but beautiful in its swells of ground, scarcely to be called hills, spotted with buildings, and varied with inlets of the sea opening in different points of view; high but infructuous cultivation cover every acre. The roads excellent, and every thing speaking the civilization, art, and toil of man; but nature answers not. Under the drought all fails: heat, with little or no moisture, generates nothing. Partial rains have this year, as often before, given hopes to the planter for his canes, and to the negro for his provisions; but the season has again failed, and their hopes are blasted. The whole is a picture of disappointment, in land, beast, and man. The negro houses are excellent, and many of them of stone;

but

CHAP. XIII. Antigua.

but no in-doors can give the face of comfort and contentment, if all is wanting beyond the threshold. The negroes having little or no provisions from their grounds, are fed by allowance from the planters, many themselves in distress, which scants that allowance. On estates in good condition, it is twelve quarts of corn, with two or three pounds of salt provision per week.

THURSDAY, February 2. Being a day which I had allotted for a holiday to the negroes, we went early to the valley of the old road. In the morning I distributed ten barrels of herrings amongst the negroes, and in the evening we had a very smart well-dressed negro ball in the hall of my old mansion. Mr. L—— and myself both impartially allowed the negroes, young men and girls, to dance better in step, in grace, and correctness of figure, than our fashionable, or indeed any couples at any ball in England; taking that ball generally, there is no one negro dances ill. I danced a country dance with old Hannah, and a minuet with long Nanny. Not a complaint remains at the old road.

FRIDAY, February 3. Returning from old road to Dr. Fairbairn's, I there saw Mr. Hoffman, the Moravian missionary, *whose blameless life still answers to his song*. The Moravian missionaries are of the highest character for moral example, as well as gentle manners; and they preach the doctrines of *peace and good will* to all men, and to all governments. They assimilate in simplicity best with the minds of the negroes, and in their assiduity and goodness, have, I fear, but few

equals

Antigua.

equals amongst the regular clergy in the West Indies. It was with difficulty I prevailed on the good, mild, and disinterested Mr. Hoffman, to receive annually for his domestick use a small barrel of sugar, and a quarter-cask of rum, as a token of my regard for his attention to my negroes on the old road estate.

SUNDAY, February 5. In the evening embarked for Martinique.

MONDAY, 6. Becalmed off Guadaloupe.

Martinique, 1792.

TUESDAY, 7. At seven in the evening came into St. Pierre's bay, and passing under the stern of an 18 gun sloop of war, she hailed us to come on board. I went on board with the captain of our schooner. The French officer commanding the sloop, on my stating that our vessel was not commercial, but merely having on board Englishmen, passengers, told me that the schooner must immediately come to an anchor under his stern, but that myself and other gentlemen might go on shore. Returning to the schooner, a serjeant of the national guards followed us in a shallop, and said he was come by orders to conduct us on shore: we went with him. On landing, he told us we must proceed to the *hotel de l'intendant,* Monsieur le Chevalier de Menerad. He marched us above a mile to the hotel, and passing within the sentinel at entrance of the court, asked for the governor, who was out, and only a black boy in the house, who knew not where the governor was to be found. The national serjeant talked in a high tone of brutal command, and said we must stay all night in the open air, or until the governor

was

CHAP. XIII. Martinique.

was found. I used every kind of language, but all in vain. I was afterwards told that I had omitted the essential argument with these liberty-corps, to wit, '*a johannes*.' About ten o'clock a Monsieur *De la Cour*, lieutenant of police, arrived, apparently on other business. I told him my name and situation. He behaved most politely, and told the serjeant he should take us to the *hotel des Americains*, the best tavern in St. Pierre, giving himself security for our forthcoming next morning. Whilst the receipt for our bodies was writing, the governor, Chevalier de Menerad, arrived: on my name being mentioned he behaved most politely, asked my whole party to supper, and offered me a bed. Having complained of the serjeant's conduct, he immediately told him to leave the room, and made a general apology, giving me plainly to understand that there was scarcely the appearance of law, government, or any authority at Martinique.

The national regiments had arrived a year before. The inhabitants were of a different party. The old corps on duty there of an uncertain or undecided character, and the constitution of the mother country being unsettled, and no persons in Martinique knowing who were finally to be uppermost, all were afraid to assume a responsibility.

I thanked the governor for his polite invitation, but declined accepting what the state of his house, and having no domesticks, proved to be a mere invitation of compliment. His wife and family were at Guadaloupe.

Monsieur

Monsieur De La Cour conducted us, at near eleven at night, to the American hotel, where, finding an excellent house and a truly Parisian cook, we laughed over our difficulties.

Monsieur De la Cour and Monsieur Pénan, our banker, next morning confirmed the state of government in Martinique, as before mentioned: all was a calm, but it was such a calm as generally precedes a hurricane. With respect to the slaves, they are perfectly quiet. For the free mulattoes and *gens de couleur* (who are twice as numerous as the white inhabitants) they too are waiting the result of ascendant parties in old France. For the whites, they are generally, as far as I can find, friends to the old government, and they declare themselves most openly; hence the new acts of the national assembly are yet unexecuted. The church remains on its ancient footing, and the convents are filled with the same people, Capuchins and Ursulins, but the Capuchins appear not in the open streets.

In this state of political diffidence, commerce has lost its activity, and credit is gone; yet money seems to be plenty; but there is little or no trade in this great and once commercial town. Instead of fifty or more large sugar ships, which should at this season be seen in the bay, there are only nine; and even these seem in general to be small. American vessels (schooners and sloops) are numerous; perhaps there may be forty.

Wednesday, February 8. We amused ourselves in walking about the town and purchasing presents

CHAP. XIII. Martinique. presents for our friends; *bijouterie* of Madame Gentier, *embroiderie* of Madame Nodau, and *liqueurs* of Grandmaison.

The town of St. Pierre extends along on the beach. It is above two miles in length, and in breadth about half a mile. The buildings are of stone, and handsome. The shops are many of them well decorated. The jeweller and silversmith's shop (Goutier's) is as brilliant as any in London or Paris. Trade being nearly extinguished in the harbour, the embers of what it has been glimmer in the shops.

Thursday, February 9. In the evening we embarked for St. Vincent's.

St. Vincent, 1792. Friday, February 10. Early this morning were in sight of St. Vincent's, off the Sugar Loaves of St. Lucie, and there close in with the land. A fine breeze springing up, we run over the channel of seven leagues in three hours, and then coasted down to windward of St. Vincent's, a beautiful and rich country, mostly in possession of the Charaibes. At four in the afternoon we anchored in Young's Bay, landed, and once more found ourselves in the comfortable mansion of Calliaqua. My voyage to Antigua has put me in full possession of the question concerning the best mode of feeding the negroes. I am speaking of the difference in their situation in regard to plenty and comfort, when fed by allowance from the master, as in Antigua; or when supported by provision grounds of their own, as in St. Vincent's. In the first case, oppression may, and certainly in some instances, and in different

ferent degrees, doth actually exist, either as to quantity or quality of food; besides the circumstance of food for himself, the negro suffers too in his poultry and little stock, which are his wealth. The maintenance of his pigs, turkeys, or chickens, must often subtract from his own dinner, and that perhaps a scanty one, or he cannot keep stock at all; and a negro without stock, and means to purchase tobacco, and other little conveniences, and some finery too for his wife, is miserable.

In the second case, of the negro feeding himself with his own provisions, assisted only with salt provisions from his master (three pounds of salt fish, or an adequate quantity of herrings, per week, as in St. Vincent's) the situation of the negro is in proportion to his industry; but generally speaking, it affords him a plenty that amounts to comparative wealth, viewing any peasantry in Europe. On my estate at Calliaqua, forty-six acres of the richest ground are set apart for the negro gardens, where they work voluntarily in the two hours they have every noon to themselves, on the half-holiday in the week, and Sundays; and their returns are such, that in my negro village, containing eighty-five huts, there is scarcely one but has a goat and kids, two or three pigs, and some poultry running about it. All this stock is plentifully fed from the negro's garden, and how plentifully the garden supplies him will appear from the following fact. From the late Guinea sales, I have purchased all together twenty boys and girls, from ten to thirteen years old. It is the practice, on bringing

bringing them to the estate, to distribute them in the huts of Creole negroes, under their direction and care, who are to feed them, train them to work, and teach them their new language. For this care of feeding and bringing up the young African, the Creole negro receives no allowance of provisions whatever. He receives only a knife, a calabash to eat from, and an iron boiling pot for each. On first view of this it looks like oppression, and putting the burthen of supporting another on the negro who receives him; but the reverse is the fact. When the new negroes arrived on the estate, I thought the manager would have been torn to pieces by the number and earnestness of the applicants to have an inmate from among them. The competition was violent, and troublesome in the extreme. The fact is, that every negro in his garden, and at his leisure hours, earning much more than what is necessary to feed him, these young inmates are the wealth of the negro who entertains them, and for whom they work; their work finding plenty for the little household, and a surplus for sale at market, and for feeding his stock. This fact was in proof to me from the solicitations of the Creole negroes in general (and who had large families of their own) to take another inmate, on conditions of feeding him, and with a right to the benefit of his work*. As soon as the young negro has passed his apprenticeship,

* Compare this with what is said on the same subject, vol. ii. p. 154. It was impossible that two persons, writing in different islands, could agree so very precisely, unless their observations were founded in truth.

CHAP. XIII. St. Vincent.

ticeship, and is fit for work in the field, he has a hut of his own, and works a garden on his own account. Of the salt provisions given out to the negroes, the finest sort are the mackarel salted from America, and the negroes are remarkably fond of them. My brother H—— (who is a manager at once properly strict, and most kind, and who is both feared and beloved by all the negroes) indulges them by studying to give a variety in their provisions; pork, beef, and fish of different sorts. A negro prefers pork to beef; one pound of pork will go as far as two pounds of beef in his mess-pot. This little attention of Mr. H—— to the negroes' wishes, shews how much of their comfort must even depend on the master's regard to them.

Wednesday, February 22. The 66th regiment reviewed by general Cuyler. The men well-looking, the manual in proper time and exact, the firing close, and the level good. The review in a word shewed this regiment to be well disciplined, and nothing hurt by residence of near seven years in the West Indies.

Monday, March 5. Embarked in the Fairy sloop of war for Tobago. Got under way at twelve.

Tuesday, March 6. At four P. M. Tobago in sight, our course close to the wind, making for the body of the island.

Wednesday, March 7. Close in with the land, and most of the day beating to windward with a strong lee current. In the afternoon were off *Man o'war* bay.

Thursday, March 8. The wind E. S. E.

CHAP. XIII. St. Vincent. and a strong lee current against us the whole night. At day-break, we found our ship nearly where she was the preceding sun-set. In the evening we weathered St. Giles's rocks and little Tobago on the N. E. end of the island. Lay to during the night.

FRIDAY, March 9. At sun-rise, were off Queen's bay, on the leeward coast, whence we ran down, with both wind and current in our favour, and anchored in Rockly-bay about twelve o'clock.

Tobago, 1792. SATURDAY, March 10. Went to Rise-land, or Sandy Point, in the S. W. part of the island, a country almost flat, but beautifully spotted with mountain cabbages, and various trees. Trinidada, at eighteen miles distance, appearing plain to the eye.

SUNDAY, March 11. This morning early, I rode five miles across the island from Rise-land to Adventure estate, in Courland-bay division. In traversing the country, and on my return, I was much struck with its beauty, from the Flat at Sandy Point gently breaking into hills, till ultimately at the N. E. end it becomes a scene of mountains and woods. I particularly noticed the great extent of provision grounds, and the fine healthy looks of the negroes in general, arising from the plenty around them. I saw no marks of the whip on their backs, at least not here nor at St. Vincent's. The punishments are either so unfrequent or so little severe, as to leave no traces for any length of time.

SUNDAY, March 15. Early in the morning set out, and in the afternoon reached the *Louis d'or* estate.

estate. Twenty-two miles from Port Louis, from the very point of the Town of Port Louis, the country becomes hilly; and as you further advance, the hills rise into mountains not broken and rugged, as the convulsed country of St. Vincent's, but regular though steep, and on a large scale of regular ascent and descent. The scene of nature is on an extensive scale, and gives the idea of a continent rather than an island. It is not alone its vicinity to the Spanish main that suggests this idea. The appearance of the island fully warrants the assumption, and the contiguity of South America, only more fully marks its being torn therefrom, and of its being, in old times, the southern point or bold promontory of the vast bay of Mexico.

Friday, March 16. This day I rode over my estate, but previous to any remarks thereon, I must notice the radical words and language of the Indian red Charaibe (Louis). There are three families of red Charaibes, settled in a corner of my Louis-d'or estate, and their history is briefly this.—Louis was five years old when his father and family fled (about fifty years past) from the persecutions of the Africans or black Charaibes of St. Vincent's. The family has since divided into three distinct ones, by increase of numbers. Louis, the chief, is a very sensible man, and in his traffick for fish and other articles, has obtained some knowledge of the French language.

The following words I took from sound, and with accuracy; for on reading over the Charaibe

CHAP. XIII.

words to Louis, he repeated them back in French to me.

Tobago.

* God—naketi, i. e. *Grandmere*	Wind—cazabal - -	Father—baba.
The Sun—vèhu - - - -	Rain—conob - - -	Mother—behee.
Moon—mòné - - - -	Thunder—wara wiarow	Son—wica.
Earth—hoang - - - -	Mountain—weib - -	Daughter—hania.
Sea—balané - - - - -	Tree—wewee - - -	Life—nee,
Fire—wat-ho' - - - -	Bird—fuss - - - -	Death—hela 'hal.
Water—tona - - - -	Fish—oto' - - - -	Devil—qualeva.

I INTERROGATED Louis as to religion: he is now a catholic, but says the Charaibe belief was always in a future state.—Formerly, they used to bury the defunct *sitting*†, with his bow, arrows, &c. "But now," says Louis, "we bury *au long* "*et droit*, which is better; for when sitting, the "body got *retreci* (this was his expression), and "could not easily start up and fly to heaven, but "being buried *long and straight*, it can fly up di-"rectly when called." This argument was possibly suggested by the catholic missionaries, to make the poor Charaibes leave the old practice. Louis's belief in a future state is however ascertained.

BUT now to remarks on the estate. On the beach at Queen's-bay, are brick and stone pillars, not unlike the great gate of an English park, whence the eye is directed up an avenue of cocoa-nut trees, and from thence, in the same straight line, through a broad and regular street of negro houses, at a mile from the gate, to the works, which terminate the avenue, and have the appearance of a church

* I questioned particularly on the signification of the word *naketi*.

† This is a curious and remarkable illustration of what is related in the appendix to book i. vol. i. p. 147.

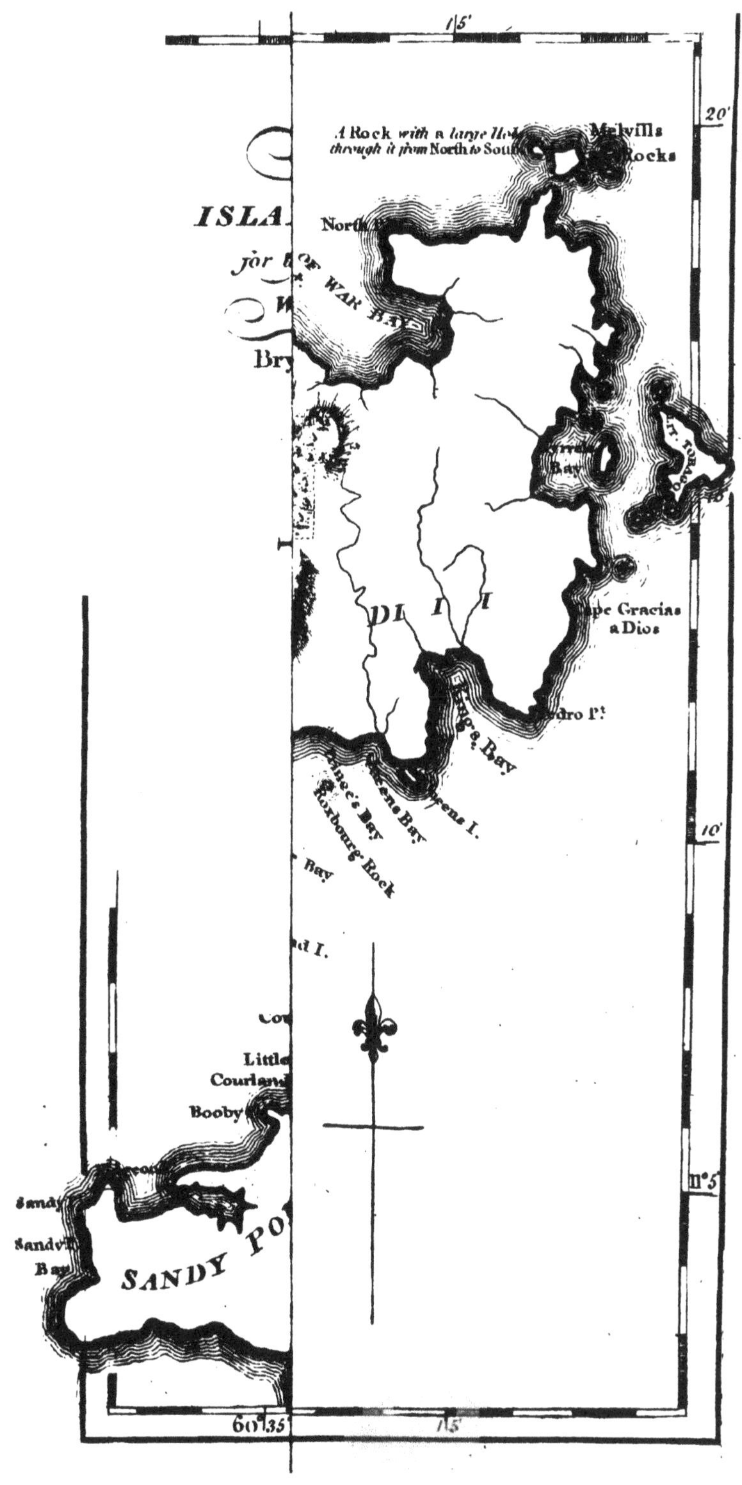

15'
20'
A Rock with a large Hole through it from North to South
Melvills Rocks
ISLA
North B
for
OF WAR BAY
Bry
St. TOBAGO
Bay
DI
ape Gracias a Dios
Pedro Pt
King's Bay
Queens I.
Prince's Bay
Roxbourg Rock
Bay
10'
d I.
Little Courland
Booby
11°5
Sandy
Bay
SANDY PO
60°35'
15'

church built in form of the letter T, with a tower raised on the centre. Over the works rise a precipice, on which stands the mansion-house, nobly commanding the whole vale. A fine river winds from the back mountains, under the point of the great ridge on which the house stands, and then pours in a direct line, nearly by the east of the negro village, into the sea. In its course it supplies a canal for turning the water-mill.

THE negroes on this estate are a most quiet and contented people; some asked me for little trifles of money for different purposes, which I gave them, but there was not one complaint, for old Castalio came to me as a kind of deputation from the rest, to tell me that "massa Hamilton was "good manager, and good massa." Indeed the negroes are generally treated as favourite children, by their masters in Tobago.

THE necessities of the island have demanded the residence of the planter; and the critical state of French government, and the wild notions and conduct of the French people in the colonies, have brought the old English settlers in Tobago, and their negroes, to a system of reciprocal regard and mutual determination to resist particular wrongs or a general attack. The planters here talk of the negroes as their resort, to be depended on against either a licentious garrison, an arbitrary governor, or the mad democracy of French hucksters.

THE negro houses throughout Tobago are much superior to those in St. Vincent's or even in Antigua,

CHAP. XIII. Tobago.

tigua. Mr. Franklyn, junior, informs me that each of his negro's houses has cost him 23 johannes, or above forty pounds sterling, including the negro's labour. These houses are built of boards, uniform throughout the estate, are about 26 feet long by 14 wide, consisting each of two apartments, besides a portico or covered walk with a seat in front, of which a closet at the end is taken from the portico to form a small kitchen or store-room. The roof is of shingles. In St. Vincent's the negro houses are of no fixed dimensions; some are very large and some very small, according to the fancy or ability of the negroes, who are however generally assisted by their masters with posts and main timbers, and occasionally supplied with boards. Thus the village is irregular, some houses boarded, some of them stone and part boards, and most of them wattled or thatched. Within, the houses are as comfortable as those at Tobago, but not so durable; and the portico of the Tobago house is a superior comfort.

SATURDAY, March 17. I passed the morning in seeing various of my negroes, particularly the women and their Creole children. This last year I have had an increase of thirteen children, of whom only one has died. I ordered, as at St. Vincent's, five yards of fine printed cotton to every woman who had reared a child, and gave ten barrels of pork among the negroes in general. Riding out, I paid a visit of some length to the red Charaibe families, of whom Louis is the head; two of the young women were really handsome.

The

The old Indian dress is lost, and they wore handkerchiefs, cotton petticoats, and jackets like the negroes. The huts were scarcely weather-tight, being wattled and thatched, crowded with all their filth and all their wealth ; the latter consisting of great variety of nets for fishing, hammocks for sleeping in, and different sorts of provision, stores, &c. &c. Beasts, stores, and people all in one room.

At two o'clock we set out for Mr. Clarke's, five miles from Louis-d'or on the road to Port Louis. Mr. Clarke's house is an excellent building, framed in England, and placed on the very pinnacle of the highest mountain in Tobago, with garden and shrubberies, abounding with birds of most splendid plumage. The variety, beauty, and number of the feathered tribes in Tobago, are indeed at once delightful and astonishing. I must observe further, on the country of Tobago, that although it is not a twentieth part cultivated, yet it is all, or for the most part, improveable. Mr. Hamilton, who has passed many successive nights in the woods, and in traversing the country, assures me there is no where a rock, or scarcely a large stone, to be found, except upon the coasts and beach. Though the season is now dry, I observed in many parts large spots or fields of Guinea grass, which would fatten cattle of the largest breed. As a timber and a victualling country, it seems valuable in an imperial, as well as commercial point of view ; a resource to armies and fleets, as well as to the merchant and planter.

WEDNESDAY,

CHAP. XIII.

Grenada, 1792.

WEDNESDAY, March 21. At 6 in the evening I embarked in the Lively schooner for Grenada.

THURSDAY, 22d. At 6 in the evening we anchored in the careenage of St. George's town, Grenada, and immediately landed.

SUNDAY, 25. In the forenoon we went to church, the governor, speaker of the assembly, officers, &c. attending, with a respectable congregation of people of all colours. In the gallery was an assemblage of girls and boys under a mulatto school-master, who sung psalms very well to the accompaniment of an excellent organ. The clergyman, Mr. Dent, read prayers, and preached with great devotion. The service was in every respect most creditable to the island. The church is plain, with a handsome steeple, and a clock given by the present governor Matthews.

ST. GEORGE'S is a handsome town, built chiefly of brick, and consists of many good houses. It is divided by a ridge, which, running into the sea, forms on one side the careenage, and on the other the bay. Thus there is the bay town, where there is a handsome square and market-place, and the careenage town, where the chief mercantile houses are situated, the ships lying land-locked, and in deep water close to the wharf. On the ridge, just above the road of communication between the towns, stands the church; and on the promontory or bluff head of the ridge, stands a large old fort, built by the Spaniards when in possession of Grenada. It is built of free-stone, is very substantially, if not scientifically constructed, and contains the

the entire 45th regiment. The 67th regiment is quartered in the new barracks, and does duty on the new fortifications of Richmond-hill; a very strong situation to the east or north-east of the town.

TUESDAY, March 27. *Louis la Granade,* chief of the Gens de couleur, and captain of a militia company, came to the government house. He seems a fine spirited, athletic fellow, and wears a large gold medal about his neck, being a gift from the colony, in reward for his various services and experienced fidelity on all occasions. The mulattoes have presented a most loyal address to the governor, stating their strong attachment to the King and the British constitution, and their abhorrence of all innovation.

FRIDAY, 29. At ten in the morning we sailed from Grenada in the Fanfan schooner, coasted the leeward side of the island from south to north; it seems well peopled, and in general it appears to be a rich sugar country; with less variety of ground indeed than St. Vincent's, and less verdure. Its mountains are but hills in comparison with those of St. Vincent. A waving surfaee, hills gently rising and falling, characterize Grenada. Deep valleys shaded with abrupt precipices characterize St. Vincent's.

St. Vincent, 1792.

SATURDAY, March 30. At three in the morning anchored in Kingston-bay, St. Vincent's, and thence rode to the villa. From Grenada to St. Vincent's, our schooner hugg'd the land of the Grenadines under their leeward side, with very small intervals of channel. The Grenadine isles

and

CHAP. XIII. St. Vincent.

and detached rocks, are supposed to be about 120 in number. Twelve of these little isles are said to produce cotton.

April 19. Had much conversation this day about the Charaibes.

The windward estates, quite to the Charaibe boundary of Bayaraw, are of the richest land in the island, but the surf on the shore is at all times so heavy, that no European vessel can continue on any part twenty-four hours with safety, and no European boat can come on shore without the danger of being swamped. Hence, until lately, the supposed impracticability of landing stores and taking off sugars, prevented the cultivation of the lands; but since the Charaibes in their canoes, have been found to accomplish what Europeans cannot effect with their boats, these lands have risen to 60*l.* sterling an acre, and every settler is growing rich. A sloop lays off and on as near as she may to the shore, and in one morning, from day-break will make forty trips to the sloop, carrying each time a hogshead of sugar, &c. &c. and the expence for the morning amounts to ten dollars, being a dollar for each Charaibe.—The Charaibes thus begin to taste of money, and are already become very industrious at this work. Moreover, they plant tobacco, and want nothing but a market to encourage them to plant more. Chatoyer's brother (Du Vallee) has nine negroes, and plants cotton. Money civilizes in the first instance, as it corrupts in the last; the savage labouring for himself, soon ceases to be a savage; to noon, a canoe manned by ten Charaibes; the

the slave to money becomes a subject to government, and he becomes a useful subject*.

Mr. B. acting collector of the customs, informed me, that the value of British manufactures exported from St. Vincent to the Spanish and French settlements, was upwards of 200,000*l.* annually. From the superior advantages of Grenada, with respect to situation, &c. the export trade of that island to the Spanish main must be much more considerable. That of Jamaica out of comparison greater. These circumstances are to be taken into the general account, of the importance of the West India Islands to Great Britain.

April 24. Went on board a Guinea ship, the Active, from Sierra Leone. On board this ship is a black boy, called Bunc, about ten years old, the

* This must be admitted with some limitation. Before a negro places such a value on money as is here supposed, he must have acquired many of the refinements and artificial necessities of civilized life. He must have found uses for money, which in his savage state, he had no conception of. It is not therefore the possession of money alone; it is the new desires springing up in his mind, from the prospects and examples before him, that have awakened his powers, and called the energies of his mind into action. I have thought it necessary to observe thus much, because the doctrine of my amiable friend, without some qualification, seems to sanctify an assertion which has been maintained by speculative writers, with some plausibility; namely, "that if the negro slaves were allowed wages for their "labour, coercion would become unnecessary." What effect a system of gradual encouragement, by means of wages, operating slowly and progressively, might produce in a long course of time, I will not presume to say; but I am persuaded that an attempt to introduce such a system among the labouring negroes in general, without great caution and due preparation, would be productive of the greatest of evils.

CHAP. XIII. St. Vincent.

the son of an African chief; he is going to England for his education, and has two slaves sent with him by his father, to pay his passage by their sale. Captain Williams has another boy on board, who was sent to England two years ago for the same purpose. This voyage he was to take him back to Annamaboe; but the boy absolutely refused landing again in Africa, and he waits on Captain Williams as a free servant, and is going back to England with him. The slaves were in high health; captain Williams is a superior man in this trade; as a fundamental trait of his character, I notice, that last year (1791) on receiving the parliamentary bounty for the good condition in which his people arrived, he gave out of his own pocket 50*l.* as a gratuity to the surgeon of his ship.

MONDAY, April 30. This day Dufond, Chatoyer's brother, and next to him in authority, particularly on the Grand Sable side of the country, made me a visit; he had been twice before when I was absent in the other islands, and on his first visit had left his own bow and arrows for me. I gave him in return a pair of handsome brass-barrelled pistols. He seems a very polite and sensible man, and speaks good French.

MAY 8. Embarked on board the Delaford, and at 5 P. M. sailed for England.

HISTORY OF THE WEST INDIES,

&c. &c.

HISTORICAL ACOOUNT

OF THE

CONSTITUTION OF JAMAICA.

JAMAICA*.

CHAP. XIV.

CHAP. XIV.

It does not appear that there was any form of civil government established in the island of Jamaica before the Restoration; when Colonel D'Oyley, who had then the chief command under a commission from the lord Protector, was confirmed in that command by a commission from King Charles, dated the 13th of February, 1661.

His commission, which recites the king's desire to give all protection and encouragement to the people of Jamaica, and to provide for its security and good government, empowers him to execute his trust according to such powers and authorities as are contained in his commission and the instructions annexed to it, and such as should from time to time be given to him by his majesty, and according

* In the former editions, this account of the constitution of Jamaica was ascribed to Governor (now Lord) Lyttelton, who was Captain General of that island in 1764, but I have since had reason to believe it was an official paper drawn up by some person in the plantation office in Great Britain, and transmitted to the Governor for his information. That it came last from the Governor's office, is a fact within my own knowledge; but Lord Lyttelton having assured me that he has no recollection of its contents, I feel myself bound to apprise my readers of the circumstance. As there can be no possible doubt concerning the authenticity of the documents annexed to it, the question by whom the introductory part was prepared is of little importance in itself, but justice towards Lord Lyttleton, and regard to truth, require me to give this explanation.

CHAP. XIV. cording to such good, just, and reasonable customs and constitutions as were exercised and settled in other colonies; or such other as should, upon mature advice and consideration, be held necessary and proper for the good government and security of the island, provided they were not repugnant to the laws of England.

It further empowers him to take unto him a council of twelve persons, *to be elected by the people* according to the manner prescribed in the instructions; and, by the advice of any five or more of them, to constitute civil judicatories, with power to administer oaths; to command all the military forces in the island, and put in force and execute martial law; to grant commissions, with the advice of his council, for the finding out new trades; and to do and perform all other orders which might conduce to the good of the island. The instructions consist of fifteen articles:

The first directs the commission to be published, and the king proclaimed.

The third regulates the manner of electing the council, eleven of which to be chosen indifferently, by as many of the officers of the army, planters, and inhabitants, as could be conveniently admitted to such election, either at one or more places; which said persons, with the secretary of the island, who was thereby appointed always to be one, were established a council, to advise and assist the governor in the execution of his trust, and five were to be a quorum.

The fourth and fifth articles direct the taking the

the oaths, and settling judicatories for the civil affairs and affairs of the admiralty, for the peace of the island, and determining controversies. CHAP. XIV.

The sixth directs the governor to discountenance vice and debauchery, and to encourage ministers, that Christianity and the protestant religion, according to the church of England, might have due reverence and exercise amongst them.

The seventh directs the fortifications at Cagway to be completed, and empowers him to compel, not only soldiers, but planters, to work by turns.

The eighth directs him to encourage the planters, and to assure them of his majesty's protection: and, by the ninth, he is to cause an accurate survey to be made of the island.

By the tenth it is directed, that the secretary shall keep a register of all plantations, and the bounds thereof; and that all persons shall be obliged to plant a proportionable part thereof within a limited time.

The eleventh and twelfth direct all encouragements to be given to such negroes and others as shall submit to the government, and to merchants and such as shall bring any trade there, and forbid monopolizing.

The thirteenth directs, that any vessel which can be spared from the defence of the island, shall be employed in fetching settlers from any other colonies, and that no soldiers be allowed to depart without licence.

The fourteenth relates to the keeping of the stores and provisions sent to the island: and the

CHAP. XIV. fifteenth directs the governor to transmit, from time to time, a state of the island, and all his proceedings.

In 1662, Lord Windsor was appointed governor of Jamaica, by commission under the great seal; which, besides containing the same powers as those contained in Col. D'Oyley's commission, directs, that, in case of Lord Windsor's dying or leaving the island, the government shall devolve on the council, or any seven of them, and appoints a salary of two thousand pounds *per annum* payable out of the exchequer.

His instructions consist of twenty-two articles. The first directs the publication of his commission: and the second, the appointment of the council, according to his commission and the instructions. But it must be observed upon this article, that no directions whatever are given, either in the commission which refers to the instructions, or the instructions themselves, as to the mode in which the council shall be appointed; BUT IT APPEARS THAT THE GOVERNOR NAMED THEM HIMSELF.

The third, fourth, fifth, sixth, and seventh articles relate to the administering oaths, establishing judicatures, and providing for the security of the adjacent isles.

The eighth directs encouragement to be given to planters to remove to Jamaica from the other colonies.

The ninth directs 100,000 acres of land to be

set apart in each of the four quarters of the island as a royal demesne, a survey to be made, and a register kept of all grants, and a militia formed.

The tenth directs the planters to be encouraged, their lands confirmed unto them by grants under the great seal, and appoints 50,000 acres of land to the governor for his own use.

The eleventh relates to the encouragement of an orthodox ministry: and the twelfth establishes a duty of five *per cent.* upon all exports after the expiration of seven years.

The thirteenth, fourteenth, fifteenth, and sixteenth articles contain general directions as to the liberty and freedom of trade (except with the Spaniards), assistance to the neighbouring plantations, and the security of the island, by obliging planters to reside in bodies together, and in contiguous buildings.

The seventeenth directs, that, as an encouragement to men of ability to go to the island, no offices shall be held by deputy; and gives a power to the governor of suspension or removal, in case of bad behaviour.

The nineteenth empowers the governor to grant royalties and manors, or lordships, to contain less than five hundred acres.

The twentieth empowers the governor, with advice of the council, to call assemblies, to make laws, and, upon imminent necessity, to levy money; such laws to be in force two years, and no longer, unless approved of by the crown.

CHAP. XIV.

See the Proclamation of the 14th of December, 1661, upon which the people of Jamaica have upon any occasion laid so much stress.

THIS proclamation was published by Lord Windsor upon his arrival; but nothing else material arises out of his short administration worth notice, for he staid but two months, and left the island, and the execution of his commission, to Sir Charles Lyttelton, who had been appointed lieutenant-governor; and who governed with the advice of a council of twelve, appointed by himself, and called an assembly, that made a body of laws, amongst which was one for raising a revenue.

Nothing, however, which appears to be material, as to the form of the constitution, occurred during his administration, which continued about twenty months; when he was superseded by the arrival of Sir Thomas Modyford, who was appointed governor in chief by a commission under the great seal, which empowered him either to constitute, by his own authority, a privy-council of twelve persons, or to continue the old one, and to alter, change, or augment it as he thought proper; to create judicatories; and make laws, orders, and constitutions, provided they did not extend to take away any right or freehold, or the interest of any person in their rights or freeholds, goods or chattels, and that they were transmitted to his majesty for allowance or disapprobation.

He was further empowered to command and discipline all military forces, to use martial law upon

upon persons im military service, and establish articles of war; to create courts of admiralty, according to such authority as he should receive from the lord high admiral; to erect forts and fortifications; to establish ports, cities, towns, boroughs, and villages; to create manors and lordships; to grant charters to hold fairs; to take surveys, and keep records of all grants of lands, under such moderate quit-rents, services, and acknowledgments, as he should think fit; and to prescribe terms of cultivation; and grants so made under the seal, and enrolled, were to be good and valid against the crown; to grant commissions for finding out new trades; to pardon all offences, except murder and treason, and in those cases to reprieve for twelve months.

He was also empowered, with the advice of the majority of council, to frame a method for establishing general assemblies, and from time to time to call such assemblies together, and with their consent to pass all manner of laws, reserving to him a negative voice; as also, upon imminent occasions, to levy money. These laws not to extend to taking away any one's freehold, or to the loss of a member, and to be in force only two years, unless approved and confirmed by the crown.

This commission appoints a salary to the governor of one thousand pounds per annum, payable out of the exchequer.

The instructions, which consist of twenty articles, relate to the encouragement to be given to planters to come from the other colonies; to the allowance settled upon himself and the other officers;

CHAP. XIV. ficers; and extend to most of the points contained in Lord Windsor's instructions; but direct, that the measure of setting out the 400,000 acres, as a royal demesne, shall be suspended; that no duties shall be laid in the island upon the import or export of any goods for twenty-one years, nor shall any duty be laid here upon the produce of Jamaica for five years.

By these instructions it appears, that the crown allowed two thousand five hundred pounds *per annum* for the support of government; and what was wanted, over and above, was to be made good by a duty on strong liquors, either made or imported, to be levied by the authority of the governor and council.

In July, 1664, Sir Thomas Modyford issued writs for electing two assembly-men for each parish; which assembly met in October following.

It does not appear that this assembly sat above a month or two before they were dissolved; but, during their session, they passed a body of laws, which was transmitted to the lord chancellor, to be laid before the crown; but, not being confirmed, they would have expired at the end of two years; but (as I find it asserted by Lord Vaughan) the governor continued them in force to the end of his administration, by an order of council. I cannot, however, find this order upon record, but after that time a great many ordinances of the governor and council, in the nature and form of laws; in some of which it was declared, that they shall continue in force until another

another assembly was called, and then to be confirmed, altered, or repealed, as that assembly should see convenient: but no other assembly was called during Sir Thomas Modyford's administration. CHAP. XIV.

In 1670, Sir Thomas Modyford was recalled, and Sir Thomas Lynch appointed lieutenant-governor and commander in chief, with the same powers as Sir Thomas Modyford had.

On the 1st of December, 1671, he issued writs for calling an assembly, to consist of two persons for each parish; which met on the 8th of January, and sat till June following, when the governor dissolved them, after having passed a body of laws, which were transmitted to England, but were not confirmed.

In May, 1673, Sir Thomas Lynch called another assembly; but upon their refusing to grant money for the fortifications, he dissolved it after sitting only a few days; and, in January following, upon consideration that two years were almost expired since making the body of laws, and that his majesty had not been pleased to signify his royal consent to them, a new assembly was called, which met the 18th of February, and, on the 14th of March, a new body of laws was passed, which were transmitted to England; but, not being confirmed by the crown, expired at the end of two years.

On the 3d of December, 1674, Lord Vaughan was appointed governor of Jamaica. A council, consisting

CHAP. XIV. consisting of twelve persons, was named in the commission, with power to him to expel or suspend any of them, and, in case of vacancies, to fill up the council to nine. He was also empowered to call assemblies, according to the usage of the island; and, with the council and assembly, to pass laws, which laws were to be in force for two years, unless the crown's pleasure was in the mean time signified to the contrary, and no longer, except they were approved and confirmed within that time. In the passing of these laws, the governor was to have a negative voice, and to dissolve any assembly, as he should think proper.

Upon Lord Vaughan's arrival in his government, he called an assembly, which met on the 26th of April, 1675, and passed a new body of laws.

It does not appear when this assembly was dissolved; but in March, 1676-7, writs were issued for a new assembly, which met on the 26th of that month; and, having passed several other laws, they were dissolved on the 26th of July: and the laws passed by both assemblies having been transmitted to England, the council took them into their consideration, and, after frequent deliberations upon them, and many alterations proposed, they were referred, with the council's observations upon them, to the attorney-general to consider thereof, and to form a new body of laws for the good government of this island.

With these laws, the council took into consideration

deration the state and constitution of Jamaica, and made the reports upon it hereunto annexed, *vide Documents, No.* 1, 2. CHAP. XIV.

THESE reports having been confirmed, a commission passed the great seal, constituting Lord Carlisle governor of Jamaica, by which, and by the instructions annexed thereto, *vide No.* 3, 4, the form of government proposed in the council's report was adopted and established.

UPON Lord Carlisle's arrival in his government, he found the people very much dissatisfied with and averse to this new form of government, as will better appear by his letters, *vide No.* 5, 6, 7, 8, 9, 10.

THESE letters and papers being taken into consideration by the council, as also a report thereon by the committee, the council, on the 4th of April, 1679, made the order *No.* 11; and, on the 28th of May following, the annexed report *No.* 12, was presented to his majesty, and, being approved, was transmitted to the Earl of Carlisle, with the annexed letter, *No.* 13.

UPON receipt of these papers, the Lord Carlisle communicated them to the assembly, who presented an address in answer to the report of the 28th of May; which address was transmitted to the council by Lord Carlisle. *Vide No.* 14, 15, 16, 17, 18, 19, 20.

ON the 5th of March, 1679-80, the council took into consideration the letters received from the Earl of Carlisle; and the annexed extracts (*No* 21 *to* 38 *inclusive*) of their proceedings, will shew

CHAP. XIV. shew their several resolutions and directions in consequence thereof.

It is impossible, at this distance of time, to judge what motives could have induced the council, after they had shewn so much firmness and resolution to support the rights of the crown, by establishing in Jamaica the Irish constitution, to give the point up, as it appears they did by the annexed explanatory commission to Lord Carlisle, *No.* 39, which contains the same power of making laws in assembly as is now given to the governor of Jamaica, and which, from that time, has been minutely the same; excepting only, that, in 1716, the governor was directed, by instructions, not to pass any laws that should repeal a law confirmed by the crown, without a clause of suspension, or first transmitting the draft of a bill; and, in 1734, this limitation was extended to all laws for repealing others, though such repealed law should not have been confirmed by the crown *(b)*.

(b) Neither of these orders are enforced, except in the case of private bills, the assembly having constantly refused to admit suspending clauses in any publick act, and the crown has long since given up the point. E.

DOCUMENTS

ANNEXED TO THE

HISTORICAL ACCOUNT.

NUMBER I.

The Right honourable the Lords of the Committee for Trade and Plantations having this day presented to the Board the ensuing Report; viz.

MAY IT PLEASE YOUR MAJESTY,

APPENDIX.

We having, according to the trust reposed in us in reference to your majesty's plantations, taken in consideration the present state and government of the island of Jamaica, particularly such matters as, from the nature of affairs as they now stand there, we have judged necessary to be recommended to the Right honourable the Earl of Carlisle, whom your majesty has been pleased to nominate and constitute governor of the said island; and having, after several meetings, agreed upon the following particulars, we most humbly crave leave to lay them before your majesty, for your royal determination.

The first point that did occur most worthy to be considered by us was, the power and manner of enacting laws for the civil, military, and ecclesiastical government; and upon taking a view of what has been practised since your majesty's happy restoration in the legislative, we find, that the methods and authorities for the framing and ordaining the said laws have been only such as were directed by your royal commission unto your majesty's several governors, or prescribed by the instructions given them from time to time; and that as the constitution and exigency of affairs have often changed, so your majesty has

CHAP. XIV.

has thought fit variously to adapt your royal orders thereunto; and, by the last commission, given unto the Lord Vaughan, your majesty was pleased to empower his lordship, with the advice of your majesty's council, from time to time to summon general assemblies of freeholders, who have authority, with the advice and consent of the governor and council, to make and ordain laws for the government of the island; which laws are to be in force for the space of two years, except in the mean time your majesty's pleasure be signified to the contrary, and no longer, unless they be confirmed by your majesty within that time. Having, therefore, directed our thoughts towards the consequences and effects which have been produced, or may arise, from this authority derived unto the said freeholders and planters, which we observe to have received a daily increase by the resolutions they have taken, less agreeable to your majesty's intention, we do most humbly offer our opinions, that the laws transmitted by the Lord Vaughan, which are now under consideration in order to be enacted by your majesty, may be intrusted in the hands of the Earl of Carlisle, who, upon his arrival in the island, may offer them unto the next assembly, that they may be consented unto as laws originally coming from your majesty; and that, for the future, no legislative assembly be called without your majesty's special directions; but that, upon emergencies, the governor do acquaint your majesty by letters with the necessity of calling such an assembly, and pray your majesty's consent and directions for their meeting; and, at the same time, do present unto your majesty a scheme of such acts as he shall think fit and necessary, that your majesty may take the same into consideration, and return them in the form wherein your majesty shall think fit that they be enacted; that the governor, upon receipt of your majesty's commands, shall then summon an assembly, and propose the said laws for their consent, so that the same method in legislative matters be made use of in Jamaica as in Ireland, according to the form prescribed by Poyning's's law; and that, therefore, the present style of enacting laws,

laws, *By the governor, council, and representatives of the commons assembled,* be converted into the style of, *Be it enacted by the king's most excellent majesty, by and with the consent of the general assembly.*

We are further of opinion, that no escheats, fines, forfeitures, or penalties be mentioned in the said laws to be applied to the publick use of the island; and that your majesty do instruct your governor to dispose thereof for the support of the government. It is also our opinion, that in all laws for levying of money, and raising a publick revenue, the clauses whereby the said levies are appropriated unto the publick use of the island, without any mention made of your majesty, or unto your majesty for the said publick use, are so far derogatory to your majesty's right of sovereignty, that they ought to be, for the future, altered and made agreeable to the style of England.

We do likewise offer it unto your majesty as necessary, that no minister be received in Jamaica without licence from the Right reverend the lord bishop of London; and that none having his lordship's licence be rejected, without sufficient cause alleged; as also, that in the direction of all church affairs, the ministers be admitted into the respective vestries.

And whereas it has upon some occasions proved inconvenient, that the members of the council have been constituted by your majesty's commission; we are of opinion, that, for the future, they be only named in the instructions of the governor; for the strengthening of whose authority under your majesty we do offer, that he may have power to suspend any of the said members, if he see just cause, without receiving the advice and consent of the council; and also, that none of the said so suspended, or by your majesty's order displaced, from that trust, may be permitted to be received into the general assembly.

And whereas nothing can contribute more to the welfare of your majesty's island, than that all means be found out for the increase

CHAP. XIV.

increase of trade; we do offer, for the encouragement thereof, that a mint be allowed in Jamaica, in such manner that no prejudice do arise unto your majesty's other dominions, or that what bullion is brought from thence may be coined here in England; provided that all such coins may bear your majesty's royal superscription, and not be imposed in payment elsewhere.

All which, &c.

FINCH,
DANBY,
WORCESTER,
ESSEX,
FAUCONBERRY,
CRAVEN,
H. COVENTRY.
Tho. Dolman.

His majesty, taking the same in consideration, was pleased to approve thereof; and did order, that the Right honourable Mr. Secretary Coventry do prepare a commission and instructions for his majesty's royal signature, for the Earl of Carlisle, according to the tenor of the said report.

NUMBER II.

At the Court at Whitehall, the 15th of February, 1677-8.

PRESENT, the King's Most Excellent Majesty in Council.

Upon reading at the board, a report from the Right honourable the Lords of the Committee for Trade and Plantations, in the words following:

May it please your Majesty,

HAVING received, on the 12th of January last past, from the Right honourable Mr. Secretary Coventry, a draft of a commission and instructions for the Earl of Carlisle, whom your majesty has appointed to be your governor of Jamaica; and having, after

after several additions and alterations, remitted the same unto Mr. Secretary Coventry, on the 2d inst. we crave leave to offer to your majesty the most material points which did occur unto us upon perusal of the said draft; which are as followeth:

1st. As we are of opinion that all members of council in Jamaica may, for the more easy passing of laws, be admitted into the assembly, if duly elected by the freeholders; so we cannot but advise your majesty, that as well the members of the said council suspended by your majesty's governor, as the members displaced by your majesty, may be rendered incapable during such suspension of being admitted into the assembly.

2d. That although your majesty has, by an order of the 16th of November last past, thought fit that no assembly be called without your majesty's especial leave and directions; we think it very important, for your majesty's service and safety of the island, that in case of invasion, rebellion, or some other very urgent necessity, your majesty's governor may have power, with the consent of the assembly, to pass acts for raising of money, to answer the occasions arising by such urgent necessities.

3d. That whereas hitherto, within your majesty's island of Jamaica, the oaths of allegiance and supremacy have not been imposed on persons that bear any part of the government, except the members and officers of the council, and all judges and justices; so, for the prevention of future inconveniences, and greater assurance of loyalty towards your majesty, we are humbly of opinion, that all persons elected into the assembly shall, before their sitting, take the oaths of allegiance and supremacy, which your majesty's governor shall commissionate fit persons, under the seal of the island, to administer unto them, and that, without taking the said oaths, none shall be capable of sitting, although elected.

We have likewise, pursuant to your majesty's orders, prepared a body of laws, such as the Right honourable the Earl of Carlisle may be empowered to carry with him, and to offer

unto

CHAP. XIV.

unto the assembly of Jamaica for their consent. Whereas we do not find, since your majesty's happy restoration, that any laws transmitted from your majesty's plantations have been confirmed by your majesty, either under the great seal of England, or any other signification of your majesty's pleasure (the act of four and a half *per cent.* in the Caribbee islands only excepted, which was confirmed by the order of council), and the intended method of enacting laws in Jamaica hath not as yet been put in practice; we humbly crave your majesty's royal determination, whether the said laws shall pass only by order of your majesty in council, or under the great seal of England, that we may accordingly be enabled fitly to present them unto your royal view.

All which, &c.

His majesty was pleased to order, that Mr. Secretary Coventry do prepare Lord Carlisle's commission and instructions concerning these matters accordingly; and as for the laws of the said island, his majesty by an order of the board, hath been pleased this day to declare his pleasure, that they shall pass under the great seal of England.

NUMBER III.

Extract of King Charles the Second's Commission to the Earl of Carlisle.

AND we do hereby give and grant unto you, with the advice and consent of the said council, full power and authority, from time to time, as need shall require, to summon or call general assemblies of the freeholders and planters within the said island, and other the territories under your government, in such manner and form as hath been formerly practised and used in the said island of Jamaica.

And our will and pleasure is, that the persons thereupon duly elected, and having before their sitting taken the oaths of allegiance and supremacy, (which you shall commissionate fit

fit persons, under the seal of our island, to administer, and without taking which none shall be capable of sitting, though elected) shall be called and held the general assembly of the said island of Jamaica, and other the territories thereon depending; and shall have full power and authority to agree and consent unto all such statutes and ordinances for the publick peace, welfare, and good government of the said island, and other the territories thereon depending, and the people and inhabitants thereof, and such others as shall resort thereunto, and for the benefit of our heirs and successors, as having been by you, with advice and consent of the said council, framed and transmitted unto us, in order to be here enacted, by our giving our consent thereunto, shall be by us approved and remitted unto you under our great seal of England; which said statutes, laws, and ordinances, are to be by you framed as near as conveniently may be to the laws and statutes of our kingdom of England.

And we do hereby, nevertheless, authorize and empower you, in case of invasion, rebellion, or some very great necessity, to pass an act or acts, by and with the consent of the general assembly, without transmitting the same first to us, to raise money within the said island, and the territories within your government, to answer the occasions arising by such urgent necessities.

And we give you likewise full power, from time to time, as you shall judge it necessary, to dissolve all general assemblies, as aforesaid.

NUMBER IV.

Extract of King Charles the Second's Instructions to the Earl of Carlisle.

AND whereas by our commission we have directed that, for the future, no general assembly be called without our special directions; but that, upon occasion, you do acquaint us by letter with the necessity of calling such an assembly, and

CHAP. XIV.

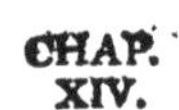

pray our consent and directions for their meeting; you shall, at the same time, transmit unto us, with the advice and consent of the council, a draft of such acts as you shall think fit and necessary to be passed, that we may take the same into our consideration, and return them in the form we shall think fit to be enacted: in and upon the receipt of our commands, you shall then summon an assembly, and propose the said laws for their consent.

And accordingly we have ordered to be delivered unto you herewith, a certain body of laws, for the use of our said island, framed in pursuance of other laws transmitted unto us by former governors, with such alterations and amendments as we have thought fit, with the advice of our privy-council here; which, upon your arrival in our said island, you shall offer unto the next assembly, that they may be consented to and enacted as laws originally coming from us.

We are willing, nevertheless, that in case of invasion, rebellion, or some very urgent necessity, you pass an act or acts, with the consent of the general assembly, without transmitting the same first unto us, to raise money within the said island, and the territories depending thereon, to answer the occasions arising by such urgent necessities.

And you shall take care that the present style of enacting laws, *By the governor, council, and representatives of the commons assembled*, be converted into the style of, *Be it enacted by the king's most excellent majesty, by and with the consent of the general assembly*.

NUMBER V.

Extract of a Letter from the Earl of Carlisle to Mr. Secretary Coventry.

I HAVE spoken with several of the council, and find some of them much dissatisfied at the alterations in the laws and manner of passing them, particularly at the latter part of the clause in the militia bill: "but that in all things he may, "upon

"upon all occasions or emergencies, act as captain-general "and governor in chief, according to and in pursuance of all "the powers and authorities given unto him by his majesty's "commission; any thing in this case, or any other, to the "contrary in anywise notwithstanding;" which they are jealous of, lest that thereby they shall make it legal to execute all instructions that either are or shall be sent to me, or any other succeeding governor; which scruple might easily be avoided, but that the great seal being affixed to the laws, I have no power to make alteration, which I might have done both to their satisfaction and the preservation of the king's rights. The act for the revenue, too, I fear will not without difficulty pass; but I shall endeavour all I can to bring them to pass, for which I have greater inducements than my being here, without any hopes from the present state of the treasury, which is exhausted and in debt for their new fortifications.

NUMBER VI.

Copy of a Letter to Mr. Secretary Coventry from the Earl of Carlisle.

St. Jago, 11th September, 1678.

Sir,

THE assembly met on the 2d instant, and, I find, are so dissatisfied with the alteration of the government, that I question whether they will pass any of these laws: they have objections against several of them; as the act for the revenue that is perpetual, and may be diverted; they are nettled at the expression in the preamble, that the revenue was raised by the governor and council; and though they cannot deny it to be truth, yet they say that council was elected by the people, and, though continued under the name of a council, yet was in effect an assembly of representatives of the people.

I have given into their hands a copy of that act and fourteen more, and gave them liberty to compare them with the original. The act of militia and some others I keep by me, till

CHAP. XIV.

I see what they will do with those they have. All the acts are not yet transcribed; for but one man can write at a time, and they are bulky; but I have enough to keep them employed. The speaker came to me on Saturday, to desire liberty to adjourn for a few days, which I consented to, and they adjourned till Thursday morning. Lieut. Col. Beeston is speaker, who I recommended to them upon Sir H. Morgan's assurances that he would behave himself well. He hath the general repute of an honest and discreet gentleman, though he signed the order about the privateer, at which so much offence was taken; but I am satisfied he was no further faulty, than in complying with the directions of the assembly: and I the rather proposed him (whom they had a mind to choose) to gain the point quietly of recommending, which my Lord Vaughan, I am told, neglected to do.

The assembly appointed a committee to compare these laws with their former: it is said they differ in many things, especially from those laws last sent from Lord Vaughan, which are most usefully framed for their present benefit.

Popular discourses here as well as in England; and I find a few men's notions have taken such place with the leading men of the assembly, that they rather set themselves to frame arguments against the present constitution, than to accommodate things under it. I cannot yet tell you what course I shall take to remove this difficulty; but I will do the best I can. I find one of the council more faulty in this than any man in the island, but am unwilling to name him till I have tried the utmost to reclaim him.

Whilst we are here busy about small matters, I doubt your hands are full of greater, and may therefore forget us. We hear the French and Dutch are agreed.

I am, Sir,

Your most humble servant,

CARLISLE.

NUMBER VII.

Extract of a Letter from the Earl of Carlisle to the Committee, 24th October, 1678.

My Lords,

I HAVE met with the difficulties here I foresaw, but could neither avoid nor prevent, in England. The general assembly meeting on the 2d of September last, I recommended and sent to them the several bills I brought over under the great seal of England, for their consent to be enacted; but being much dissatisfied at the new frame of government, and their losing their deliberative part of power in altering and amending laws, they would not pass any one of them, but threw them all out; but prepared an address, with a bill of impost upon wines and other strong liquors for one year, without giving me notice thereof, in such terms and form as was not fit for me to pass it: but afterwards changing the style of enacting, as directed in my instructions, with some other amendments to this bill, the public necessities of the island, having contracted many debts from new fortifications and salaries already due, requiring it, I gave the royal assent; and then, on the 12th this instant October, I dissolved them. My earnest suit to all your lordships is, that you'll please to have me in your thoughts, and the present state of this colony under your lordships consideration, for some expedient which may be elucidatory to the power given me by my commission and instructions, which may quiet the minds of persons generally dissatisfied in this island, which is most certainly under the greatest hopes of improvement of all the islands in the West Indies, and therefore most fit for to be encouraged, with the king's countenance and support, with good and acceptable laws.

What bills I shall send to Mr. Secretary Coventry, I pray may be dispatched speedily when brought before your lordships and received; an order to be passed through all offices without delay, being in part of what is so very much wanting towards the support of the good government of this island.

NUMBER VIII.

Copy of a Letter from the Earl of Carlisle to the Committee.

My Lords,

A FORTNIGHT ago I gave you an account upon what terms I had parted with the assembly. I have since thoroughly considered of what might in this place most conduce to his majesty's service, and could not think of any better expedient than to send the bearer, Mr. Atkinson, to wait upon your lordships. He was Secretary to Sir Thomas Lynch and my Lord Vaughan, and has been enough acquainted with all my proceedings since my arrival, so as perfectly able to satisfy your lordships in any thing you may desire to know concerning the place, and to lay before you all the several interests of his majesty relating to it.

My lords, I find that the present form appointed for the making and passing of laws, considering the distance of the place, is very impracticable, besides very distasteful to the sense of the people here, as you may observe by the assembly's address to me; and if your lordships will please to move his majesty to send me a general instruction to call another assembly, and to re-enact and make what laws are fit for this place, I could then order the matter to conclude effectually to his majesty's service. I have, by Mr. Atkinson, sent you the drafts of such bills as are the most fundamental, and chiefly concern his majesty's interest; and I do assure you, that I will not in any material point vary from them. He will, when your lordships order him to attend you, lay them all before you, and, I believe, give your lordships such thorough satisfaction, that you will rest assured that what I desire is for his majesty's service, and that I shall be enough enabled by it to settle every thing upon so good a foundation, that neither his majesty nor your lordships will ever repent of having made any deference to my opinion: in it, my lords, much success depends upon the dispatch, and of the circumstances Mr. Atkinson

Atkinson will give you an account. His business is wholly to attend your lordships, and, I believe, he will always be in the way. He has prayed me to intercede with your lordships, to excuse what errors he may commit, as having been a West Indian for these eight years past, and do on his behalf beg that favour of your lordships; but hope that he will prove so discreet, as to give your lordships no manner of offence. I thought it the readiest and best way to have all things rightly understood, and do hope that issue will be produced from it.

I am, your Lordships' most

humble, and obedient servant,

CARLISLE

St. Jago de la Vega, Nov. 15, 1678.

NUMBER IX.

Extract of a Letter from the Earl of Carlisle to Mr. Secretary Coventry.

ON the 2d of September last, the general assembly met; but under so much dissatisfaction from the new frame of government, and their losing their deliberative part of power, in framing, altering, and amending laws, that they spent near a fortnight very uneasily about some of the laws, and would have begun with the bill of revenue to have thrown that out first, as a mark of their disallowing the new method of government, being so highly incensed that they were near questioning the king's power and authority to do it: insomuch, that I, taking the maintenance thereof to be in my charge, and finding some of the council equally disgusted at the change of government, and foreseeing that it was like to encourage discontent in the assembly, to take them off, and leave the assembly upon their humour by themselves, I thought it absolutely necessary to put this question to each of the counsellors, in these words: "Do you submit and consent to this present "form of government which his majesty hath been pleased to "order for this island of Jamaica?" To which the chief-justice,

CHAP. XIV.

justice, Col. Long, refused to answer, with two more, Col. Charles Whitfield and Col. Thomas Freeman. The chief-justice, being a man of very great influence upon the assembly, I presently suspended, and gave the other two (less dangerous) till morning to consider on it: and then the chief-justice sent to me his submission under his hand, and Col. Freeman submitted; but Col. Charles Whitfield, otherwise a very good man, went away into the country.

The assembly received and examined all the laws I brought over, and drew up their reasons against passing them; of each, many were very frivolous, and the best was, because they were not compared with and amended by the last laws of my Lord Vaughan's, now with you, and received some two days before my coming away, the fleet then staying in the downs, and my departure much pressed upon the expectation of war. These reasons against the revenue bill I answered individually; but no means or endeavours either I myself, the council, or both could use, would prevail with them to pass any one of them; and I look upon this to be their chief reason, that by not passing them they might the better shew their dislike of that new way of government; though they urge this for their enjoying a power of altering and amending laws, the necessity of changing them as often as occasions do require, and the distance from this place is so great, that before the king's approbation can be obtained to a law, and returned hither, it may be fit for the public good either to lay that law aside, or much to change and alter it; and, indeed, in this part of the objection I think they are in the right, for that they will want temporary laws till the colony be better grown: and, upon thorough consideration of the whole matter in this part, I am of opinion it is very advisable and requisite that there should be leave and power from the king to make laws (not relating to his majesty's power or prerogative) to endure for some term till his royal approbation may be had therein; and of this I do earnestly entreat your care.

Having used all methods possible with the several members apart, and jointly with the body of the assembly, for the passing the

the laws, I was, after many conferences and debates, and several adjournments, frustrated, and they threw them all out. Afterwards, in a full body, by the speaker they gave me the inclosed address, and presented to me a bill for a publick impost, prepared, without giving me notice thereof, in such terms and forms as was not fit for me to pass it in; but at last in some part consented to such amendments as I and the council thought fit, changing the style of enacting as directed in my instructions, but restraining it to one year, from a fear that if they should have made it perpetual, they should be assembled no more, but be governed by governor and council as they were in Col. D'Oyley's time, when they enacted laws, not only for the revenue but other occasions, by governor and council, and some part of Sir Charles Lyttleton's time, as appears by our council-book upon the place; and Sir Thomas Modyford had an instruction to continue this revenue by order of governor and council, the assembly in his life-time passing it perpetual; and in Sir Thomas Lynch's time the assembly made it perpetual, but, for want of the king's consent, they both are fallen; but now, the assembly say, they are of a better understanding than to give the reins out of their own hands.

To this bill, the island's affairs being under great pressures from publick debts contracted for the new fortifications and salaries already due, I gave the royal assent; and then, being the 12th instant, I dissolved them.

Which having done, and not being satisfied with the behaviour of the assembly in their proceedings in relation to the government I stood charged with, most of them being in military trusts, I put this question to each of them: "Do you "submit to this form of government which his majesty hath "been pleased to order for this island of Jamaica?" to which several of them neither gave me a dutiful nor cheerful answer; some did, and at this some are much dissatisfied.

CHAP. XIV.

NUMBER X.

May it please your Excellency,

WE, the members chosen by his majesty's writ to be the general assembly for this his island of Jamaica, do, with a great deal of thankfulness, acknowledge the princely care which his majesty hath been ever pleased to have of this his colony, and of which your excellency hath likewise given to us very late and fresh assurances: and, in obedience to his majesty's commands, we have perused the several bills which your excellency sent us; and, having duly examined the matters contained in them, we could not give our consent to any of them, there being divers fundamental errors, which we particularly observed, and did cause them to be entered into our journal; and from the consideration of them we cannot but reflect, and do humbly beg your excellency to represent unto his most sacred majesty, the great inconveniencies which are like to redound unto this his island by this method and manner of passing of laws, which is absolutely impracticable, and will not only tend to the great discouragement of the present planters, but likewise put a very fatal stop to any further prosecution of the improvement of this place, there being nothing that invites people more to settle and remove their family and stocks into this remote part of the world, than the assurance they have always had of being governed in such manner as that none of their rights should be lost, so long as they were within the dominions of the kingdom of England: nor can we believe that his majesty would have made this alteration, had he been truly informed of his own interests, and of that which is proper and natural for the constitution of this island.

My lord, you that are now our governor, and here upon the place, cannot but distinguish both, and plainly see that which, at great distance, is impossible to be known, being always distinguished with the false colours of interest and design. It is to you, therefore, we address ourselves; and do humbly beg you to assure his majesty, which we do from the bottom

bottom of our hearts unfeignedly declare, that we are his true, faithful, and loyal subjects. In the next place, sir, we humbly beg you to lay before his majesty the true condition of this island, and the several circumstances wherein it stands: the situation and natural advantages of the place will very probably, by God's blessing, in a very short time, make it very considerable. It were pity, therefore, that any stop in its infancy should be put to it, which may hinder its future growth, and disappoint those hopes which his majesty hath ever had, and which will no doubt of it come to pass, that, if this island be encouraged by good government and wholesome laws, it will effectually serve very many interests, both of his majesty's crown and the nation's trade.

Sir, the present form of the government, as it is now appointed, has these plain and manifest inconveniencies in it.

1st. That the distance of this place renders it impossible to be put in practice, and does not in any manner fall under the same consideration as Ireland does, from which we conclude the example is taken.

2d. The nature of all colonies is changeable, and consequently the laws must be adapted to the interest of the place, and must alter with it.

3d. It is no small satisfaction that the people, by their representatives, have a deliberative power in the making of laws; the negative and barely resolving power being not according to the rights of Englishmen, and practised no where but in those commonwealths where aristocracy prevails.

4th. This manner of form of the government brings all things absolute, and puts it into the power of a governor to do what he pleases, which is not his majesty's interest, and may be a temptation for even good men to commit great partialities and errors.

5th. The method which has been always used, both in this island and all other colonies, in the making of laws, was a greater security to his majesty's prerogative than the present form; for a governor durst not consent to any thing against his interest; and if he did, the signification of the king's pleasure

CHAP. XIV. pleasure determined the laws, so that his majesty had thereby a double negative.

Thus, sir, we have truly laid before your excellency our real sense; and do hope that your excellency, being thoroughly satisfied of the mischiefs which will certainly arise to this place from the reasons we have given, will in that manner represent our condition to his majesty, that he may be thereby induced to give an instruction to your excellency, to pass such laws as are municipal and fit for us, and in the same manner which has ever been practised in this island and other his majesty's colonies; we having no other claim in it than to express our duty to the king, and our unfeigned service and gratitude to your excellency, for mediating that which is so much for his majesty's and the island's interest.

And we do here likewise present unto your excellency a bill for the raising a publick impost unto his majesty, his heirs and successors, for the support of this his government; and do hereby beg your excellency to accept of it as a real demonstration of our loyalty to our prince and service to your excellency, with assurance that we shall, upon all occasions, be ready to express such further testimonies of the same as may be suitable to our duty and allegiance.

NUMBER XI.

At the Court at Whitehall, 4th of April, 1679.

Present, the King's Most Excellent Majesty in Council.

Whereas the Right Honourable the Lords of the Committee for Trade and Plantations did this day make Report unto his Majesty in Council,

THAT having, in pursuance of his majesty's order, considered the present state and constitution of Jamaica, and the government thereof, as it is settled by his majesty's command, their lordships see no reasons why any alterations should be made

made in the method of making laws according to the usage of Ireland, for which their lordships are preparing reasons to evince the necessity and legality of the same. And that whereas a ship is now lying in the Downs, bound for that island, their lordships advise that the Right Honourable Mr. Secretary Coventry do, by this conveyance, inform the Earl of Carlisle of his majesty's pleasure herein, with directions that all things be disposed to this end; and that, in the mean time, the present laws enacted by Lord Vaughan be continued by proclamation, or otherwise, until his majesty's pleasure be further known; as also that his lordship do, by the first conveyance, send over an authentick copy of the act for a publick impost, lately enacted there, according to his lordship's instructions for matters of that nature.

APPEN-DIX.

His majesty, having thought fit to approve thereof, was pleased to order, as it is hereby ordered, that the Right Honourable Mr. Secretary Coventry do signify his majesty's pleasure unto the Earl of Carlisle, according to the said report.

NUMBER XII.

At the Court at Whitehall, the 28th of May, 1679.

PRESENT, the King's Most Excellent Majesty in Council.

Whereas there was this day read at the Board a Report from the Right Honourable the Lords of the Committee for Trade and Plantations, in the words following; viz.

May it please your Majesty,

WE have, in obedience to your majesty's commands, entered into the present state of your majesty's island of Jamaica, in order to propose such means as may put an end to the great discouragement

CHAP. XIV.

discouragement your majesty's good subjects there lie under by the unsettled condition thereof, occasioned by the refusal of the laws lately offered by the Earl of Carlisle to the assembly for their consent; at which proceedings dissatisfaction appears to have risen in the manner following:

By the commission granted by your majesty unto the Lord Vaughan and several preceding governors, it was your royal pleasure to entrust the assembly of Jamaica with a power to frame and enact laws, by the advice and consent of the governor and council; which laws were to continue in force for the space of two years, and no longer: but so it hath happened, that your majesty, finding the inconveniencies which did attend that power and manner of making laws, by the irregular, violent, and unwarrantable proceedings of the assembly, was pleased, with the advice of your privy council, to provide, by the Earl of Carlisle's commission, that no laws should be enacted in Jamaica, but such as, being framed by the governor and council, and transmitted unto your majesty for your royal approbation, were afterwards remitted to Jamaica, and consented unto by the assembly there; and, in pursuance thereof, the Earl of Carlisle carried over a body of laws under the great seal of England; which laws, upon his lordship's arrival there, have been rejected by the general assembly, upon grounds and reasons contained in an address to your majesty's governor, and in divers letters received from his lordship in that behalf.

1st. In the first place, we find they are unsatisfied with the clause in the militia bill, whereby it is provided, that the governor may, upon all occasions or emergencies, act as governor in chief, according to and in pursuance of all the powers and authorities given unto him by your majesty's commission; fearing that thereby they shall make it legal to execute all instructions that either are or shall be sent your majesty's governor.

2dly. They have likewise rejected the bill for raising a publick revenue, as being perpetual, and liable (as they say) to be diverted.

3dly.

3dly. It is objected, that the said laws contain divers fundamental errors.

4thly. That they were not compared with, and amended by the last laws sent over by Lord Vaughan.

5thly. That the distance of the place renders the present method of passing laws wholly impracticable.

6thly. That the nature of all colonies is changeable, and consequently the laws must be adapted to the interest of the place, and alter with it.

7thly. That thereby they lose the satisfaction of a deliberative power in making laws.

8thly. That this form of government renders your governor absolute.

9thly. That by the former method of enacting laws your majesty's prerogative was better secured.

These being the objections and pretences upon which the assembly has, with so much animosity, proceeded to reject those bills transmitted by your majesty, we cannot but offer, for your majesty's information and satisfaction, such a short answer thereunto as may not only give a testimony of the unreasonableness of their proceedings, but also furnish your governor, when occasion shall serve, with such arguments as may be fit to be used in justification of your majesty's commission and powers granted unto him.

1st. It is not without the greatest presumption that they go about to question your majesty's power over the militia in that island, since it has been allowed and declared, even by the laws of this your kingdom, that the sole supreme government, command, and disposition of the militia, and of all forces by sea and land, and of all forts and places of strength, is residing in your majesty, within all your majesty's realms and dominions.

2d. The objection made against the bill for the public revenue hath as little ground, since its bei g perpetual is no more than what was formerly offered by them unto your majesty,

CHAP. XIV.

majesty, during the government of Sir Thomas Lynch, in the same measure and proportion as is now proposed; nor can it be diverted, since provision is thereby expressly made, that the same shall be for the better support of that government; besides, that it is not suitable to the duty and modesty of subjects, to suspect your majesty's justice or care for the government of that colony, whose settlement and preservation have been most particularly carried on by your majesty's tender regard, and by the great expence of your own treasure.

3d. It cannot with any truth be said, that these laws contain many and great errors, nothing having been done therein but in pursuance of former laws, at divers times enacted by the assembly, and with the advice of your majesty's privy council, as well as the opinion and approbation of your attorney-general, upon perusal of the same.

4th. To the fourth objection it may be answered, that, if any thing had been found of moment or importance in the last parcel of laws transmitted by the Lord Vaughan, your majesty's tender care of your subjects' welfare would have been such as not to have sent those bills imperfect, or defective in any necessary matter.

5th. As to the distance of the place, which renders (as they say) the present method of making laws altogether impracticable, your majesty having been pleased to regulate the same, by the advice of your privy council, according to the usage of Ireland, such care was taken as that no law might be wanting which might conduce to the well-being of the plantation, and that nothing might be omitted which in all former governments had been thought necessary; nor is it likely that this colony is subject to greater accidents than your kingdom of Ireland, so as to require a more frequent and sudden change of laws in other cases than such as are already provided for upon emergencies, or in other manner than is directed by your majesty's commission; whereby the inhabitants have free access to make complaints to to your governor and council, of any defect in any old law, or to give reasons for any new one, which, being modelled by the governor and council into form of law, and transmitted unto your majesty, if by your majesty and council found reasonable, may be transmitted back thither to be enacted accordingly. APPENDIX.

6th. It was sufficiently apparent unto your majesty, that laws must alter with the interest of the place, when you were graciously pleased to lodge such a power in that government, as might not only, from time to time, with your majesty's approbation, and by the advice both of your privy-council here and of the governor and council there, enable the assembly to enact new laws answerable to their growing necessities, but even, upon urgent occasions, to provide, by raising money, for the security of the island, without attending your majesty's orders or consent.

7th. It is not to be doubted but the assembly have endeavoured to grasp all power, as well as that of a deliberative voice, in making laws: but how far they have thereby intrenched upon your majesty's prerogative, and exceeded the bounds of their duty and loyalty, upon this pretence, may appear by their late exorbitant and unwarrantable proceedings during the government of the Lord Vaughan, in ordering and signing a warrant under the marshal of the island, your majesty's officer of justice, for the stopping and preventing the execution of a sentence passed, according to the ordinary forms of law, upon a notorious pirate and disturber of your majesty's peace: and they have further taken upon them, by virtue of this deliberative power, to make laws contrary to those of England, and to imprison your majesty's subjects; nor have they forborne to raise money by public acts, and to dispose of the same according to their will and pleasure, without any mention made of your majesty, which has never in like case been practised in any of your majesty's kingdoms. How far, therefore, it is fit to intrust them with a power which they have thus abused, and to which they

CHAP. XIV.

have no pretension of right, was the subject of your majesty's royal commission, when you were pleased to put a restraint upon those enormities, and to take the reins of government into your own hands, which they, in express words, against their duty and allegiance, have challenged and refused to part with.

8th. It cannot with any truth be supposed, that, by the present form of government, the governor is rendered absolute, since he is now, more than ever, become accountable unto your majesty of all his most important deliberations and actions, and is not warranted to do any thing but according to law and your majesty's commission and instructions, given by advice of your privy council.

9th. And whether your majesty's prerogative is prejudiced by the present constructions, is more the concernment of your majesty, and subject of your own care, than of their considerations.

Lastly, and in general: We humbly conceive, that it would be a great satisfaction to your subjects there inhabiting, and an invitation to strangers, when they shall know what laws they are to be governed by, and a great ease to the planters, not to be continually obliged to attend the assemblies to re-enact old laws, which your majesty has now thought fit, in a proper form, to ascertain and establish; whereas the late power of making temporary laws could be understood to be of no longer continuance than until such wholesome laws, founded upon so many years experience, should be agreed on by the people, and finally enacted by your majesty, in such manner as hath been practised in either of your majesty's dominions to which your English subjects have transplanted themselves. For as they cannot pretend to further privileges than have been granted to them, either by charter or some solemn act under your great seal, so, having from the first beginning of that plantation been governed by such instructions as were given by your majesty unto your governors, according to the power your majesty had originally

over

over them, and which you have by no one authentic act ever yet parted with, and having never had any other right to assemblies than from the permission of the governors, and that only temporary and for probation, it is to be wondered how they should presume to provoke your majesty, by pretending a right to that which hath been allowed them merely out of favour, and discourage your majesty from future favours of that kind, when what your majesty ordered for a temporary experiment, to see what form would best suit the safety and interest of the island, shall be construed to be a total resignation of the power inherent in your majesty, and a devolution of it to themselves and their wills, without which neither law nor government, the essential ingredients of their subsistence and well-being, may take place among them.

Since, therefore, it is evident, that the assembly of Jamaica have, without any just grounds, and with so much animosity and undutifulness, proceeded to reject the marks of your majesty's favour towards them, and that your majesty's resolutions in this case are like to be the measure of respect and obedience to your royal commands in other colonies; we can only offer, as a cure for irregularities past and a remedy against all further inconveniencies, that your majesty would please to authorize and empower your governor to call another assembly, and to represent unto them the great convenience and expediency of accepting and consenting unto such laws as your majesty has under your great seal transmitted unto them; and that, in case of refusal, his lordship be furnished with such powers as were formerly given unto Col. D'Oyley, your first governor of Jamaica, and since unto other governors, whereby his lordship may be enabled to govern according to the laws of England, where the different nature and constitution of that colony may conveniently permit the same; and, in other cases to act, with the advice of the council, in such manner as shall be

 held

held necessary and proper for the good government of that plantation, until your majesty's further orders; and that, by all opportunities of conveyance, the governor do give your majesty a constant and particular account of all his proceedings, in pursuance of your instructions herein.

All which is most humbly submitted, &c.

Upon reading of which report, and full debate thereupon, his majesty was pleased to approve the same; and the Right honourable Mr. Secretary Coventry is hereby directed to prepare such suitable orders and instructions as may answer the several parts and advices contained in the said report.

Robert Southwell.

NUMBER XIII.

Extract of a Letter from the Committee to the Earl of Carlisle.

AFTER our very hearty commendation unto your lordship, we have received two letters from you, the one of the 24th of October, the other of the 15th of November, 1678; both of which gave us an account of the distaste the assembly had expressed at the new frame of government, and of their throwing out all the bills transmitted under the great seal; and your lordship having therein recommended unto us the speedy dispatch of the bills sent to Mr. Secretary Coventry, for passing them through the offices here, we did thereupon take the same into our consideration: but finding that they contained such clauses as we had formerly (your lordship being present) disallowed in the laws enacted by the Lord Vaughan, as most prejudicial to his majesty's rights and prerogative, one of them appropriating and disposing of the quit-rents in the same terms as was formerly done, so much to his majesty's dissatisfaction; another, declaring the laws of England to be in force, which clause (your lordship cannot but

but remember) was postponed here, upon very serious deliberation; besides divers other particulars, altogether unfit to be passed by his majesty: we have, withal, perused the several letters which your lordship had written to Mr. Secretary Coventry, in relation to your government: and as for the laws, we could not advise his majesty to proceed in any other manner, than by giving power to call another assembly, and to offer unto them the same laws your lordship carried over, as being the most usefully framed and settled for the good of the island and his majesty's service; and that, in case of refusal, you might be enabled to govern according to commissions and instructions given unto former governors, as your lordship will more fully understand by our report unto his majesty, and the order of council thereupon, to which we refer your lordship, as setting forth at large the grounds and reasons inducing the resolutions his majesty has now taken.

NUMBER XIV.

Extract of a Letter from the Earl of Carlisle to Mr. Secretary Coventry.

St. Jago de la Vega, 30*th Aug.* 1679.

YOUR packet by Captain Buckingham, having inclosed his majesty's letter of the 31st of May last, and an order in council of the 28th of May, 1679, together with the animadversions of the council upon several points of the 22d of May last, and two letters from yourself, I received the 26th inst. at night. The next morning I read them in council. The assembly then having sat some seven days, to renew the bill for a revenue, the last being just expiring, I sent for the general assembly, and read the order of council and the king's letter thereupon to them, which I hope will have some good effect, but they came in as good time so much contrary to their expectation. I herewith send you a copy

copy of their address thereupon, which they presented to me the 28th; and finding them nettled and warm, I thought it discretion to let them take time to digest their thoughts; and, having continued the revenue bill for six months longer from the 1st of September next, I passed it, and then prorogued them till the 28th of October following.

NUMBER XV.

Copy of a vote of the Assembly, Aug. 22. 1679.

DIE VENERIS.

The committee appointed to examine Mr. Martyn's accounts reported, that Mr. Martyn, appearing before them, said, that my lord had ordered him to come and tell them, that, both from the king and from my lord, he was not obliged to shew his accounts to the assembly; but that he had given them unto my lord, and his excellency had told him, that, if any of the assembly had a mind to see them, they might see them there.

The house, considering the return of the committee ordered to inspect Mr. Martyn's accounts, re-assumed that debate, and thereupon did vote, that, notwithstanding my lord's answer by Mr. Martyn to that committee, it was and is their undoubted and inherent right, that as all bills for money ought and do arise in their house, so they ought to appoint the disposal of it, and to receive and examine all the accounts concerning the same.

Vera Copia.

ROWLAND POWELL.

APPEN-DIX.

NUMBER XVI.

Extract of a Letter from the Earl of Carlisle to the Committee.

St. Jago de la Vega, 15th Sept. 1679.

My Lords,

YOUR lordships letters of the 25th of March, 4th of April, and 31st of May last, I received on the 26th of August, as also your lordships orders and reports to his majesty, touching the laws and government of Jamaica; which I communicated to the council (the assembly then sitting to continue the revenue bill, expiring the 2d of September) on the 27th of August; and afterwards, the same day, I communicated, the council being present, his Majesty's letter of the 31st of May last, and your lordships order and report of the same date, to the assembly; which came to me as seasonably as they received them surprisedly, making me the next morning the inclosed address; upon which, having passed a bill of impost for six months, I prorogued them, by advice of the council, till the 28th of October next, hoping in that time they would fall of their heat, and, upon recollection, better bethink themselves of their duties and allegiance, and upon my offering them again the laws, which I propose to do upon their first meeting, better demonstrate their obedience by readily giving their consent that they might be enacted.

But, from what I can learn from the chief leaders among them, I find the same averseness as formerly, averring that they will submit to wear, but never consent to make, chains, as they term this frame of government, for their posterities; so that I scarce expect better success; of which I have writ at large to Mr. Secretary Coventry.

CHAP. XIV.

NUMBER XVII.

Extract of a Letter from the Earl of Carlisle to Mr. Secretary Coventry.

St. Jago de la Vega, 23d *November*, 1679.

Sir,

THE assembly meeting on the 28th of October, I, with the council, went to them; commanded the council's report of the 28th of May, and his majesty's letter of the 31st of May last, to be read again to them; pressed them very much to consider how much it imported at this juncture for the interest of the island, that they should pass these laws I brought to them under the great seal of England, or at least part of them; desiring that any one or more of the assembly would there and then argue the reasonableness of their objection, which none of them would undertake; and so I left the body of laws with them. They having the last session passed a vote, that the raising money and disposing of it, was the inherent right of the assembly (of which I had no account either from the members or their speaker, in fourteen days afterwards, they presuming it to be their privilege that their proceedings should be kept secret from me). I then appointed and swore them a clerk, which before used to be of their own choice; and this they are very uneasy under.

They proceeded to read over the body of laws: notwithstanding the great care, pains, and trouble I had taken with them, both apart individually as well as assembled together, they threw out and rejected all the laws, again adhering to their former reasons, rather than admitting or honouring those from their lordships for rules of obedience.

I thereupon presently, with the council, framed a bill of revenue indefinite, and sent that to them: but that had no better success; and they then attended me with the address, to be presented to his majesty, which I herewith send you; as also the humble desire of justification of his majesty's council

council thereupon, which I and they earnestly desire your favour in humbly presenting to his majesty, being unanimously agreed to by all the council: but Col. Samuel Long (chief-justice of the island, whom I have found all along since my arrival here to be a most pertinacious abettor and cherisher of the assembly's stubbornness in opposing this new frame of government, having had a hand, being their speaker, in the leaving the king's name out of the revenue bill) refuses to join with the council in this their genuine act, and has sufficiently possessed himself of the opinion of the assembly, by advising and assisting them in the framing of their address: thinking their resolutions to be unalterable as his own, he is withdrawn to his plantation, some thirty miles off from this town, where at this juncture we have most need of council.

Upon serious and deliberate consideration of all which, I have sent him his *quietus;* and appointed Col. Robert Byndloss chief-justice in his place, of whose fidelity to the king's interest I have many proofs, having formerly executed the place, and was now one of the judges of the supreme court.

I have also suspended Col. Long from being one of the council, purposing, by the advice of the council, to bring or send him, with six more of the assembly, to attend the king and council in England to support their own opinions, reasons, and address, wherein they are not ordinarily positive; and this I do from the council here unanimously agreeing, that there is no other nor better expedient for the settlement of this government to a general consent.

NUMBER XVIII.

Extract of a letter from the Earl of Carlisle to the Committee.

St. Jago de la Vega, 23d *Nov.* 1679.

My Lords,

MINE of the tenth of September last to your lordships I hope you have received; and what I therein sent your lordships,

CHAP. XIV. ships, as my conjectures in prospect, since the general assembly's meeting, on the 28th of October last, have found to be no vain prophecy.

Upon the assembly's meeting on that day, I, with the council, went to the place where they were met, and again, in the presence of the council and the assembly, commanded to be read your lordship's report of the 28th of May last past made to his majesty, as also his majesty's commands to myself of the 31st of the same; and thereupon offered to the assembly the body of laws brought over under the great seal of England for their consent; at the same time declaring to them the great expediency it would be to all the officers of the island, and reason to persuade his majesty they were another people than represented at home; that it would induce the king to gratify them in what was necessary; and that, otherwise, they could not appear but in great contempt, to the lessening of the island's interest in his royal favour: and what I urged in general to them at their meeting, I had not been wanting to press to them apart individually before it: then swore them a clerk of my appointing, which they took not well, alledging it was their right to choose their own clerk, I told them no: for that the king did grant by patent the clerk of the parliament, so that they were uneasily overruled. The reason of my doing this was from their having an opinion that the votes of the house should be kept a secret from me, and their passing a vote the former sessions, that to raise money, and dispose of the same, was a right inherent in the assembly, of which I had no notice, in some fourteen days after, from any of them or their speaker.

I much urged the whole assembly freely to argue, in the presence of the council and their own members, for the reasonableness of the matter commanded by the king, that, upon their discoursing it openly and freely, they might be the better convinced of the necessity of their being dutiful therein: but none of them, in my presence and the council's, would undertake it; so we left them, and the body of laws with them.

Some

Some days they spent in reading over again the body of laws under the great seal left with them; but rejected the many arguments I had laboured them with, and threw all the laws out again: whereupon they appointed a committee to draw up an address, to be presented by me to his majesty on their behalfs: and in that time, with the council, I drew a bill of revenue indefinitely, and gave it myself to their speaker; but that bill had no better success, but was rejected also.

Upon this, on the 14th instant, the speaker and assembly being sent for to attend me in council, to shew cause why they did reject the bill of revenue so framed by us in pursuance of his majesty's pleasure therein, they gave me no answer; but, by their speaker, desired to present to me their address, the speaker contending to give it its due accent by reading it himself; a copy whereof is here sent inclosed.

This address is founded greatly upon the advice of Lieutenant-Colonel Samuel Long, chief-justice of the island, and one of the king's council, who principally contends for the old frame of government, of whom the assembly is highly opiniated, and esteem him the patron of their rights and privileges as Englishmen, who had a hand in leaving the king's name out of the revenue bill, being then speaker, and denies not his having a hand in framing and advising some parts of the address, which in whole is not truth; for,

1st. Whereas they alledge, that the civil government commenced in my Lord Windsor's time; it is generally known and recorded in our council-book, fifteen months before, in Colonel D'Oyley's time, and will be proved by Sir Thomas Lynch, who then himself had an occasion of a trial by jury, the foreman of which was Colonel Byndloss.

2dly. They alledge the readiness of governors to use martial law, particularly in Sir Thomas Lynch's time; which is here contradicted, for there was only an order in council for the putting it in force upon condition of any actual descent or invasion, and not otherwise; neither was it on foot really all this time here, as I am credibly informed upon good enquiry.

3dly. As

CHAP. XIV.

3dly. As for its being in force in my time, it was not from my affecting, but the council advising and their desiring it; as also the putting off the Courts till February, in favour generally of the planters. Then, for their alledging so much to be done during the martial law, wholly at the charge of the country; that it is done is true, but the charge thereof they would clog the revenue bill with, amounting to twelve hundred and twenty-eight pounds, when, *communibus annis*, the bill of impost is but fifteen hundred pounds; of which twelve hundred and twenty-eight pounds there is not yet made payment of one farthing, nor any prospect how it may, since the revenue is so much anticipated from the want of money in the treasury, occasioned by my Lord Vaughan's letting fall the bill of revenue before his departure.

NUMBER XIX.

To his Excellency Charles Earl of Carlisle, captain-general, governor, and commander in chief of his majesty's island of Jamaica, &c.

The humble address of the assembly of this his majesty's island, in answer to the report of the right honourable the lords of the committee of trade and plantations, made to his majesty's council; which we entreat his excellency may be humbly presented to his most sacred majesty and his council.

WE, his majesty's most loyal and obedient subjects, the assembly of this his island of Jamaica, cannot without infinite grief of mind read the report made to his majesty by the right honourable the lords of the committee for trade and plantations; wherein, by the relations made by their lordships unto his majesty, they have represented us as a people full of animosity, unreasonable, irregular, violent, undutiful, and transgressing both the bounds of duty and loyalty; the bitterness of which characters were we in the least part conscious

to

to have deserved, we should, like Job, have said, "*Behold, we* "*are vile; what shall we answer? we will lay our hands upon* "*our mouths.*"

But, lest our silence should argue our guilt, we shall, in all humility, endeavour to make appear we have always demeaned ourselves as becometh good and obedient subjects, and those who acknowledge and are truly sensible of the many favours received from his majesty; the truth of which resting only on matter of fact being related, and the false colours which hitherto have been thrown on us being washed off, we shall not doubt but his majesty will soon entertain a better opinion of his subjects of this island.

We must, therefore, humbly beg that his majesty will with patience be pleased to hear the account of our proceedings; which truly to manifest we must be forced to look back so far as Sir Charles Lyttleton's and Sir Thomas Modyford's entrance upon their government:

At which time, we humbly conceive, the island began really to take up the form of a civil government, and wholly to lay aside that of an army, which, until that time, was deemed the supreme authority; when after, upon their several arrivals, by order from his majesty, and according to the method of his majesty's most ancient plantations, they called assemblies, and settled the government of the island in such good form, that, until his excellency the Earl of Carlisle's first arrival, his majesty thought not fit to alter it, though several governors in that time were changed, which must necessarily infer the goodness and reason of it, as well as the satisfaction of the people (since, from that time, they betook themselves to settle plantations), especially the merchants, by which means the estates here are wonderfully increased, as is evident by the great number of ships loaden here by the industry of the planters; and the satisfaction they received by those wholesome laws then began, and until that time continued, the change of which laws we had no reason to expect, being done on such mature deliberation from home.

2 But

CHAP. XIV.

But to return to answer: the first thing their lordships are pleased to accuse us of is, presuming to question his majesty's power over the militia; which, how much they are misinformed in it, will hereunder appear: but we must first repeat the clause against which, we humbly conceive, we had just reasons to take exceptions, which clause is as followeth:

"Provided always, and it is hereby further enacted and de-"clared by the authority aforesaid, that nothing in this act "contained be expounded, construed, or understood, to di-"minish, alter, or abridge, the power of the governor or com-"mander in chief for the time being; but that in all things he "may, upon all occasions or exigencies, act as captain-general "and governor in chief, according to and in pursuance of all "the powers and authorities given to him by his majesty's "commission; any thing in this act or any other to the con-"trary in anywise notwithstanding."

In their lordships observations, in which they take no notice that the power given by that clause extends as well to the governor as captain-general, nor of the words "any "thing in this act or any other to the contrary notwithstand-"ing," which words, being plain, need no references to expound them, being consented to, there is no occasion of making any other law, because that makes all the powers and authorities given by his majesty's commission, and, by that commission, the instructions which shall be after given to him, shall be law, though it be to the nulling of any beneficial law, made either here or in England, by which we are secured both in life and in estate; the like of which was never done in any of his majesty's dominions whatsoever, and is in effect to enact will to be law, and will be construed (we fear) to bind us by the old rule of law, that every man may renounce his own right: and if their lordships had been pleased to have as well remembered the other clauses of the act of the militia, we cannot think they would have said we had questioned his majesty's power over it, for no act of England gives his majesty the like power over the militia as ours doth; for,

for, on any apprehension of danger, the general with his council of officers have power to put the law martial on foot for what time they please, and to command us in our own persons, our servants, negroes, horses, even all that we have, to his majesty's service; which having been so often put in practice will need the less proof: but how readily and willingly we have obeyed, and in that faith is best justified by works, it will not be amiss to instance some times, and what hath been done in those times, by the charge and labour of his majesty's subjects here, under the several governors; none of which have left unexperimented the strength of his majesty's commission, and the virtue or force of that act, upon the least seeming occasion.

In the government of Sir Thomas Modyford, in the years 1665 and 1666, the whole island was put under law martial for many months together; in which time, by the inhabitants and their blacks, Port-Charles was made close, which to that time wanted a whole line, and also the breast-work at Port-Royal was built, with a very small charge to his majesty.

In the time of Sir Thomas Lynch, in the year 1673, the law martial was again set on foot; Fort-James built by the contributions of the gentlemen of his majesty's council and assembly, and several other of his majesty's good subjects in this island, which amounted to a very considerable sum of money; a breast-work thrown up at Old-Harbour and several other places; and guns mounted on a platform placed at Port-Morant.

In Lord Vaughan's time, though there was no probability of war, yet he wanted not the trial of his power also in the militia, and our obedience to it; for he commanded out a company of the inhabitants in search of a Spanish *barqua longa*, who was said to have robbed a sloop belonging to this island upon the coast of Cuba: he, likewise, in favour of the royal company, commanded out to sea two vessels, with a company of the militia and their captain, from Port-Royal, to seize an interloper riding in one of his majesty's harbours, and there by force seized her.

CHAP. XIV.

In the time of Sir Henry Morgan being commander in chief, we were again put under martial law; in which time Fort-Rupert, Fort-Carlisle, and a new line at Fort-James, were built.

Lastly, in his excellency the Earl of Carlisle's time (the present governor) the law martial was again put in force for about three months; in which time Fort-Morgan with its platform, and another line at Fort-James, and the breast-work reinforced very considerably in thickness and height, and new carriages were made for the guns, those that came out of England not being fit for land service; all which fortifications are substantially built with stone and brick, at the charge and labour of the country.

Neither have we ever been wanting in due respect to his majesty's governors; the militia having always waited on them to church, in their progresses, and on all publick occasions: and we may safely affirm with truth, that no militia in his majesty's dominions undergo the like military duty as his subjects in Jamaica; as is evident to all men that ever set foot in Port Royal, which cannot be distinguished from a garrison, either in time of peace or war, but by their not being paid for their service.

To answer their lordships objections to the bill of revenue, wherein his majesty's name was left out, there are several members of this assembly now sitting who were members when that bill passed three times in form in the assembly; and, upon the best recollection of their memories, they are fully persuaded and do believe the bill was again sent down with that amendment from the governor and council, according as it is passed at the last: but, should it have risen in the assembly, they are very unfortunate if they must bear the censure of all mistakes that may happen in presenting laws to be passed, when both the governor and his council have their negative voices, which, had either of them made use of in this point, would have been readily consented to by the assembly, as they had formerly done, both under the

government

government of Sir Thomas Modyford and Sir Thomas Lynch, before whose time it had been raised without mentioning his majesty's name, and that without check; and we always concluded the governor's name in the enacting part to be of the same effect as his majesty's is in England, whom, in this particular, he seems rather to personate than represent: for which reasons we hope, it ought not to have been imputed to the assembly as their crime altogether, being consented unto us by his majesty's governor, without any debate, and all applied by the act whereby it was raised, to the very same public use his majesty directs; and we are certain no instance can be given of any money disposed of to any private use, but was always issued by the governor's warrant, for the payment of his own and other his general officers' salaries in this island, with some small contingent charges of the government.

Their lordships also affirm, that the assembly offered this bill, in the same measure and proportion as it is now proposed, to Sir Thomas Lynch: in which their lordships are misinformed; for his majesty's instructions were, that the laws should be in force for two years and no longer, which their lordships also acknowledge in the prior part of the report; so that the assembly needed not to have expressed any time, and the particular uses therein appointed.

But had their lordships known how great sums of money have been raised here, and how small a part hath been applied to his majesty's service for the defence and strengthening the island, we humbly conceive their lordships would have been of opinion, that we have no reason to bar ourselves to perpetuity, and pass the said act without limitation of uses or time; nor can we be so presumptuous as to imagine the king can be hindered from making such use of his own money as he shall think fit, and apply it where he finds most necessary.

It is very true the laws contain many and great errors, as their lordships may see by the assembly's journal; so that were the assembly as much petitioners to his majesty for this new form as they are to be restored to their old, above half the body of these laws, without amendment, would never be reasonable to pass.

As, to instance some few amongst many: in the act for preventing damages by fire, a single justice of the peace hath power of life and death; and the act of the militia empowers the governor and council to levy a tax on the whole island; and in the act directing the marshal's proceedings, there is a clause that makes it felony for any person to conceal his own goods, left in his own possession, after execution levied by that law, so that a man may be hanged for being poor, which, though inconvenient, was never till then accounted capital; with others too long to be repeated.

And whereas their lordships are pleased to say, that there is nothing imperfect or defective in these bills transmitted hither; yet we humbly conceive, that no notice being taken in this body of laws how or in what nature we are to make use of the laws of England, either as they have reference to the preservation of his majesty's prerogative or the subject's rights, we ought not in reason to consent to these bills; for, nothing appearing to the contrary, the governor is left, *ad libitum*, to use or refuse as few or as many as he pleases, and such as suit with his occasions; there being no directions in them how to proceed according to the laws of England, either in causes criminal or testamentary, and in many other cases which concern the quiet of the subject, both in life and estate.

We conceive also, that, whatsoever is said to the contrary by their lordships in answer to the distance of places, this very last experiment is sufficiently convincing of the truth of that allegation; since it is a year since this model came over and was debated, and before their lordships report came back, notwithstanding one of the advices went home by an express. And,

Whereas their lordships say, we cannot be subject to more accidents

accidents than his majesty's kingdom of Ireland; to that we object, that advice and answers thence may be had in ten or fourteen days, and that kingdom is already settled, our plantation but beginning. But further, we cannot imagine that the Irish model of government was, *in principio*, ever intended for Englishmen: besides, their lordships cannot but know, that that model was introduced amongst them by a law made by themselves in Ireland, and so consequently bound them, which, being now generally known to all those who remove thither, they have no cause to repine at, that being their choice to live under it or stay from it, and was made for the preservation of the English against the Irish faction. As there is not the same cause, so there is not the same reason, for imposing the same on us, unless we did it ourselves, who are all his majesty's natural-born subjects of his kingdom of England; which is the reason the parliament give, in all their acts concerning the plantations, for obliging us by them to what, and with whom, and in what manner, we made trade, and impose a tax on us here in case of trade from one colony to another; and it is but equity then, that the same law should have the same power of loosing as binding.

His majesty giving a power, on urgent occasions, to raise monies the old way, only secures the king's officers their salaries, which else they had been disappointed of; the act of the militia which was heretofore consented to, ever providing, that, on alarm or invasion, the commander in chief should have unlimited power over all persons, estates, and things, necessary on such urgencies.

As to the 7th, the assembly say, they never desired any power but what his majesty's governors assured them was their birth-rights, and what they supposed his majesty's most gracious proclamation allowed them: also his majesty was graciously pleased to write a letter to his governor Sir Thomas Lynch, after the double trial of one Peter Johnson, a pirate, signifying his dislike that any thing should be done that should cause any doubt in his subjects, in not enjoying all the

 privileges

CHAP. XIV.

privileges of subjects of the kingdom of England, or to that effect.

But as to the obstructing of justice against Brown, the pirate, what they did, though not justifiable in the manner, was out of an assurance, that we had no law in force then to declare my lord chancellor of England's power, and our chancellor's here equal, in granting commissions in pursuance of the statute of Henry the eighth; which also his majesty and council perceiving, have, in the new body of laws, sent one to supply that want: and if they, not meddling with the merits of the cause, endeavoured to preserve the form of justice, and justice itself, and, after denial of several petitions, joined with the council, were led beyond their duty (for which they were sharply reprimanded by the then governor) they do hope for and humbly beg his majesty's pardon.

And as for the act upon which he came in, it arose not in the assembly, but was sent from the council, to be consented to by them, which was accordingly done.

And as to the imprisonment of Mr. Thomas Martyn, one of their members, for taking out process in chancery in his own private concern against several other members, and of the council, the assembly then sitting, and for other misdemeanors and breach of the rules of the house; they hope it is justifiable, the king's governor having assured them, that they had the same power over their members which the house of commons have, and all speakers here praying, and the governors granting, the usual petitions of speakers in England.

Seeing the governor hath power to turn out a counsellor, and turning out incapacitates him from being an assembly-man, no counsellor dares give his opinion against the governor, under danger of less penalty than losing that which he thinks his birth-right: also, a governor being chancellor, ordinary, and admiral, joined with his military authority, lodges so great a power in him, that being united and executed in one person to turn it *totum in qualibet parte*, so that he may invalidate any thing done under his own commission.

There

There is no doubt but, by this new way, it is in the assembly's power to consent to and perpetuate such laws as are wholly of benefit to them, and leave unpassed all that may be thought most necessary for his majesty; which advantage they not laying hold on, hope it will be an evidence they are careful of his majesty's prerogative, as it is the duty of every good subject to be.

It is without controversy that the old form of government, which was ordered so like his majesty's kingdom of England, must of consequence be of greater encouragement to all his majesty's subjects, as well as strangers, to remove themselves hither. Upon his majesty's proclamation in my Lord Windsor's time, and by those gracious instructions given to Sir Thomas Modyford, all or most part of the sugar plantations have been settled; and the major part of the said planters being such who arrived here and settled upon the general liking of the model first constituted, and in belief that they lost not any of the privileges of his majesty's subjects of the kingdom of England by their removal hither, and having by no act, as we believe, either provoked his majesty or forfeited our rights, or ever desiring or attempting to lessen or question his majesty's prerogative, the preservation whereof we ever deemed the best means of preserving our own privileges and estates, we shall presume to hope for the continuance of his majesty's favour, which is impossible for us ever to forget.

And whereas their lordships are pleased to offer their advice to his majesty, to furnish his governor with such powers as were formerly given to Colonel D'Oyley and others, in whose time the then accounted army was not disbanded, but so continued till Lord Windsor's arrival, who brought over the king's royal donative, and order to settle the civil government: we hope their lordships intend not that we are to be governed by or as an army, or that the governor be empowered to levy any tax by himself and council; since his majesty having discharged himself and council, by an act of parliament, of any such power over any of his majesty's subjects of his kingdom

CHAP. XIV.

dom of England, as we undoubtedly are, it will be very hard to have any imposition laid on us but by our own consents; for their lordships well know, that no derived power is greater than the primitive.

However, if his most gracious majesty shall not think fit to alter this model, but we are to be governed by the governor and council, according to their lordships' advice, yet we humbly beseech his majesty to do us the grace to believe, that we are so sensible of our duty and allegiance, that our submission to and comportment under his majesty's authority shall be such as that, we hope, he, in his due time, will be graciously pleased to restore unto us our ancient form of government, under which it hath hitherto pleased God to prosper us; ending with our hearty prayers for his majesty's long and happy reign over us, and most humbly begging his majesty's pardon of all our errors and mistakes, and a gracious interpretation of this our answer; protesting, from the bottom of our hearts, that we are and resolve to die his majesty's true, loyal, and obedient subjects.

A true copy.

ROWLAND POWELL, *Cl. Conc.*

NUMBER XX.

The humble desire and justification of the members of his majesty's council, to his Excellency the Governor in Jamaica.

THE alterations of the frame of government in this his majesty's island of Jamaica unto that of his kingdom of Ireland, which his majesty, the best and greatest of kings, hath graciously commanded us to submit unto and own, we his majesty's truly loyal and dutiful subjects, hitherto have and yet do, by a willing readiness, and ready willingness, declare our entire obedience and hearty conformity thereunto, because his majesty commands,

And

And although his majesty's great perspicuity and truly royal prudence is best able to determine what government is the fittest for his subjects in this island, yet with all due submission, in all humility, we beg leave to represent to his majesty the great inconvenience attending the present frame, in transmitting our laws home.

The vast distance of place will of necessity require a great expence of time, between the first framing our laws here and the transmitting and return of them hither again: so that, before they can be passed into laws by the assembly here, there will probably as great cause arise to alter as there were at first to make them.

And, with all due submission, we judge it even impossible to adapt laws to the present constitution, so as not to admit of often and great alterations; for, according to our experience hitherto, we have found urgent occasions to alter and amend the laws, that have more immediately concerned us here, at the least every two years; and we cannot foresee but we shall lie under the same necessity still; so that if his majesty graciously please to take it into his princely consideration, and either restore to us our former power and way or method of passing laws, or at least remit that part of the present method of making laws which only concerns us here, as they may pass without transmitting the same, we hope, by our present submission and entire obedience to all his laws here, his majesty will be a glorious prince and his subjects here an happy people.

And whereas the gentlemen of the assembly, in their address to his majesty read here in council the 15th of November, 1679, do declare, that as to the bill of revenue wherein his majesty's name was left out, that there are several of the members of their assembly now sitting who were members when the bill passed three times in form in the assembly, and, upon the best recollection of their memories, they are fully persuaded and do believe the bill was again sent down with that amendment from the governor and council, according as it passed at the last: we, the gentlemen of his majesty's council

CHAP. XIV.

council here present at the passing of the bill, do most humbly and with all seriousness aver and declare, that we were so far from consenting the said bill should pass without his majesty's name in it, that we do not remember it was ever debated or mentioned in council; and further, that, to the best of our respective knowledge, it was read three times, and passed the council-board, with his majesty's name in it: and we are the rather induced to this our confidence, because we find the original act was razed, and, by the then speaker's own hand, interlined; and moreover, the several amendments of the said bill, that were made in council, were all taken notice of in the minutes in our council-books, and no mention made of this; and the gentlemen of the assembly do produce nothing out of their journal to justify the reflections upon us; therefore it is to be presumed they cannot.

And we do further humbly and unanimously declare, we never did at any time, either jointly or severally, make any complaint to the assembly, or any of them, of the power given by his majesty to his excellency our present governor to suspend any of his majesty's council here: for as we have hitherto yielded all due obedience and submission to his majesty's royal will and pleasure concerning us, so we hope we shall approve ourselves such, and, as in duty bound, ever pray for his majesty's long life, and that he may prosperously and triumphantly reign over us.

This was unanimously agreed to in council by the respective members thereof who were present at the passing the bill of revenue: Colonel Thomas Ballard, Colonel John Cope, Colonel Robert Byndloss, Colonel Thomas Freeman, Colonel William Joy, Colonel Thomas Fuller, John White, Esquire;

And consented to by the whole council, excepting Lieutenant-Colonel Samuel Long.

Received from the Earl of Carlisle, 26th February, 1679-80.

NUMBER

NUMBER XXI.

Extract of an order in council.

JAMAICA.

At the committee of trade and plantations, in the council-chamber at Whitehall, the 5th of March, 1679-80,

PRESENT,

Prince Rupert,	Marquis of Worcester,	Mr. Hyde,
Lord President,	Earl of Bridgewater,	Mr. Sec. Coventry,
Lord Privy Seal,	Earl of Essex,	Sir Leolin Jenkins.

A LETTER from the Earl of Carlisle to the committee, dated 23d of November last, is read, wherein his lordship acquaints the committee, that, having called the council and assembly together, he had caused their lordships report of the 28th of May to be publickly read; which their lordships think to be disagreeable to the directions of the report, which was only presented to his majesty for his information, and in order to furnish the Earl of Carlisle, when occasion should serve, with such arguments as might be fit to be used in justification of his majesty's commission and instructions; and their lordships particularly take notice, that it was neither necessary nor convenient for him to expose his instructions to the assembly: and as to the clerk of the assembly, which his lordship had appointed, the committee does very much approve his lordship's proceedings therein, and will desire him to continue the same method for the future.

And whereas Colonel Long is represented to have a hand in leaving out the king's name in the late bill of revenue, and in framing and advising the address of the assembly now transmitted to his majesty; their lordships will report, that the Earl of Carlisle may be ordered to send him to England, to answer what is laid to his charge.

The

CHAP. XIV.

The address of the assembly of Jamaica to his majesty, in answer to a report of the committee approved on the 28th of May last, being read, their lordships observe, that there are many falsities and mistakes contained therein.

First, it is alledged by the assembly, that the island took up the civil form of government in the time of Sir Thomas Modyford and Sir Charles Lyttelton; whereas it is certain, that Colonel D'Oyley had a commission, soon after his majesty's restoration, to govern by the civil power.

As to their denial of having left out his majesty's name in the revenue bill, it is evident, by the justification of the council, and assurance of the Lord Vaughan, that the bill passed the governor and council with his majesty's name, which was afterwards left out, or erazed, as may be supposed by the interlineation that yet appears upon the original bill.

And whereas it is said, that their lordships are misinformed, in affirming that the assembly had before offered the bill of revenue in the same measure and proportion as is now proposed, since the laws were to be in force for two years, and no longer: the assembly have quite forgotten, or pretended to be ignorant of, the powers settled by his majesty's commission to Sir Thomas Lynch, whereby the laws were to be in force for two years, and no longer, unless confirmed by his majesty within that time; so that the bill transmitted by Sir Thomas Lynch wanted only his majesty's approbation to render it perpetual.

The assembly further mentions the great sums raised in Jamaica, which had not been employed to his majesty's service; but does not instance the misapplication of any part of the revenue by any of the governors.

It is also to be observed, that the law for preventing damages by fire, of which they complain, was first made by them; as also the act directing the marshal's proceedings cannot be but very reasonable, and for the advantage of the planters, since it gives them the use of their goods after execution, and enables them the better to pay their debts.

And

And whereas the assembly complains, that there is no law transmitted to them for ascertaining the laws of England; it is thought reasonable, that his majesty should retain within himself the power of appointing the laws of England to be in full force in that island, as he shall find it necessary.

The delays and length of time, alledged by them in reference to the model prescribed by his majesty, were wholly occasioned by the refractoriness of the assembly, and not by the distance of places, or other reasons.

What they object concerning Ireland, in reference to Jamaica, is frivolous: since the English there have right to the same privileges as those of Jamaica, and are bound up by acts of parliament in England, as well as the inhabitants of Jamaica,

To the 7th objection it is replied, that nothing has been done to take away their enjoyment of all the privileges of English subjects, since they are governed by the laws and statutes of this realm.

Their unwarrantable proceedings in obstructing of justice against Brown the pirate is confessed, and his majesty's pardon prayed by them.

Their lordships think the imprisonment of Martyn, and the articles preferred against him, altogether unjustifiable, not only as he was his majesty's collector, but as the assembly ought not, by the pretensions of privilege, to shelter themselves from justice, there being no such usage in Barbadoes and other plantations.

In the 9th place, it is altogether erroneous in the assembly to think it is, by the present model, in their own power, to accept such laws as are wholly of benefit to themselves, and to reject such as are most necessary for his majesty; since the governor yet retains a negative voice, after the consent of the assembly.

And whereas they very much insist upon his majesty's proclamation in my Lord Windsor's time: his majesty has not in any instance withdrawn the effects of his promise to them,

nor

CHAP. XIV.

nor imposed several rules and instructions that were prescribed in Sir Thomas Modyford's commission and instructions, whereby he had power, with the advice of the council, to raise money on strong liquors: and the assembly can as little believe they have not provoked his majesty to keep a strict eye upon them, after their several unwarrantable proceedings during the government of the Lord Vaughan, and since of the Earl of Carlisle, by their votes and otherwise.

In the last place, it is falsely insinuated by the assembly, that the government remained under an army in Colonel D'Oyley's time: since it appears plainly by his commission, that it was otherwise provided, and that the martial law was then laid aside; so that, upon the whole matter, they have reason to beg his majesty's pardon for all their errors and mistakes.

The justification of the council of Jamaica, in answer to the imputation of the assembly, of their leaving out the king's name in the revenue bill, is also read; and to be made use of by the governor, to disprove the allegations of the assembly in their own behalf.

NUMBER XXIII.

Extract of an order in council.

JAMAICA.

At the committee of trade and plantations, in the council-chamber at Whitehall, Monday the 8th of March, 1679-80,

PRESENT,

Lord Privy Seal, Earl of Bridgewater, Sir Leolin Jenkins.

THE Lord Vaughan attends, concerning the charge against Colonel Long, of Jamaica, for razing out the king's name in the act of revenue; and declares, that he is very confident that the bill came up from the assembly to the council with the

the king's name in it, and that it was not put out by the council, nor by his privity: and that when Mr. Martyn came to Jamaica with the king's patent to be collector, his lordship then sent for the act, and perceived the interlineation to be in Colonel Long's hand; and that his lordship does absolutely agree with the council of Jamaica, in the matter of their justification.

NUMBER XXIV.

Extract of an order in council.

JAMAICA.

At the committee of trade and plantations, in the council-chamber at Whitehall, Thursday the 11th of March, 1679-80,

PRESENT,

Lord President,	Marq. of Worcester,	Sir Leolin Jenkins.
Lord Privy-Seal,	Earl of Bridgewater,	

THEIR lordships take into consideration the state of the government in Jamaica, and agree to refer the queries following to Mr. Attorney and Mr. Solicitor General, for their opinions therein; *viz.*

1st. Whether, from the past and present state of Jamaica, his majesty's subjects inhabiting and trading there have a right to the laws of England, as Englishmen, or by virtue of the king's proclamation, or otherwise?

2d. Whether his majesty's subjects of Jamaica, claiming to be governed by the laws of England, are not bound as well by such laws as are beneficial to the king, by appointing taxes and subsidies for the support of the government, as by other laws, which tend only to the benefit and ease of the subject?

3d. Whether the subsidies of tonnage and poundage upon goods that may by law, or shall be directly carried to Jamaica, be not payable, according to law, by his majesty's subjects inhabiting

CHAP. XIV. habiting that island, or trading there, by virtue of the acts of tonnage and poundage, or other acts made in England?

4th. Whether wine or other goods, once brought into England and transported from thence, upon which the respective abatements are allowed upon exportation, according to law, the same being afterwards carried to Jamaica and landed there, shall not be liable to the payment of the full duty of tonnage and poundage which it should have paid if consumed in England, deducting only such part of the said duty as shall not be repaid in England upon exportation of the said goods from thence?

Which queries were accordingly transmitted to Mr. Attorney and Mr. Solicitor General, with a paper containing the past and present state of Jamaica, in relation to the government.

NUMBER XXV.

Letter to Mr. Attorney and Mr. Solicitor General.

Council-chamber, 11th March, 1679-80.

Gentlemen,

THE right honourable the lords of the committee for trade and plantations, upon consideration of the affairs of Jamaica, have stated the questions following; *viz.*

[*Here were recited the queries stated in the preceding number.*]

To which questions their lordships desire your answer in writing, with all convenient speed: and, for your information, I have inclosed *a paper, containing a short account of the past and present state of the government in Jamaica;* and in case you should require any further satisfaction therein, or touching the queries referred unto you, I am ordered by the lords of the committee to attend you at any time or place you shall think fit to appoint.

I am, with all respect, gentlemen, &c.

NUMBER

NUMBER XXVI.

Extract of an order in council.

JAMAICA.

At the committee of trade and plantations, in the council-chamber at Whitehall, the 27th of April, 1680,

PRESENT,

Prince Rupert,	Earl of Essex,	Mr. Hyde,
Lord President,	Visc. Fauconberg,	Mr. Sec. Jenkins.
Earl of Sunderland,		

MR. Attorney and Mr. Solicitor General having likewise acquainted the committee, that, upon consideration of the four questions concerning Jamaica, referred unto them the 11th of March, they did find them of such difficulty and moment as to deserve the opinion of the judges: it is agreed that they be accordingly referred unto the judges; upon whom Mr. Attorney and Mr. Solicitor General are desired to attend with them; Mr. Attorney having first delivered his opinion, "that "the people of Jamaica have no right to be governed by the "laws of England, but by such laws as are made there, and "established by his majesty's authority." But whereas Mr. Solicitor General doth deliver his opinion, that the word "do-"minion," in the act of parliament for tonnage and poundage, may seem rather to imply the dominion of Wales and Berwick upon Tweed only, than to extend to the plantations; and more especially, as Mr. Attorney alledges, since the islands of Guernsey and Jersey are not concerned in that act: their lordships order the two first questions only to be sent unto the judges, without any mention to be made of the two last, which particularize the act of tonnage and poundage.

NUMBER

CHAP. XI

NUMBER XXVII.

References to the judges about Jamaica.

Council-chamber, 27th April, 1680.

Gentlemen,

I AM commanded by the right honourable the lords of the privy-council appointed a committee of trade and foreign plantations, to signify their desires that you attend his majesty's judges with the questions following:

1st. Whether from the past and present state of Jamaica, his majesty's subjects inhabiting and trading there have a right to the laws of England, as Englishmen, or by virtue of the king's proclamation, or otherwise?

2d. Whether his majesty's subjects of Jamaica, claiming to be governed by the laws of England, are not bound as well by such laws as are beneficial to the king, by appointing taxes and subsidies for the support of the government, as by other laws, which tend only to the benefit and ease of the subject?

Which questions their lordships desire his majesty's judges to consider and answer in writing, and to return the opinions to the committee with convenient speed.

I am, with respect, &c.

NUMBER XXVIII.

Order to the judges about the question of Jamaica.

At the court at Whitehall, the 23d of June, 1680,

PRESENT,

His Majesty,

Prince Rupert,	Lord Chamberlain,	Mr. Coventry,
Abp. of Canterbury,	Earl of Sunderland,	Mr. Sec. Jen-
Lord Chancellor,	Earl of Clarendon,	kins,

Lord

Lord President,	Earl of Bath,	Mr. Chancellor of
Lord Privy-Seal,	Ld. Bp. of London,	the Exchequer,
D. of Albemarle,	Mr. Hyde,	Mr. Godolphin.
Marq. of Worcester,	Mr. Finch,	
Earl of Ossory,	Lord Chief Justice North,	

IT is this day ordered in council, that Mr. Attorney and Mr. Solicitor General do attend his majesty's judges, and desire them to assemble with all convenient speed, and, being assembled, to confer with them concerning this question, *viz.*

Whether, by his majesty's letter, proclamation, or commissions, annexed, his majesty hath excluded himself from the power of establishing laws in Jamaica, it being a conquered country, and all laws settled by authority there being now expired?

And that, upon receiving the opinions of his majesty's judges, *under their hands in writing*, they do report the same to the lords of the privy-council appointed a committee for trade and foreign plantations.

NUMBER XXIX.

Extract of an order in council.

JAMAICA.

At the committee of trade and plantations, in the council-chamber at Whitehall, the 7th of September, 1680,

PRESENT,

Lord President,	Marquis of Worcester,	Mr. Sec. Jenkins.

MR. Secretary Jenkins acquaints the committee, that Colonel Long, of Jamaica, had some days before surrendered himself to him, upon a bond of ten thousand pounds given to the Earl of Carlisle to that purpose; and that he had taken his security for the like sum, that he would attend the first council, on Friday next, being the 10th instant.

NUMBER XXX.

Copy of an order in council.

JAMAICA.

At the committee of trade and plantations, in the council-chamber at Whitehall,

PRESENT,

Prince Rupert,	Marquis of Worcester,	Earl of Bath,
Lord President,	Earl of Clarendon,	Mr. Sec. Jenkins.

THE Earl of Carlisle is called in, and delivers a paper containing a charge against Colonel Long, which is read, consisting chiefly in three points; *viz.* That he had razed the king's name out of the act for raising a public revenue; that he had granted an *habeas corpus*, being judge, for a person condemned by law; and had opposed the settlement of the country pursuant to the king's orders.

And his lordship declaring, that he had nothing more to say against Colonel Long than was contained in that paper, only reserving to himself the liberty of explaining what he had therein mentioned, Colonel Long is called in, and the paper read to him; whereupon he positively denies that he had done any thing to the bill without the directions of the assembly; and that he believes the razure happened, inasmuch as the clerk of the assembly had transcribed the bill passed in Sir Thomas Lynch's time, which was now blotted out by the agreement of the governor, council, and assembly, and the words written in his hand were only added to make up the sense, which otherwise would have been wanting, which he did as speaker of that assembly from whom he had directions; which is confirmed by the letters of Major Molesworth, Mr. Bernard, Mr. Ashurst, Mr. Burton, and of the clerk of the assembly.

As to the granting an *habeas corpus*, he declares he did not know the person was condemned; and that it is usual for the judges

judges to sign blank *habeas corpus*'s, which the clerk gives out in course. APPENDIX.

And that he never opposed the king's orders, otherwise than by expressing his opinion, that they were not for his majesty's service, nor the good of the country.

NUMBER XXXI.

Extract of an order in council.

JAMAICA.

At the committee of trade and plantations, in the council-chamber at Whitehall, Tuesday the 12th of October, 1680,

PRESENT,

Prince Rupert,	Earl of Sunderland,	Mr. Hyde,
Lord President,	Earl of Clarendon,	Mr. Godolphin,
Lord Privy-Seal,	Earl of Halifax,	Mr. Sec. Jenkins,
Marquis of Worcester,	Visc. Fauconberg,	Mr. Seymour.

THE Earl of Carlisle attending, acquaints the committee, that the act for raising a publick revenue will expire in March next, and that the government will be left under very great necessities, in case the king do not give Sir Henry Morgan leave to pass a temporary bill, until the full settlement of affairs shall be agreed on, which is like to take up a considerable time; and therefore proposes, that the order in council, dated the 14th of January last (which is read) forbidding the governor to raise money by any other act or order whatsoever than by the bill transmitted by his majesty, which the assembly will not be willing to pass until the government be entirely settled in such manner as may be more agreeable to them than the Irish model, be suspended. His lordship proceeds to give an account of his transactions with the assembly, to persuade them to pass the revenue bill, and reads the objections of the assembly, and his answer to them; whereof, and of the coun-

CHAP. XIV. cil-books, his lordship is desired to give a transcript to the committee.

There having been two laws read which were entered therein, the one made by Colonel D'Oyley and the council, for raising imposts on liquors, the other by Sir Charles Lyttelton and his council, being a supplemental act to the former:

And his lordship acquainting the committee, that, as for licences of taverns, he had set them on foot before he passed any bill of revenue:

It is thereupon thought fit, by some of their lordships, that the assembly of Jamaica be induced to pass a perpetual bill, by having leave to appropriate the revenue to the support of the government.

And the committee is appointed to meet again on this business on Thursday, at nine o'clock in the morning; when Colonel Long, and the other assembly men lately come over, are to attend.

NUMBER XXXII.

JAMAICA.

At the committee of trade and plantations, in the council-chamber at Whitehall, Thursday the 14th of October, 1680,

PRESENT,

Prince Rupert,	E. of Clarendon,	Visc. Fauconberg,
Lord President,	E. of Essex,	Ld. Ch. Just. North,
Lord Privy-Seal,	E. of Halifax,	Mr. Sec. Jenkins.
Marq. of Worcester,		

THE Earl of Carlisle attends, and produces an entry in the council-book of Jamaica, of a law passed by Colonel D'Oyley and the council, for raising a publick revenue, and of another passed by Sir Charles Lyttelton and the council, being a supplemental act to the former, both which are indefinite, and not determined by the commissions of Colonel D'Oyley

of

or my Lord Windsor, whose deputy Sir Charles Lyttelton was.

After which, Colonel Long and Mr. Ashurst are called in (the other gentlemen of Jamaica being in the country) and being asked, Why they were not willing that a perpetual bill of revenue should pass in Jamaica? they made answer, that they have no other way to make their aggrievances known to the king, to have them redressed, than by the dependance of the governor upon the assembly, which is preserved by passing temporary bills of revenue; and that, a perpetual bill being passed, all the ends of government would be answered, and there would be no further need of calling assemblies. To which my Lord of Carlisle replies, that, notwithstanding any act for raising an impost on liquors should be passed in that manner, yet the necessities and contingencies of the government are such as to require the frequent calling of assemblies, for raising money by other means, and doing publick works, the present revenue coming far short of the expence of the government.

Their lordships tell Colonel Long, that in case they be willing and pass the act of revenue indefinitely, the king may be induced to settle other perpetual laws, which they shall propose as beneficial to them.

The gentlemen of Jamaica being withdrawn, their lordships enter upon a debate concerning a continuance of the two laws made by Colonel D'Oyley and Sir Charles Lyttelton before mentioned, and *how far the English laws and methods of government ought to take place in Jamaica; and it is there alleged, " that the laws of England cannot be in force in another " country, where the constitution of the place is different from " that of England."*

Upon the whole matter, the committee desire my Lord Chief Justice North to report his opinion in writing, on Monday next, upon the question following; *viz.*

1st. Whether the king, by his proclamation published during my Lord Windsor's government, *his majesty's letter dated*

15th

15th of January 1672-3, or any other act, appearing by the laws of England or any laws of Jamaica, or by his majesty's commissions or instructions to his governors, has divested himself of the power he *formerly had* to alter the forms of government in Jamaica?

2d. Whether any act of the assembly of Jamaica, or any other act of his majesty or his governors, have totally repealed the acts made by Colonel D'Oyley, and Sir Charles Lyttelton, for raising a publick revenue, or whether they are now in force?

Memorandum, His majesty being present, my Lord Chief Justice North was added to the committee.

Memorandum, Colonel Long having mentioned some transactions of my Lord Vaughan's during his government, his lordship is to be summoned for the next meeting.

NUMBER XXXIII.

JAMAICA.

At the committee of trade and plantations, in the council-chamber at Whitehall, on Monday the 18th of October, 1680,

PRESENT,

Lord President,	Earl of Halifax,
Lord Privy Seal,	Lord Visc. Fauconberg,
Lord Chamberlain,	Lord Chief Justice North,
Earl of Essex,	Mr. Secretary Jenkins,
Earl of Clarendon,	Mr. Seymour.

MY Lord Chief Justice North having acquainted the committee, that he had considered of the two questions proposed by their lordships; and that, although some further time would be requisite for him to give in his answer, yet, in respect of the haste

haste that was necessary for settling the revenue, his lordship undertakes to return his answer at the next meeting upon the second question; wherein his lordship is desired to take to his assistance some other of his majesty's judges; *viz.* APPEN-DIX.

Whether any act of the assembly of Jamaica, or any act of his majesty or his governors, have totally repealed the acts made by Colonel D'Oyley and Sir Charles Lyttelton, for raising a publick revenue, or whether they are now in force?

NUMBER XXXIV.

JAMAICA.

At the committee of trade and plantations, in the council-chamber at Whitehall, on Wednesday the 20th of October, 1680,

PRESENT,

Lord President,	Lord Chief Justice North,
Earl of Sunderland,	Lord Bishop of London,
Earl of Bridgewater,	Mr. Secretary Jenkins,
Earl of Essex,	Mr. Seymour.
Earl of Halifax,	

MY Lord Chief Justice North, having delivered his opinion in writing upon the question recommended to him at the last meeting, Colonel Long, Mr. Beeston, Mr. Ashurst, and other planters and merchants of Jamaica, together with the Earl of Carlisle, are called in, and his lordship's opinion is read to them; whereby his lordship concludes, that the act of revenue made in 1663 by Sir Charles Lyttelton, is yet in force, as being not repealed by any subsequent acts, which were limited to the term of two years by his majesty's commands. But Colonel Long objects, that there was a law made by Sir Thomas Modyford, which declares all laws passed at Sir Charles Lyttelton's assemblies void, for want of due form in the writs, and other particulars:

CHAP. XIV. particulars: whereupon they are bid to withdraw; and whereas, my Lord Chief Justice North was not present when this objection was made, their lordships think fit that he be acquainted therewith, and desired to renew his opinion; and the gentlemen of Jamaica are also desired to be ready with the objections they have to make to his lordship's report, at the next meeting, which is appointed for to-morrow at three in the afternoon.

NUMBER XXXV.

JAMAIÇA.

At the committee of trade and plantations, in the council-chamber at Whitehall, Thursday 21st of October, 1680,

PRESENT,

Prince Rupert,	Viscount Fauconberg,
Lord President,	Mr. Hyde,
Marquis of Worcester,	Lord Chief Justice North,
Earl of Bridgewater,	Mr. Secretary Jenkins.
Earl of Clarendon,	

THE lords, being met to consider the business of Jamaica, order the proclamation published in my Lord Windsor's time to be read: and thereupon their lordships express their opinion, that his majesty did thereby assure and settle the property of the inhabitants, *but not the government and form;* thence these questions did arise; *viz.*

1st. Whether, upon the consideration of the commission and instructions to Colonel D'Oyley, and Sir Charles Lyttelton, and the *constitution of the island thereupon,* the acts of council made by Colonel D'Oyley and Sir Charles Lyttelton were perpetual laws, binding to the inhabitants of the island?

2d. Whether, supposing those laws good and perpetual, any

of

of the subsequent laws, or the proclamation in my Lord Windsor's time, have taken away the force of these laws? APPENDIX.

And because the gentlemen of Jamaica made divers objections against the validity of those laws, as being made by the governors and council without an assembly, and against the perpetuity of them, as being repealed by subsequent laws; their lordships do therefore think it most conducing to his majesty's service, that Colonel Long, Major Beeston, and Mr. Ashurst, do attend my Lord Chief Justice North, in order to explain to his lordship what is chiefly expected by them, whereby they may be induced to settle the revenue for the support of the government, to the end matters may be brought to an accommodation.

NUMBER XXXVI.

JAMAICA.

At a committee of trade and plantations, in the council-chamber at Whitehall, Wednesday the 27th of October, 1680,

PRESENT,

Lord Privy-Seal,	Earl of Bath,
Earl of Bridgewater,	Earl of Halifax,
Lord Chamberlain,	Mr. Chan. of the Exchequer.

MY Lord Chief Justice North reports, that he has been attended by the gentlemen of Jamaica, who have declared themselves willing to grant the perpetual bill for the payment of the governors, and another bill for the payment of contingencies to continue for seven years, provided they may be restored to their ancient form of passing laws, and may be assured of such of the laws of England as may concern their liberty and property.

Their lordships taking notice, that the revenue of Jamaica will

CHAP. XIV.

will expire in March next, direct a letter to be prepared, for the approbation of the council, empowering Sir Henry Morgan to call an assembly, and to endeavour the passing a temporary bill, with their consent, for the revenue; and, in case of their refusal, to raise the same in such manner as hath been done by former governors.

Memorandum, At a council on the instant, a draught of the aforementioned letter was read:

And upon reading the petition of the planters, merchants and inhabitants of Jamaica, praying to be restored to their ancient method of making laws; the lords of the committee are ordered to meet *de die in diem*, until they shall have agreed on such a method for the making of laws, and the settlement of the government, as they shall find most convenient for his majesty's service.

NUMBER XXXVII.

JAMAICA.

At the committee of trade and plantations, in the council-chamber at Whitehall, on Thursday the 28th of October, 1680,

PRESENT,

Prince Rupert,	Earl of Halifax,
Lord Privy-Seal	Viscount Fauconberg,
Lord Chamberlain,	Bishop of London,
Earl of Bridgewater,	Mr. Hyde,
Earl of Sunderland,	Lord Chief Justice North,
Earl of Clarendon,	Mr. Secretary Jenkins.
Earl of Essex,	

THEIR lordships having considered that part of the letter from the council of Jamaica, dated 20th May last, that concerns the laws, and having read the petition of the merchants and planters of Jamaica, presented in council on the , as also a paper prepared by Mr. Blackwayt, concerning the manner of making laws in Jamaica, their lordships, upon full consideration and debate of what may best conduce to his majesty's service, agree, *that the present method of making laws in Barbadoes, as settled by the commission of Sir Richard Dutton, be proposed unto his majesty in council:* and that powers be drawn up for the Earl of Carlisle, with instructions suitable to that scheme, and with respect to the present circumstances of Jamaica; and that the assembly may be the more easily induced to grant a revenue for the support of the government, their lordships are of opinion, that his majesty's quit-rents, and the tax on the wine-licences, as well as all other levies which now are or shall be made, be appropriated to the support of the government, and to no other use whatsoever.

NUMBER XXXVIII.

JAMAICA.

At the committee of trade and plantations, in the council-chamber at Whitehall, on Saturday the 30th of October, 1680,

PRESENT,

Prince Rupert,	Earl of Clarendon,
Duke of Albemarle,	Earl of Essex,
Lord Chamberlain,	Viscount Fauconberg,
Earl of Bridgewater,	Earl of Halifax,
Earl of Sunderland,	Mr. Secretary Jenkins.

COLONEL Long and the other gentlemen of Jamaica attend, and are acquainted with the resolutions of the committee to report to his majesty, that they may enjoy the same method of making laws as is now appointed for Barbadoes; with which the gentlemen express themselves very well satisfied.

NUMBER

NUMBER XXXIX.

Copy of powers to the Earl of Carlisle for making laws.

Charles the Second, by the grace of God, king of England, Scotland, France, and Ireland, Defender of the Faith, &c.

To our right trusty and right well-beloved cousin Charles Earl of Carlisle, our captain-general and governor in chief in and over our island of Jamaica, and other the territories depending thereon; and to our deputy-governor and commander in chief of our said Island; and, in case of their death or absence, to our council of Jamaica.

WHEREAS, by our royal commission bearing date the first of March, in the thirtieth year of our reign, we having thought fit to constitute and appoint you, Charles Earl of Carlisle, captain-general and governor in chief in and over our island of Jamaica, and the territories depending thereon, thereby commanding and requiring you, or in your absence our deputy-governor, or our council, to do and execute all things belonging to the said command, and the trust reposed in you, according to the several powers or directions granted or appointed you by the said commission and the instructions therewith given you, or by further powers and instructions to be granted or appointed you under our signet and sign manual, as by our said commission (reference being thereunto had) doth more at large appear: and whereas it is necessary that good and wholesome laws and ordinances be settled and established for the government and support of our island of Jamaica: we do hereby give and grant unto you full power and authority, with the advice and consent of the said council, from time to time, as need shall require, to summon or call general assemblies of the freeholders and planters within the said island, in manner and form as is now practised in Jamaica. And our will and pleasure is, that the persons thereupon duly elected by the major part of the freeholders of the respective parishes and places, and so returned (having, before their sitting, taken the oaths of allegiance and supremacy, which you shall commissionate fit persons, under the public seal of that island, to administer, and without taking which none shall be capable of sitting, though elected) shall be called and held the general assembly of our island of Jamaica; and that they, or the major part of them, shall have full power and authority, with the advice and consent of yourself and of the council, to make, constitute, and ordain laws, statutes, and ordinances, for the public peace, welfare, and good government of the said island, and of the people and inhabitants thereof, and such other as shall resort thereto, and for the benefit of our heirs and successors; which said laws, statutes, and ordinances, are to be (as near as conveniently may be) agreeable to the laws and statutes of our kingdom of England: provided, that all such laws, statutes, and ordinances, of what nature or duration whatsoever, be, within three months, or by the first conveyance after making the same, transmitted unto us under the public seal, for our allowance and approbation of them, as also duplicates thereof by the next conveyance: and in case all or any of them (being not before confirmed by us) shall at any time be disallowed and not approved, and so signified by us, our heirs or successors, under our or their sign manual or signet, or by order of our or their privy-council, unto you, the said Earl of Carlisle, or to the commander in chief of our said island for the time being, then such or so many of them as shall be so disallowed and not approved shall from thenceforth cease, determine, and be utterly void and of none effect, any thing to the contrary thereof notwithstanding. And, to the end nothing may be passed or done in our said island by the said council or assembly to the prejudice of us, our heirs or successors,

CHAP. XIV.

cessors, we will and ordain that you, the said Charles Earl of Carlisle, shall have and enjoy a negative voice in the making or passing of all laws, statutes, and ordinances, as aforesaid; and that you shall and may likewise, from time to time, as you shall judge it necessary, dissolve all general assemblies, as aforesaid; any thing in our commission bearing date as aforesaid to the contrary hereof notwithstanding. And our will and pleasure is, that, in case of your death or absence from our said island, our deputy-governor for the time being exercise and enjoy all and singular the powers and authorities hereby granted unto you, or intended to be granted you, the said Charles Earl of Carlisle; and in case he likewise happen to die, or be absent from our said island, we do hereby authorize and empower our council of Jamaica to execute the powers hereby given you, until we shall declare our further pleasure therein.

Given at our court at Whitehall, this 3d day of November, in the thirty-second year of our reign.

HISTORY

HISTORY OF THE WEST INDIES, &c.

HORTUS EASTENSIS:

OR

A CATALOGUE OF EXOTIC PLANTS, in the Garden of Hinton East, Esq., in the Mountains of Liguanea, in the Island of Jamaica, at the time of his decease. By Arthur Broughton, M. D.

N. B. This Garden is now the Property of the Public.

HORTUS EASTENSIS:

&c.

Classis I.

MONANDRIA.

MONOGYNIA.

CANNA	*indica var. lutea*	Yellow Indian Shot	East-Indies	Mr. Shakespear, 1780
AMOMUM	*Granum paradisi**	Guinea Pepper	Guinea	Tho. Hibbert, Esq. 1785
	Zingiber	Common Ginger	East-Indies	
CURCUMA	*longa*	Turmerick	East-Indies	Z. B. Edwards, Esq. 1788
KÆMPFERIA	*Galanga*	Galangale	East-Indies	Dr. Tho. Clarke, 1775
THALIA	*geniculata*	Indian Arrow-root	South-America	

Classis II.

DIANDRIA.

MONOGYNIA.

NYCTANTHES	*Sambac*	Arabian Jasmine		
	var. fl. pleno	Double Arabian Jasmine	East-Indies	H. East, Esq. 1775
JASMINUM	*officinale*	Common Jasmine		
	lanceolatum ?	Narrow-leav'd Jasmine	East-Indies	H. East, Esq. 1787
	azoricum	Azorian Jasmine	Madeira	H. East, Esq. 1787
	odoratissimum	Yellow Indian Jasmine	Madeira	M. Wallen, Esq. 1787
OLEA	*europæa*	European Olive	Europe	M. Wallen, Esq. 1783
	fragrans	Sweet-scented Olive	China	H. East, Esq. 1783
SYRINGA	*vulgaris*	Common Lilac	Persia	M. Wallen, Esq. 1774
	persica	Persian Lilac	Persia	M. Wallen, Esq. 1785
JUSTICIA	*sp. nov. arborea*		Italy	Tho. Hibbert, Esq. 1787
DIANTHERA	*americana*	American Balsam	Virginia	

* This plant has now several times perfected its seed, from which it appears to be the true Guinea or Malagita Pepper and Grains of Paradise of the Shops; it is not however an AMOMUM, but approaches nearer to the LIMODORUM than any other known Genus.

ROSMARINUS	*officinalis*	Rosemary	Europe	
SALVIA	*officinalis*	Garden Sage	S. of Europe	
	africana	African Sage	C. of G. Hope	Dr. Tho. Clarke, 1775
	coccinea	Scarlet Sage	East-Florida	Dr. Tho. Clarke, 1775
	Solarea	Clary	Syria	H. East, Esq.

TRIGYNIA.

PIPER	*nigrum*	Black Pepper	East-Indies	Tho. Hibbert, Esq. 1787

Classis III.

TRIANDRIA.

MONOGYNIA.

VALERIANA	*Locusta*	Lamb's Lettuce	Portugal	H. East, Esq.
TAMARINDUS	*indica*	Tamarind Tree	India. America	
CROCUS	*sativus*	Spring Crocus	England	M. Wallen, Esq. 1779
IXIA	*rosea*	Rose-coloured Ixia	C. of G. Hope	H. East, Esq.
	chinensis	Spotted Ixia	China	H. East, Esq. 1789
GLADIOLUS	*communis*	Common Flag	S. of Europe	M. Wallen, Esq. 1774
ANTHOLYZA	*æthiopica*		C. of G. Hope	H. East, Esq. 1788
IRIS	*pumila*	Dwarf Iris	Austria	H. East, Esq.
WACHENDORFIA	*thyrsiflora*		C. of G. Hope	H. East, Esq. 1790
LYGEUM	*Spartum*	Rush-leaved Lygeum	Spain	H. East, Esq. 1791.

DIGYNIA.

AVENA	*sativa*	Oats		M. Wallen, Esq. 1773
ARUNDO	*Bambos*	Bamboo Cane*	East-Indies	M. Wallen, Esq.
HORDEUM	*vulgare*	Barley		M. Wallen, Esq. 1773

Classis IV.

TETRANDRIA.

MONOGYNIA.

SCABIOSA	*cretica*	Cretan Scabious	Candia	H. East, Esq. 1788
	atropurpurea	Sweet Scabious	Italy	M. Wallen, Esq. 1772
	stellata	Starry Scabious	Spain	H. East, Esq. 1788.
RUBIA	*tinctorum*	Madder	S. of Europe	Mr. Thame, 1790
BUDLEJA	*globosa* †		Chili	H. East, Esq. 1788
PLANTAGO	*lanceolata*	Rib-wort Plantain	Britain	M. Wallen, Esq. 1772
CISSUS	*quadrangularis*		India	H. East, Esq. 1791
OLDENLANDIA	*umbellata*	Chè	India	H. East, Esq. 1791
ALCHEMILLA	*vulgaris*	Ladies Mantle	Britain	H. East, Esq. 1791

TETRAGYNIA.

ILEX	*aquifolium*	Common Holly	Britain	H. East, Esq. 1774
	Cassine	Paraguay Tea	Carolina	Mr. Gale, 1772
	nov. Sp.		Madeira	Tho. Hibbert, Esq. 1787

* This most valuable production is now successfully cultivated in all parts of Jamaica.
† *Hort. Kewensis*, vol. i. p. 150.

Classis V.

PENTANDRIA.

MONOGYNIA.

Heliotropium	*peruvianum*	Peruvian Turnsole	Peru	H. East, Esq. 1788
Anchusa	*officinalis*	Bugloss	Europe	H. East, Esq. 1774
Cynoglossum	*officinale*	Hound's-tongue	Britain	M. Wallen, Esq. 1775
Borago	*officinalis*	Borage	England	M. Wallen, Esq. 1772
Primula	*veris*	Primrose	Britain	M. Wallen, Esq. 1780
	auricula	Auricula	Austria	H. East, Esq. 1790
Cyclamen	*persicum*	Persian Cyclamen	Candia	H. East, Esq. 1787
Azalea	*viscosa*	White Azalea	N. America	H. East, Esq.
Plumbago	*rosea*	Bengal Lead-wort	Bengal	H. East, Esq. 1787
Phlox	*glaberrima*	Smooth Lychnidea	N. America	Mr. Thame, 1787
Convolvulus	*Scammonia*	Scammony Bind-weed	Levant	Dr. Tho. Clarke, 1775
	purpureus major	Large purple Bind-w.	America	H. East, Esq.
	minor	Small purple Bind-w.	America	H. East, Esq.
	tricolor	Trailing Bind-weed	Spain	H. East, Esq.
	canariensis	Perennial Bind-weed	Canary Islands	
	speciosus	Broad-leav'd Bind-w.	East-Indies	
Ipomoea	*Quamoclit*	Indian Creeper	East-Indies	
Campanula	*rotundifolia*	Bell-flower	Britain	M. Wallen, Esq. 1772
Cinchona*		Hispaniola Bark	Hispaniola	Mr. Thame, 1790

Coffea	*arabica*	Coffee-Tree	Arabia	
Lonicera	*Periclymenum*	Common Honeysuckle	Britain	M. Wallen, Esq. 1773
	symphoricarpos	St. Peter's Wort	Carolina	H. East, Esq.
	tartarica	Tartarian Honeysuckle	Russia	H. East, Esq.
Mirabilis	*Jalapa*	Marvel of Peru	E. & W. Indies	
Verbascum	*Thapsus*	Great Mullein	Britain	H. East, Esq. 1772
Datura	*Metel*	Hairy Thorn Apple	Africa	
Nicotiana	*Tabacum*	Virginian Tobacco	America	
Physalis	*Alkekengi*	Winter C	S. of Europe	H. East, Esq. 1779
Solanum	*tuberosum*	Common Potato	Peru	
	Melongena	Egg Plant	India	
	Sodomæum *	Bolangena	Africa	
Rhamnus	*Jujuba*	Jujube-tree	East-Indies	Dr. Tho. Clarke, 1790
Diosma	*ciliata*	Ciliated-Diosma	C. of G. Hope	H. East, Esq. 1788
Mangifera	*indica* †	Mango Tree	East-Indies	Lord Rodney, 1782
Ribes	*grossularia*	Gooseberry	Europe	M. Wallen, Esq. 1772

* *Affinis Cinchonæ Caribeæ.*

† The Mango is inserted in its usual Place, although in reality it is Polygamious, and hitherto very imperfectly described.—*N. B.* This Plant, with several others, as well as different Kinds of Seeds, were found on board a French Ship (bound from the Isle de France for Hispaniola) taken by Captain Marshall of his Majesty's Ship Flora, one of Lord Rodney's Squadron, in June 1782, and sent as a Prize to this Island. By Captain Marshall, with Lord Rodney's approbation, the whole Collection was deposited in Mr. East's Garden, where they have been cultivated with great assiduity and success.

RIBES	*rubrum*	Red Currant	Britain	M. Wallen, Esq. 1772
	nigrum	Black Currant	Britain	M. Wallen, Esq. 1772
VITIS	*vinifera*	Grape		
CELOSIA	*cristata*	Cockscomb	Asia	
	var.	Cocksc.	Asia	H. East, Esq. 1774
GARDENIA	*florida*		China	Dr. Tho. Clarke, 1775
	Thunbergia	Gardenia	C. of G. Hope	Dr. Tho. Clarke, 1775
ALLAMANDA	*cathartica*	Galarips	South America	Tho. Hibbert, Esq. 1789
VINCA	*rosea*	Red Periwinkle	East-Indies	
	*alba**	White Periwinkle		Mr. Thame
NERIUM	*Oleander fl. rubro*	Red South-Sea Rose	Spain. Portugal	
	fl. albo	White South-Sea Rose		H. East, Esq. 1787
	fl. pleno	Double Oleander		

DIGYNIA.

ASCLEPIAS	*fruticosa*	Shrubby Swallow-wort	Africa	H. East, Esq.
	gigantea	Auricula Tree		
STAPELIA	*variegata*	Variegated Stapelia	C. of G. Hope	Tho. Hibbert, Esq. 1787
BETA	*hybrida*	Mangel Wursel	Europe	H. East, Esq. 1790
	vulgaris	Common Beet	England	
DAUCUS	*Carota*	Garden Carrot	Britain	
GOMPHRENA	*globosa*	Globe Amaranth	India	
CORIANDRUM	*sativum*	Coriander	England	Mr. Thame, 1787
PASTINACA	*sativa*	Garden Parsnip	England	
ANETHUM	*graveolens*	Dill	Spain. Portugal	H. East, Esq.
	Fœniculum	Fennel	England	

CARUM	*Carvi*	Caraway	Britain	Mr. Thame, 1787
PIMPINELLA	*Anisum*	Anise	Egypt	Mr. R. Lloyd, 1787
APIUM	*Petroselinum*	Parsley	Sardinia	
	graveolens	Celery	Britain	
CASSINE	*capensis*	Hottentot Cherry	C. of G. Hope	H. East, Esq. 1788
SAMBUCUS	*Ebulus*	Dwarf Elder	Britain	M. Wallen, Esq. 1773
	nigra	Black-berried Elder	Britain	M. Wallen, Esq. 1773
RHUS	*Coriaria*	Elm-leav'd Sumach	S. of Europe	Tho. Hibbert, Esq. 1787
	typhinum	Virginian Sumach	Virginia	Mr. Gale, 1772

PENTAGYNIA.

LINUM	*usitatissimum*	Common Flax	Britain	M. Wallen, Esq. 1773
	maritimum	Sea Flax	Italy	H. East, Esq. 1788

Classis VI.

HEXANDRIA.

MONOGYNIA.

TRADESCANTIA	*discolor* †	Purple Spider-wort	Honduras	Mr. Shakespeare, 1782
NARCISSUS	*odorus*	Sweet-scented Narciss.	S. of Europe	Mr. Thame, 1773

* This Plant first appeared here on a dunghill where the red had been thrown out, and has since continued steady from seed.

† *Hort. Kewensis*, vol. i. p. 403.

NARCISSUS	*Tazetta*	Polyanthus Narcissus	Spain. Portugal	Mr. Thame, 1773
	Jonquilla	Jonquil	Spain	Mr. Thame, 1773
HÆMANTHUS	*puniceus*	Blood-Flower	Guinea	H. East, Esq. 1785
CRINUM	*Americanum*	American Crinum	S. America	
	Zeylanicum?	Ceylon Crinum	East-Indies	
	Asiaticum	Indian Crinum	East-Indies	
	Africanum	African blue Lily	C. of G. Hope	H. East, Esq. 1770
AMARYLLIS	*Atamasco*	Atamasco Lily	N. America	H. East, Esq.
	formosissima	Jacobea Lily	S. America	M. Wallen, Esq. 1772
	reginæ	Mexican Lily	S. America	H. East, Esq. 1790
	Belladonna	Belladonna Lily	S. America	M. Wallen, Esq. 1774
	aurea	Golden Amaryllis	China	H. East, Esq. 1785
	longifolia	Long-leav'd Amaryllis	C. of G. Hope	H. East, Esq. 1789
	radiata	Snow-drop Amaryllis		H. East, Esq. 1789
	vittata	Striped Lily		H. East, Esq. 1789
ALLIUM	*ascalonicum*	Jerusalem Shallot	Asia	H. East, Esq.
	gracile *	African Garlick	Africa	Dr. Tho. Clarke, 1775
	sativum	Garlick		
	Porrum	Leek		
	Cepa	Onion		
LILIUM	*bulbiferum*	Orange Lily	Italy	H. East, Fsq. 1774
	pomponium	Pomponian Lily	Siberia	H. East, Esq.
	Chalcedonicum	Scarlet Martagon Lily	Levant	H. East, Esq. 1790
	Martagon	Purple Martagon Lily	America	Mr. Thame, 1789
GLORIOSA	*superba*	Superb Lily	East-Indies	H. East, Esq. 1788
TULIPA	*gesneriana*	Tulip	Levant	M. Wallen, Esq.
ORNITHOGALUM	*pyrenaicum*	Star of Bethlehem	England	H. East, Esq. 1782

	nutans	Neapolitan Do	Italy	H. East, Esq. 1782
Asphodelus	*ramosus*	Branchy Asphodel	South of Europe	H. East, Esq. 1784
Asparagus	*officinalis*	Asparagus	England	
Dracæna	*Draco*	Dragon Tree	East-Indies	Dr. Tho. Clarke, 1775
	ferrea	Purple Dracæna	China	H. East, Esq. 1787
Polyanthes	*tuberosa fl. pleno*	Tuberose	East-Indies	
Hyacinthus	*orientalis*	Hyacinth	Levant	M. Wallen, Esq. 1773
Aletris	*capensis*	Cape Aletris	C. of G. Hope	H. East, Esq. 1788
	hyacinthoides	Ceylon Aloe	Ceylon	H. East, Esq. 1790
Yucca	*gloriosa*	Superb Aloe	N. America	Dr. Lindsay
	aloifolia		South-America	
	draconis		South-Carolina	
Aloe	*perfoliata*			
	var. barbad.	Barbadoes Aloe		
Berberis	*vulgaris*	Berbery	Britain	Mrs. Brodbelt, 1770

DIGYNIA.

Oryza	*sativa*	Common Rice		M. Wallen, Esq.

TRIGYNIA.

Rumex	*obtusifolius*	Blunt-leav'd Dock	Britain	M. Wallen, Esq. 1773

* *Hort. Kewensis*, vol. i. p. 429; said to be a native of Jamaica, but erroneously.

Classis

Classis VII.

HEPTANDRIA.

MONOGYNIA.

ÆSCULUS	*Hippocastanum*	Horse Chesnut	Asia	Mrs. Brodbelt, 1770
	flava	Yellow-flower'd Ches.	N. Carolina	H. East, Esq. 1790
	Pavia	Scarlet-flower'd Ches.	N. America	M. Wallen, Esq. 1774

Classis VIII.

OCTANDRIA.

MONOGYNIA.

TROPÆOLUM	*minus*	Indian Cress	Peru	M. Wallen, Esq. 1774
MELICOCCA	*bijuga*	Genip	South-America	
XIMENIA	*inermis*	Smooth Ximenia	East-Indies	H. East, Esq. 1784
FUCHSIA	*tryphylla*	Scarlet Fuchsia	Chili	H. East, Esq.
LAWSONIA	*inermis*	Smooth Lawsonia	Africa	Mons. Nectoux*, 1789
	spinosa	Prickly Lawsonia	East-Indies	H. East, Esq. 1785
VACCINIUM	*Arctostaphylos*	Madeira Whortle-Berry	Madeira	Tho. Hibbert, Esq. 1787
ERICA	*multiflora*	Many-flower'd Heath	S. of Europe	M. Wallen, Esq. 1784

Oenothera	*pumila*	Dwarf Primrose	N. America	M. Wallen, Esq.
Nov. Gen.†		The Akee	Africa	Dr. Tho. Clarke, 1778

* Botanist to the French King at Hispaniola.

† This Plant was brought here in a Slave Ship from the Coast of Africa, and now grows very luxuriant, producing every Year large Quantities of Fruit; several Gentlemen are encouraging the Propagation of it. I do not know that it has hitherto been described; its Characters are as follows:

Cal. Perianthium pentaphyllum inferum, foliolis ovatis acutis concavis, persistentibus villosis.

Cor. Petala quinque oblongo-lanceolata, acuta, villosa, ad basin sursum flexa et receptaculo adpressa, calyce alterna et eo longiora.

Stam. Filamenta octo brevissima, pilosa, ad basin Germinis receptaculo glanduloso inserta. Antheræ oblongæ in circa Germen dispositæ et ejusdem fere longitudinis.

Pist. Germen subovatum triquetrum pilosum. Stylus longitudine Germinis, cylindricus, pilosus. Stigma obtusum.

Per. Capsula carnosa, oblonga, utrinque obtusa, trigona, trilocularis, trivalvis, apice dehiscens.

Sem. Tria, orbicularia, nitida, appendice aucta.

Arbor hæc quinquaginta pedes altitudine plerumque superat; Truncus cortice subfusco scabro tegitur ramis numerosis longis crassis irregularibus, inferioribus ad terram fere dependentibus. Folia habet pinnata, foliolis ovato-lanceolatis venosis integerrimis oppositis lævibus superne nitidis, spithamæis, utrinque quatuor vel quinque, petiolis brevibus tumidis. Racemi simplices stricti [illegible] ori axillares, longitudine fere pinnarum, pedunculis propriis unifloris, stipulis lanceolatis, rufo-tomentosis, persistentibus. Flores parvi albidi inodori. Fructus magnitudinis ovi anserini, colore flavo, rubro, aurantiaco, vel ex utrisque mixto. Semina tria nitida nigra magnitudinis Nucis moschatæ, quorum unum

TRIGYNIA.

TRIGYNIA.

SAPINDUS	*edulis*	Litchi Plumb	China	Dr. Tho. Clarke, 1775

Classis IX.

ENNEANDRIA.

MONOGYNIA.

LAURUS	*Cinnamomum* *	Cinnamon Tree	Ceylon	Lord Rodney, 1782
	Camphora	Camphire Tree	Japan	Dr. Tho. Clarke, 1775
	nobilis	Sweet Bay-Tree	Italy	Mr. Kuckan, 1770
	indicæ	Royal Bay-Tree	Madeira	H. East, Esq. 1788
	fœtens	Madeira Laurel	Madeira	Tho. Hibbert, Esq. 1787
	Benzoin	Benjamin Tree	Virginia	Tho. Hibbert, Esq. 1787
	Borbonia	Carolina Bay-tree	Carolina	Mr. Gale, 1772
	Sassaphras	Sassaphras Tree	N. America	M. Wallen, Esq. 1772

TRIGYNIA.

RHEUM	*rhaponticum*	Bastard Rhubarb	Asia	Mr. Thame, 1786
	palmatum	True Rhubarb	China	Mr. Thame, 1786

Classis X.

DECANDRIA.

MONOGYNIA.

BAUHINIA	*purpurea*	Purple Bauhinia	East-Indies	H. East, Esq. 1790
	scandens	Climbing Bauhinia	East-Indies	H. East, Esq. 1790
	variegata	Variegated Bauhinia	East-Indies	H. East, Esq. 1790
CASSIA	*Senna*	Senna Tree	Ægypt	H. East, Esq. 1787
	Fistula	Sweet Cassia	E. & W. Indies	
POINCIANA	*pulcherrima*			
	var. fl. flavo	Yellow Flower-fence	Honduras	Mr. Shakespeare, 1782
GUILANDINA	*Moringa* †	Horse-radish Tree	East-Indies	H. East, Esq. 1784

unum sæpissime abortit. Semini singulo adnascitur materies albida (Semen magnitudine excedens) consistentiæ pinguedinis bovinæ et aqua leniter cocta Medullæ haud absimilis. Ab Incolis in Guinea ad mensas apponitur vel per se vel Jusculo vel Pulmento elixa.

* This Tree will doubtless, in a few years, become a very valuable Acquisition to the Island: some samples of the Bark lately sent to England prove it to be the true Ceylon Cinnamon, and of the best Kind. It is now cultivated with great Attention in many parts of the Island.

† This Tree has hitherto been generally considered as a species of the Genus *Guilandina*, but very erroneously, as will appear from the following characters:

CAL.

RUTA

Ruta	*graveolens*	Garden Rue	S. of Europe	M. Wallen, Esq.
Melia	*Azederach*	Bead Tree	East-Indies	
Quassia	*amara*	Bitter Quassia	Guiana	Mons. Nectoux, 1789
Kalmia	*latifolia*	Broad-leav'd Kalmia	N. America	H. East, Esq. 1786
	angustifolia	Narrow-leav'd Kalmia	N. America	H. East, Esq. 1786
Rhododendron	*maximum*		N. America	H. East, Esq. 1786
	ponticum		Gibraltar	H. East, Esq. 1786
Arbutus	*Unedo*	Strawberry Tree	Ireland	H. East, Esq. 1785

DIGYNIA.

Saxifraga	*umbrosa*	London Pride	England	M. Wallen, Esq. 1789
Dianthus	*barbatus*	Sweet-William Pink	Europe	M. Wallen, Esq. 1772
	caryophyllus	Clove July-flower	England	M. Wallen, Esq. 1772
	var.	Carnation		
	Chinensis	China Pink	China	M. Wallen, Esq. 1772
	superbus	Superb Pink	France	M. Wallen, Esq. 1772
Nov. Gen*		Mandarin Orange	East-Indies	H. East, Esq. 1788

Cal. Perianthium pentaphyllum, foliolis oblongis obtusis concavis, tribus superioribus reflexis, duobus inferioribus patentibus.

COR. Petala quinque. Petala duo superiora magnitudine foliolorum calycis, plana obtusa reflexa obovata; lateralia duo paulo majora concava obovata lunata minus reflexa; inferius spatulato-obovatum obtusum concavum, lateralibus majus, et genitalibus approximatum, patens.

STAM. Filamenta novem, quorum quinque tantum fertilia, ad basin crassa villosa, versus apices contorta, longitudine inæqualia, antheræ quinque bicapsulares subrotundæ. Sterilia quatuor minora longitudine etiam inæqualia, antheris minimis vel nullis, omnia petalis fere dimidio breviora.

PIST. Germen oblongum. Stylus filiformis leviter curvatus, petalis et staminibus longior. Stigma acutum.

PER. longum triangulare trivalve, utrinque acutum.

SEM. trialatum, alis lineis oblongis sibi invicem junctis. Nux fragilis rotunda. Nucleo rotundo trisulcato.

Arbor viginti pedalis, cortice cinereo; Rami patentes numerosi. Folia tri vel quadripinnata sessilia, foliolis ovalibus obtusis tri-linearibus teneris integerrimis pedicellatis; glandula parva pedicellata intra singulas foliolorum divisiones. Racemi axillares semipedales, calycis foliola subcarnea, petalis albis ad basin leviter purpureis. Pericarpium pedale sulcatum, angulis acutis. Calycis foliola et petala sæpe irregulariter reflexa et numero varia, sed Petalum inferius semper rectum et genitalibus approximatum.

---

* This Shrub has been introduced into our Gardens here from England under the above Title, but I do not know on what Authority: the following are its Characters, as nearly as I have been able to ascertain them:

CAL. Perianthium pentaphyllum inferum, foliolis parvis ovatis erectis.

COR. Petala quinque, laciniis ovatis vel subrotundis, erectis inferis, calyce duplo longioribus.

STAM. Filamenta decem circa Germen compressa, erecta, longitudine Corollæ. Antheræ parvæ simplices.

PIST.

TRIGYNIA.

Silene	*Armeria*	Lobel's Catchfly	England	H. East, Esq. 1773

PENTAGYNIA.

Spondias		South-Sea Plum	Asia	Lord Rodney, 1782
Agrostemma	*coronaria*	Rose Campion	Italy	H. East, Esq.
Sedun	*Anacampseros*	Evergreen Orpine	S. of France	H. East, Esq. 1791

Classis XI.

DODECANDRIA.

MONOGYNIA.

Portulaca	*triangularis*	Triangular-stalked Purslane	St. Vincent	Tho. Hibbert, Esq. 1787
Malesia	*tetraptèra*	Snow-drop Tree	Carolina	H. East, Esq. 1789
Garcinia	*cornea ?**	Small Mangostein	East-Indies	Lord Rodney, 1782

TRIGYNIA.

Reseda	*odorata*	Mignionette	Ægypt	M. Wallen, Esq. 1773

Classis XII.

ICOSANDRIA.

MONOGYNIA.

CACTUS	*cochinillifer*	Cochineal Cactus	South America	Mons. Nectoux, 1789
	Pereskia	Spanish Gooseberry	South-America	
PHILADELPHUS	*coronarius*	Dwarf Syringa	S. of Europe	H. East, Esq.
	aromaticus	Sweet-scented Syringa	New Zealand	H. East, Esq. 1787
EUGENIA	*Jambos*	Rose-Apple	India	Z. Bayly, Esq. 1762

PIST. Germen subrotundum. Stylus vix ullus. Stigma compressum.
PER. Bacca lucida membrano tenui obtecta, pulpa paucissima.
SEM. Duo, membrano proprio tecta, striata, pisi magnitudine, ita ut duo applicata sphærum constituunt, et sorte semen unicum in duo fissile.

Frutex quatuor pedalis inordinate ramosa, folia petiolata lanceolata-ovata alterna glabra integerrima; flores axillares congesti subsessiles. Corolla alba. Germen facie æmulat fructum juniorem Citri Aurantii.

* This Tree was at first supposed to be the true Mangostein, but having perfected its fruit, on comparison with the description given of the true Mangostein, we judge it to be the G. *cornea*. Male and Hermaphrodite flowers are found on ~~the same~~ Tree.

Genus	Species	English name	Native	Introduced by
MYRTUS	*communis*			
	var. romana	Broad-leav'd Myrfle		M. Wallen, Esq. 1773
	belgica	Dutch Myrtle		
		Narrow-leav'd Myrtle		
PUNICA	*Granatum fl. pleno*	Double-flower'd Pomegr.	Spain	M. Wallen, Esq. 1774
AMYGDALUS	*Persica*	Peach Tree		M. Wallen, Esq.
	var. Nectarina	Nectarine Tree		M. Wallen, Esq.
	communis	Almond Tree	Africa	Dr. Tho. Clarke
PRUNUS	*Armeniaca*	Apricot Tree		Mr. Kuckan, 1773
	Cerasus	Cherry Tree	England	M. Wallen, Esq.
	domestica	Plum Tree	England	M. Wallen, Esq. 1789

DIGYNIA.

Genus	Species	English name	Native	Introduced by
CRATÆGUS	*Oxycantha*	Hawthorn	Britain	H. East, Esq. 1773
	Crus Galli	Cockspur Hawthorn	N. America	H. East, Esq.

PENTAGYNIA.

Genus	Species	English name	Native	Introduced by
MESPILUS	*germanica*	Dutch Medlar	England	H. East, Esq. 1774
	Pyracantha	Evergreen Thorn	Italy	H. East, Esq. 1774
PYRUS	*Malus*	Apple Tree	Britain	
	communis	Pear Tree	England	M. Wallen, Esq.
	Cydonia	Quince Tree	Germany	M. Wallen, Esq. 1773

MESEMBRYANTHEMUM	*crystallinum*	Ice-Plant	Greece	H. East, Esq. 1787
SPIRÆA	*Ulmaria*	Meadow-Sweet	Britain	M. Wallen, Esq. 1772

POLYGYNIA.

ROSA	*lutea*	Yellow Austrian Rose	Germany	H. East, Esq.
	cinnamomea	Cinnamon Rose	S. of Europe	H. East, Esq.
	centifolia	Hundred-leav'd Rose	Spain	H. East, Esq.
	damascena	Damask Rose	France	M. Wallen, Esq.
	gallica	Red Rose	S. of Europe	M. Wallen, Esq.
	muscosa	Moss Rose	France	H. East, Esq.
	moschata	Musk Rose	Italy	H. East, Esq.
	alba	White Rose	Europe	H. East, Esq.
	rubiginosa	Sweet-Brier Rose	Britain	M. Wallen, Esq.
RUBUS	*idæus*			
	var. ruber.	Red Raspberry	Britain	M. Wallen, Esq. 1773
	albus	White Raspberry	Britain	M. Wallen, Esq. 1773
FRAGARIA	*vesca*			
	var. chiloens.	Chili Strawberry	Chili	M. Wallen, Esq. 1772
	pratens.	Hboy Strawberry	Britain	M. Wallen, Esq. 1772

Classis

Classis XIII.

POLYANDRIA.

MONOGYNIA.

CAPPARIS	*spinosa*	Caper Shrub	Italy	H. East, Esq. 1774
PAPAVER	*Rhœas*	Red Poppy	Britain	H. East, Esq. 1773
THEA	*viridis*	Green Tea-Tree	China	Dr. Tho. Clarke, 1775
	Bohea	Bohea Tea-Tree	China	Mr. Baker, 1771
CARYOPHYLLUS	*aromaticus* *	Clove Tree	Molucca Islands	Dr. Tho. Clarke, 1789
CISTUS	*populifolius*	Poplar-leav' Cistus	Portugal	H. East, Esq. 1779
	incanus	Hoary-leav'd Cistus	Portugal	H. East, Esq. 1779
	crispus	Curled-l Cistus	Portugal	H. East, sq. 1779
	Tuberaria	Plantain d Cistus	Portugal	H. East, Esq. 1779
DELPHINUM	*grandiflorum*	Great- d Larksp.	Siberia	H. East, Esq. 1774
	Consolida	Branching arkspur	England	M. Wallen, Esq. 1772
	elatum	Bee Larks	Siberia	M. Wallen, Esq. 1773
		Chinese L pur	China	H. East, Esq. 1773
ACONITUM	*Napellus*	Wolfsban	France	

PENTAGYNIA.

AQUILEGIA	*vulgaris*	Columbine Flower	Britain	M. Wallen, Esq. 1772
NIGELLA	*damascena*	Fennel Flower	Spain	M. Wallen, Esq. 1772

POLYGYNIA.

ILLICIUM	*floridanum*	Aniseed Tree	Florida	H. East, Esq. 1787
LIRIODENDRON	*Tulipifera*	Tulip Tree	N. America	H. East, Esq. 1776
MAGNOLIA	*grandiflora*	Laurel-leav'd Magnol	Carolina	Mr. Gale, 1772
	glauca	Swamp Magnolia	N. America	Mr. Gale, 1772
	acuminata	Blue Magnolia	N. America	H. East, Esq. 1788
ANNONA		Cherimoya	S. America	H. East, Esq. 1786
ANEMONE	*hortensis*	Garden Anemone	Italy	M. Wallen, Esq. 1773
ATRAGENE	*indica*		S. America	H. East, Esq. 1788
CLEMATIS	*Flammula*	Virgin's Bower	S. of France	
ADONIS	*autumnalis*	Flos Adonis	England	M. Wallen, Esq.
RANUNCULUS	*auricomus*	Wood Crowfoot	Britain	M. Wallen, Esq. 1773

Classis XIV.

DIDYNAMIA.

GYMNOSPERMIA.

SATUREJA	*hortensis*	Garden Savory	Italy	
HYSSOPUS	*officinalis*	Hyssop	S. of Europe	
NEPETA	*Cataria*	Catmint	Britain	H. East. Esq.
LAVANDULA	*Spica*	Common Lavender	S. of Europe	M. Wallen, Esq. 1774

* Two of these Plants were presented to Doctor Clarke by Monsieur Nectoux, from the King's Garden at Port au Prince; they appeared in a very luxuriant State of Growth on their Arrival, but have since died.

LAVANDULA	*Stœchas*	[illegible]avender	S. of Europe	H. East, Esq. 1787
	dentata	T[illegible]eav'd Lav.	S. of Eur[illegible]	H. East, Esq. 1787
	multifida	C[illegible]vender	Canary Islands	Dr. Tho. Clarke, 1784
SIDERITIS	*candicans*	Ir[illegible]	Madeira	H. East, Esq.
MENTHA	*viridis*	Sp[illegible]t	England	
	piperita	Pep[illegible]nt	England	
	Pulegium	Pen[illegible]	Britain	
GLECOMA	*hederacea*	Grou[illegible]	Britain	
BETONICA	*officinalis*	Woo[illegible]y	Britain	H. Fast, Esq.
MARRUBIUM	*vulgare*	Horeh[illegible]	Britain	M. Wallen, Esq.
ORIGANUM	*Onites*	Pot Mar[illegible]	Sicily	
	Majorana	Sweet M[illegible]m		
THYMUS	*vulgaris*	Garden [illegible]	Italy	
	mastichina	Mastick [illegible]	Spain	H. East, Esq.
MELISSA	*officinalis*	Balm	Britain	
DRACOCEPHA-LUM	*Ruyschiana*		Sweden	H. East, Esq. 1788
	Moldavica	Moldavian [illegible]	Moldavia	M. Wallen, Esq. 1774
OCYMUM	*Basilicum*	Sweet Basil	Persia	M. Wallen, Esq.

ANGIOSPERMIA.

ANTIRRHINUM	*majus*	Snap-dragon	England	M. Wallen, Esq. 1773
	asarina	Toad-flax	Italy	H. East, Esq. 1773
DIGITALIS	*purpurea*	Purple Fox-glove	Britain	H. East, Esq. 1787
	ambigua	Yellow Fox-glove	Switzerland	H. East, Esq. 1784

BIGNONIA	*Catalpa*	Trumpet-flower	Carolina	H. East, Esq. 1788
BROWALLIA	*elata*	Upright Browallia	Peru	Dr. Tho. Clarke, 1775
SESAMUM	*orientale*	Vanglo, or Oil Plant	East-Indies	
BARLERIA	*prionites*	Thorny Barleria	India	H. East, Esq. 1788
VITEX	*Agnus Castus*	Chaste Tree	Sicily	Mons. Nectoux, 1789
PEDALIUM	*Murex*	Prickly-fruited Pedal.	East-Indies	Tho. Hibbert, Esq. 1787
MELIANTHUS	*major*	Honey-flower	C. of G. Hope	H. East, Esq. 1784

Classis XV.

TETRADYNAMIA.

SILICULOSA.

LEPIDIUM	*latifolium*	Pepper-wort	Britain	H. East, Esq. 1788
	sativum	Garden Cress	Germany	
COCHLEARIA	*officinalis*	Scurvy-gr	Britain	H. East, Esq. 1773
	Armoracia	Horse-rad	England	
IBERIS	*umbellata*	Candy-tuft	S. of Europe	H. East, Esq. 1775
ALYSSUM	*halimifolium*	Sweet Alysson	Italy	H. East, Esq. 1774
	incanum	Hoary Alysson	Italy	H. East, Esq. 1788
LUNARIA	*annua*	Honesty	Germany	H. East, Esq. 1773

SILIQUOSA.

SILIQUOSA.

SISYMBRIUM	*Nasturtium*	Water-cress	Britain	
CHEIRANTHUS	*Cheiri*	Wall-flower	Britain	M. Wallen, Esq. 1772
	incanus	Queen's Stock	Italy	M. Wallen, Esq. 1772
	annuus	Ten-week Stock	Spain	H. East, Esq. 1772
HESPERIS	*tristis*	Night-smelling Rocket	Hungary	H. East, Esq. 1772
SINAPIS	*alba*	White Mustard	Britain	M. Wallen, Esq.
	nigra	Black Mustard	Britain	
BRASSICA	*Rapa*	Turnep	England	
	oleracea	Common Cabbage	England	
	var. 1.	Red Cabbage		
	2.	Savoy Cabbage		
	3.	Cauliflower		
	4.	Brocoli		
	5.	Turnep-rooted Cabbage		
RAPHANUS	*sativus*	Garden Radish	China	
	var. 1.	Turnep Radish		
	2.	Black Radish		

Classis XVI.

MONADELPHIA.

PENTANDRIA.

GERANIUM	*malacoides*	Mallow-leav'd Geran.	S. of Europe	H. East, Esq. 1788
	alchimilloides	Mantle-leav'd Geran.	C. of G. Hope	H. East, Esq. 1788

	coriandrifolium	Coriander-leav'd Ger.	C. of G. Hope	H. East, Esq. 1788
	zonale	Horse-shoe Geran.	C. of G. Hope	
	quercifolium	Oak-leav'd Geran.	C. of G. Hope	H. East, Esq. 1788
	Radula		C. of G. Hope	H. East, Esq. 1788
	vitifolium	Balm-scented Geran.	C. of G. Hope	M. Wallen, Esq.
	capitatum	Rose-scented Geran.	C. of G. Hope	M. Wallen, Esq.
	betulinum	Birch-leav'd Geran.	C. of G. Hope	H. East, Esq. 1788
	Bohemicum		C. of G. Hope	H. East, Esq. 1778
	lævigatum		C. of G. Hope	H. East, Esq. 1788
	Hermannifolium		C. of G. Hope	H. East, Esq. 1788
	palmatum		C. of G. Hope	H. East, Esq. 1788

DODECANDRIA.

PENTAPETES	*phœnicea*	Scarlet Pentapetes	East-Indies	Dr. Tho. Clarke, 1775

POLYANDRIA.

ADANSONIA	*digitata*	Monkies-Bread	Senegal	H. East, Esq.
SIDA	*indica*	Indian Mallow	India	H. East, Esq.
ALCEA	*rosea*	Holly-hock	China	M. Wallen, Esq. 1774
MALVA	*capensis*	Cape Mallow	C. of G. Hope	H. East, Esq. 1787
	crispa	Curl'd Mallow	Syria	H. East, Esq. 1774
	rotundifolia	Dwarf Mallow	Britain	Capt. Jones
LAVATERA	*thuringiaca*	Great-flower'd Lav.	Hungary	M. Wallen, Esq. 1773

HIBISCUS

HIBISCUS	*populneus*	Poplar-leav'd Hibisc.	East-Indies	H. East, Esq. 1784
	mutabilis	Changeable Rose	East-Indies	M. Wallen, Esq.
	Rosa sinensis	China Rose	China	M. Wallen, Esq.
	syriacus	Althæa frutex	Syria	M. Wallen, Esq.
	ficulneus	Fig-leav'd Hibiscus	Ceylon	H. East, Esq. 1788
	Trionum	Bladder Hibiscus	C. of G. Hope	H. East, Esq. 1788
	Sabdariffa	Sorrel Hibiscus	India	
CAMELLIA	*japonica*	Japan Rose	Japan	H. East, Esq. 1787

Classis XVII.

DIADELPHIA.

DECANDRIA.

ERITHRINA	*herbaca*	Herbaceous Coral tree	Carolina	Mr. Gale, 1772
	grandiflora	Large flowering C. tree		H. East, Esq.
SPARTIUM	*junceum*	Spanish Broom	South of Europe	M. Wallen, Esq. 1773
	scoparium	Common Broom	Britain	M. Wallen, Esq.
	monospermum	White-flower'd Broom	Portugal	M. Wallen, Esq.
GENISTA	*candicans*	Hoary Genista	S. of Europe	H. East, Esq. 1788
ULEX	*europæus*	Furze or Whin	Britain	M. Wallen, Esq.
	capensis	Cape Furze	C. of G. Hope	H. East, Esq. 1782
CROTALARIA	*juncea*	Chinese Crotalaria	China	Dr. Tho. Clarke,
	retusa	Wedge-leav'd Crot.	East-Indies	
	verrucosa	Blue-flower'd Crot.	East-Indies	H. East, Esq.

	*pallida**	Pale-flower'd Crotal.	Africa	Dr. Tho. Clarke, 1775
	laburnifolia	Shrubby Crotalaria	Asia	H. East, Esq. 1791
	quinquefolia		India	H. East, Esq: 1791
Ononis	*rotundifolia*		Switzerland	H. East, Esq. 1791
Arachis	*hypogæa*	Earth Nuts or Pindars	South-America	
Lupinu	*albus*	White Lupine		M. Wallen, Esq. 1773
	varius	Blue Lupine	Sicily	M. Wallen, Esq. 1773
	angustifolius	Narrow-leav'd Lupine	Spain	H. East, Esq. 1780
	luteus	Yellow Lupine	Sicily	M. Wallen, Esq. 1773
Phaseolus	*vulgaris*	Kidney Bean	India	
Dolichos	*Lablab*	Black-seeded Dolichos	Ægypt	H. East, Esq. 1789
	sinensis	Chinese Dolichos	East-Indies	H. East, Esq. 1789
Glycine	*triloba*		India	H. East, Esq. 1791
Clitoria	*ternatea*	Blue Clitoria	East-Indies	
	fl. albo	White Clitoria		
Pisum	*sativum*	Garden Pea	S. of Europe	
Lathyrus	*odoratus*	Sweet Pea	Sicily	M. Wallen, Esq. 1773
	var.	Painted Lady Pea	Ceylon	H. East, Esq. 1781
	tingitanus	Tangier Pea	Africa	H. East, Esq. 1781
	latifolius	Broad-leav'd Pea	England	H. East, Esq. 1781
Vicia	*Faba*	Garden Bean	Ægypt	
Cytisus	*Laburnum*	Common Laburnum	Austria	M. Wallen, Esq. 1773
	Cajan	Pigeon Pea	East-Indies	
Robinia	*hispida*	Rose-Acacia	Carolina	H. East, Esq. 1786
	grandiflora	Large-flower'd Acacia	East-Indies	H. East, Esq. 1782

* *Hort. Kewensis*, vol. iii. p. 20.

Robinia

Robinia	*mitis*		East-Indies	H. East, Esq. 1792
Coronilla	*valentina*	Shrubby Coronilla	Spain	H. East, Esq. 1788
	arabica	Arabian Coronilla	Arabia	H. East, Esq. 1788
	minima	Small Coronilla	S. of Europe	H. East, Esq. 1788
Æschynomene	*grandiflora*	Pea-Tree	East-Indies	J. G. Kemys, Esq. 1774
	Sesban	Egyptian Pea-Tree	Ægypt	Dr. Tho. Clarke, 1775
	aquatica	Swamp Pea-Tree	East-Indies	H. East, Esq. 1780
Hedysarum	*gyrans*	Moving Plant	East-Indies	Dr. Tho. Clarke, 1775
Galega	*purpurea*	Purple Galega	East-Indies	H. East, Esq. 1790
Lotus	*jacobæus*	Dark-flower'd Lotus	Azores	H. East, Esq. 1790
Medicago	*polymorpha*			
	var. scutellata	Snail Medick	Europe	H. East, Esq.
	intertexta	Hedge-hog Medick	Europe	M. Wallen, Esq.

Classis XVIII.

POLYADELPHIA.

PENTANDRIA.

Theobroma	*Cacao*	Chocolate Nut-Tree	S. America	
Ambroma	*augusta*	Maple-leav'd Ambroma	New S. Wales	H. East, Esq. 1791

DODECANDRIA.

Monsonia	*speciosa*	Fine-leav'd Monsonia	C. of G. Hope	H. East, Esq. 1791

ICOSANDRIA.

CITRUS	*Media*	Citron-Tree	Asia	
	var. 1.	Lemon-Tree		
	2.	Lime-Tree		
	3.	Sweet Lime-Tree		
	4.	Forbidden-fruit-Tree		
	5.	Grape-fruit-Tree		
	Aurantium	Seville Orange-Tree	India	
	var.	China Orange-Tree		
	Decumana	Shaddock-Tree	India	

POLYANDRIA.

HYPERICUM	*balearicum*	St. John's-wort	Majorca	H. East, Esq. 1788
	monogynum	Chinese St. John's-wort	China	H. East, Esq. 1788

Classis XIX.

SYNGENESIA.

POLYGAMIA ÆQUALIS.

SONCHUS	*oleraceus*	Sow-thistle	Britain
LACTUCA	*sativa*	Garden Lettuce	

Leontodon	*Taraxacum*	Dandelion	Britain	M. Wallen, Esq. 1774
Cichorium	*Endivia*	Endive		
	var. crispa	Curled-leav'd Endive		
Cynara	*Scolymus*	French Artichoke	S. of France	
	Carduncculus	Cardoon Artichoke	Candia	
Crepis	*barbata*	Spanish Hawk-weed	S. of France	
Spilanthus	*Acmella*	Balm-leav'd Spilanthus	Ceylon	H. East, Esq. 1788

POLYGAMIA SUPERFLUA.

Tanacetum	*vulgare*	r Tansey	Britain	M. Wallen, Esq.
Artemisia	*Abrotanum*	ıwood	S. of Europe	
	Absinthium	mwood	Britain	
Gnaphalium	*fœtidum*	Everlasting	C. of G. Hope	H. East, Esq. 1788
Xeranthemum	*speciosissimum*	themum	C. of G. Hope	H. East, Esq. 1775
Aster	*fruticosus*	bby Aster	C. of G. Hope	H. East, Esq. 1784
	chinensis	ese Aster	China	M. Wallen, Esq. 1775
	Amellus		Italy	H. East, Esq. 1780
Bellis	*perennis*		Britain	M. Wallen, Esq. 1773
Tagetes	*patula*	ygold	Mexico	
	erecta	c Marygold	Mexico	
Zinnia	*multiflora*		N. America	H. East, Esq. 1772
Chrysanthemum	*coronarium*	rysanthemum	Sicily	H. East, Esq. 1774
Anthemis	*nobilis*	Camomi	Britain	Mrs. Duncomb, 1783
Achillea	*millefolium*	i, Yarrow	Britain	M. Wallen, Esq.

POLYGAMIA FRUSTRANEA.

HELIANTHUS	*annuus*	Common Sun-flower	Mexico	
	indicus	Dwarf Sun-flower		H. East, Esq.
	tuberosus	Jerusalem Artichoke	Brazil	H. East, Esq.
RUDBECKIA	*laciniata*		Virginia	H. East, Esq. 1789
	hirta	American Sun-flower	Canada	H. East, Esq. 1790
CENTAURE	*Cyanus*	Blue-bottle	Britain	M. Wallen, Esq. 1774

POLYGAMIA NECESSARIA.

CALENDULA	*officinalis*	Garden Marygold	S. of Europe	M. Wallen, Esq. 1773
ARCTOTIS	*calendulacea*	Marygold Arctotis	C. of G. Hope	H. East, Esq. 1783

MONOGAMIA.

LOBELIA	*siphilitica*	Blue Cardinal-flower	Virginia	Mons. Nectoux, 1789
VIOLA	*odorata*	Sweet Violet	Britain	M. Wallen, Esq. 1773
	var.	Double-flower'd Violet	Britain	H. East, Esq. 1789
	tricolor	Heart's-ease, or Pansies		Mrs. Brodbelt, 1769
IMPATIENS	*Balsamina*	Garden Balsam	East-Indies	M. Wallen, Esq. 1773

Classis

Classis XX.

GYNANDRIA.

DIANDRIA.

LIMODORUM	*tuberosum*	Tuberous-rooted Lim.	N. America	
	Tankervilliæ	Chinese Limodorum	China	H. East, Esq. 1787
EPIDENDRUM	*Vanilla*	Vanilla	S. America	Mr. Thame, 1787

TRIANDRIA.

SISYRINCHIUM	*bermudiana*		N. America	

PENTANDRIA.

PASSIFLORA	*maliformis ?*	Water Lemon	Barbadoes	
	cærulea	Passion Flower	Brazil	M. Wallen, Esq. 1780

POLYANDRIA.

ARUM	*bicolor* *	Painted Arum		H. East, Esq.
CALLA	*æthiopica*		C. of G. Hope	H. East, Esq. 1787

Classis XXI.

MONOECIA.

MONANDRIA.

Casuarina	*equisetifolia*		East-Indies	H. East, Esq. 1788
Artocarpus	*integrifolia*	Indian Jaca Tree	East-Indies	Lord Rodney, 1782

TRIANDRIA.

Typha	*latifolia*	Large Reed-mace	Britain	
Coix	*Lacryma Jobi*	Job's Tears	East-Indies	M. Wallen, Esq.
Phyllanthus	*Niruri*	Annual Phyllanthus	East-Indies	H. East, Esq. 1782

TETRANDRIA.

Buxus	*sempervirens*	Box-tree	England	M. Wallen, Esq.
Urtica	*dioica*	Common Nettle	Britain	M. Wallen, Esq.
	urens	Lesser Nettle	Britain	H. East, Esq.
Morus	*alba*	White Mulberry Tree	China	H. East, Esq. 1784
	nigra	Common Mulb. Tree	Italy	M. Wallen, Esq.
	rubra	Red Mulberry Tree	Carolina	H. East, Esq. 1774
	papyrifera	Paper Mulberry Tree	Japan	H. East, Esq. 1779

* *Hort. Kewensis*, vol. iii. p. 316.

PENTANDRIA.

AMARANTHUS	*melancholicus*	Two-colour'd Amar.	East-Indies	M. Wallen, Esq. 1773
	tricolor	Three-colour'd Amar.	East-Indies	M. Wallen, Esq. 1773
	cruentus	Bloody Amaranth	East-Indies	M. Wallen, Esq. 1773

POLYANDRIA.

QUERCUS	*Ilex*	Evergreen Oak Tree	S. of Europe	H. East, Esq. 1787
	Suber	Cork Tree	S. of Europe	H. East, Esq.
	rubra	Red Oak Tree	N. America	Mr. Thame, 1788
	alba	White Oak Tree	Virginia	Mr. Thame, 1788
	Robur	Common Oak Tree	Britain	M. Wallen, Esq. 1773
JUGLANS	*regia*	Walnut Tree	Persia	M. Wallen, Esq. 1774
	alba	White Hickery Tree	N. America	M. Wallen, Esq. 1786
	nigra	Black Walnut Tree	N. America	Mr. Jones, 1786
FAGUS	*Castanea*	Chesnut Tree	England	Mrs. Brodbelt
	pumila	Dwarf Chesnut Tree	N. America	M. Wallen, Esq.
CORYLUS	*Avellana*	Hazel-nut Tree	Britain	M. Wallen, Esq. 1775
PLATANUS	*orientalis*	Oriental Plane Tree	Levant	M. Wallen, Esq.
	occidentalis	America Plane Tree	N. America	Mr. Thame, 1775

MONADELPHIA.

PINUS	*sylvestris*	Common Pine Tree	Europe	M. Wallen, Esq. 1775
	Pinaster	Cluster Pine Tree	Europe	M. Wallen, Esq. 1775

	Pinea	Stone Pine Tree	Europe	M. Wallen, Esq. 1775
	Cembra	Siberian Pine Tree	Siberia	M. Wallen, Esq. 1778
	Strobus	Weymouth Pine Tree	N. America	M. Wallen, Esq. 1775
	Cedrus	Cedar of Libanon	Levant	H. East, Esq. 1788
	Larix	White Larch Tree	Germany	H. East, Esq. 1788
THUJA	*orientalis*	Chinese Arbor Vitæ	China	H. East, Esq. 1775
CUPRESSUS	*sempervirens*			
	var. stricta	Upright Cypress Tree	Candia	H. East, Esq. 1773
	horizontalis	Spreading Cypr. Tree	Candia	Mr. Thame, 1786
	disticha	Deciduous Cypr. Tree	N. America	Mr. Salt, 1786
	juniperoides	African Cypress Tree	C. of G. Hope	H. East, Esq. 1789
CROTON	*sebiferum*	Tallow Tree	China	John Ellis, Esq. 1765

SYNGENESIA.

MOMORDICA	*Balsamina*	Smooth Cerasee	India	
	Charantia	Hairy Cerasee	East-Indies	
CUCURBITA	*Pepo*	Pumpkin Gourd		
	Melopepo	Squash Gourd		
	Citrullus	Water Melon	S. of Europe	
CUCUMIS	*Melo*	Common Melon		
	Dudaim	Apple-shap'd Cucum.	Levant	H. East, Esq.
	sativus	Common Cucumber		
	flexuosus	Turkey Cucumber		
SICYOS	*angulata*	Chocho Vine	America	

 Classis

Classis XXII.

DIOECIA.

MONANDRIA.

Pandanus	*odoratissimus*	Screw Pine	Ceylon	Lord Rodney, 1782
		DIANDRIA.		
Salix	*babylonica*	Weeping Willow	Italy	H. East, Esq. 1783
		TETRANDRIA.		
Myrica	*cerifera*	Candleberry Myrtle	Carolina	Dr. Tho. Clarke, 1775
		PENTANDRIA.		
Pistacia	*officinarum*	Pistachia Tree	Greece	H. East, Esq. 1783
	Terebinthus	Turpentine Tree	S. of Europe	H. East, Esq. 1790
	Lentiscus	Mastick Tree	S. of Europe	H. East, Esq. 1789
Spinacia	*oleracea*	Garden Spinage		
Cannabis	*sativa*	Hemp	India	M. Wallen, Esq.
		HEXANDRIA.		
Smilax	*Sarsaparilla*	Sarsaparilla	America	Z. Bayly, Esq. 1765 *

OCTANDRIA.

Populus	*balsamifera*	Tacamahac Poplar Tree	Siberia	H. East, Esq. 1791

DECANDRIA.

Schinus	*molle*	Peruvian Mastick Tree	Peru	H. East, Esq. 1783

Classis XXIII.

POLYGAMIA.

MONOECIA.

Nov. Gen.?		Bichy Tree †	Guinea	

* It was first planted by Mr. Bayly, at Nonsuch Plantation, in St. Mary's parish, and grew with great luxuriancy, but seems not to have been generally cultivated with that care which it merits.

† This Tree is noticed by Sir Hans Sloane in his Natural History of Jamaica, as having been imported from the Coast of Guinea, and planted in the mountains of Liguanea; it still continues to grow there, as well as in many other parts of the South Side of the Island: the following Characters were taken from a Tree growing in the Garden, which perfected its fruit.

Herma-

Terminalia

Terminalia	*Catappa*		East-Indies	Dr. Tho. Clarke, 1790
Acer	*Pseudo Platanus*	Sycamore Tree	Britain	H. East, Esq. 1787
	rubrum	Red Maple	Virginia	H. East, Esq. 1790
Mimosa	*sensitiva*	Sensitive Plant	Brazil	
	farnesiana	Sweet-scented Mimosa	East-Indies	H. East, Esq. 1788
	nilotica	Gum Arabic Tree	Egypt	Dr. Tho. Clarke, 1775
	Lebbeck	Ægyptian Sensitive	Egypt	Lord Rodney, 1782
	Senegal	Gum Senegal Tree	Arabia	Tho. Hibbert, Esq. 1787

DIOECIA.

Fraxinus	*Ornus*	Manna Ash	Calabria	Dr. Tho. Clarke, 1775

TRIOECIA

Ceratonia	*Siliqua*	St. John's Bread	Sicily	Dr. Tho. Clarke, 1775
Ficus	*Carica*	Fig Tree	S. Europe	

PALMÆ.

Cycas	*circinalis*	Sago Palm	East-Indies	Dr. Tho. Clarke, 1775
Phoenix	*dactylifera*	Date Palm Tree	Levant	

Hermaphroditus Flos.

Cal. Nullus

Cor. Monopetala quinquepartita infera, laciniis ovatis acutis crassis subvillosis, striatis patento-erectis. Nectarium concavum, includens Germen, margine decem-dentato.

Stam. Filamenta decem brevissima vel nulla. Antheræ didymæ in orbem dispositæ et extus Nectarii dentibus coalitæ.

Pist. Germen subrotundum quinque-sulcatum hirsutum. Stigmata quinque crassa reflexa subcontorta, germini incumbentia.

Per. Capsula magna subovata gibbosa, leniter incurvata, unilocularis, bivalvis, sutura dorsali prominente.

Sem. Plura angulata imbricata, singulum cortice coriaceo proprio obtectum.

Masculi Flores.

Cal. & Cor. ut in Flore hermaphrodito, sed $\frac{1}{3}$ majores.

Stam. ut in Flore hermaphrodito.

Pist. Germen nullum. Stigmatum quinque rudimenta parva è medio Nectarii orta.

Arbor inelegans ramosa, cortice subfusco truncus tegitur; folia habet alterna pedicellata integra oblonga venosa glabra acuminata, margine undulato, sicca, laurina, ad extremitatem ramulorum congesta; pedicellis utrinque tumidis vel ganglionosis. Racemi compositi breves, plerumque è ramis majoribus orti. Corolla lutea, laciniæ singulæ striis tribus purpureis intus notatæ; odor valde ingratus. A Nigritis in Jamaica vocatur Bichy vel Colu, et ibi semina per se vel cum Sale et Capsico commista ad dolores ventriculi pro remedio habentur.

POSTSCRIPT

TO THE

HISTORICAL SURVEY

OF

ST. DOMINGO,

Containing a brief Review of the Transaction and Condition of the British Army there, during the Years 1795, 6, 7, and 8, until the final Evacuation of the Country.

FOUR years have elapsed since I closed the details of the military operations of the British army in St. Domingo, and I grieve to say, that what was then prophetic apprehension, is now become historical fact. This once opulent and beautiful colony, the boast of France, and the glory of the new hemisphere, is expunged from the chart of the civilized world! The prospect of such lamentable ruin might give occasion for many observations and reflections, and I shall present to my readers, in the following very imperfect sketch (for such it is in every sense) a few that occur to me: more than this I dare not attempt. Were it in my power (as in truth it is not) to continue, in a regular series, the history of those sad events which have led to this miserable catastrophe,

catastrophe, I should indeed decline a task which would be equally disgusting to my readers, and painful to myself. In a climate where every gale was fraught with poison, and in a contest with uncounted hosts of barbarians, what could the best efforts of our gallant countrymen effect? Their enemies indeed fled before them, but the arrows of pestilence pursued and arrested the victors, in their career of conquest! Scenes like these, while they afford but small cause of gratulation to the actors themselves, furnish no topicks to animate the page of the historian; who would have little else to display but a repetition of the same disasters—delusive promises, unrealized hopes, unavailing exertions; producing a complication of miseries, disease, distraction, contagion, and death!

At the same time (although I know not that the reader will derive any great degree of consolation from the circumstance) it is incumbent on me to observe, that, during the disastrous period of which I treat, I have not heard that any misconduct or neglect was ever fairly imputed to those persons who had the direction of the enterprize, either in the public departments of Great Britain, or in the scene of action itself. The names of Williamson, Forbes, Simcoe, Whyte, and Maitland, carry with them a demonstration that neither courage, nor energy, nor military talents, was at any time wanting in the principal department. Reinforcements of troops too, were sent by the British government with a more liberal hand than in former years. Towards the latter end of April 1795, the 81st and 96th regiments (consisting together of 1,700 men) arrived

arrived from Ireland; the 82d, from Gibraltar, landed 980 men in August; and in April 1796, the 66th and 69th regiments, consisting of 1,000 men each, with 150 artillery, arrived from the same place, under the command of General Bowyer; so that the whole number of effective men which had landed in St. Domingo, down to this period (including some small detachments sent up at different times from Jamaica) amounted to 9,800. In June following, four regiments of infantry, and a part of two others*, arrived from Cork, under the command of General Whyte. These were soon afterwards followed by seven regiments of British†, together with three regiments of foreign cavalry‡; besides two companies of British, and a detachment of Dutch artillery; making in the whole a further reinforcement of about 7,900§.

But what avail the best concerted schemes of human policy against the dispensations of Divine Providence? A great part of these gallant troops, most of them in the bloom of youth, were conveyed, with little intermission, from the ships to the hospital; from the hospital to the grave! Of the 82d regiment, no less than 630 became victims to the climate, within the short space of ten weeks after

* The 17th, 32d, 56th, and 67th, with part of the 93d and 99th.

† The 13th, 14th, 17th, 18th, 21st, 26th, and 29th.

‡ The York, Hompesch and Rouen Hussars.

§ Out of this number are however to be deducted the 32d infantry and the 26th dragoons; the former of which were sent from St. Domingo to Bahama, and the latter to the Windward Islands.

after their landing. In one of its companies, no more than three rank and file were fit for duty. Hompesch's regiment of hussars were reduced, in little more than two months, from 1,000 to 300, *and the 96th regiment perished to a man!* By the 30th of September, 1796, the registers of mortality displayed a mournful diminution of no less than 7,530 of the British forces only; and towards the latter end of 1797, out of the whole number of troops, British and foreign, which had landed and were detained in this devoted country, during that and the two preceding years, (certainly not far short of 15,000 men) I am assured that not more than 3,000 were left alive and in a condition for service *.

During this dreadful sacrifice of human life, the necessary operations in the colony were productive of such an expenditure of treasure to the British government, as excited the utmost astonishment in the minds of the king's ministers; who ought however to have foreseen, that the cost of raising, feeding, arming, clothing, and paying colonial regiments, both black and white, in a country where every article was three times as dear as in Europe, and the expence of fitting out armed vessels to transport troops and stores from one part of the colony to another part, (both of them measures of absolute necessity) must unavoidably be very great †. The charges attending the

* The loss of seamen in the ships employed on the coast are not included. It may be stated very moderately at 5,000 men.

† The colonial troops, black and white, embodied by General Williamson, amounted at the end of 1795 to 8,170.

the hospital service, were alone found to amount to 10s. a day for each invalid. For the payment of these, and other services, the Governor was authorized to draw bills of exchange on the British treasury; and the bills thus drawn, to the first of May, amounted to 4,383,596*l*. 8*s*. 2*d*. sterling.

But, notwithstanding this enormous expence, both of blood and treasure, the prospect of subduing the whole of this great island, and annexing it, in a profitable condition, to the British dominion, was more distant than ever. The weakness and diminution of our troops, inspired the enemy with renewed confidence. They were not unobservant of our situation, and took advantage of it. Those among the white inhabitants who were secretly disaffected, became encouraged and confirmed in their hostile purposes, and were easily prevailed upon to declare openly against a cause, which they plainly foresaw must, in a short time, work its own destruction.

It is not however to be understood that the British army was suffered to remain, during this time, in desponding inactivity. The case was far otherwise. Every man who was in a condition for service, had full employment assigned to him, and undoubtedly very vigorous efforts were made to distress the enemy, and extend our footing in the country, until, unhappily, every succeeding exertion, like the labours of Sysiphus, terminated in new disappointment.

At one period very sanguine expectations prevailed from the co-operation and services of the colonial

colonial corps, which General Williamson had caused to be organized. Their knowledge of the country, and their habitude to the climate, were supposed to render them a useful and formidable body. They had been formed in a great degree under the Baron de Montalembert, (an officer of whose military merit it is not easy to speak in terms too favourable) and, immediately after the arrival of the 82d regiment from Gibraltar, such of them as were brought to a sufficient state of discipline, commenced operations, under that officer's command, in the western province: being reinforced by the Baron's own regiment, and a detachment from the British 82d, they proceeded for a time very successfully, driving the enemy out of many fortified posts, and taking possession of a great extent of country, even as far as the Spanish frontiers. Nothing could exceed the noble spirit of emulation which animated their conduct. Unhappily, the want of a sufficient number of men to garrison the posts which the enemy had abandoned, rendered all their successes ultimately abortive. Their progress, therefore, was productive of no lasting impression: it was like that of a vessel traversing the ocean;—the waves yielded indeed for the moment, but united again as the vessel passed.

In the meanwhile a very considerable body of the revolted negroes (the whole of whom had now separated themselves altogether from the people of colour) continued to maintain their position in a strong post, on the heights which overlook Port au Prince towards the south. This party of brigands were commanded by a negro named Dudo-

nait,

nait, who had contrived to cut off the streams by which the town was usually supplied with fresh water. The distress to which the garrison was reduced by this measure, and the disgrace of suffering the insults of such an enemy to remain unpunished, induced the General, in the month of December, to make formidable preparations for attacking Dudonait in his camp; when an extraordinary circumstance occurred, which, as it displays the state of parties among the revolters, deserves recital. On the first of January 1796, this negro chief sent a flag to the General, signifying that it was his intention to present the British with a supply of water, by way of a new-year's gift; and accordingly the springs were cleared, and the streams suffered to run in their usual channel, to the great relief of the town and the garrison. This measure, on the part of the enemy, was followed by overtures for a negociation; and Dudonait soon afterwards transmitted the heads of a treaty in writing, offering therein to bring the chief part of his army over to the English, on certain conditions; one of which was, that the English troops should co-operate with their new negro allies, *utterly to cut off and extirpate the people of colour throughout St. Domingo.*

As it was impossible that General Williamson could listen to propositions of this nature, although he had no reason to doubt the sincerity of Dudonait, the preparations for driving the enemy from his position were continued. Light artillery was provided to be carried up the mountains on mules. The enterprize however was attended with

with so many difficulties, that it was not until the 28th of February the attack was made; when the British had the satisfaction, in the course of a few hours, to see the brigands, who had so long hemmed in and insulted them, fly from their chain of formidable posts in all directions. General Bowyer was at the head of the column, at the place where the chief attack was made, and he carried the lines by storm.*

HAD I the means of resounding in detail the many other enterprizes, in the prosecution of which the honour of the British flag was ably maintained and supported, notwithstanding the cruel ravages which the diseases of the climate hourly made among the troops, the recital of them should not be omitted.—I should dwell with infinite satisfaction on the merits of the Generals Churchill, Bowyer, Montalembert; the Colonels Spencer, Stuart, Dessource, and other officers in high command. It is universally acknowledged, that the services of all these gentlemen that I have mentioned were eminently conspicuous; and I regret that my information is not sufficiently minute and particular, to enable me to bestow that distinct and appropriate tribute of applause on the conduct of each, which justice and gratitude would otherwise demand. This general acknowledgment therefore is all that I can offer; but my regret is heightened by the mournful reflection,

* The negro commander, Dudonait, was soon afterwards surprized by the Mulatto General Rigaud, who had heard of his negociation with the English, and ordered him to immediate execution.

that

that such exertions and talents were employed in so unprofitable a service; a warfare in which all human efforts were unavailing, and success itself unattended with lasting advantage or renown.

In the month of March 1796, Sir Adam Williamson embarked for Great Britain, having resigned the command of the troops to General Forbes, who was himself superseded by the arrival of General Simcoe, as chief governor, in March 1797. One great object the king's ministers had in view, by the appointment last mentioned, was, as I have heard, to obtain a full and accurate representation of the state of the colony, the actual situation of the British army there, and the prospects which remained of the ultimate success of the enterprize. No man was better qualified to form a correct, comprehensive, and unbiassed opinion on those points, than General Simcoe. He was instructed, withal, to carry into effect a plan of reform and retrenchment in the disposal and application of the public money. Abuses under this head were loudly, and I believe very justly, complained of, the correction of which, it was said, could be effected only by a proper exertion of firmness, energy, and decision in the commander in chief; qualities which eminently distinguish that officer's character. It is unpleasant to relate, but it is too notorious to be denied, that among the French colonists, our allies, many of the principal men, in return for the tender of their services, had stipulated for, and obtained very extraordinary salaries and appointments. Some of these gentlemen,

gentlemen, without doubt, had acquired a just claim to liberal remuneration; but there were others among them, who set, I am afraid, a very exaggerated value on their own merits. In the present forlorn and sad condition of the army, however, the measure of retrenching expences and allowances, of what nature soever, proved a painful and perilous undertaking. The whole body of our allies were alarmed and discontented in consequence of it. Their efforts became every where palsied; and it is alleged, that some important posts were surrendered to the enemy, without an effort being made to save them It is certain that officers of high rank resigned their commissions and quitted the country. Thus, whilst disease was rapidly thinning the ranks, disgust and disaffection spread with equal rapidity among the survivors. The prospect, on every side, was gloomy; and the mournful exclamation, *tout est perdu*, resounded equally from disappointed selfishness, and desponding loyalty.

General Simcoe, by the moderation and firmness of his conduct, succeeded in restoring order and subordination; and, in some degree, in reviving confidence; but the state of affairs was irretrievably desperate, and the General probably thought, that the greatest service he could render his country was to return to Great Britain, fully and faithfully to represent in person to the king's ministers, the result of his experience and observations. For this purpose (as it is supposed) he embarked for Europe in July.

What report the General made, on his arrival

in London, to the British administration, is not known to me but by conjecture. It is certain that government soon afterwards came to the determination of reducing the number of British posts in St. Domingo, (by ordering the most distant and less important ones to be abandoned), and of concentrating and directing all our force to the maintenance of certain places only, the permanent possession of which might afford security to our navigation and commerce, and deter the enemy from attempting predatory excursions against the British settlements in the neighbourhood.

This determination appears to me to have been suggested by wisdom, or rather it was founded on necessity; and in order to carry it into full effect, suitable instructions were prepared for General Nesbit, who was appointed successor to General Simcoe in December 1797.

The command of the troops in the meanwhile had devolved on General Whyte, an officer of great experience, local knowledge, and approved bravery; but neither experience nor courage in the commander could enable the army to do more than to maintain itself within the garrison. The war was no longer a war of conquest, but of self-preservation. The rebel negroes were at the gates, and no alternative remained but to stand on the defensive until General Nesbit's arrival.

Respecting the forces of the enemy, and the interior state of the colony, at the period of General Simcoe's departure, it was known that the men in arms were become divided into two principal

cipal factions, under different leaders. The republican troops which had been sent at different times from France, having been reduced by sickness and famine to about 700, had made a sort of junction with the revolted negroes of the northern province; reserving to themselves only the privilege of forming a distinct regiment, and of being commanded by white officers; but the General or Commander in Chief of the whole of this northern army, white and black, was a negro named Toussaint L'Ouverture. This man, at the commencement of the revolt in 1791, was a slave to Monsieur Noé, a considerable planter in the neighbourhood of Cape François, now residing in London. Having taken an active part in the rebellion, Toussaint had acquired, in a short time, great weight among the negroes, and at length obtained such an ascendancy among his adherents, as invested him with absolute and undisputed authority over them. His attachment, however, to the French government was thought extremely doubtful; and in truth he seemed to have no other immediate object in view, than that of consolidating his own power, and securing the freedom of his fellow negroes. His black army in 1797 was estimated at 18,000 infantry, and a troop of horse of about 1,000.

THE other principal body was composed chiefly of Mulattoes, collected from different parts of the colony, and negro slaves whom they had compelled to join them. The Mulattoes, spurning the idea of serving under a negro General, had resorted to the southern province, and enrolled themselves with their brethren of colour in that part of the country, under Andrew Rigaud, a General of their own cast, of whom mention has already been made. His army, (comprehending also such of the lower class of white inhabitants of the southern and western provinces, as found it necessary, either for their daily support, or personal protection, to enlist under his banner) was said to amount to about 12,000; and they declared themselves in the interest of the republican government established under the French Directory.

Between these two bodies, however, as the reader must have perceived, there existed the most inveterate and rancorous animosity, which had already manifested itself in many conflicts; and nothing but the presence of an invading enemy in the country restrained it, in any degree, from proceeding to that extremity of civil contest—a war of utter extermination—in which mercy is neither to be given nor accepted. On the departure of the English, Toussaint made a public declaration, signifying that it was his intention not to leave a Mulatto man alive in the country; and, with respect to such of these unhappy people as have since fallen into his hands, I am assured that he has kept his word; not an individual of them has been spared.

But although these great factions were the two most considerable, they were not the only bodies of armed men that associated in this unfortunate country, and acted without any co-operation with each other. Separate hordes, composed of revolted slaves, and ruffians of every description, appeared

appeared in different parts (chiefly in the northern and western provinces) supporting themselves by depredation and plunder. Against the cruelties and enormities committed by these parties, the few remaining whites had no means of safety, but by purchasing the protection of Toussaint: and thus an extraordinary revolution had taken place;—the very chief whose original intent was the total extirpation of the whites, had checked his career of massacre, and was now become their defender and protector. In the southern province were parties of brigands of a similar description, some of which made piratical excursions at sea in canoes, and captured many small vessels, both American and English, which were found near the coast. On these occasions, the savages put all the white seamen to instant death; but where any women were unhappily found on board, these they carried away with them in a state of captivity, for purposes which perhaps made them envy the more immediate fate of the murdered seamen. It must not be omitted, however, that Rigaud published an indignant proclamation against these pirates, and hanged up all such of them as were apprehended under it.

Such was the state of affairs in St. Domingo, during the latter part of 1795, and the whole of the years 1796 and 1797, until the mortality among the British forces was so great, as in truth to leave no alternative to the sad survivors, but to retire from a contest, in which victory itself was disappointment and defeat!

On the 22d of April 1798, therefore, Brigadier Maitland,

Maitland, (who in consequence of General Whyte's return to Europe, and the death of General Nesbit in his voyage outwards, had succeeded to the chief command) came to the resolution of evacuating the towns of Port au Prince and St. Marc, with their respective dependencies, together with the parish of Arcahaye; a measure which, by a judicious negociation with Toussaint, he happily effected without loss, and withdrew with the troops to Mole St. Nicholas.

The whole number of white troops, English and foreign, at this period in the British service, under General Maitland's command, did not exceed 2,500, including even the sick and convalescent. Of the British, not more than 1,100 were left alive. Part of these held possession of Grand Ance under Brigadier General Spencer, the remainder embarked with General Maitland for the Mole.

The great importance of the post at Mole St. Nicholas, to which our troops now retreated, has been pointed out on a former occasion;* but it was also remarked that the fortifications there, however defensive they might prove in the case of a maritime attack (for which alone they were constructed), could not easily be maintained against an attempt on the side of the land, being completely commanded by the hills adjacent. This circumstance could not possibly have escaped General Maitland's notice; for the same observation occurred to myself, and must have occurred to every other man who has visited the place. Very

* Historical Survey of St. Domingo, p. 140.

serious

serious apprehensions must therefore have been felt, that the British forces would, at no distant period, be compelled to abandon this post, as they had abandoned the others.

It is probable, that considerations of this nature induced General Maitland to form the design of repossessing the no less important post of Cape Tiburon; which, as the reader has already been told, was taken from the British by a force under Rigaud, on the 25th of December 1794. It was thought that, with the neighbouring port of Jeremie, and the bay of Irois, already in our possession, the capture of Tiburon would not only command the district of Grand Ance, and secure the navigation of the windward passage, equally with the Mole St. Nicholas, but afford also, in a very considerable degree, protection to Jamaica; in case the enemy should meditate attempts on the coasts of that island. At the same time, it was not intended, I presume, to evacuate the Mole, but under circumstances of imperious necessity.

In the beginning of June 1798, such of the troops as could be spared for the intended expedition against Tiburon, assembled in the bay of Irois. The first brigade was commanded by Colonels Spencer and Grant, and the second by Colonel Stuart; a third brigade, under the command of Colonel Dessource, consisting of colonial troops, moved forwards by land on the 11th; the other brigades embarked, at the same time, in the squadron appointed to co-operate with them, consisting of the York, Adventure, Tourterelle, Rafter, and Drake, under the command of Captain Ferrier.

So far the whole business seems to have been judiciously conducted, and to have promised a successful termination; but the issues of war are in the hands of the Almighty. Owing to the prevalence of strong south-easterly winds, it was found impossible, after many unavailing attempts for that purpose, to effect a landing of the troops; and the General, not from the resistance of the enemy, but from the rage of the elements, was ultimately obliged to relinquish the attack, and return with the toops to Mole St. Nicholas.

The failure of this attempt on Tiburon, was soon afterwards followed by a design of the enemy on the Mole itself. Towards the summit of one of the hills commanding the fort, the British had established a post of 60 men, chiefly colonial troops. On the 21st of July this post was attacked by a horde of brigands, and (to the great astonishment of the garrison below) was carried, without much resistance, the major part of the detachment stationed there having deserted to the enemy. The few British among them, however, by keeping up a well-directed retreating fire, reached the garrison in safety.

But the triumph of the brigands on this occasion was of short duration; for the mortars of the garrison having been brought to play against the spot, the enemy was soon driven from the post, and a detachment of British, under Colonel Stewart, again took possession of it.

A more daring attempt however was made, about the same time, at another post called the

Gorge;

Gorge; where the brigands appeared in great force; and although by the gallantry and good conduct of the troops sent against them, they were finally repulsed, their defeat was not effected without an obstinate resistance on their part, and considerable loss on ours.

It was now evident to every man, that, unless possession could be obtained of the surrounding hills, and a chain of strong posts, with lines of great extent, established on their summits, it was not within the reach of human skill, or human courage, to preserve the garrison itself from destruction, in the event of a still more formidable attack from the enemy, of which the garrison was in hourly expectation.

For the erection of such works and defences, General Maitland, whatever might have been his wishes, certainly did not possess the necessary means; neither had he troops enough to man them, even if the means had been within his reach.

It is plain, therefore, that no sort of alternative remained to General Maitland on this occasion, but to consider of a speedy and secure retreat for the wreck of his worn-out veterans, and to abandon for ever a country which, after five bloody years of hopeless warfare within its borders, has furnished its invaders with just space enough, and no more, for the graves of about 20,000 brave soldiers and seamen; sacrificed to the vain project of seizing on a territory, which, after obtaining it, we must have newly peopled, to render it productive!

Such a retreat General Maitland, in the month of October 1798, happily effected*. Of the means by which it was accomplished, and the arrangements which it is believed were made, about the same time, with the negro chief Toussaint, for the future safety of the British trade, and the security of the British possessions in this part of the world, I can give no certain information to my readers. On those points the king's ministers have hitherto withheld all manner of communication. Enough is known however, (and more than enough) to demonstrate to every unprejudiced mind, that the final evacuation of most parts of St. Domingo, was not a matter of mere prudence and discretion, but of absolute and uncontroulable necessity. To have attempted the further prosecution of offensive war in this devoted country, (after such experience as five years had already furnished) would have argued,

* The troops at the Mole and those at the Grand Ance under Colonel Spencer, were removed to Jamaica. They did not amount all together to one thousand. The negro regiments embodied by General Williamson were disbanded, and the men left to dispose of themselves as they thought proper. This measure was, I believe, unavoidable; nevertheless, it was a mortifying circumstance to behold this fine body of men turned adrift, and compelled by necessity to join the enemy. They were purchased originally at a prodigious expence; had been trained up to arms with surprising success; were proud of their character as soldiers; and, without doubt, when kept in constant employment, were troops the best suited of any in the world for the country and climate. Whether any great dependence might be placed on the proper subordination and loyalty of such a body of men in time of peace, or on their fidelity in time of war, with people of their own cast, (and in cases where no white troops could be brought to co-operate with them) I will not venture to decide.

argued, not merely an unwarrantable excess of mistaken zeal in the minds of its conductors, but the pitiable and impotent rage of incurable insanity!

And thus terminated this most disastrous enterprize against St. Domingo. Nevertheless, dreadful as the consequences of it have proved, I am persuaded that no human being was ever actuated, on any occasion, by motives more pure and patriotic, than was General Williamson on this. Certainly it was on his recommendation and advice that the project was originally adopted by government; and if, in this case, he erred in his judgment, concerning persons and circumstances, even his errors proceeded from his virtues. Unsuspicious in his nature, and incapable of deception himself, he mistrusted not the fraudulent views and arrogant pretensions of others. Here indeed he failed. It was his misfortune to place too great reliance on the venal and unfounded assurances of a few adventurers from St. Domingo; men who had neither property nor consideration in that island, nor any sort of authority from the resident planters, to invite a British invasion. It was this ill-placed confidence that induced General Williamson to recommend the measure to the king's ministers; and afterwards, on receiving their sanction, to undertake the conduct of it himself, with means so infinitely disproportioned to the end, that disappointment and discomfiture were its necessary and natural consequences! Let me add. at the same time, that instead of procuring any pecuniary advantage to himself, General Williamson

Williamson injured his private fortune, in the prosecution of this very service. His health was the sacrifice, and poverty his reward!

The history of this unfortunate experiment will hereafter, it is hoped, furnish a profitable lesson to men in power. They may learn from it the extreme danger of giving a willing ear, in time of war, to the representations of designing foreigners, concerning the disposition and principles of the great body of their countrymen; and the state of the country from which (whether unjustly or not is nothing to the purpose) they have probably been driven. To expect a fair and impartial report from such men, in such a case, were to suppose that the human mind has changed its character. This unhappy credulity has been a distinguished feature in the conduct of the present war, and the case of St. Domingo affords a melancholy proof of its effects.

The account which I have given will likewise furnish additional confirmation to the cases already recorded in history, demonstrating the fatal folly of prosecuting aggressive war, for the acquisition of territory, in the climate of the West Indies. The dreadful expence of human life in such enterprizes, is beyond all the compensation that the most splendid victory can afford. The hand of Omnipotence is uplifted against the measure, and no one nation on earth has ever made the attempt, without having had occasion afterwards to lament its commencement, and to deplore its consequences*!

* "In these adventures," observes Mr. Burke, "it is not an enemy we have to vanquish, but a cemetery to acquire. In

carrying

Such are the reflections and observations which have occurred to me on this painful topick. With a few remarks of a less general, but, perhaps, of no less interesting a nature, I shall quit the subject.

So long as the two great parties which now exist in St. Domingo, shall continue the prosecution of civil warfare against each other, there is not, I suppose, much danger to be apprehended that either of them will have leisure to make many depredations on the British shipping trading in that part of the world, or any very serious attempts on the coasts of the neighbouring islands. This state of things cannot, however, be of extensive duration. The war is of too violent a nature to last many

carrying on war in the West Indies, the hostile sword is merciful: the country itself is the dreadful enemy:—there the European conqueror finds a cruel defeat in the very fruits of his success. Every advantage is but a new demand for recruits to the West Indian grave." Let us hear also on this subject the poet of the Seasons:

" Then wasteful forth
Walks the dire Power of Pestilent Disease;
Sick nature blasting; and to heartless woe
And feeble desolation, casting down
The towering hopes, and all the pride of man!
Such as of late at Carthagena quenched
The British fire.—
——————— Gallant Vernon saw
The miserable scene, ———————
Heard nightly plung'd amid the sullen waves
The frequent corse!" THOMSON.

This miserable scene, however, has been frequently repeated since the siege of Carthagena. It was exhibited at the Havannah in 1762; at the river St. Juan; and lately in the Windward Islands; but no where I believe with greater force and effect than in St. Domingo.

many years; and it is probable the first general conflict will decide the fate of one of the two contending factions.

By the last accounts, Toussaint appears to have at present the superiority. His army is undoubtedly more numerous than that of Rigaud; but I suspect it is worse appointed and provided. The Mulattoes too have infinitely the advantage of the blacks in point of general knowledge and military discipline. Rigaud himself is a man of sagacity and experience; but above all, there is this circumstance attending the Mulattoes, (which I think must ultimately turn the scale in their favour), that they have no possibility of retreat, and are well assured they must either subdue their enemies, *or perish themselves to a man.* My opinion therefore is, that the Mulattoes will finally become masters of all the sea coast, and the cultivatable parts of the country; and the fugitive negroes seek a refuge in the mountainous and interior districts. If such shall be the termination of the present civil contest in St. Domingo, the island of Jamaica must have a vigilant eye to its own safety. Its trade, both outwards and homewards, will be exposed to capture; and such devastation may be spread over the windward parishes by hordes of banditti, coming thither in open canoes from the southern parts of St. Domingo, as may destroy the labour of years, before the squadron at Port Royal can give the smallest assistance to the inhabitants. Of this impending danger to Jamaica, the British government is without doubt sufficiently apprized, and I believe that measures are in contemplation how avert the threatened evil. I will venture however to pronounce, from circumstances within my own knowledge, that nothing can afford solid and permanent security to Jamaica, twt tranquillity at home. Let peace be re-established between England and France, and all apprehensions from St. Domingo will vanish. The Mulattoes having, after a long and bloody struggle, established their claim to all the rights of French citizens, have now nothing to desire but to be considered and acknowledged as faithful subjects of France: and if the French government, whatever form it may hereafter assume, entertains the most distant hope of restoring, in any degree, order and subordination in the country, and of deriving any advantage from it as a colony, it will receive them as such, and avail itself of their services in suppressing the remains of revolt and rebellion throughout the island. Peace, therefore, between England and France, will convert the Mulattoes of St. Domingo, from formidable enemies, into harmless and inoffensive neighbours to the British West Indies; for it will not then be any longer the business of our fleets and armies to heighten and extend the miseries of war on this theatre of bloodshed, and thus invite retaliation on our own possessions. If indeed Great Britain judges rightly, she will consider the restoration of order in St. Domingo, as the only certain pledge of future security to her West Indian colonies.

HISTORY

OF THE

WAR IN THE WEST INDIES,

FROM ITS COMMENCEMENT IN FEBRUARY 1793.

CHAPTER I.

Preliminary Observations.—Commencement of the War.—Capture of Tobago.—Fruitless Attempt against Martinico.—Determination of the British Ministry thereon, and consequent Preparations for a large Armament to be sent to the West Indies.—Sir CHARLES GREY *appointed to the Command of the Land Forces, and Sir* JOHN JERVIS *to the Command of the Fleet.—New Arrangement.*

CHAP. I.

Preliminary Observations.

WHOEVER has made himself acquainted with the history of the West Indian Islands, cannot fail to have observed that, whenever the nations of Europe are engaged, from whatever cause, in war with each other, those unhappy countries are constantly made the theatre of its operations. Thither the combatants repair, as to the arena, to decide their differences; and the miserable planters, who are never the cause, are always the victims of the contest!

WHEN, at the pacification of 1763, the claims of Great Britain and France to the neutral Islands

 of

CHAP. I.

Preliminary Observations.

of St. Lucia, Tobago, St. Vincent, and Dominica, were adjusted by a division of the spoil, many circumstances concurred to induce a hope, that the contending parties would remain satisfied with their booty, and not hastily involve the world again in devastation and bloodshed. One of the causes of former contests between France and England (the claim to those islands) having been removed, there was certainly reason to suppose that the remembrance of recent calamities, the pressure of poverty, and the various other distresses which the war had brought on all the belligerent powers, were circumstances highly favourable to a continuance of the peace. The short experience of ten years proved the fallacy of this expectation. The martial spirit of Great Britain sickened for employment; and pretences being wanting for directing it towards her ancient enemies, it was turned, in an evil hour, against her own subjects in North America. Wise men foresaw and predicted, that the restless and intriguing genius of France would not allow that kingdom to continue an indifferent spectator of such a contest. Accordingly, in the year 1778, she rushed into another war with England, without even affecting to have sustained the shadow of provocation; and the consequence of her injustice, and our insanity, was the loss not only of those of the sugar islands, which had been assigned to us in 1763, but of almost all the rest; the dismemberment of the empire, and a combination of dangers from which, at one moment, death seemed our only refuge.

Of

CHAP. I. Preliminary Observations.

Of the capture of the sugar islands in that war, and their restoration to Great Britain at the peace of 1783, I have sufficiently treated elsewhere. America alone derived advantage from the contest. As the French had engaged in the war without provocation, so they retired from the field, not only without benefit, but with manifest loss. They contracted an enormous debt, to the payment of which their ordinary revenues were inadequate; and perhaps to this circumstance, more than to any other, the ruin of their ancient government must immediately be attributed. So true is the observation of our great dramatic poet (and it is equally applicable to nations and to individuals) that

——Even-handed justice
Commends th' ingredients of our poison'd chalice
To our own lips. SHAKSPEARE.

To a philosopher, speculating in his closet, it might seem that such an event could not fail to operate both as a terrible example, and a profitable lesson, to the nations of the earth; but above all, to those few envied states who have every thing to lose, and nothing to gain, by a change in their situation. Posterity will either mourn over that page of our history, or doubt its fidelity, which shall record the melancholy truth, that, in the year 1792, the government of Great Britain (too proud to learn wisdom from the misfortunes of others) adopted towards France the same infatuated line of conduct, which, a few years before, the French government, nearly under the same circumstances, had pursued towards Great Britain.

CHAP. I.

Britain. Our conduct was similar; may the mercy of Divine Providence avert from us a similar issue!

February 1793.

WAR being thus renewed (first proclaimed, I admit, on the part of France, but provoked undoubtedly by the rash counsels and imperious language of the British administration), the West Indies became, as usual, the scene of military enterprize; and Great Britain had the advantage (if an advantage it might be called) of making the first onset. On the 10th of February 1793, a few days only after notice had been received of the French declaration of war, directions were transmitted to Major General Cuyler, the commander in chief of the British troops in the Windward Islands, and to Sir John Laforey, who commanded in the naval department, to attempt the reduction of Tobago. As most of the proprietors in that island were English, it was supposed that an English armament would be favourably received by the inhabitants; and the event justified this expectation. The island surrendered, without any great struggle, on the 17th of April.

Of the territory thus re-annexed to the British dominion, I shall give the best account I am able to collect in a subsequent chapter. At present, I am unwilling to interrupt the narrative of military transactions, by disquisitions either on its past history, or its present importance; and shall, therefore, proceed to the next attempt of the British forces in this part of the world, which I am sorry to observe had a less favourable termination.

It was an attack on Martinico; an enterprize

of great magnitude; for the labours and ingenuity of man had co-operated with the hand of nature, in rendering that island one of the strongest countries in the world. In 1759, it had successfully resisted a formidable British armament of ten ships of the line, besides frigates and bomb ketches, having on board 5,800 regular troops; and although the island surrendered, three years afterwards, to a much superior force, yet the gallant and vigorous resistance which the garrison was enabled to make on that occasion, for upwards of three weeks, ought surely to have induced great caution and consideration, with regard to future expeditions against a country so amply provided, both by nature and art, with the means of defence.

In the present conjuncture, the whole of the British force in the Windward Islands was known and allowed to be, of itself, vastly inadequate to the object in view; but such representations had been spread throughout the army, concerning the disaffection of the greater part of the inhabitants of all the French islands towards the republican government, recently established on the ruins of their monarchy, as to create a very general belief, that the appearance of a British armament before the capital of Martinico would alone produce an immediate surrender. General Bruce, on whom the chief command of our troops had devolved in the interim, was indeed assured, by a deputation from the principal planters of the island, that "a body of 800 regular troops would be more than sufficient to overcome all possible resistance."

These representations (as the General himself informed

CHAP. I. 1793.

informed the king's ministers) induced him, in conjunction with Admiral Gardner, to undertake the expedition; and the land forces having been embarked in the ships of war, the armament arrived off Cape Navire on the 11th of June 1793. On the 16th the British troops, in number eleven hundred, made good their landing; and having been joined by a body of about eight hundred French royalists, took possession of a very strong post within five miles of St. Pierre, it being the General's intention to attack the two forts which defended that town. The plan however did not succeed, and I regret that I am unable to furnish a satisfactory account of the causes of its failure. Whatever information might have been contained in the dispatches from the commander in chief to government, all that has been communicated to the public lies in a narrow compass, and I shall repeat the substantial part in the General's own words: "The morning of the 18th (he observes) "was the time fixed for the attack, and we were "to move forward in two columns, the one con- "sisting of the British troops, the other of the "French Royalists; and for this purpose, the "troops were put in motion before day-break; "but unfortunately, some alarm having taken "place amongst the royalists, they began, in a "mistake, firing on one another; and their com- "mander being severely wounded on the occasion, "his troops were disconcerted, and instantly re- "tired to the post from which they had marched." "This conduct (continues the General) strongly "proved that no dependance could be placed on "the

"the royalists, and that the attack against St. "Pierre must have been carried on solely by the "British troops, to which their numbers were not "equal. They were therefore ordered to return "to their former posts, from whence they re-em- "barked," &c.

This is the whole, or nearly the whole, of what the British administration thought proper to furnish for the gratification of the public curiosity, concerning the conduct and failure of this unfortunate expedition; and indeed it is sufficient to demonstrate, that the strong assurances which had been given, and the sanguine expectations which had been formed, of support and assistance from the greater part of the French inhabitants, consisting in the whole of upwards of 10,000 whites, were not justified by the event. It reflects therefore great honour on the liberal and humane disposition of the British commanders, that they did not suffer the disappointment, which they must have felt on this occasion, to operate to the disadvantage of those of the French planters, by whom such assurances were held forth, and who, though mistaken as to their countrymen, manifested the sincerity of their own professions by their subsequent conduct. "As they would certainly have "fallen victims," observes General Bruce, "to "the implacable malignity of the republican "party, as soon as we quitted the island, it be- "came in a manner incumbent on us, in support "of the national character, to use our utmost ex- "ertions to bring these unhappy people from the "shore; and although the necessity of impressing "such

CHAP. I. 1793.

"such vessels as could be found, and the purchasing provisions from the merchant vessels, "will incur a great expence, I have nevertheless "ventured upon it, trusting for my justification "to the generous and humane disposition exhibited by the British nation on similar occasions. "We were therefore employed in embarking these "people, from the 19th to the 21st," &c. &c.

NOTWITHSTANDING this discouraging account, the British ministers, on receiving intelligence of General Bruce's miscarriage, considered themselves imperiously called upon to vindicate the honour of the English arms, by enterprizes of greater magnitude in the same quarter. They resolved to send thither, forthwith, such an armament, as, in addition to the British force already in the West Indies, should be sufficient not only for the conquest of Martinico, but even "to dislodge the "enemy from every one of their possessions in that "part of the world." Such was their declaration.

THE necessity of dispatching to that part of the king's dominions a considerable reinforcement, could not indeed admit of doubt or delay. The preservation of many of our sugar islands, rendered such a measure indispensable; but the question whether it was consistent with prudence and good policy to prosecute offensive war in that quarter, rather than confine our attention solely to the defence of the British territories there, involves in it many great and weighty considerations. A few reflections which have occurred to me on this head will be found towards the conclusion of my narrative.

SUCH,

CHAP. I. 1793.

SUCH, however, whether wisely or not, was the system approved by the British ministers; and it must I think be admitted that, if a war of conquest in the West Indies was, at all hazards, a proper and justifiable measure, the comprehensive plan, which embraced the whole possessions of the French in the Windward Islands, originated in sound policy: certainly it was wise, either to attempt the conquest of all of them, or to leave all of them unmolested. Every man who is acquainted with the relative situation of the French and British colonies in those islands, the condition of each, and their affinity to each other, will allow that, in this case, there was no medium.

IT must likewise be admitted, that the preparations which the ministers caused to be made, in consequence of this determination, corresponded to the magnitude and extent of their views. Orders were issued for the immediate embarkation of fourteen regiments of infantry, consisting of near eleven thousand men; a fleet composed of four first-rate ships of war and nine frigates, besides sloops, bomb-ketches, and transports, was appointed to convey them to the scene of action, and act in conjunction with them. And that no possible doubt might arise in the public mind, concerning the judicious application of this great armament to its proper object, the whole was placed under the direction of two of the most distinguished officers which any age or nation has produced; the chief command being assigned to Sir CHARLES GREY, General of the land forces; and the naval department to vice-admiral Sir JOHN

JERVIS.

CHAP. I. 1793. JERVIS. Neither must it pass unobserved, in justice to the different public offices of this kingdom, that the whole was ready for its departure in less than three months after the receipt of General Bruce's dispatches.

How much it is to be lamented that this great and decisive plan was not persisted in to the last, the circumstances which I shall hereafter record, will mournfully demonstrate. It is with pain I relate, that a few days only before Sir Charles Grey expected to sail, a new arrangement was made, by which no less than 4,600 of the troops that had been placed under his orders, were detached from the rest, and employed on another service; the ministers apologizing to the General, by intimating that it was not expected of him to accomplish all the objects for which the more extensive armament had been judged necessary.

ALTHOUGH it cannot easily be supposed that this unexpected diminution of his army, any more than the apology which was made for it (by which it was evident that the original plan was abandoned by government), could be matter of satisfaction to the commander in chief, yet he silently acquiesced in the measure; and, as the secretary of state afterwards very honourably and handsomely observed in the House of Commons, "did nevertheless complete all the conquests which were in contemplation before any reduction of his force had taken place."

THE reader's first impression therefore will naturally be, that, although a less force was actually employed than was allotted for this expedition, the

the deficiency was abundantly supplied by the spirit and energy of the army and navy, and the wisdom and decision of the commanders; that the objects in view being fully obtained, though with less means than were at first suggested, the original system was in truth carried into full effect; and of course the reduction of the army, justified by subsequent events.

How far this reasoning can be supported, the sequel will shew. I shall proceed in the next chapter with a detail of military transactions in the order they occurred.

CHAP.

CHAP. II.*

Sir Charles Grey arrives at Barbadoes, and sails for the Attack of Martinico.—Proceedings of the Army and Navy, until the Surrender of that Island.

CHAP. II. January 1794.

ON the 26th of November 1793, the armament, reduced as was stated in the latter part of the preceding chapter, sailed from St. Helen's, and on the 6th of January 1794, the squadron cast anchor in Carlisle Bay, in the island of Barbadoes: it was afterwards reinforced by the Asia, of 64 guns, and some additional frigates.

AFTER a month's stay at Barbadoes (an interval which was usefully employed in preparing gun-boats, in training the seamen for land service, and in attendance on the sick) the squadron sailed for the attack of Martinico; having on board, of land

* It is proper to observe, that most of what is related in this chapter, concerning the proceedings of the army and navy, in the attack and conquest of Martinico, is copied from the public dispatches of the respective commanders. The few particulars which I have interwoven in some places, and added in others, are derived partly from the comprehensive and circumstantial account which was published by the Rev. Cooper Willyams; and partly from private communications from officers who were in actual service in this campaign. I have arranged the whole after my own manner, in the view (as I hoped) of giving the detail greater clearness and perspicuity, than can be expected from dispatches written commonly in great haste on the spur of the moment.

forces

forces (including a detachment of negro dragoons) 6,085 effective men.

February 1794.

On Wednesday, the 5th of February, the fleet approached the south-eastern coast of that island, and the General (having previously made the necessary arrangements with Sir John Jervis) divided the army into three detachments, with a view to land them at three separate and distinct quarters. These were Gallion Bay on the northern coast, Case de Navires nearly opposite, on the south, and Trois Rivieres towards the south-east. The first detachment was commanded by Major General Dundas, the second by Colonel Sir Charles Gordon, and the third by the General himself, assisted by Lieutenant General Prescott. The measure was well concerted; for, by inducing the enemy to divide his force, it enabled the British to effect their landing at each place, with very little loss.

On the evening of the same day, Major General Dundas, with his detachment, escorted by Commodore Thompson and his division, arrived off the bay of Gallion: Capt. Faulkner in the Zebra led, and immediately drove the enemy from a battery on Point a'Chaux. The troops then disembarked without further opposition, about three miles from the town of Trinité, and halted for the night. Early the next morning they began their march, but were somewhat annoyed in their progress by a fire of musketry from the cane-fields, where a body of the enemy lay concealed. The aim of the Major General was to take Morne-Le Brun, a strong post, situated on an eminence immediately

CHAP. II. 1794. ately over the town. This he happily effected; and instantly detaching Lieutenant Colonel Craddock with the second battalion of grenadiers, and Major Evatt with three companies of light-infantry, to attack Trinité Fort, the enemy fled, and our troops took possession of it, with the cannon and stores. Commodore Thompson possessed himself at the same time of the vessels in the harbour, but the town itself was destroyed by the enemy; for Bellegarde, the popular leader of the Mulattoes, being obliged to evacuate a fort bearing his own name, maliciously set fire to Trinité as he retired, and the best part of the houses, with a quantity of stores of all kinds, were consumed by the flames.

On the evening of the 7th, Major General Dundas, leaving Major Skirrett and a party of marines to command at Trinité Fort, proceeded with his brigade to Gros Morne, a situation of great importance, commanding the principal pass between the northern and southern parts of the island; but although the fortifications were strong and extensive, the Major General found the place entirely evacuated, the enemy having retired at his approach. Pushing forward again, the Major General on the 9th, took possession of a strong situation called Bruneau, about two leagues north of Fort Bourbon, the enemy retreating as before. From thence, Major General Dundas detached Lieutenant Colonel Craddock with three companies of grenadiers to seize Fort Matilde, which covered a good landing within two miles of his left, and where the enemy appeared in consider-

able

able force; but on Lieutenant Colonel Craddock's approach, they evacuated the place. Of this post the British troops, being reinforced with a company of grenadiers, held quiet possession that night, and the whole of the ensuing day; but in the night between the 10th and 11th, they were attacked by 800 of the enemy, under the command of Bellegarde, the Mulatto General. Our troops were rather taken by surprize; but recovering themselves, the enemy was totally repulsed, and compelled to take shelter in Fort Bourbon. In this action Captain M'Ewen of the 38th, and seven privates, were killed, and nineteen wounded.

Colonel Sir Charles Gordon, with the brigade under his command, was not able to make good his landing at Case de Navires; but on the morning of the 8th he landed at Cape Pilotte; when, finding that the enemy were masters of the great road and the heights above it, he made a circuitous movement through the mountains, and ascended until, by day-break of the 9th, he had gained, unmolested by the enemy, the most commanding post in that part of the country: Colonel Myers, descending from the heights, took possession of La Chapelle, and a post established by the enemy above it. On his return the column proceeded, through very difficult ground, to the heights of Berne, above Ance La Haye; the enemy keeping a constant fire in the meantime from the batteries of St. Catherine. Sir Charles Gordon had now a position which gave him an easy communication with the transports; when on the 12th, observing that the battery and works at St. Catherine,

CHAP. II. 1794.

Catherine, and the posts which guarded the first ravine, were abandoned by the enemy, he took possession of them, while Colonel Myers, with five companies of grenadiers, and the forty-third regiment, crossed four ravines higher up, and seized all the batteries by which they were defended. The enemy now fled on every side, and our troops were soon in possession of the five batteries between Cas de Navires and Fort Royal. They then proceeded and occupied the posts of Gentilly, La Coste, and La Archet, within a league of Fort Bourbon.

In the meanwhile, the commander in chief, with Lieutenant General Prescott, and that part of the army which had landed at Trois Rivieres, had marched from thence across a very difficult country, to the river Saleé, and entered the town of the same name, situated on the banks of the river. On the march, Brigadier General Whyte was detached with the second battalion of light-infantry, to force the batteries of Cape Solomon and Point a Burgos, in order to obtain possession of Islet aux Ramiercs, or Pigeon Island, an important object, the attainment of which was necessary to enable our ships to get into the harbour of Fort Royal. Those batteries were accordingly stormed, and the Brigadier General being reinforced with a detachment of Royal and Irish artillery, and 200 seamen, sent Colonel Symes with the seamen, and two companies of the 15th regiment, to ascend the heights, and take possession of Mount Matharine, which commanded Pigeon Island at the distance of 400 yards. This

was

was happily accomplished on the 9th, and batteries erected on it. These were completed during the night of the 10th, and on Tuesday morning, the 11th, they were opened, and so well pointed and incessant a fire was kept up, under the direction of Capt. Pratt of the Irish artillery, that in two hours the garrison struck their colours, and surrendered at discretion, with the loss of 15 men killed and 25 wounded.

The Islet aux Ramieres, or Pigeon Island, is situated on the south side of the bay of Fort Royal, about two hundred yards from the shore. It is in itself a steep and barren rock, inaccessible except in one place only, where the ascent is by a ladder, fixed against a perpendicular wall; and the summit is 90 feet above the level of the sea. There were found on it, 11 forty-two pounders, 6 thirty-two pounders, 14 thirteen-inch mortars, and one howitzer, with an immense quantity of stores and ammunition of all kinds, and a stove for heating shot.

On the capture of this fortress, the squadron immediately took possession of the bay and harbour of Fort Royal; and most of the transports and store-ships got up to Cohee, a harbour at the north-east end of the bay, from whence they had a communication, by a chain of posts, with the troops at Bruneau; and the next object of attention was St. Pierre, the capital of the island, in the attack of which, the co-operation of the forces, both by sea and land, was indispensably necessary.

In consequence of an arrangement for this enterprize,

CHAP. II. 1794. terprize, Col. Symes, with three light companies, and Major Maitland, with the 30th regiment, embarked on board a detachment of the squadron, which were ordered for the bay of St. Pierre.

On the 14th the commander in chief moved forward with his army to Bruneau, where he left Major Gen. Dundas, and on the evening of the same day the Major Gen. marched from thence to Gros Morne with the 2d battalion of grenadiers, the 33d and 40th light companies, and the 65th regiment. From Gros Morne he detached Col. Campbell through the woods by Bois le Bue, with the two light companies and the 65th regiment, to the attack of Montigne, proceeding himself towards the heights of Capot and Callebasse, from both which the enemy retired. From the latter the Major Gen. had a distant view of Col. Campbell's detachment, and the mortification to see them attacked by a great body of the enemy strongly posted about half a mile short of Montigne. The Major Gen. immediately pushed forward his advanced guard under the command of the Hon. Capt. Ramsay, who, by extraordinary exertions, came up with the enemy while engaged with Col. Campbell's detachment, and silenced their fire, but the Colonel himself had unfortunately fallen early in the engagement. Capt. Ramsay being joined by the second battalion of grenadiers, now took possession of Montigne, and the Major Gen. took post on Morne Rouge. The same evening, the Major Gen. observing several bodies of the enemy moving towards his front, and forming under a small redoubt, ordered four companies

companies of grenadiers to advance, and a smart engagement ensued; the enemy was covered by a brisk fire, from two field-pieces on Morne Bellevieur. The action continued for about half an hour, when the enemy retreated, and during the night abandoned the fort on Morne Bellevieur, of which our troops immediately took possession.

Our army had now arrived within two leagues of St. Pierre, from whence at day-break, on the 16th, the enemy sent a flag, requiring three days to consider of a capitulation. The Major General returned for answer, that instead of three days he would allow them only three hours; and leaving a company of grenadiers in possession of Bellevieur, he immediately moved on towards St. Pierre. At this juncture, the detachment of the squadron arrived in the bay, and began their operations. Colonel Symes, with the troops and seamen who were to land with him, had, previous to their entering the bay, embarked on board the Zebra and Nautilus sloops, which drawing little water could land them without difficulty. In the evening of the 16th, these vessels approached the north part of the bay, the other men of war standing in to cover them from the fire of the enemy. Capt. Hervey, in the Santa Margarita, perceiving the troops were likely to be much annoyed by two batteries with heated shot, steered close under the guns of the most considerable of them, and effectually silenced it. About four in the morning of the 17th, the troops made good their landing, and immediately advanced towards St. Pierre; but the conflict was at an end, for the enemy seeing the

 British

CHAP. II. 1794.

British approach both by sea and by land, evacuated the town, leaving their colours flying, which were immediately hauled down, and the British colours placed in their room. By ten o'clock the whole of Colonel Symes's detachment had marched into the town, and were soon afterwards joined by General Dundas and his army.

No injury was done, nor outrage offered, to the inhabitants; the women and children sat at their doors to see the soldiers march in, as peaceably and cheerfully as the inhabitants of an English village behold a regiment pass through their streets. One instance only occurred, of an attempt to pillage; for which the offender was immediately hung up by the Provost Marshal, at the gate of the Jesuits' College.

The town of St. Pierre being thus captured*, and many important posts in different parts of the country already in possession of the British troops, it might have been supposed that the surrender of the island was speedily to have followed; but so great was the natural and artificial strength of the country, and so obstinately was it defended on this occasion by the inhabitants, that much remained to be done before this event took place. The two great forts of Bourbon and Fort Royal (the former commanded by Rochambeau the Governor

* Lieut. Malcolm of the 41st grenadiers was appointed Town Major, in consideration of his distinguished conduct and active services at the head of a body of riflemen, which was composed of two men selected from each company of the first battalion of grenadiers. We shall have occasion to mention this officer hereafter.

of

of the Island) were still to be conquered; and it was impossible closely to invest Fort Bourbon, without first possessing the heights of Sure or Sourier, a situation eminently strong and difficult, and defended by a large body of the enemy, under the command of the mulatto General Bellegarde. The commander in chief, therefore, proposed to attack this post from his camp at Bruneau, on the night of the 18th, and to depend for success solely on a vigorous use of the bayonet; but, a few hours previous to the time he had fixed for the enterprize, Bellegarde himself, with part of his troops, descended the heights, and attacked the General's left. His intention was, if possible, to cut off the communication between the British army and navy. The attempt was bold, but it was ruinous. The General immediately perceived the advantage to be derived from it, and seized it in the moment; for, directing Lieut. Gen. Prescott to keep the enemy in check, he ordered from his right Lieut. Col. Buckeridge, with the third battalion of grenadiers, and Lieut. Colonels Coote and Blundell, with the 1st and 2d battalions of light infantry, to attack Bellegarde's camp on the left. In this service this detachment displayed such spirit and impetuosity as proved irresistible, and possession being taken of Bellegarde's camp, his own cannon were turned against him. This unfortunate man and his second in command, with about 300 of their followers, surrendered themselves to the General a few days afterwards, the two leaders desiring to be sent to North America, on condition of never serving against his majesty; and in this

CHAP. II. 1794. this request they were gratified. Their followers were sent on board the king's ships as prisoners of war.

From the 20th of February, Forts Bourbon and Louis, with the town of Fort Royal, were completely invested, and the General was busily employed in erecting batteries on his first parallel. On the north-east side, the army under General Prescott broke ground on the 25th of February, and on the west side towards La Caste, fascine batteries for mortars and cannon were erecting with all possible expedition. In this business the seamen eminently distinguished themselves; and the siege was carried on with unremitted exertion by night and day; the most perfect co-operation prevailing between the army and navy; the exertions of both being animated by the presence and approbation of his Royal Highness Prince Edward, who arrived from Quebec the 4th of March, and taking the command of Sir Charles Gordon's brigade, set an admirable example of discipline and good conduct to the whole army, by his behaviour, during the remainder of the campaign. The advanced batteries were at length brought within five hundred yards of Fort Bourbon, and not more than two hundred from the redoubt; when on the 17th of March, the General concerted measures with the Admiral for a combined assault, by the naval and land forces, upon the fort and town of Fort Royal. Scaling ladders being provided, and the necessary arrangements settled, the ships destined for the service took their stations on the morning of the 20th of March.

March. The Asia, and the Zebra sloop, with Captain Rogers, and a body of seamen in flat boats (the whole under the command of Commodore Thompson), composed the naval force; the land force consisted of the first battalion of grenadiers, the first and third light infantry, with the third grenadiers.

About 10 o'clock the Asia and Zebra got under way. The Zebra led in, towards the mouth of the harbour, receiving the enemy's fire, without returning a shot. The Asia had got within the range of grape shot, when, to the surprize of the whole fleet, she wore and made sail from the fort. She stood in a second time, and again put about*. Now then it was that Captain Faulkner of the Zebra acquired immortal honour; for perceiving that he could not expect any assistance from the Asia (a ship of the line) he determined to undertake the service alone in his small sloop of 16 guns, and he executed this design with matchless intrepidity and good conduct; for running the Zebra close to the walls, and leaping overboard at the head of his sloop's company, he scaled the ramparts; and drove the enemy from the fort. "No language of mine (says Admiral Jervis) "can express the merit of Capt. Faulkner on "this occasion; but as every man in the army "and squadron bears testimony to it, this incom- "parable action cannot fail of being recorded in "the

* It is said that a French loyalist, named Toureller, who had formerly been lieutenant of Fort Louis, was employed by Capt. Brown as pilot on this occasion, and that this man, under pretence of shoals, refused to carry the ship any farther.

CHAP. II. 1794. "the page of history." Col. Symes, in the same triumphant moment, entered and took possession of the town.

This signal success determined the fate of the Island; for General Rochambeau, perceiving that all was lost, immediately sent a flag from Fort Bourbon, offering to surrender on capitulation. The terms were accordingly adjusted on the 23d, and on the 25th, the garrison, reduced to 900 men, marched out prisoners of war. To the gallantry with which this fortress was defended, General Grey bore an honourable testimony, by observing, that "the British troops, on entering "the place, could scarcely find an inch of ground "which had not been touched by their shot or "their shells."

Thus was achieved the conquest of Martinico, with the loss on the part of the British of 71 men killed, 193 wounded, and of three that were missing. The limits I have prescribed to myself will not allow me to enumerate the particular merits of all those gallant men, whose services, both by sea and land, were conspicuous on this occasion. History will not fail to record them, and above all to give due honour to that zealous co-operation, to that admirable spirit of unanimity and concord between the sea and land service, which were particularly observable during the whole siege; and for want of which, in other cases, both numbers and courage have oftentimes proved unavailing.

_ Immediately on the surrender of the Island, the following proclamation was issued in General Orders :

Head Quarters, Fort Royal,
25th March 1794.

Parole, FORT GEORGE. C. S. FORT EDWARD.

Field Officer, COLONEL COOTE.

THE Commander in Chief orders Fort Bourbon now to bear the name of Fort George, and Fort Louis to bear the name of Fort Edward : and to be called so in future. The commander in chief, with heartfelt satisfaction, congratulates the army on the complete conquest of the Island of Martinico, a most important acquisition to his Majesty's crown. He begs permission to return the army in general his warmest thanks for their zeal, perseverance, gallantry, and spirit, so eminently distinguished, and never before exceeded, by every rank, from the general to the soldier, throughout this service ; and this justice he cannot fail to do them in the strongest language to his Majesty.

CHAP.

CHAP. III.

Conquest of St. Lucia.—Description of Guadaloupe.—Proceedings against that Island.—Its Surrender completes the Conquest of the French West India Colonies.—Cause of the subsequent Reverses.—Mortality among the British.—Arrival of a French Squadron with Troops at Guadaloupe.—Their Successes: followed by the Reduction of the whole Island.—Inhuman Barbarity of Victor Hugues to the Royalists.—Sir C. Grey and Sir J. Jervis, succeeded by Sir J. Vaughan and Admiral Caldwell.

CHAP. III. March 1794.

VICTORY having thus far crowned the British arms, General Grey determined, without loss of time, to persevere in his career of glory; wherefore, leaving five regiments under the command of General Prescott, for the protection of Martinico, he and the brave Admiral proceeded, on the morning of the 31st of March, to the attack of St. Lucia. This island had not the means of a formidable defence; and on the 4th of April, his Royal Highness Prince Edward, after a fatiguing march of fourteen hours from the landing place, hoisted the British colours on its chief fortress Morne Fortuné; the garrison, consisting of 300 men, having surrendered on the same terms of capitulation as those that had been granted to General Rochambeau. Ricard, the officer commanding in St. Lucia, desired and obtained permission, as Rochambeau

chambeau had done before him, to embark for North America; but the garrisons of both, of St. Lucia and Martinico, were sent to France immediately on their surrender*.

After the completion of this service, General Grey, having left the sixth and ninth regiments, with detachments of artillery and engineers, as a garrison for St. Lucia, and appointed Sir Charles Gordon governor of that island, returned to Martinico; and the spirit of enterprize among the soldiers being thus kept alive and encouraged, the General turned his attention in the next place to the large and fertile colony of Guadaloupe.

It is necessary the reader should be apprized in this place, that Guadaloupe consists in fact of two islands, divided from each other by a narrow arm of the sea, called La Riviere Salee, (Salt River) which is navigable for vessels of 50 tons; the eastern island, or division, being called Grande Terre, and the western, Basse Terre. Adjoining the former, is a small island called Desirade, and near

* So rapid were the movements of the British army, that his Royal Highness Prince Edward reimbarked in the Boyne at the end of 58 hours after he had landed at St. Lucia. It is impossible to mention this island without lamenting that it has proved in every war a grave to thousands of brave men! On the present occasion a circumstance occurred which demonstrates, in a very striking manner, the extreme unwholesomeness of the climate. The night after the troops had landed, the first battalion of grenadiers took possession of some negro huts: the second battalion had no such accommodation, or rather chose to remain in the open air. The consequence was, that while the former continued healthy, 40 of the best men of the latter were returned the next morning on the sick list.

CHAP. III. 1794. to the latter a cluster of little islands called Les Saintes. At some distance from these, towards the east, is another island called Marie Gallante; all these were dependencies on Guadaloupe, and comprized in its government.

On Tuesday the 8th of April, such of the troops as remained after the necessary garrisons for the conquered islands were formed, embarked in transports, and the fleet sailed from the Bay of Fort Royal. A detachment of the squadron having been sent in the first place to attack the little islands above mentioned, called Les Saintes, that service was executed with much spirit and gallantry by a party of seamen and marines; and about noon on the 10th, the Boyne and Veteran cast anchor in the Bay of Point a Petre, in the division of Grande Terre; a fresh wind and lee current preventing many of the transports from getting in until the day following.

Without waiting however for the arrival of all the troops, the General effected the landing of a considerable detachment, with the addition of 500 marines, at Grosier Bay, at one o'clock in the morning of the 11th, under cover of the Winchelsea man of war, the Captain of which, Lord Viscount Garlies, being the only person that was wounded on the occasion. "He received a bad "contusion (observes Admiral Jervis) from the "fire of a battery against which he had placed his "ship, *in the good old way*, within half musket "shot." The battery however was soon silenced, and early on the morning of the 12th, the Fort of La Fleur d'Epée was carried by assault, and the greatest

greatest part of the garrison put to the sword. Fort St. Louis, the town of Point à Petre, and the new battery upon Islet à Cochon, being afterwards abandoned, and the inhabitants flying in all directions, the possession of Grande Terre was complete.

The reduction of Basse Terre was effected the 21st of the same month; for the strong post of Palmiste being carried by the gallantry of Prince Edward and Col. Symes, and that of Houelmont by Major Gen. Dundas, the French governor (Collot) immediately capitulated; surrendering the whole of Guadaloupe and all its dependencies to the king of Great Britain, on the same terms that were allowed to Rochambeau at Martinique, and Ricard at Lucia. It is pleasing to add, that this conquest was happily effected with the loss on the part of the British of only seventeen men killed, and about fifty wounded*.

This gallant and successful enterprize completed the entire conquest of the French possessions in the West Indian Islands; and the primary views and declarations of the British ministers were thus wonderfully, and I believe unexpectedly, realized by British energy and valour. Happy, if the scene had shut at this period, and no envious cloud overcast the close of a campaign, the opening and progress of which had shone with so bright a lustre in the eyes of all Europe!

* From a return found among General Collot's papers, it appeared that the number of French troops in Guadaloupe was 5877.

CHAP. III. 1794. But now it was that the measure of reducing the army at the outset of the expedition, began to manifest those unhappy consequences, which it was then predicted would ensue from it. In allotting garrisons for the security of the several islands which had surrendered, the deficiency of troops for that purpose was at once obvious and alarming. It was discovered that the mortality had been so great (more from sickness, the never-failing effect of extraordinary exertion in tropical climates, than the sword of the enemy), as to have reduced the ranks to nearly one-half their original numbers; and of the troops which remained alive, a very large proportion were so worn down by unremitting fatigue, as to be rendered absolutely incapable of efficient service. Unfortunately, the numerous enterprizes in which the British forces were engaged, and especially the fatal, and never enough to be lamented, attempt on St. Domingo, left it not in the power of the king's ministers to send such a reinforcement to the Windward Islands as the occasion required.

So early, however, as the 22d of March, four regiments, consisting of 2,377 men, had sailed from Cork for Barbadoes. They were intended indeed for St. Domingo, but authority was given to General Sir Charles Grey to detain two of them, if circumstances should render it necessary, to serve under his own command in the Windward Islands.

These regiments arrived at Barbadoes on the 5th of May, and the General detained the eight battalion companies of the 35th, one of the four regiments, but observing the extreme anxiety which

which the British minister expressed in his dispatches for prosecuting the enterprize against St. Domingo, and trusting (as he writes) "that effectual care would be taken at home to prevent the enemy in the conquered islands receiving assistance from Europe," he replaced those battalion companies with eight flank companies from his own army, which was thus rather diminished than augmented by the exchange *.

From this period, the tide which had hitherto flowed with so rapid and prosperous a current, began

* These flank companies proceeded first to Jamaica, and from thence to Port au Prince; and nothing can afford a more striking demonstration of the sad consequence of tropical warfare, than the account which has been given of this reinforcement on its arrival at the place of its destination. "On the 8th of June, "eight flank companies belonging to the 22d, 24th, 35th, and "41st regiments, arrived at Port au Prince, under the command "of Lieutenant Colonel Lenox. They consisted, on their embarkation, of about seventy men each, but the aggregate number, when landed, was not quite three hundred. The four "grenadier companies, in particular, were nearly annihilated. "The frigate in which they were conveyed, became a house of "pestilence. Upwards of one hundred of their number were "buried in the deep, in the short passage between Guadaloupe "and Jamaica, and one hundred and fifty more were left in a "dying state at Port Royal. The wretched remains of the "whole detachment discovered, on their landing at Port au "Prince, that they came not to participate in the glories of conquest, but to perish themselves within the walls of an hospital! So rapid was the mortality of the British army, after "their arrival, that no less than forty officers, and upwards of "six hundred rank and file, met an untimely death, without a "contest with any other enemy than sickness, in the short space "of two months after the surrender of the town."

Historical Survey of St. Domingo, Chap. xi. p. 174.

CHAP. III. 1794. gan to run in a contrary direction. The sickness which had for some time prevailed in the army, was become exasperated to pestilence. The troops sunk under it in great numbers, and among its most distinguished victims, was major general Dundas, the governor of Guadaloupe. On the 4th of June the commander in chief (being at that time with the admiral, inspecting the state of St. Christopher's) received the melancholy account of this gallant officer's death, and early on the morning of the 5th further intelligence arrived, which rendered his loss at that juncture doubly afflicting. This was nothing less than the very unexpected information, that a French armament of considerable force was, at that moment, off Point a Petre!

On receipt of this intelligence, the admiral made immediate sail for Guadaloupe, and arrived there on the afternoon of the 7th, and having put the commander in chief ashore at Basse Terre, he proceeded with the ships to Point a Petre; but found that the enemy had not only made good their landing, but had also forced Fort Fleur d'Épée on the preceding day, and were actually in possession of the town, and the forts by which it was defended. They had likewise secured their shipping at safe anchorage in the harbour. It was now discovered that this armament consisted of two frigates, a corvette, two large ships armed *en flute*, and two other vessels; having brought with them 1500 regular troops*.

* This armament sailed from Rochfort on the 25th of April.

The

The success of the French on this occasion was the more surprising, as there was at this time in Guadaloupe a larger proportion of British troops than in either of the other conquered islands; it is asserted by a respectable author*, who collected his observations on the scene of action, that the progress of the enemy was greatly accelerated by the misconduct of several of the French royalists then in the fort, a party of whom (misinformed perhaps as to the real number of the invaders) offered their services to sally on the besiegers, and marched out for that purpose, under the command of Captain M' Dowall of the 43d, but on approaching the enemy they were panic struck, and deserted to the town. Thirty of them only out of 140 returned to Fleur d'Epée with Captain M'Dowall. The British merchants and sailors from the town of Point a Petre, had thrown themselves into this fort to co-operate with the garrison. This little band, under the command of Lieutenant Colonel Drummond of the forty-third regiment, did all that gallant men could do; twice they repulsed the assailants; but the French royalists who remained in the fort, conceiving the vain hope of obtaining mercy for themselves by a surrender, insisted at length that the gates should be thrown open. This was no sooner done, than the enemy poured in from all sides, and the few surviving British soldiers (not more than 40 in number) were obliged to make the best retreat they could to Fort Louis. This

* Rev. Cooper Willyams, chaplain to the Boyne.

 place

CHAP. III. 1794.

place not being tenable after the loss of Fleur d'Epée, was soon abandoned by them, and they crossed over to Basse Terre*.

The commander in chief, the moment the strength of the enemy was ascertained, had transmitted orders to the commanders in the different islands to send from thence whatever force could be spared; and the legislature of St. Christopher, immediately on receiving notice of the enemy's appearance, raised a considerable body of volunteers at the expence of the colony, and dispatched them, with great expedition, to co-operate in this important service.

* The celebrated Brigadier General Arnold, being on business of a mercantile nature at Point a Petre, was captured at the time the place fell into the hands of the republicans, and, being apprehensive of ill treatment, changed his name to Anderson. He was put on board a prison-ship in the harbour, and had considerable property in cash with him, of which, it is supposed, Fremont and Victor Hugues were informed, as he received an intimation from one of the French sentries, that he was known, and would soon be guillotined. On this alarming intelligence, he determined to attempt an escape, which he effected in the following manner: At night he lowered into the sea a cask containing clothes and valuables, with a direction on it, that if it floated to the shore of our camp at Berville, it might be known, and restored to him; he then lowered down his cloak-bag to a small raft which he had prepared, on which also he got himself, and proceeded to a small canoe, in which he pushed for the British fleet, directed by the admiral's lights. On his making towards the mouth of the harbour, he was challenged by the French row-guard, but by the darkness of the night escaped from them, and arrived on board the Boyne by four o'clock on Monday morning, the 30th of June.

See the Rev. Cooper Willyams's Account of the Campaign in the West Indies.

All

ALL the force that could be thus obtained, being at length collected at Bassè Terre, detachments were landed on the side of Fort Fleur d'Epée, and many skirmishes took place with the enemy, between the 19th of June and the beginning of July, the particulars of which it is not necessary to relate. The weather was now become insupportably hot, and the tropical rains being already set in, the General determined to make an effort to finish the campaign at a blow. It was planned that a large body of troops, under Brigadier General Symes, should march during " the night, and make themselves masters of Morne government, and the other commanding heights round the town of Point a Petre; the General himself, at the head of the rest of his army, remaining in readiness on the heights of Mascot, to storm Fort Fleur d'Epée, on receiving a signal from the brigadier: the failure of this enterprize was a fatal circumstance; and many animadversions having been made on the conduct of it; I shall recite the particulars in General Grey's own words: "On the evening of the 1st "instant Brigadier General Symes marched from "Morne Mascot with the 1st battalion of grena-"diers, the 1st and 2d battalions of light infantry, "and the 1st battalion of seamen commanded by "Captain Robertson, to attack the town of Point "a Petre before day-break on the 2d instant; but "being misled by their guides, the troops entered "the town at the part where they were most ex-"posed to the enemy's cannon and small arms, "and where it was not possible to scale the walls "of

CHAP. III. 1794.

"of the fort; in consequence of which, they suffered considerably from round and grape-shot, "together with small arms fired from the houses, "&c. and a retreat became unavoidable." It gives me great concern, observes the General, to add, that Brigadier General Symes was wounded; and that Lieutenant Colonel Gomm, and some other meritorious officers, were killed on this attack, as was also Captain Robertson of the navy, a valuable officer, and whose death was a great loss to the service.*

The meditated attack on Fort Fleur d'Epée, being thus rendered abortive, and the British troops so reduced or debilitated as to be absolutely unfit for further exertion, (exposed as they were to the sun and the rains) it was resolved, at a consultation held on the 3d, between the commander in chief and the admiral, to relinquish all further attempts for the present on Grand Terre; and to remove the artillery and stores, and to reinforce, with the troops, the posts in Basse Terre. This determination, dictated by a necessity which left

* Brigadier General Symes died of his wounds a short time afterwards: exclusive of whom, the total loss of the British in this unfortunate affair, and some preceding attacks, is stated as follows:

1 lieutenant colonel, 4 captains, 7 lieutenants, 7 serjeants, 2 drummers, 91 rank and file, *killed;* 1 major, 3 captains, 7 lieutenants, 13 serjeants, 8 drummers, 298 rank and file, *wounded;* 1 serjeant, 3 drummers, 52 rank and file, *missing*. One of the French frigates in the harbour did great execution, killing 3 officers and 36 privates of the light infantry, by a single discharge of grape shot. They were unfortunately drawn up in a street, which was effectually commanded by her guns.

no

no alternative, was carried into effect without loss, on the night of the 5th. "I now" said the general in his letter of the 8th, "occupy with my whole force, the ground between St. John's Point and Bay Mahault, and having erected batteries with 24-pounders, and morter batteries, at Point Saron and Point St. John, opposite to the town of Point a Petre, my situation gives perfect security to Basse Terre."

MANY arrangements, however, were yet to be made for the maintenance of this position during the approaching hurricane months, and until a reinforcement should arrive from Great Britain. These being at length completed, the general embarked on board the Boyne, and sailed for St. Pierre in the island of Martinique, where he established his head-quarters, leaving Brigadier Graham to command in his absence at Basse Terre.

THE head-quarters of the British army in Guadaloupe were at camp Berville, which was placed on commanding ground; flanked by the sea on one side, and on the other by an impassable morass. About a mile on the rear, was a narrow pass, by which alone the camp could be approached, and in front was the river Saliée, on the furthermost banks of which stands the town of Point a Petre; but the situation of this encampment, so favourable in other respects, proved to be, in the highest degree, unhealthful. The baneful effects of the climate at this season of the year were aggravated by putrid exhalations from the neighbouring swamps, and a dreadful mortality

lity

CHAP. III. 1794.

lity ensued among the troops. By the middle of August, the numbers on the sick list constituted the majority of the camp. During the month of September, the army was inadequate to the supply of guards for the different batteries. Several companies could not produce a single man fit for duty; and the 43d regiment could not even afford a corporal and three men, for the protection of their own camp in the night.

In order, therefore, to keep up the appearance of force in front of the enemy, the different islands were completely drained of troops, and a body of French loyalists were selected to perform military duty at the post of Gabarre; where they conducted themselves with much spirit and fidelity.

The commissioner from the French convention, and now commander in chief of the French troops in Guadaloupe, was Victor Hugues, a man of whom I shall hereafter have frequent occasion to speak. It is sufficient in this place to observe, that though his name has since become proverbial for every species of outrage and cruelty, he was not deficient either in courage or capacity. Observing how severely his own troops, as well as ours, suffered from the climate, he conceived the project of arming in his service as many blacks and mulattoes as he could collect. These men, inured to the climate, and having nothing to lose, flocked to his standard in great numbers, and were soon brought into some degree of order and discipline. With the co-operation of these auxiliaries, apprized at the same time of the debilitated state of the British army, the French commissioner determined

determined to attack the British camp at Berville. For this purpose, on Saturday the 26th of September, he embarked a large body of troops in small vessels, which passing our ships of war unperceived, under cover of a dark night, made good their landing in two detachments; the one at Goyave, the other at Bay Mahault. The detachment which took possession of the place last mentioned, immediately marched to Gabarre, in the view of surrounding the French royalists stationed there, and it was with great difficulty that they escaped to Berville. The other detachment which had landed at Goyave, began its march to Petit Bourg. Lieut. Col. Drummond, of the 43d regiment, with some convalescents from the hospital, and a party of royalists, advanced to meet them, but perceiving their great superiority, found it advisable to retreat; and they took post at a battery upon the shore, called Point Bacchus, where however they were soon surrounded, and the whole party made prisoners. By the possession of this post, the enemy entirely cut off all communication between the British camp and shipping. They then proceeded to possess themselves of the neighbouring heights, and formed a junction with the other detachment which had landed at Bay Mahault: by this means the camp at Berville was completely invested by land; its whole strength, including the sick and convalescent, consisted of no more than two hundred and fifty regular troops, and three hundred royalists. All that courage, perseverance, and despair could effect, was performed by the united exertions of this gallant

band

CHAP. III. 1794.

band. In the first attack on the morning of the 29th, after a conflict of three hours, the republicans were defeated with great loss. They were again repulsed in two subsequent attacks, on the 30th of the same month and the 4th of October. But their numbers continually increasing, and the manifest impossibility of opening a communication with the British fleet, depriving the garrison of all proper succour, General Graham, on the representation of his officers, consented on the 6th of October to send a flag to the French commissioner, offering to capitulate. Towards the British, the terms granted by the enemy were sufficiently liberal, but the condition demanded for the French royalists, that they should be treated as British subjects, was declared inadmissible; all the favour that could be obtained for them, was the sanction of a covered boat, in which twenty-five of their officers escaped to the Boyne. The rest of the miserable royalists, upwards of 300 in number, were left a sacrifice to the vengeance of their republican enemies. Finding themselves excluded from the capitulation, they solicited permission to endeavour to cut their way through the enemy, an attempt which must have ended only in the destruction both of themselves and the British. There was a faint hope entertained, however, that Victor Hughes (whose character was not at that time sufficiently developed) would relent on their surrender. In this expectation, however, these unfortunate people were cruelly disappointed, and their sad fate cannot be recorded without indignation and horror. The republicans erected a

guillotine,

guillotine, with which they struck off the heads of fifty of them in the short space of an hour. This mode of proceeding, however, proving too tedious for their impatient revenge; the remainder of these unhappy men were fettered to each other, and placed on the brink of one of the trenches which they had so gallantly defended: the republicans then drew up some of their undisciplined recruits in front, who firing an irregular volley at their miserable victims, killed some and wounded others; leaving many, in all probability, untouched: the weight however of the former, dragged the rest into the ditch, where the living, the wounded, and the dead, shared the same grave; the soil being instantly thrown in upon them *.

Thus was the whole of this fertile country (the single fortress of Matilda excepted) restored to the power of France, and placed under the denomination of a revengeful and remorseless democracy. General Prescott, who commanded the Matilda Fort, sustained a long and most harassing siege, from the 14th of October to the 10th of December. His conduct throughout, as well as that of the officers and men under his command, was above all praise. He maintained his position until the fort was no longer tenable, and having no other means of saving his reduced and exhausted garrison from the sword, he was obliged at length to abandon it by silent evacuation. Three line of battle ships had indeed arrived in the

* Rev. Cooper Willyams's account of the campaign, &c.

interim

CHAP. III. 1794.

interim from Great Britain, but they came only to behold the triumph of the enemy. With this adverse stroke of fortune, closed the campaign of 1794: its career for a while was glorious beyond example; and if the very unhappy measure of reducing the number of the troops at the outset, had not taken effect, or if, as soon as the news of the capture of Martinico had reached England, a strong reinforcement had been sent to the scene of action, it cannot be doubted that Guadaloupe would have still continued in possession of the English, and the page of history remained undefiled with those dreadful recitals of revolt, devastation, and massacre, which I shall soon have the painful task of recording, to the shame and everlasting dishonour of the French character, and the disgrace of human nature. Our gallant commanders were fortunate, in being allowed to withdraw in time from an atmosphere polluted by such enormities. Worn down by constant exertion both of body and mind, assailed by an unprincipled faction with the basest calumnies, and oppressed by the melancholy and daily prospect of a gallant army perishing of disease, they were happily relieved from infinite anxiety by the appearance of the reinforcement before mentioned, in which arrived Gen. Sir John Vaughan and Vice-Admiral Caldwell; to the former of whom Sir Charles Grey, and to the latter Sir John Jervis, surrendered their respective commands, and on the 27th of November sailed for Great Britain.

CHAP. IV.

Savage Indignities of Victor Hugues to the remains of General Dundas.—His unprecedented Cruelty to his British Prisoners.—Meditates Hostilities against the other Islands.

CHAP. IV. 1794.

THE first measure of the French commissioner, on taking possession of Fort Matilda, displayed in the strongest manner the baseness and ferocity of his character. The body of Major General Dundas had been buried within the walls of that fortress, and a stone placed over it with a suitable inscription. This humble memorial, which a generous enemy, in every civilized part of the earth, would have held sacred, was immediately destroyed by orders of this savage despot, and the remains of the deceased hero dug up and thrown into the river Gallion. This mean and cowardly display of ineffectual vengeance, was made the subject of boasting and triumph in a public proclamation, worthy only of its author*.

* So much has been heard of Victor Hugues, that it may be agreeable to the reader to be informed of his origin and early pursuits. He was born of mean parents in some part of old France, and was placed out when a boy, as an apprentice to a hair dresser. In that occupation he went originally to Guadaloupe, where he was afterwards known as a petty inkeeper at Basse Terre. Failing in that pursuit, he became master of a small trading vessel, and at length was promoted to a lieutenancy in the French navy. Being distinguished for his activity in the French Revolution, he was afterwards deputed, through the

CHAP. IV. 1794.

The miseries of war seem, indeed, to have been wantonly aggravated by this man, to an extent never known among the rudest and most barbarous nations. In the village of Petit Bourg lay many sick and wounded British soldiers, who had been taken prisoners with Colonel Drummond at Point Bacchus. These unhappy men made an humble application to Victor Hugues for medical assistance and fresh provisions. Their petition was answered by a death-warrant. The vindictive conqueror, instead of considering them as objects of mercy and relief, caused the whole number in the hospital, and among them it is said "many women "and some children," to be indiscriminately murdered by the bayonet; a proceeding so enormously wicked, is, I believe, without a precedent in the annals of human depravity*.

After such conduct towards men who were incapable of making either resistance or escape, it may well be supposed that revenge was not tardy in the pursuit of its victims among the inhabitants

the influence of Robespierre, to whose party he was strongly attached, to the National Assembly. In 1794 he obtained the appointment of Commissioner at Guadaloupe, with controuling powers over the commanders of the army and navy; and proved himself in every respect worthy of his great patron and exemplar, being nearly as savage, remorseless, and bloody, as Robespierre himself.

* I am unwilling to give this anecdote to the public, without quoting my authority. I relate it on the testimony of the Rev. Cooper Willyams, chaplain of the Boyne, who quotes Colonel Drummond himself, and it is confirmed by a declaration drawn up by General Vaughan and Vice-Admiral Caldwell. Colonel Drummond himself was confined to a prison ship, and by particular orders from Victor Hugues, to swab the decks like the meanest seamen.

of the country. To be accused of actions, or suspected of principles, hostile towards the new government, was to be convicted of treason. Accordingly, persons of all conditions, without respect to sex or age, were sent daily to the guillotine by this inexorable tyrant, and their execution was commonly performed in sight of the British prisoners.

Victor Hugues, having taken these and other measures for securing their quiet possession of Guadaloupe, determined in the next place (his force being inadequate to a regular attempt against any of the other islands) to adopt a system of hostility against some of them, which, though well suited to his character and disposition, was not less outrageous and sanguinary than unprecedented among civilized states. To this end he directed his first attention towards Grenada and St. Vincent's, expecting to find in each of those islands, adherents fit for the project which he meditated. * * * * * * * * * *
* * * * * * * * * * * * * * *
* * * * * * * * * * * * * * *
* * * * †

† N. B.—At this interesting period the history closes.—Death abruptly terminates the author's labours.

T. Gillet, Printer, Wild-Court, Lincoln's-Inn-Fields.

Lightning Source UK Ltd.
Milton Keynes UK
UKHW021743080219
336804UK00007BA/587/P

9 780365 297635